The Cuban Missile Crisi

This volume brings together a collection of leading international experts to revisit and review our understanding of the Cuban missile crisis, via a critical reappraisal of some of the key texts.

In October 1962, humankind came close to the end of its history. The risk of catastrophe is now recognised by many to have been greater than realised by protagonists at the time or scholars subsequently. The Cuban missile crisis remains one of the mostly intensely studied moments of world history. Understanding is framed and informed by Cold War historiography, political science and personal experience, written by scholars, journalists and surviving officials. The emergence of Soviet (later Russian) and other national narratives has broadened the scope of enquiry, while scrutiny of the operational, especially military, dimensions has challenged assumptions about the risk of nuclear war.

The Cuban Missile Crisis: A critical reappraisal brings together leading world scholars from the US, the UK, France, Canada, and Russia to present critical scrutiny of authoritative accounts and to recast assumptions and interpretations. The book aims to provide an essential guide for students of the missile crisis, the diplomacy of the Cold War and the dynamics of historical interpretation and reinterpretation. Offering original ideas and agendas, the contributors seek to provide a new understanding of the secrets and mysteries of the moment when the world went to the brink of Armageddon.

This book will be of great interest to students of the Cuban missile crisis, Cold War Studies, nuclear proliferation, international history and International Relations in general.

Len Scott is Professor of International History and Intelligence Studies at Aberystwyth University.

R. Gerald Hughes is Director of the Centre for Intelligence and International Security Studies (CIISS) at Aberystwyth University.

Series: Cold War History
Series Editors: Odd Arne Westad and Michael Cox

In the new history of the Cold War that has been forming since 1989, many of the established truths about the international conflict that shaped the latter half of the twentieth century have come up for revision. The present series is an attempt to make available interpretations and materials that will help further the development of this new history, and it will concentrate in particular on publishing expositions of key historical issues and critical surveys of newly available sources.

The Cuban Missile Crisis

A critical reappraisal

**Edited by Len Scott and
R. Gerald Hughes**

LONDON AND NEW YORK

First published 2015
by Routledge
2 Park Square, Milton Park, Abingdon, Oxfordshire OX14 4RN

and by Routledge
711 Third Avenue, New York, NY 10017

First issued in paperback 2016

Routledge is an imprint of the Taylor & Francis Group, an informa business

British Library Cataloguing in Publication Data
A catalogue record for this book is available from the British Library

Library of Congress Cataloging-in-Publication Data
The Cuban missile crisis : a critical reappraisal / edited by Len Scott
and R. Gerald Hughes.
  pages cm. – (Cold war history)
  1. Cuban Missile Crisis, 1962. 2. Cuban Missile Crisis, 1962–
Historiography. 3. Nuclear crisis stability. 4. Cold War.
  I. Scott, L. V. (Leonard Victor), 1957–, editor. II. Hughes,
  R. Gerald, editor.
  E841.C8447 2015
  972.9106'4–dc23   2014039828

ISBN 13: 978-0-415-78716-1 (pbk)
ISBN 13: 978-1-138-84092-8 (hbk)

Typeset in Baskerville
by Wearset Ltd, Boldon, Tyne and Wear

To Lucy, James and Frances
For Owen and in memory of Dave Barnes and Dave Martyn

Contents

Contributors

Barton J. Bernstein is Professor of History at Stanford University, having received his PhD in history from Harvard University. His books include *The Atomic Bomb; The Truman Administration: A Documentary History; Towards a New Past: Dissenting Essays in American History; Politics and Policies of the Truman Administration;* and *Twentieth-Century America: Recent Interpretations.*

Peter Catterall is Reader in History at the University of Westminster. In 1998 he founded the journal *National Identities,* which he continues to edit. He has published widely on twentieth-century British history, not least as editor of the diaries of former Prime Minister Harold Macmillan, which were published in two volumes in 2003 and 2011. He is currently completing a monograph on the Labour Party and the churches between the wars.

Campbell Craig is Professor in International Politics at Aberystwyth University, where he writes on the history of US foreign policy, the Cold War, historical and theoretical aspects of the nuclear revolution, and contemporary international politics. He is the author of: *Glimmer of a New Leviathan: Total War in the Thought of Niebuhr, Morgenthau and Waltz* (Columbia University Press, 2003); *The Atomic Bomb and the Origins of the Cold War* (Yale University Press, 2008, co-written with Sergey Radchenko); and *America's Cold War: The Politics of Insecurity* (Harvard University Press 2009, co-written with Fredrik Logevall).

R. Gerald Hughes is Director of the Centre for Intelligence and International Security Studies at Aberystwyth University. He is the author of *Britain, Germany and the Cold War: The Search for a European Détente, 1949–1967* (2007) and *The Postwar Legacy of Appeasement: British Foreign Policy Since 1945* (2014). He is reviews editor of the journal *Intelligence and National Security,* the author of a number of articles (most recently in the *Journal of Contemporary History* and in *Diplomatic History*), and co-editor of *Intelligence, Crises and Security: Prospects and Retrospects* (2008); *Exploring Intelligence Archives: Enquiries into the Secret State* (2008); and

Intelligence and International Security: New Perspectives and Agendas (2011). R. Gerald Hughes is a Fellow of the Royal Historical Society.

Robert Jervis is Adlai E. Stevenson Professor of International Politics at Columbia University. His most recent book is *Why Intelligence Fails: Lessons from the Iranian Revolution and the Iraq War* (Cornell University Press, 2010), and his other books include *American Foreign Policy in a New Era* (Routledge, 2005), *System Effects: Complexity in Political Life* (Princeton University Press, 1997), and *The Meaning of the Nuclear Revolution* (Cornell University Press, 1989). He was President of the American Political Science Association in 2000–1 and has received career achievement awards from the International Society of Political Psychology and the International Studies Association's Security Studies section. In 2006 he received the National Academy of Science's tri-annual award for behavioral sciences contributions to avoiding nuclear war.

Don Munton specializes in contemporary foreign policy and international relations, especially on intelligence and security issues. His current research focuses on the British-Canadian-American intelligence collection and sharing in Cuba in the 1960s and 1970s. He has published more than one hundred articles and book chapters and is co-author of *The Cuban Missile Crisis: A Concise History*, co-editor of *Canadian Foreign Policy: Selected Cases* and of *Rethinking National Security: The Public Dimension*, and editor of *Hazardous Waste Siting and Democratic Choice.*

Benoît Pelopidas is a lecturer in International Relations at the University of Bristol and an affiliate of the Center for International Security and Cooperation (CISAC), Stanford University. His research focuses on the authority of experts in international security issues, the political uses of nuclear history and memory, renunciation of nuclear weapons as a historical possibility and French nuclear history and policy. He is currently completing an edited book manuscript on the global nuclear crisis of 1962 with a focus on the awareness of nuclear vulnerability at the time. He has been awarded two international prizes for his research, has published a co-authored book in three languages and scholarly articles in journals including the *Nonproliferation Review*, the *Cambridge Review of International Studies*, the *European Journal of Social Sciences*, *The Bulletin of Atomic Scientists*, *Esprit* and *Critique Internationale.*

Sergey Radchenko is Reader in International Politics at Aberystwyth University. He specialises in the history of the Cold War, with a particular focus on the history of Russia's and China's foreign relations, and international relations in Northeast Asia. He also has a lasting attachment to Central Asia and Mongolia. His publications include *Unwanted Visionaries: The Soviet Failure in Asia at the End of the Cold War* (New York: Oxford University Press, 2014); *Two Suns in the Heavens: The Sino-Soviet Struggle for Supremacy, 1962–1967* (Washington DC and Stanford, CA: Woodrow

Wilson Center Press and Stanford University Press, 2009) and *The Atomic Bomb and the Origins of the Cold War* (New Haven, CT: Yale University Press, 2008, co-written with Campbell Craig).

Len Scott is Professor of International History and Intelligence Studies at Aberystwyth University. His publications include *An International History of the Cuban Missile Crisis: A 50-year Retrospective*, co-edited with David Gioe and Christopher Andrew (Routledge, 2014); *The Cuban Missile Crisis and the Threat of Nuclear War* (Continuum Books, 2007) and *Macmillan, Kennedy and the Cuban Missile Crisis: Political, Military and Intelligence Aspects* (Macmillan Palgrave, 1999). He is a Fellow of the Royal Historical Society and a Fellow of the Royal Society of Arts.

Sheldon M. Stern taught US history at the college level for more than a decade before becoming a historian at the John F. Kennedy Library in Boston, Massachusetts from 1977 to 2000. He was the first non-member of the ExComm, as well as the first historian, to listen to and evaluate all the secret White House tape recordings made during the 1962 Cuban missile crisis. Stern is the author of *Averting 'The Final Failure': John F. Kennedy and the Secret Cuban Missile Crisis Meetings* (Stanford University Press, 2003), *The Week the World Stood Still: Inside the Secret Cuban Missile Crisis* (Stanford University Press, 2005) and *The Cuban Missile Crisis in American Memory: Myth Versus Reality* (Stanford, CA: Stanford University 2012).

Foreword

Len Scott and R. Gerald Hughes

> History is the sum total of all the things that could have been avoided.
>
> (Konrad Adenauer)

In October 1962, humankind came close to the end of its history. Recent research makes clear that this risk of catastrophe was greater than understood by protagonists at the time or by scholars subsequently. The Cuban missile crisis remains one of the mostly intensely (and imaginatively) studied moments of world history. Understanding these moments is framed and informed by authoritative, and indeed seminal, texts. These are drawn from Cold War historiography, political science and personal experience, written by scholars, journalists and surviving officials. The emergence of Soviet (later Russian) as well as Cuban and other national narratives has broadened the scope of enquiry, while scrutiny of the operational, especially military, dimensions has challenged assumptions about the risk of nuclear war.

The aim of this collection is to provide a critical reappraisal of key texts on the crisis. New research and interpretation compels a thoroughgoing reappraisal of authoritative accounts, and the recasting of assumptions, arguments and conclusions. In short, the book is intended as an essential guide for students of the missile crisis, those exploring the nuclear history and diplomacy of the Cold War, and those concerned with the dynamics and trajectories of historical interpretation. Not all new work compels revision, and an important goal is to understand where traditional accounts and interpretations remain valid, in whole or part. Further, the emergence of new texts itself invites critical scrutiny of method and substance in new interpretations.

The Cuban Missile Crisis: A Critical Reappraisal brings together leading international experts to revisit and review our understanding of when the world came closest to Armageddon. *The Cuban Missile Crisis: A Critical Reappraisal* builds upon a special issue of the journal *International Relations*, published to mark the fiftieth anniversary of the crisis in 2012. Four articles by Peter Catterall, Campbell Craig, Don Munton and Sergey

Radchenko have been revised and extended. Further chapters have been added by Barton Bernstein, Robert Jervis, R. Gerald Hughes, Benoît Pelopidas and Sheldon Stern. A concluding chapter is provided by Len Scott. These authors provide expertise in international history, political science, and international relations and are drawn from the USA, the UK, Canada, Russia and France.

As the project has taken shape we have been ever more conscious that no one collection can do justice to the vast historiography on the crisis. For, as Nicholas Howe has noted: 'If nature abhors a vacuum, historiography loves a void because it can be filled with any number of plausible accounts.'[1] With regard to the Cuban missile crisis, the task we set our contributors was to fill the 'void' in historical truth by identifying, at the very least, the most probable past from the plausible paths proffered since October 1962. This is no easy task in so well-traversed a subject as the Cuban missile crisis. It is nonetheless a vital task for, as Samuel Butler once observed, 'God cannot alter the past, though historians can.'[2] And, if the past informs the present, and the future, the importance of the task of the scholar engaged in the study of history is plainly apparent. Over many years, various texts and projects have guided and challenged our interpretations, perhaps most notably the path-breaking work of James Blight, David Welch and Bruce Allyn which helped revitalise and sustain scholarly interest in the subject in the 1980s and 1990s. Others such as Jutta Weldes have brought new perspectives and insights. The contributions of the Woodrow Wilson Center at Washington University and the National Security Archive at Georgetown University have likewise generated an invaluable stream of important new evidence and interpretation. That we failed to provide assessments of such work is intended neither to disparage nor marginalise their contributions. The constraints of space proved such that we were forced to omit one chapter from the original issue of *International Relations* and turn away a major contribution to the history and historiography of the crisis by Barton Bernstein.

If, as editors, we are held responsible for our sins of omission we feel entitled to some credit for assembling an array of world-class scholars whose contributions, we believe, will enrich the study of world politics, and inspire further research and debate on what is unquestionably one of the most important episodes in the history of humankind.

Notes

1 Nicholas Howe, 'Anglo-Saxon England and post-colonial void' in Ananya Jahanara Kabir and Deanne Williams (eds), *Postcolonial Approaches to the European Middle Ages: Translating Cultures* (Cambridge: Cambridge University Press 2005) p. 25.
2 J. David Markham, 'Introduction' in J. David Markham and Mike Resnick (eds), *History Revisited: The Great Battles – Eminent Historians Take On the Great Works of Alternative History* (Dallas, TX: Benbella 2013) p. 2.

Acknowledgements

This book began with Ken Booth's invitation to mark the fiftieth anniversary of the missile crisis with a special issue of *International Relations*. To Ken and David Mainwaring, then at SAGE, we express our appreciation. We also thank David Mainwaring and SAGE for giving permission for the chapters by Peter Catterall, Campbell Craig, Don Munton and Sergey Radchenko, which have been subsequently revised and developed. We wish to thank Andrew Humphrys and Hannah Ferguson from Routledge for their help. Special thanks also go to Sheldon Stern for his endeavours on our behalf.

Len Scott would to thank Lucy, James and Frances for their love and support in difficult times.

R. Gerald Hughes would like to thank Arddun Hedydd Arwyn, Rima Devereaux, Amy Ekins-Coward, Michael Foley and Kathleen Kennedy. As ever, he acknowledges the unceasing support of his family: Ma, Arnie, David, Owen and Rachel.

Len Scott and R. Gerald Hughes
Aberystwyth
Autumn 2014

Abbreviations

ASW	Anti-Submarine Warfare
BBC	British Broadcasting Corporation
BST	British Summer Time
C3I	Command, Control, Communications and Intelligence
CIA	Central Intelligence Agency
C-in-C	Commander-in-Chief
CINCLANT	Commander-in-Chief Atlantic
CINCSAC	Commander-in-Chief Strategic Air Command
COMOR	Committee on Overheard Reconnaissance
CPSU	Communist Party of the Soviet Union
CWIHP	Cold War International History Project
DCI	Director of Central Intelligence
DDI	Deputy Director of Intelligence
DEFCON	Defense Condition
DIA	Defense Intelligence Agency
DoD	Department of Defense
EST	Eastern Standard Time
ExComm	Executive Committee of the National Security Council
FBI	Federal Bureau of Investigation
FKR	*Frontovaya Krylyatnaya Raketa* (Front Cruise Missiles)
FOIA	Freedom of Information Act
FROG	Free Rocket Over Ground
FRUS	*Foreign Relations of the United States*
GLCM	Ground Launched Cruise Missile
GMT	Greenwich Mean Time
GOP	Grand Old Party
GRU	*Glavnoye Razvedyatelnoye Upravlenie* (Chief Intelligence Directorate of the Soviet General Staff)
ICBM	InterContinental Ballistic Missile
IRBM	Intermediate Range Ballistic Missile
JCS	Joint Chiefs of Staff
JFK	John Fitzgerald Kennedy
JFKL	JFK Library

JIC	Joint Intelligence Committee
KGB	*Komitet Gosudarstvennoy Bezopasnosti* (Soviet Committee for State Security)
KT	Kiloton
MiG	Mikoyan (Soviet aircraft manufacturer)
MRBM	Medium Range Ballistic Missile
MOD	Ministry of Defence
MT	Megaton
NAC	North Atlantic Council
NATO	North Atlantic Treaty Organisation
NIE	National Intelligence Estimate
NSA	National Security Agency
NSA	National Security Archive
NSC	National Security Council
OAS	Organisation of American States
PRC	People's Republic of China
RAF	Royal Air Force
RFK	Robert Francis Kennedy
SAC	Strategic Air Command
SAM	Surface to Air Missile
SLBM	Submarine-launched Ballistic Missile.
SNIE	Special National Intelligence Estimate
SSBN	Nuclear-powered Ballistic Missile Submarine
SSK	Conventionally powered General-purpose Attack Submarine
SSM	Surface to Surface Missile
SSN	Nuclear-powered General-purpose Attack submarine
TNA	The National Archives
UK	United Kingdom
UN	United Nations
USA	United States of America
USAF	United States Air Force
USN	United States Navy
USSR	Union of Soviet Socialist Republics

1 The Cuban missile crisis

What can we know, why did it start, and how did it end?[1]

Robert Jervis

As is true for many events, the more we know about the Cuban missile crisis the more puzzling some aspects of it become. So much has been written about it that rather than trying to provide complete coverage, I will cover topics that have either been under-explored or remain in dispute: the extent and role of uncertainty and surprise in the crisis; the particularly political nature of the disputes over the major issues; Khrushchev's motives; how the blockade brought pressure to bear on both sides; and the place of threats and promises in resolving the crisis, especially the role of the removal of the Jupiter missiles from Turkey, which was more complicated and subtle than is normally portrayed. I will close by pointing out five ways in which the crisis was typical of Cold War interactions.

Knowledge and uncertainty

Before and during the crisis, the leading actors had different degrees of knowledge, ignorance, and misinformation about what was happening, but all were surprised by how it unfolded. Most obviously, the US was taken by surprise, which was Khrushchev's intention (although in retrospect, seeking surprise may have been a mistake). But when a U-2 flight revealed the secret and the US reacted, it was Khrushchev and Castro who were surprised. These surprises were not only reciprocal, but in a sense the second caused the first. 'We missed the Soviet decision to put missiles into Cuba because we could not believe that Khrushchev could make such a mistake,' declared the leading American intelligence analyst who had been responsible for earlier estimates that had confidently predicted that the USSR would not deploy missiles.[2] Although self-serving, the statement is essentially correct. If Khrushchev had known how strongly – or dangerously – the US would react, he would not have proceeded. Even if the crisis did bring some gains, the risk was not worth it. For the Americans as well, the risks were perhaps not worth the gains, or even the losses avoided. On the day that he learned what Khrushchev had done, Kennedy told his colleagues: 'Last month I said we weren't going to [allow it]. Last month I should have said we don't care.'[3] No doubt he was joking, but like every good joke this reveals an element of truth. At the very least, had Kennedy understood that Khrushchev was so reckless and so highly motivated (leaving aside for the moment the content of the motivation), he surely would have behaved differently, although exactly what he would have done is unclear.

Not only the start of the crisis but its course took everyone by surprise. At no point could anyone be confident of what would unfold within the next 24 hours, and that uncertainty drove the felt need to end the crisis as soon as possible. Indeed, events moved much more quickly than Kennedy, and probably Khrushchev, had expected, and the former's initial speech talked about the need for 'self-sacrifice and self-discipline' over a period of several months.

Of course not all was unexpected, and each side had some inkling of what the other would do. If the US had been completely confident that the Soviets would not put missiles in Cuba, it would not have collected intelligence reports or staged U-2 flights.[4] If Khrushchev had been confident that the US would accept the emplacement of missiles, he would not have acted in secret. Most importantly, throughout the crisis, both Kennedy and Khrushchev were confident that the other did not intend to start a nuclear war (which brings up the question of what they did fear, which I will discuss later).

Although Kennedy and Khrushchev often acted boldly – and even in retrospect it is not clear what would have been cautious – they acknowledged the uncertainties. It is striking how much the record is filled with statements to the effect that how the other will react is crucial, but is also unknown. While the participants had hunches, the very fact that they had already been taken by surprise gave them unusual humility. This must have induced great psychological tension because only rarely did someone on either side claim to have what game theorists call a dominant strategy – i.e. one that would be best no matter how the other played the game. Thus the Americans had to debate whether the Soviets would react more strongly to bombing the missile sites or to boarding their ships, and whether Khrushchev would be willing to stand by his first conciliatory letter of Friday night and settle for a no-invasion pledge or whether it was necessary to promise to remove the Jupiter missiles from Turkey. Such debates are typical, but what is less so is that the participants were rarely dogmatic in their assertions, frequently changed their minds, and did not hesitate to acknowledge uncertainty. The phrase 'I don't know' appears with great frequency. As Kennedy told the ExComm when the blockade was about to take effect, 'what we are doing is throwing down a card on the table in a game which we don't know the ending of'.[5] When he told Congressional leaders that his initial decision for a blockade was based on his belief that attacking the missiles would be much more dangerous, he admitted, 'Now, who knows that? . . . We just tried to make good judgments about a matter about which everyone is uncertain.'[6]

As they took their steps, or even more, contemplating using greater violence, they admitted they were looking into a void. Even the self-confident McGeorge Bundy said that 'after we've done a violent thing we, none of us, know where it will go'.[7] The Deputy Director of Central Intelligence, Marshall Carter, spoke for many when he said that an attack on the missiles sites 'just frightens the hell out of me as to what goes beyond.... This isn't the end; this is the beginning, I think'.[8] Whether escalation would occur or not could not be foreseen, and its perceived likelihood was a crucial factor separating those who were more inclined to favour using force (whether it be an airstrike or an invasion) because they thought that Khrushchev was at such a military disadvantage that he would have to acquiesce, from those who believed that he would feel great pressures to respond militarily in some way and would probably do so.[9]

The uncertainty loomed largest and most frightening when the increase in pressure or use of force was being contemplated, but it inhibited diplomatic initiatives as well because once launched, no one could be sure of their result. Would concessions lead to further demands? Would allies become demoralized –or, conversely, would they see an America that was standing firm as unduly reckless? Kennedy famously said that an American attack on Cuba would be 'one hell of a gamble' and Soviet ambassador Anatoly Dobrynin referred to the president as 'a hot-tempered gambler', but the pejorative connotations were tied to an understanding that anything they did was a gamble.[10]

Uncertainty is normal in international politics. But here the decision-makers, at least in the American side, were openly at sea, and although available Soviet and Cuban records are much less complete, their great thirst for every scrap of information indicates that their leaders also knew how little they knew. The situation was unprecedented, and the fact that each side was taken by surprise destabilized everyone's expectations and made it hard for anyone to feel that he understood the other side or could predict what it would do.[11] If major beliefs about the other side had just been shown to be wildly incorrect, what other ideas needed to be modified or discarded? On what basis could either side now estimate how the adversary would respond? For the US the problem was especially acute because the two established interlocutors (Ambassador Anatoly Dobrynin and Georgi Bolshakov, the intelligence agent who provided a back-channel) had been exposed as uninformed or duplicitous.

Kennedy's openness and willingness to acknowledge uncertainty undoubtedly brought out these characteristics in his colleagues, but more than they Kennedy realized that while they could not predict the future, it was important to understand the past in order to resolve the crisis. Throughout, and especially during the meeting the first evening of the crisis, he pressed for answers as to why Khrushchev had deployed the missiles. He never got much of an answer, and perhaps he gave up too soon.[12] But he realized that because the established assumptions about

Khrushchev's perceived self-interest, calculations, and view of the world had just been disconfirmed, it was important to put them on a more secure footing as a prelude to taking action. In fact, the ExComm's refusal to delve into Khrushchev's motives (understandable, perhaps, in light of the need to rapidly establish a policy) reduced members' sensitivity to some of the diplomatic tools the US could deploy, most obviously a pledge not to invade Cuba.

The uncertainty discussed so far refers to the behaviour of others. While this was central, two other forms were important as well. One was uncertainty of a more factual sort. Most obviously, while Kennedy and his colleagues knew quite a bit about what the Soviets had done, they did not know everything – as they well understood. They realized that they could not be certain about the extent of the Soviet deployment or whether nuclear warheads had arrived (and, if so, whether they had been mated to the missiles). Even more hidden were the activities of Soviet submarines, which posed a menace to the warships that might stop and search Soviet vessels. But the Americans were not uncertain enough: they never thought that the submarines might be armed with nuclear torpedoes or worried that they had vastly underestimated Soviet ground forces in Cuba (and, until late in the crisis, that these forces included tactical nuclear weapons) and that the resistance to an invasion would be much greater than they calculated.[13] More uncertainty surrounded the American estimates of how many airstrikes it would take to wipe out the Soviet missiles, and indeed whether all of them could be destroyed before they could be launched. What was crucial to the decision to opt for a blockade and to the sense that if that failed airstrikes would have to be combined with an invasion was the estimate that even a large strike might leave some missiles untouched. This knowledge of the inability to confidently predict the physical, let alone the political, effects of bombing played a large role in turning the tide against an airstrike, and at least some subsequent analysis indicates that the American leaders may have overestimated the difficulties of an attack on the Soviet missiles and exaggerated the ease and speed with which they could be moved.[14]

Ever since the publication of James Fearon's path-breaking 'Rationalist Explanations for War', political scientists have returned to the bargaining problems – and opportunities – caused by the well-known fact that incentives to misrepresent mean that adversaries cannot be certain of each other's intentions and resolve.[15] Fearon's basic point is that states have 'private information' about their resolve, but often lack credible means to convey it, and the actors in 1962 were aware of how hard it was to judge what others would do. But it is a mistake to believe that states always know their own resolve.[16] In fact neither Kennedy nor Khrushchev appears to have known much more about the risks he was willing to run than he knew about the other's tolerance for danger. One advisor hinted at this when he said that the blockade gave the Soviets 'a couple of days while they make up their own minds what their intentions are'.[17] Indeed, resolve came and went, and moved sideways. Khrushchev first was ready to remove the missiles in return for a no-invasion pledge and then a few hours later decided to try for more; Kennedy and his colleagues had decided to retaliate if a reconnaissance aircraft was shot down, but then thought better of it in the event. And while we can speculate about what either Kennedy or Khrushchev would have done had the crisis not ended when it did, neither leader had a clear course of action charted out – and even if he had, he might not have followed it.

The fact that resolve is not known to the person ahead of time is only the tip of an iceberg that is a major and largely unrecognized hazard to scholars. We rely heavily on documents as well as behaviour for our analysis. One reason why we think we understand American decision-making during the Cuban missile crisis better than we do other episodes is the treasure trove of tape recordings. Although they are sometimes indistinct and often hard to interpret, not all meetings were recorded, and there are no records of the numerous private conversations that occurred, historians and political scientists are used to such gaps, and know they cannot have everything. What they are less aware of is that even when people are honestly trying to describe their own motives and reasons for reaching their conclusions, they are often unable to do so. A great deal of our mental processing is unavailable to us because it occurs below the level of consciousness, and we often go about understanding why we are behaving as we do or holding our preferences in exactly the same manner that we use when analysing others – and these accounts are likely to be no more accurate. Shortly before he was assassinated, Kennedy noted that 'the essence of ultimate decision remained impenetrable to the observer – often, indeed, to the decider himself'.[18] We try to make sense of what we have done, but this is a reconstruction. One does not have to be Freudian to recognize that, in a deep sense, we are 'strangers to ourselves'.[19] Statements by Kennedy, Khrushchev, and their colleagues about why they held their views and why they thought others would act in specified ways may be simultaneously completely honest and untrue. Self-knowledge is inevitably limited.

The political nature of the debates

Much of the scholarly disagreement about the missile crisis centers on the beginning and the end: Khrushchev's motives for putting the missiles into Cuba and the conditions under which he withdrew them. I will discuss these issues shortly, but first want to note that these debates, like many in our field, are highly political. Very few scholars are agnostic about the fundamental issues of the Cold War, and it is almost inevitable that their views of the crisis tend to mirror their analyses of the general conflict. Those in the 'traditional' camp who see Stalin's paranoia and/or aggressiveness as responsible for the start of the Cold War and the US as largely reactive and defensive believe that Khrushchev's main motive was to nullify the American nuclear advantage and prepare the ground for renewed pressure on Berlin and that he withdrew largely because he was met by a President who made his resolve clear and who had many more usable military options than he did. Most revisionists who argue that Stalin's control over Eastern Europe was largely a response to the American unwillingness to respect Soviet security interests and treat it as a legitimate great power see Khrushchev as acting mainly to protect its small ally against the American threat to overthrow it.

The revisionist narrative about the end of the crisis, however, has changed in accord with both new documents and the preferred interpretation of the end of the Cold War. Initially the argument was that Kennedy had been irresponsible in starting with threats rather than diplomacy and in pushing Khrushchev to the wall and making only minor concessions throughout. But subsequent evidence from the Soviet side indicates that a purely diplomatic approach would have failed (at least if it did not include attractive offers), and, more importantly, American records show that Kennedy in fact made more concessions than were public. I will discuss the substance of the controversies about the removal of Jupiter missiles from Turkey later, but here just want to note that while the more traditional accounts downplay both what Kennedy promised and its impact on Khrushchev, revisionists now see the removal as essentially accepting Khrushchev's offer in his 'second letter' of 27 October and as crucial to ending the crisis. This version makes Kennedy more of a negotiator and less of a hardliner, and fits with a revisionist account of the end of the Cold War in arguing that episodes like the missile crisis cannot be explained by a 'triumphalist' narrative of American might and virtue prevailing but rather were negotiations (albeit not necessarily among equals) in which the US did not enjoy unalloyed victories.

One could imagine a consistent revisionist narrative in which the US was unyielding in seeking to contain, rollback, and ultimately destroy Soviet power. In fact, I think there is much to this, but for most scholars it is psychologically, morally, and politically unacceptable to view the US as both aggressive and successful. Logic would also lead to the expectation that those who believe that Khrushchev's main motive was to protect Cuba would also believe that the American pledge not to invade would have satisfied him. But in fact people with this diagnosis of the situation usually argue for the importance of Kennedy's promise to take the Jupiters out of Turkey, thus producing a view of the crisis as caused by American aggressiveness in the Caribbean and ending, not in a Soviet retreat, but in a fairly equal bargain that Kennedy insisted on keeping secret, a narrative that denies both halves of the story that puts the US in a favourable light, which I believe explains its popularity among revisionist historians.

Khrushchev's motives

We sometimes use the name of the leader as shorthand for the country, but when we talk about the Soviet decision to deploy missiles to Cuba it really *was* Khrushchev's decision. This complicates the search for motives because while we have his and his son's recollections, the deliberative records that could be useful are unavailable not because they remain sealed but because there were no deliberations. Although the fact that it took two meetings before the Presidium agreed may show some resistance (the records are too sparse to reveal this), there is no doubt that Khrushchev was in charge.[20] Furthermore, sorting out motives may be particularly difficult in Khrushchev's case. Because he was notoriously impulsive and an improviser and failed to think through the implications of much that he did, pointing out that the likely consequences of his acts were at variance with some posited motives does not mean that the latter were not driving.[21]

Related to motivation is the question of 'who started it', to put it crudely but I think accurately. The traditional explanation fits with the version propounded by American officials in seeing the crisis as beginning with the Soviet deployment of missiles to Cuba – thus the name the Cuban missile crisis. In his letter of 23 October replying to Khrushchev's claims that the missiles were meant to deter an American attack on Cuba and so the deployment was reactive, Kennedy declared that 'I think you will recognize that the step which started the current chain of events was the action of your government secretly furnishing offensive weapons to Cuba'.[22] The implication was that Khrushchev had drastically and without provocation altered the status quo. To the contrary, by stressing Khrushchev's desire to protect Cuba revisionists implicitly endorse the Soviet name for the episode, 'the Caribbean Crisis', which started with the American attempt to overthrow the Cuban revolution. (Interestingly, the Cubans call it 'the October Crisis' which gestures toward the American blockade but does not imply that the missiles were emplaced to ward off an American attack, which is consistent with the Cuban view that they were not needed for that purpose.) But starting points are not only crucial, they are highly subjective and usually involve judgments, often implicit, about counterfactuals. Would Khrushchev have refrained from asking Castro to accept missiles if the US had been less threatening? Or would a Berlin settlement have precluded this move? Claims about the actor or events that started a conflict also draw on unstated assumptions about what the status quo is, its political if not moral legitimacy, and the naturalness of the resistance to changing it. Kennedy's statement just quoted assumes not only that the deployment of the missiles was not a response to a previous American move, but also that the blockade, which after all in at least some sense did mark the start of the crisis, was not a real choice on the part of the US but was something it had to do to counter the Soviet move.

The most obvious complication in assessing motives is that people can be and usually are moved by multiple ones. Doctors have a saying that 'the patient can have as many diseases as he damn well pleases' to remind them of one of the troubling obstacles to moving from symptoms to diagnosis and treatment. Of course scholars (historians more than political scientists) are fully aware of this, at least in the abstract, and often decry 'single-factor' explanations. Nevertheless, we want to move beyond saying multiple impulses were at work to trying to establish their relative weights and how they combined.

Seeing multiple motives as operating raises the question of whether behaviour is over-determined. That is, arguing that several strong motives were at work, while reasonable, implies that the behaviour would have followed even if one of them had been absent. In any single case this is logically possible, just as a person may be stabbed, poisoned, and shot simultaneously with any one of these insults by itself being sufficient to have caused death. But there is something odd about a world in which most behaviour is over-determined, since this implies that behaviour follows only from a plethora of relevant impulses, which means that it would not have occurred without each of them, which in turn means that the behaviour was not over-determined. Nevertheless, hindsight, which is both valuable and dangerous, often allows us to find multiple motives once we know that the behaviour occurred. It is striking that although almost no one expected Khrushchev to take this action, after he did we have no trouble in finding lots of motives. The problem for historical explanation, then, is often not in finding the appropriate motive, but in dealing with the excess of them.[23] Furthermore, psychology comes in because it is quite common for people to bolster decisions they have made by later adding additional considerations to their judgments without understanding what they are doing. Decision-makers will then honestly believe that multiple impulses were driving even if this is not the case, and this is especially likely when the decision in fact lacks sufficient justification. William Taubman's characterization of the Cuban case is quite accurate and not unusual: Khrushchev prescribed 'a cure-all, a cure-all that cured nothing'.[24]

So it is perhaps not surprising that we are faced with an embarrassment of riches in terms of possible motives. Although the defense of Cuba and the desire to develop a stronger military posture that would force the West to change the status of West Berlin to a 'free city' are the most obvious ones, also important could be the general desire to rectify the military balance, especially urgent after the speech by Deputy Secretary of Defense Roswell Gilpatric in October 1961 making it clear that the US knew that Khrushchev had been vastly exaggerating his nuclear strength. Indeed Khrushchev's memoirs say that 'in addition to protecting Cuba, our missiles would have equalized what the West likes to call "the balance of power"', his son says that while defending Cuba was the 'principal aim of the operation', 'of course [he] did think that [it] had a certain strategic importance', and this is what Khrushchev's confidant Anastas Mikoyan told the Warsaw Pact ambassadors in Washington in November 1962.[25] The nuclear balance was particularly pressing for Khrushchev because, like Eisenhower with the 'New Look', he counted on these forces to allow him to cut the military budget, which he needed to do to bolster the Soviet civilian economy and raise the standard of living.

Parity in status as well as in military power was sought. The Soviet Union had long strived to be treated as a fully fledged superpower, and the double standards of the US had always rankled.[26] If the US could encircle the USSR and place missiles in neighboring countries, then it was surely appropriate and fitting to the Soviet position in the world that it could do the same. If the USSR could not do what the US did, then how could it be a fully fledged superpower? Aleksandr Alekseev, the Soviet ambassador to Cuba whom Khrushchev closely consulted, later reported the Chairman as telling him: 'The Americans are going to have to swallow this the same way we have had to swallow the pill of the missiles in Turkey.... We can do the same thing the Americans do.'[27] Furthermore, being a superpower brought with it the responsibility to protect allies. If the US could shield Western Europe from a purported Soviet threat, then if the USSR was to play a similar role in the world, it had the right and the duty to stand up for Cuba.[28]

At the time, American leaders believed that Khrushchev's main if not sole motive was to put pressure on Berlin. The question is whether this reflected their preoccupation or Khrushchev's.[29] Although there was no special reason for them to have been fearful, such misperceptions are not unusual, but in this case the perceptions seemed not only reasonable at the time but remains so in retrospect. While Khrushchev had solved the most pressing aspect of his Berlin problem by erecting the Wall, both the contemporary diplomatic records and declassified Soviet documents indicate that Khrushchev was not satisfied and that he hoped for more. The Western presence in Berlin was troublesome as a mark of Soviet (and East German) inferiority, as a base for espionage, albeit at a much reduced level thanks to the Wall, and as a destabilizing contrast between life on each side of the dividing line.[30] The stubborn refusal of the Americans to recognize the permanence and legitimacy of East Germany was a continuing problem.

Khrushchev's son Sergei argues that the multiple Soviet statements in the summer and fall of 1962 that the USSR would reopen the Berlin issue after the American elections were a ploy to distract the US from realizing that the fear for Cuba was leading it to take drastic action.[31] This is ingenious but unconvincing. Some of the officials dropping these hints were ignorant of the planned deployment and knew more about Berlin than they did about Cuba; this maneuver might have led the Americans to ask themselves what Khrushchev could be doing in the interim to gain bargaining leverage, and the expectation of renewed pressure on Berlin would only stiffen the US resistance to allowing the missile to stay in Cuba. More importantly, Soviet records point to the continued importance of Berlin, showing that Khrushchev did not regard the erecting of the Wall as ending the problem, that he was committed to trying to push the US out of West Berlin, and that he felt he could do so by ratcheting up the tension (what he called his 'meniscus' approach). When he explained this policy to his associates in January 1962 he believed that the Soviet ICBM program was proceeding well, but the next month he learned that the Soviet missiles were crude and vulnerable compared to the American ones. This generation of missiles, even if produced in large numbers, could not lead to strategic parity. It is likely that this realization spurred Khrushchev's search for shortcuts, which in turn inspired the idea of placing missiles into Cuba.[32] Furthermore, as the build-up proceeded Khrushchev inflated his foreign policy goals, especially in West Berlin, and in May the intriguing but unfortunately terse Presidium notes say that the deployment 'would be an offensive policy'.[33]

This fits with Khrushchev's pattern of not being satisfied with gains he had made and to keep pushing to see if he could get more. This explains why he sent his 'second letter' to Kennedy demanding the withdrawal of missiles from Turkey after he had originally been willing to settle for a no-invasion pledge: he thought he could get more and felt he should try ('one last haggle', as Bundy termed it).[34] Those who argue that Khrushchev was not concerned with making further gains in Berlin seem to regard such a motive as in some way disreputable or as showing Soviet aggressiveness. I do not think these associations are necessary, however. In competitive international politics states always seek more and the Soviet desire to rectify the military imbalance in order to squeeze the West out of Berlin and put the East German regime on a firm footing would hardly be unusual or reflect badly on the Soviet Union. Had Khrushchev really abandoned this goal after erecting the Wall, he could have either traded an acknowledgment of the status quo for American concessions elsewhere, perhaps in the economic arena, or have used his new stance to relax international tensions. But at this point he had not given up, nor was there any good reason for him to do so.

The argument that Khrushchev's main motive was to defend Cuba gains most of its support from the retrospective accounts by Khrushchev, his son, and other officials. One reason this was given no credence in the West at the time was the widespread belief that after the failure of the Bay of Pigs invasion the US posed no serious challenge to the Cuban regime, a view that not only ignores the fact that states may see threats where they do not exist but is brought to the ground by declassified records showing how committed to overthrowing Castro the US was. A second objection is that Khrushchev would not have taken such a risk to protect a less than vital interest. But it is clear that Khrushchev did not understand the magnitude of the risks he was running, and in any event this objection would apply with equal force to the argument that the motive was to seek gains in Berlin. Furthermore, Prospect Theory from psychology indicates that actors are more willing to run risks to avoid losses than to make gains, something that points to Cuba rather than Berlin.[35]

The notes of the Presidium meetings after the missiles were discovered reveal no arguments that withdrawing the missiles would mean the end of the plans to change the status quo in Berlin or, more broadly, to alter the balance of military power.[36] Instead, there was a great deal of discussion of protecting Cuba, and pride in the fact that thanks to the crisis 'the whole world is focused on Cuba'.[37] In parallel, it is significant that as far as we can tell from the fragmentary records, the discussion in the Presidium authorizing the deployment, although not truly deliberative, focused on protecting Cuba and did not mention Berlin.[38] The advantages of rectifying the strategic balance, however, may have been so obvious as not to have required explication, and Berlin had been the subject of earlier Presidium discussions.

The fact that Khrushchev sent ground forces, supported by tactical nuclear weapons, also points to the defense of Cuba as the motive because while they could make invasion extremely costly, they could not protect against American airstrikes that could have destroyed the Soviet strategic assets. But this leads back to the question of why, if this was his motive, Khrushchev sent the strategic missiles at all. Not only were they highly provocative, but it is not only in hindsight that we can see how disadvantaged Khrushchev would be if they were discovered before the deployment was complete. On the other hand, ground forces would seem to have provided a quite effective deterrent to invasion, as Khrushchev himself explained to his colleagues when he decided to withdraw the strategic forces.[39] Such a deployment could not have warded off covert assassination attempts or continuing low-level sabotage, but neither could the strategic missiles have done so. The temptation to conclude that forces that threatened the US were incompatible with a defensive mission needs to be resisted, however: the US and its allies thought that parallel forces were needed in Europe to deter against a Soviet attack.

Much of the skepticism toward the defensive account stresses the perceived disproportion between the risks of the deployment and the value of Cuba. While it is safe to say that the later was underestimated by American decision-makers at the time and by many scholars for a subsequent period, remains hard to estimate. The weight currently put on this factor by many analysts both reflects and supports the conception of Khrushchev as revolutionary romantic. It is clear that much more than Stalin and probably Brezhnev, Khrushchev sought to increase Soviet influence the spread of Communist regimes in the Third World. To separate er-political from ideological/identity motives is probably impossible e, but the latter have gained most currency over the years, and are epitomized by Mikoyan's remark that 'we have been waiting all our lives for a country to go Communist without the Red Army, and it happened in Cuba. It makes us feel like boys again!' Although Sergey Radchenko perceptively notes that these and related 'snippets' gain much of their plausibility by being so vivid and frequently repeated even if the ultimate source remains unclear,[40] they are indeed plausible. Furthermore, not only does Prospect Theory imply that Khrushchev and his colleagues would grow attached to any country that had come over to their side, but more than defense was involved because to have lost Cuba would have been the end of Soviet ambitions in Latin America, if not in the rest of the Third World, and to have increased Khrushchev's vulnerability to Chinese attacks. In addition, the great efforts to which Khrushchev went to repair relations with Castro after the crisis instead of washing his hands of a leader who had showed himself to be dangerously irresponsible points to the considerable value he placed in the regime. Much of Khrushchev's behaviour is consistent with a commitment to Cuba, and what later scholars called revolutionary romanticism is another name for the 'harebrained schemes' that his colleagues saw as an ineradicable character trait that required removing him from office.

Nevertheless, to protect Cuba by measures that turned out to increase the danger to it does seem odd. That such oddities are a staple of international politics, however, should be apparent even to those who do not see the security dilemma as central. Perhaps better evidence that Cuba was far from the whole story is provided by the fact that Soviet Foreign Minister Andrei Gromyko did not follow up when Kennedy, and later Secretary of State Rusk, told him that the US had no intention of invading Cuba and would be willing to make a pledge not to do so. Kennedy repeated the promise three times and added, as Gromyko reported, 'If Mr. Khrushchev addressed me on this issue, we could give him corresponding assurances on that score.'[41] Even more, when Khrushchev realized that he could end the crisis by withdrawing his missiles in return for an American pledge not to invade, he did not declare victory and leave the field. Although Oleg Troyanovsky, Khrushchev's translator and foreign policy assistant, reports that on receiving Kennedy's initial letter demanding the missiles' removal and instituting a blockade, Khrushchev immediately exclaimed 'we've saved Cuba!',[42] his initial replies did not offer to withdraw the missiles in exchange for Cuba's security. If Cuba had been his main concern, the pledge would have been much more than a face-saving device: it would have given him what he really cared about, and the missiles would have served their purpose. But after proposing this bargain he upped the ante without waiting for Kennedy's response, and when he decided to settle for the pledge he and his colleagues did so with a sense of relief, without any apparent elation for having reached their main goal. The Soviet reaction supports the conclusion of Arnold Horelick, a Soviet expert and later intelligence official, that 'to regard the outcome of the

Cuban missile crisis as coinciding in any substantial way with Soviet intentions or interests is to mistake the skillful salvage of a shipwreck for brilliant navigation'.[43]

We should also not neglect the role of the increasingly troublesome rivalry with China, which magnified the need to protect Cuba as well as to secure a favourable settlement in Berlin.[44] To pull off a major coup and show Soviet power and role in the world might not convince Mao to fall into line, but surely would diminish the power of the Chinese critique of Soviet leadership.

Trying to combine all of this into a coherent judgment may be not only difficult, but misguided. Aside from the fact that multiple impulses and motives are possible, Khrushchev, more than many political leaders, was impulsive and an improviser. He had objectives, but often they were not supported by coherent plans. His associates, even those who admired him, were keenly aware that he often failed to think things through. Politicians are less disturbed by inconsistencies than are academics, and this was particularly true for Khrushchev. We may be looking for coherence where it is absent, and what is maddeningly inconsistent to us may just be Khrushchev's normal way of proceeding.

How did the blockade work?

Why Kennedy chose the blockade has been discussed more than exactly how it worked to bring pressure to bear on Khrushchev. The two questions are linked, of course. While critics of the blockade pointed out that even if successful it could only prevent additional strategic forces from arriving at the island but not remove those already in place, proponents believed it would, or at least might, bring Khrushchev to his senses. In part, this was a debate between those who felt that only brute force could be effective and those who thought that coercion might suffice. As Thomas Schelling pointed out two years before the crisis, threats and force can not only protect or seize territory and weaken the adversary's military capabilities (brute force), they can also be used to threaten or inflict pain on the other side and make it worthwhile for him to make concessions (coercion). The latter became much more important with nuclear weapons, especially in the form of mutual second-strike capability, when military victory was out of reach.[45] Although the members of the ExComm did not use the terms 'brute force' and 'coercion', this is part of what they were arguing about. The blockade's proponents did not fully explain how it would contribute to coercion, however. My sense is that they had some intuitive understanding of it but also felt that a full articulation would be less than completely convincing, even to themselves. Indeed on Friday 26 October Kennedy told the ExComm that 'we're either going to trade [the missiles] out, or we're going to have to go in and get them out ourselves'.[46] Even at this late date, Kennedy did not fully appreciate that the pressures generated by the fear of an American invasion and the danger that things would get out of control could reach his goal without the necessity for either brute force or a trade.

Despite the ExComm's criticisms and doubts, it is clear in retrospect that the blockade served two functions which, when supplemented by the build-up that underscored the threat to invade if necessary, proved effective. The first mechanism was to signal the American commitment to seeing that the missiles were removed. In this way it was like a loud and rude diplomatic note. Kennedy put Khrushchev, allies, and the American public on notice that the missiles simply had to go. As Schelling had made clear, such commitments work by increasing the price that the actor will pay if he fails to live up to his word.[47] The blockade pledged the US to seeing that the missiles were removed and so implicitly promised that even harsher measures would follow if the Soviets did not comply. This I infer was the thinking behind the common statements in the ExComm that the blockade would give the Soviets reason to reevaluate their policy. And this was how the Soviets interpreted things. From the start, Khrushchev and his colleagues realized that by taking such a public stand, Kennedy had made it hard for him to retreat even if he wanted to. As Dobrynin put it toward the end of the crisis, 'a certain danger of the situation is that the President has largely engaged himself before the public opinion of America and not only America'.[48] One reason for the need to maintain secrecy was that if Khrushchev knew that the US had discovered the missiles, he could have made a public announcement making clear that he would not pull back. In a game of Chicken the first player to commit itself wins.

The announcement of the blockade was indeed a strong message of commitment, but its implementation was more than that. And something more was needed because in September, before the missiles were discovered, Kennedy had said that the US would not permit such an emplacement, and Khrushchev's response was not to pull back but to send more tactical nuclear weapons to the island.[49] The blockade upped the ante because once ships, planes, and men were put into motion no one could be sure what would happen next. Knowledgeable people – and both Kennedy and Khrushchev were knowledgeable – understood that events could get out of control. This meant that nuclear war could have occurred even though neither leader wanted it.

Indeed, if complete control were guaranteed, the crisis would not have been dangerous, and the balance between the need to minimize danger and the need to use it to exert pressure was a central dilemma throughout the crisis, as it was throughout the Cold War. Nuclear war was what Kennedy called 'the final failure' – the worst possible outcome, much worse than having to back down – and in parallel from the time when Khrushchev decided that he would send missiles to Cuba, he emphasized that these would never be used.

Every idiot can start a war, but it is impossible to win this war ... therefore the missiles have one purpose – to scare [the Americans], to
restrain them so that they have appreciated this business [and] to give
them back some of their own medicine.[50]

At the Vienna summit meeting, Khrushchev derided the notion of accidental war.[51] During the crisis, however, he not only understood the
danger, but described it most eloquently in a letter to Kennedy:

Mr. President we and you ought not now to pull on the end of the
rope in which you have tied the knot of war, because the more the two
of us pull, the tighter the knot will be tied. And a moment may come
when that knot will be tied so tight that even he who tied it will not
have the strength to untie it. And then it will be necessary to cut that
knot, and what that would mean is not for me to explain to you,
because you yourself understand perfectly well of what terrible forces
our countries dispose.[52]

The blockade was then not only a signal of commitment; it was what
Schelling called a 'threat that leaves something to chance'.[53] As Soviet
ambassador to the UN, Valerian Zorin, put it in reporting his conversation
with UN Secretary General U Thant on the day the crisis reached its
climax, 'we emphasized that it is necessary to act quickly, since our ships
cannot remain on the open sea for an indefinite period of time, and since
the situation cannot be allowed to get out of control'.[54] Everyone affirmed
that the situation could not be allowed to get out of control, but this was
premised on the realization that it could get out of control. In fact, as Len
Scott has argued, if a nuclear weapon were fired in the crisis, this decision
probably would have been made by a military subordinate, not by either of
the leaders.[55] Khrushchev tried to keep his own soldiers in Cuba under
close command, and Kennedy expended great energies on overseeing and
monitoring what the Navy was doing. But both realized that there were
severe limits on what they could do – and they were right. As Sergei
Khrushchev characterizes it, the line between upholding the Soviet
'dignity of a great power ... [and] making a fatal miscalculation ... was ...
almost invisible'.[56] This is why, contrary to American fears, Khrushchev did
not respond to the blockade by exerting pressure on Berlin, rebuking a
colleague who suggested this: 'keep that kind of advice to yourself. We
don't know how to get out of one predicament and you drag us into
another'.[57] Kennedy also sought to be cautious, but not all American
actions conformed. He did not understand the dangers involved in dropping signaling depth charges on Soviet submarines, nor did he think to
suspend test flights of missiles and U-2 missions over the Arctic or understand that the US fighters scrambled to protect the plane that stayed over
Soviet territory were armed with nuclear tipped air-to-air missiles.[58]

Khrushchev's abilities to control his forces in Cuba and in the submarines, let alone Fidel Castro, were even less. Indeed it was an unauthorized shooting down of a U-2 flight over Cuba (ordered not by Castro, as the American thought, but by the Soviet officer on the scene) that deeply disturbed both sides. Sergei Khrushchev reports that 'it was at that very moment – not before or after – that Father felt the situation slipping out of control.... As Father said later, that was the moment when he felt instinctively that the missiles had to be removed, that disaster loomed'.[59] Perhaps at least as important was Castro's letter arguing the invasion was about to start and that the Soviet Union should launch a pre-emptive nuclear strike. Khrushchev regarded this as crazy and feared that the Cuba leader would take some rash action that might trigger a war.[60] The situation was then simply too dangerous to be allowed to continue: as Fyodor Burlatsky, Khrushchev's speech writer, put it later, 'he had decided that it was enough'.[61]

In parallel, at the end Kennedy felt such a sense of urgency that he did not wait to see whether Khrushchev might withdraw the missiles in return for a no-invasion pledge before simultaneously sending his brother to Ambassador Dobrynin to sweeten the pot with the Jupiters in Turkey (along with a very tough warning that an immediate reply was needed). Just as Khrushchev's worry was reflected in his decision to stop haggling, Kennedy told Khrushchev that he was sending his acceptance via public broadcast, as Khrushchev had done with his last message, 'because of the great importance I attach to moving forward promptly to the settlement of the Cuban crisis. I think that you and I ... were aware that developments were approaching a point where events could have become unmanageable'.[62]

In such a situation, both leaders had to balance the imperative to avoid war with the need to show resolve, partly by denying the danger. So in order to demonstrate that he did not feel that the risks were excessive and that he was not unduly moved by the American threat, Khrushchev strived to keep up appearances that all was normal. 'It doesn't pay to show that we are nervous.'[63] But while both sides feared undesired escalation, the pressures were greatest on Khrushchev because he had information on three frightening matters that Kennedy lacked. The first really was misinformation – Khrushchev and his colleagues, misunderstanding the American government, worried that the Pentagon would either act without authorization or bend the weak and inexperienced President to its will. At the climax of the crisis, Dobrynin reported that Robert Kennedy had hinted that his brother could no longer be confident of controlling the military, and the seeds of Khrushchev's concern that the military might act on its own were planted not only by general Soviet beliefs about the American political system, but by Bolshakov's report six months earlier that the Attorney General told him about the power and independence of the Joint Chiefs of Staff.[64]

Second, Khrushchev but not Kennedy knew that Castro was increasingly panicky and difficult to control. The Soviets had assured the Americans that it was they rather than Castro who were in control, and the Americans accepted this. But as the crisis went on, Khrushchev had reason to worry about what Castro would do. The Americans remained blissfully ignorant of this danger.

They also were ignorant of the number Soviet forces in Cuba, estimating them at something like a third of the actual figure. Toward the end of the crisis, they were told but did not focus on the fact that these forces were equipped with tactical missiles that likely had nuclear warheads (although they never learned that there were two types of such weapons, one of which was being positioned to attack Guantánamo). Khrushchev knew this very well, and understood as the Americans did not that an invasion would lead to a major clash between American and Soviet forces, one in which the latter might use tactical nuclear weapons even if Khrushchev withheld authorization. It remains a mystery to me why the likelihood that an invasion would face tactical nuclear weapons did not stop the ExComm's deliberations in its tracks. But the fact remains that it did not, and although the Americans realized that an invasion would be dangerous and bloody, they did not come to grips with the extent to which this was true.[65]

In all likelihood, furthermore, Khrushchev guessed that Kennedy did not share the last two of these worries. He then realized that Kennedy did not feel all the pressures to back down that he did, with the resulting decrease in his bargaining leverage. In addition, although Kennedy felt that escalation to nuclear war would be the worst outcome, he also realized that the nuclear balance was very much in the American favour. It is striking that as far as we can tell, neither side's leaders asked for briefings on the likely consequences of a nuclear war.[66] This does not mean that they did not think about it, and the Americans knew both that they might not escape damage in a nuclear war (especially if they did not pre-empt) and that the Soviet situation was even worse. In fact, it was much worse than Kennedy realized; the American estimates that the Soviets had something like 75 ICBMs was off by roughly a factor of four. Khrushchev then knew that while the USSR would be destroyed the US would suffer much less (whether either he or Kennedy thought about the Soviets' capacity to destroy Western Europe is not known, and few observers noted that the American stance that it valued Western Europe so much that it would treat an attack on it as an attack on the US – enshrined in Article V of the NATO treaty – implied that the Soviet ability to hold the Continent hostage was equivalent to the ability to destroy much of the US). Khrushchev may have also assumed that the combination of spy satellites and human agents (Oleg Penkovsky's spying had recently been uncovered) had led Kennedy to believe that the US had first-strike capability and could come through a nuclear war without significant damage.

Although a full discussion of the role of the strategic balance is beyond the scope of this paper, Kennedy was probably less influenced by American nuclear superiority than Khrushchev was by Soviet inferiority. To the extent that the latter sought to put missiles into Cuba in part in order to rectify the strategic balance, he would have been highly sensitive to how far behind the Soviets were and why it mattered. That at their June 1961 meeting in Vienna Khrushchev so quickly agreed with Kennedy's (incorrect) statement that the two sides had equal nuclear power[67] is not surprising (although Kennedy's statement is), for this at minimum is what he was seeking. He knew his country was not there yet, however. The influence of the strategic balance on Kennedy is less certain. As most of the ExComm members stressed later, everyone believed that even a single bomb going off in an American city would be a disaster that would not be compensated for by the utter destruction of the Soviet Union. On the other hand, in the presidential campaign Kennedy had said he would move vigorously to close the 'missile gap' and was relieved on assuming office to discover that it was in the American favour. When Richard Nixon became president he frequently bemoaned the fact that the balance he inherited was so much less favourable than the one in October 1962 and implied that Kennedy was able to act strongly then because of the nuclear advantage. The participants in the crisis might have sincerely denied this, but as I noted above people often are unaware of the influences on their own behaviour. Perhaps Kennedy and his colleagues gained confidence by the balance (and by the knowledge that Khrushchev was aware of how badly outgunned he was), and this may even have contributed to their commitment to having the missiles removed because they had reason to believe that they had the leverage to do this.

For the Soviets it was not only the threat that leaves something to chance in the form of the blockade and the aerial reconnaissance that generated pressure. The looming danger was that the US would invade Cuba, and neither Khrushchev nor Castro had any doubt that the US could overwhelm the island. For Khrushchev, this would be a three-fold disaster as it would be a humiliating defeat, bury any hope for détente (needed, among other things, for Khrushchev to be able to reduce the crushing burden of military expenses), and could well escalate. While some American hardliners, especially but not only in the military, wanted to overthrow Castro, Kennedy saw the grave dangers in an invasion and probably believed that even if it did not lead to a wider war, the Soviets might take Berlin or, at minimum, would end the search for better relations with the US. So Kennedy strongly resisted arguments for invasion, but he could not dismiss them and feared that if the crisis did not end soon he might have to take this step. Khrushchev was even more worried, so he avidly and nervously watched for all signs that the US would invade, including a spurious tip from a bartender at the Washington Press Club that the force was about to sail.[68] According to some accounts, the fear was fuelled by an equally false report that Kennedy was about to make another nationwide address, which Khrushchev thought would announce the attack. Indeed the movement of troops and other preparations might have been sufficient to induce the Soviets to pull back even without the blockade, and without the fear of invasion it is possible that Khrushchev would have preferred an air attack to withdrawal. Kennedy wanted to avoid an invasion, but Khrushchev had to. To say that he retreated under these pressures is not to say that he was weak or foolish; far from it, he was sensible.[69]

How did the crisis end?

Most of the debate about how the crisis ended centers on the nature and impact of Kennedy's commitment to withdraw the Jupiter missiles from Turkey. Was this a bargain, and if so was it an implicit or explicit one, was it an agreement, was it an arrangement, was it an understanding, was it a 'hedged promise'[70] – and is there a real difference between these? Because 'arrangement' is the most neutral term, I will use it. The scholarly debate about exactly what the arrangement was is particularly difficult, not only because the record is incomplete, but because the point was not an outcome, but how each side (or each person in each side) interpreted it. Unlike other unresolvable debates, such as that concerning Khrushchev's motivations for deploying missiles to Cuba, this one makes literally no sense as it is usually posed as a question of what was agreed to because there is no real arrangement aside from what the participants believed about it.

The controversy should not obscure seven areas of agreement, however. First, Kennedy considered the possibility of something along these lines from the first days of the crisis.[71] The fact that Khrushchev raised it did not come as a surprise to him, and he was very annoyed that the State Department had not done more to lay the foundation for the arrangement during if not before the crisis.[72] Interestingly, on 19 October (i.e. before it was public that the US knew of the missiles), Dobrynin told Moscow that on the 16th (i.e. the day Kennedy learned of the emplacement), in a closed meeting with media executives and reporters Kennedy talked about the Soviet military presence in Cuba and said that 'There can be no deal struck with the USSR regarding its renunciation of bases in Cuba in exchange for the USA's renunciation of bases in other parts of the world (in Turkey, for example).'[73]

Second, the missiles were seen by the civilian leaders as obsolete by the time they were installed, and the necessary target coverage could be supplied in a more secure fashion by the Polaris submarines that were soon to move into the Mediterranean. Although Kennedy had not ordered the Jupiters to be removed, he did want them out, had called for a study to be done, on the first day of the crisis mused that this 'gives us an excuse to get them out of Turkey and Italy', and during the final day's deliberation said that 'we last year tried to get the missiles out of there because they're not militarily useful'.[74] Even the members of the ExComm who vigorously opposed a trade did so because of the bad impression it would make, not because they thought the US was losing a military asset. (The missiles had no military value to the US because they were highly vulnerable, which meant that they were of no use as a retaliatory force, and indeed the lack of this kind of utility made them provocative. But this does not mean that the Soviets did not see them as a threat because they could have been used for a first strike. Nevertheless, although the evidence is not as clear, it does appears that Khrushchev thought these missiles were militarily insignificant, knew that this was the US view, and understood that Polaris submarines would soon replace them, thus presumably increasing his confidence that Kennedy would accept a trade).[75]

Indeed, even without the crisis and without the bargaining, the missiles probably would have been withdrawn quite soon. These two aspects should be separated. The pre-crisis deliberations of both the Kennedy and the Eisenhower administrations and the amount of attention paid to the Jupiters even before Khrushchev raised the issue make it clear that the leading figures in the government felt that the alliance was better off without these missiles, especially when the Polaris submarines were available. But the issue had not seemed urgent, especially in light of the Turks' desire to keep them, and so they might have remained in place for another couple of years had there been no crisis. But even without having to make the arrangement, the crisis itself heightened the sense of urgency on the part of Kennedy in a way that I think allows us to be fairly confident that the missiles would have been removed within something like a year even had Khrushchev not raised the issue. In this regard, it is telling that the US removed the missiles from Italy as well as from Turkey even though Khrushchev never called for this.[76] (Why both sides focused on the missiles in Turkey and ignored those in Italy is a puzzle, although at least some of the reason is the obvious parallel between the former and Cuba due to the geographical proximity to the threatened superpower.)[77] If there was a trade, it was not an equal one since what Khrushchev gave up was important to both him and Kennedy and what Kennedy surrendered was not. As in much international politics, the outcome was roughly congruent with the distribution of power.

A third area of agreement is that in the tense debate following the arrival of Khrushchev's letter calling for a missile swap Kennedy was alone in believing that the US almost surely would have to accept it and that the harm to the NATO alliance would be slight, in part because NATO could be maneuvered into endorsing it as a way of avoiding more dangerous actions. Whether this difference of opinion is to be explained by differences in individual views and willingness to run risks or whether it is more attributable to the roles that people had, with the President having ultimate responsibility and therefore seeing the world differently, is impossible to determine. Whatever the source, his views were insistent and unequivocal.[78]

The fourth and related point is that while Kennedy was influenced by the argument of his Soviet expert Llewellyn Thompson that Khrushchev would back down without any arrangement about the Jupiters, he was not convinced that this would work, and so after the ExComm meeting he gathered a small group of colleagues and decided that Robert Kennedy would tell Dobrynin that if the Soviets withdrew their missiles, the Jupiters would soon be removed. In passing we should note that Kennedy's approach to this issue shows the limits of the ExComm as he ignored its advice and kept it in the dark about what he was doing.[79]

Fifth, we will never know exactly what Robert Kennedy said to Dobrynin or what the latter heard (these can be different, of course), and we do not have a record, let alone a tape-recording, of the meeting in which President Kennedy and his colleagues decided on what message his brother would carry. We have Dobrynin's long cable to Moscow and a shorter memo by Robert Kennedy to Rusk, but the memo was clearly circumspect and the cable is subject to normal ambassadorial biases. While diplomats are trained to report accurately, not only do their expectations and needs influence what they hear, but what they write is often colored by the desire to have their home governments adopt the policy they favour. Although this complicates the lives of both scholars and policy-makers, it is not surprising that the participants' memos of conversations are often different. We have to resign ourselves to the fact that while we know more about this interaction than we do about many others, we will never know what was said, let alone the tone of voice and body language that can create important impressions and expectations.

Perhaps the details do not matter because for Kennedy and his colleagues the fate of the Jupiters was much less important than that the discussion not be revealed. Secrecy had to be maintained; allies and the general public had to be deceived. It would then be a mistake to say that Kennedy accepted Khrushchev's offer, because the latter involved a public trade. I will come back to why this mattered.

Finally, the arrangement almost surely was not responsible for Khrushchev's response. He was ready to settle for the promise not to invade Cuba earlier and does not seem to have been committed to the sweetener. Although there is some doubt on this point, it appears that Dobrynin's report only reached the Presidium after Khrushchev had announced his decision, and according to Troyanovsky the Soviets were more impressed by the reports that Kennedy might yield to Pentagon pressure than they were by the promise to remove the Jupiters.[80] Indeed, if Sergei Khrushchev is correct, his father did not consider what he heard to be a significant concession, and in fact concluded that 'a trade was no longer feasible. There was no use harping on the Turkish missiles. They were not what counted. The idea of a trade would have to be given up. It was a shame. But life was more important than prestige'.[81] As far as we can tell, Khrushchev never bragged to his colleagues that the removal of the Jupiters was a great victory and that it showed that the Soviet Union could no longer be bullied. Instead, he seems mostly to have been relieved that the crisis ended without an invasion and to have been impressed by what he thought was Kennedy's ability to stand up to the military, something that paved the way for the mini-détente in 1963.

These points are probably more important than the remaining disputes about how the arrangement should be characterized. Central to the latter is whether Robert Kennedy merely informed Dobrynin that the missiles in Turkey would soon be out, whether he promised to withdraw them as a quid pro quo for the Soviets removing their missiles from Cuba, or whether it was something in between. Later accounts by members of the small group that set the policy say that Robert Kennedy was instructed to say the former,[82] but Dobrynin's report is a bit different:

> 'And what about Turkey?' I asked R. Kennedy.
> 'If that is the only obstacle to achieving the regulation I mentioned earlier, then the president doesn't see any unsurmountable [*sic*] difficulties in reconciling this issue,' replied R. Kennedy. 'The greatest difficulty for the president is the public discussion of the issue of Turkey. Formally the deployment of missiles in Turkey was done by special decision of the NATO Council. To announce now a unilateral decision by the president of the USA to withdraw missile bases from Turkey – this would damage the entire structure of NATO and the US position as the leader of NATO, where, as the Soviet government knows very well, there are many arguments. In short, if such a decision were announced now it would seriously tear apart NATO.'
> 'However, President Kennedy is ready to come to agree on that question with N.S. Khrushchev, too. I think that in order to withdraw these bases from Turkey,' R. Kennedy said, 'we need 4–5 months. This is the minimal amount of time necessary for the US government to do this, taking into account the procedures that exist within the NATO framework.... However the president can't say anything public in this regard about Turkey,' R. Kennedy said again.[83]

There is some discrepancy between this version and Robert Kennedy's briefer report to Dean Rusk:

> He then asked me about Khrushchev's other proposal dealing with the removal of missiles from Turkey. I replied that there could be no *quid pro quo* – no deal of this kind could be made. This was a matter that had to be considered by NATO and it was up to NATO to make the decision. I said it was completely impossible for NATO to take

such a step under the present threatening position of the Soviet Union. If some time elapsed – and per your [Rusk's] instructions, I mentioned four or five months – I said I was sure these matters could be resolved satisfactorily.[84]

The last sentence was crossed out by hand, but is confirmed by Dobrynin's.

Other differences between the two accounts are subtle but real. It does not concern the fate of the Jupiters – as I noted, despite Khrushchev's complaints, neither he nor the American leaders considered the missiles to have any military value. Rather the sparring then and later concerned not what the US would do, but why it was doing it. Not surprisingly, ambiguity is high here, and indeed facilitated the arrangement, which each side could interpret as it chose. This is not uncommon because actors want to project desired images, something that often involves seeking acceptance of their motives.[85] In particular, states do not want to be seen as having given in to pressure. The reason is obvious, although its wisdom can be debated: to do so is to imply that you are weak and that further pressure in this or other encounters will lead to further concessions. So after an arrangement has been made, each side often will play up the importance of what the other has done and play down the importance of its moves if they might be portrayed as concessions (although when reciprocity is expected the actor may exaggerate the value of what she has given up). States then bargain over how they had bargained, and formulations are often awkward. For example, the fighting between Hamas and Israel in November 2012 ended in a ceasefire in which Hamas claimed that in return for its restraint Israel had agreed to relax the blockade on Gaza. Israel denied this, and a month later when it allowed building material in, stressed not only that this was for the private sector and not the government, but also that the transfer was conducted 'against the background of the talks with the Egyptians and the quiet that has prevailed on the border' rather than being the fulfillment of a settlement with Hamas.[86] Was this a bargain, an arrangement, an understanding, a unilateral move, or a combination, rendered ambiguous on purpose?

It is therefore interesting that while Robert Kennedy's version has him explicitly denying that there would be a quid pro quo, his memo does not say that he told Dobrynin that the decision to withdraw the Jupiters had been made earlier, and Theodore Sorensen felt the need to add this to Kennedy's account for *Thirteen Days*.[87] This was the version the US wanted to have accepted because it minimized the extent to which the Soviets had gained anything from placing missiles in Cuba, and it corresponds to Bundy's and Rusk's account of the formulation that the latter proposed that had made Kennedy's advisors comfortable about offering an arrangement to Dobrynin.[88] If the Soviets believed that the Americans had already decided to remove the missiles, or even that they were looking for an opportunity to do so, then they would not have concluded that the US had retreated. Regardless of exactly what Robert Kennedy said, it is clear that his brother wanted the missiles out; it was not removing them but doing so under pressure that was troublesome. This means that, for the US at least, the appearance was the substance. Even in principle, we cannot peel off layers of faulty memories, distorted communications, and imprecise statements to find an underlying reality. What mattered was how the parties interpreted the arrangement. Khrushchev wanted to minimize the extent to which audiences, both domestic and foreign, believed that he had been reckless in placing missiles in Cuba and feckless in withdrawing them at the first whiff of gunpowder. Kennedy needed to be seen as tough, but not irresponsible. The fate of the Jupiters mattered only for impression management, and so success or failure necessarily resided in the minds of various perceivers.

Two days later Khrushchev sent an unsigned letter formalizing the arrangement.[89] This triggered an urgent visit by Robert Kennedy to return it, explaining (according to Dobrynin) that there was always a danger that even the most confidential of records would become public and that 'the appearance of such a document could cause irreparable harm to my political career in the future'.[90] Dobrynin and, later, Khrushchev agreed to the letter's return without protest, perhaps eased by the fact that Kennedy gave a selfish reason that did not reopen questions of Soviet and American resolve. Dobrynin did press Kennedy to confirm the 'understanding' (a term his cable used repeatedly), however, and even after Kennedy had done so Dobrynin reports that 'I asked him again about whether the President really confirms the understanding with N.S. Khrushchev on the elimination of American missile bases in Turkey. Robert Kennedy said once again that he confirmed it, and again that he hoped that their motivations would be properly understood in Moscow', although whether the latter phrase refers to the motives for the arrangement or to the need for secrecy remains unclear, as does whether Khrushchev sought a formal exchange of letters because he worried that Kennedy would renege, wanted to convince Kennedy that the Soviets considered that this had been a quid pro quo, or hoped to make gains by publicizing the arrangement.

In this regard it is interesting that Dobrynin notes parenthetically that 'the greatest suspicion in the two Kennedy brothers was elicited by the part of Khrushchev's letter which speaks directly of a link between the Cuban events and the bases in Turkey', but in fact Khrushchev's letter only alludes to a link rather than clearly stating it, and Dobrynin's concern in the meeting was to have Kennedy reaffirm that the missiles would be removed rather than to stress that this was a trade, which implied that for Dobrynin at least the Jupiters themselves did matter. Robert Kennedy's notes of what he planned to tell the ambassador include the statement that there was 'no *quid pro quo* ... as I told you [at the meeting of 27 October]'.[91] So while Dobrynin's term 'understanding' has great appeal, in fact it is far from clear that the two sides shared an understanding of the extent and kind of linkage that was involved and of the magnitude of the American concession (or whether there was a real concession at all). If the words that Sorensen added to Robert Kennedy's *Thirteen Days* reflected the understanding of the Americans involved, it was more of an explanation of what would happen than it was a concession.

Aside from this exchange, neither Kennedy nor Khrushchev attempted to convince the other to accept his desired interpretation of the arrangement, or even to convince the other that he held a certain view of it. Part of the reason was that they were consumed by the subsequent bargaining over the bombers and other weapons whose status remained ambiguous,[92] and part was that so few people on either side were knowledgeable that any discussion would have had to be reserved for special channels, and this did not seem a good use of these resources, especially since the dialogue was not likely to yield any advantage.

The muted tussle over interpretations was related to but not identical with the short-lived dispute about whether the arrangement would be kept secret. Secrecy facilitated each side holding different interpretations because there was no need to spell out the arrangement. But public statements are not entirely incompatible with ambiguity and multiple interpretations. If the Shanghai communiqué by the US and the People's Republic of China (PRC) in 1972 was extreme in this regard, with each side stating its views and acknowledging the disputes, many agreements, even formal ones, are quite ambiguous and some are accompanied by statements by one or both sides about how they interpret it. Secrecy was important for the Americans because it allowed them to portray the crisis as more of an American victory than it actually was. This point should not be exaggerated, however. The American no-invasion pledge was public, and for those who were committed to overthrowing Castro this was a major concession (one that Kennedy had resisted giving),[93] in fact a more important one than removing obsolete missiles from Turkey that the administration wanted removed. But Kennedy and his colleagues did not want the American public or allies to know that he had moved at least part of the way to meet Khrushchev's demands, and the fact that the arrangement was kept secret both points to the centrality of the interpretation of why the US acted as it did rather than what the US did and underscores American power in its ability to resist an open trade.

Although it seems odd for Robert Kennedy to have talked about his own political future at this juncture, it was obvious that the Republicans and even Democratic hawks would have used the arrangement to disparage those who were associated with it. Perhaps at least as important was the belief that although the allies usually urged the Americans to be less stiff-necked towards the Soviet Union, they would have been alarmed at the arrangement. This was especially true of the West Germans, who suspected (correctly) that Kennedy was willing to make what were for them unacceptable concessions over West Berlin. Throughout the Cold War, the US believed that its allies both lacked resolve and were hypersensitive to the US making deals behind their backs. While the US view of allies seems illogical, seeing them as both too ready to make concessions and as afraid that the US would do so, the allies did indeed hold these contradictory fears.

For Kennedy, then, what was at stake was largely his reputation for standing up to Soviet pressure and threats. Although whether and how states acquire reputations is the subject of dispute in the IR literature, there is little doubt that states believe that others do judge them and are influenced by their reputations.[94] The American attitude, then, was not unusual. What was a bit odd, however, is that reputation is usually believed to be most important in the eyes of adversaries, although the views of allies matter as well. Here, of course, Khrushchev knew of the arrangement, and if Kennedy and his colleagues carefully thought about it they probably would have guessed that Khrushchev regarded it as a greater concession than they did. Although the refusal to make the arrangement public could contribute to an American reputation for resolve, what the Soviets knew – or believed – about it was beyond retrieval. So even if reputation in Soviet eyes was most significant to Kennedy, only the allied views could be affected at this point. And it is not out of the question that this concern was more important to Kennedy even before he made the arrangement. He was deeply aware of the fissures in the alliance and the distrust of the US. Furthermore, he probably instinctively understood what a former British Minister of Defence said: 'It takes only 5% credibility of American retaliation to deter the Soviets, but 95% credibility to reassure the Europeans.'[95] He was right, and Harold Macmillan, the British Prime Minister who almost always urged American presidents to be flexible and negotiate, believed that 'anything like this deal would do great injury to NATO'.[96]

Also very important was Kennedy's reputation with the American public, especially in light of his re-election concerns. Although his pledge not to invade Cuba did not come in for extensive domestic criticism, perhaps because only a few people outside of Washington thought that the US ever would invade and so regarded this as a concession, the fact that Kennedy's desire to get rid of the Jupiters had been kept secret meant that it would have been impossible to have portrayed their withdrawal as anything other than giving in to Soviet pressure. Kennedy probably would have been willing to pay the price if this had been required in order to end the crisis (using the UN or the NATO Council as a cover to reduce the damage), but avoiding it if at all possible was an imperative in light of the series of foreign policy failures that had beset the administration. At minimum, a public deal would have made it much more difficult for him to follow the conciliatory diplomatic path he embarked on in the spring.

The other message that Robert Kennedy conveyed also shows the actors' concern with interpretations, but here they were conspiring or conniving[97] with each other rather than struggling. In both Kennedy's and Dobrynin's accounts it is obvious that the former gave an ultimatum, and Khrushchev labels it as such in his memoirs.[98] Kennedy gave a deadline for compliance and made clear that if it were not forthcoming the US would attack. But ultimata are simply not acceptable in modern diplomacy, at least not among states of roughly equal power and standing, because acceding to one is seen as humiliating and a clear indication of weakness. So Kennedy and Dobrynin agreed that the ultimatum was not an ultimatum. In Kennedy's word's, 'this was not an ultimatum … but just a statement of facts'. Dobrynin reports that he 'noted that it went without saying that the Soviet government would not accept any ultimatums and it was good that the American government realized that'.[99] (The very fact that Dobrynin had to stress that he was not interpreting the American message as an ultimatum indicates that any sensible observer would recognize it as one.) By volunteering that this was not an ultimatum and allowing Dobrynin to underscore this, Kennedy made acceptance easier, and indeed the fact that Dobrynin went out of his way to say that it was not an ultimatum implied that he thought his government would accept it as long as it was not so labelled. This was not a matter of saving face in the sense of sparing Soviet feelings; if the US had defined its message as an ultimatum, then by withdrawing the missiles the Soviets would have been bowing to superior American power rather than carrying out a statesman-like act to bring the crisis to a close. In a similar spirit, in his initial response to the blockade Khrushchev told Kennedy that 'I would like to give you a friendly warning that the measures announced in your statement represent a grave threat to peace and security in the world'.[100] Obviously there was nothing friendly about this, but saying it was, was itself a placating gesture. The other side of this coin is that in his next letter Khrushchev refers to the American demands as an ultimatum.[101] Obviously this was technically incorrect, as Kennedy had specified neither a deadline nor the action that the US would take if need be. But he did demand that the missiles be withdrawn, and by calling this an ultimatum Khrushchev signaled that he would not comply.

Final observations

Although in the end the arrangement about the Jupiters was a side-show, the diplomacy surrounding it was fascinating and ingenious, and it does shed light on the participants' priorities and calculations. Kennedy's flexibility both illuminates his general outlook and, as I will discuss below, some general characteristics of the Cold War, and Khrushchev's desire to salvage as much as he could from the crisis in parallel reveals something of his character. But we should not lose sight of the fact that what drove each side was the fear of war, which bore down even more heavily on Khrushchev than on Kennedy. Available Soviet records indicate that his willingness to make concessions and to do so quickly varied directly with his fears of an invasion and things getting out of control. He avidly consumed the numerous intelligence reports, most of them unfounded, concerning whether or not an invasion was imminent. When he thought it was not, he would 'look around' to see if he had more time and leverage to exact concessions.[102]

Although the missile crisis stands out for its drama and danger, it is typical of the Cold War in six ways, some of which contradict general IR theories. First, the bargaining over symbols and the struggle for interpretations that were so important in the final phases were common during the Cold War. Ironically, the very power of nuclear weapons meant that confrontations over matters of real value had to be minimized, and in the absence of the willingness to use such weapons, surrogate struggles were needed to show credibility. Psychology and symbolism were thus central to the ways in which nuclear weapons had influence.[103] Bloody struggles of course existed, most obviously in Korea and Vietnam. But these were never fights over material resources and military assets. They were attempts at impression management.

Second, judgments of relative military power mattered in the crisis as it did throughout the Cold War, but communication was also central, although this need not imply cooperation. At every stage of this episode the two sides puzzled over what the other would do next and how it would react to various moves the state might make, and in parallel tried to convince the other about how it would act – sometimes accurately and sometime misleadingly. This came up most sharply when McNamara explained to the Chief of Naval Operations that following Navy standard operating procedures was not adequate because this was not simply a blockade but 'a means of communication between Kennedy and Khrushchev',[104] and when Robert Kennedy shrewdly pointed out that any American ship that might intercept a Soviet vessel should have on board at least one person who spoke Russian. Much of the Cold War was about each side communicating what was most important to it, what it would and would not tolerate, and the risks it was willing to run. Of course this was not simple because each side had incentives to deceive the other and in fact did not know how it would respond to a major challenge. But the constant search for credibility, most obvious on the American side, was driven by and carried out through communication.

Third, credibility was central to the crisis at all stages, as it was to the Cold War. Considerations of the military balance in the sense of the relative advantage and disadvantages that would accrue were a war to be fought were not unimportant, but were framed by the felt need to convince adversaries and allies that the state would fight if need be. As far as we can tell, Khrushchev's decision to place missiles in Cuba, whatever his motives, was not preceded by any detailed military analysis. He knew that his military strength would be increased, but this was less important in terms of brute force than it was for bolstering his credibility, although whether for defending Cuba, putting pressure on West Berlin, or generally establishing a larger role for the USSR (or all three) is hard to determine. Eisenhower's decision to put Jupiters into Italy and Turkey was sparked by the need to reassure allies after the Soviets launched sputnik, and Kennedy's re-evaluation of the decision was cut short by his weak performance at the Vienna summit.[105] During the missile crisis itself, of course, the sides jostled to bolster the credibility of their threats, and the bargaining over the arrangement for the Jupiters was driven by fears and hopes about how adversaries and allies (and domestic audiences) would see the credibility of Soviet and American threats and promises in the aftermath. It explains why Kennedy was willing to make the arrangement but insisted on keeping it secret and why he refused to do so as part of his opening bid, believing that Adlai Stevenson's proposal to do so at the start would only lead to further Soviet demands.[106]

Concern with credibility can be found throughout history, but, like the willingness of each side to make concessions in order avoid war, was heightened by nuclear weapons. The very fact that resort to all-out war would be, in Kennedy's words quoted earlier, the 'final failure' meant that states were preoccupied by how they could make the threat to fight at all believable. Given the dreadful consequences of war, threats did not have to be anything like completely believable to be effective, but no one could be sure how much credibility was enough, which helps explain why both sides constantly sought ways to protect and build their reputations for resolve.[107] Most of the scholarship here has concentrated on the American preoccupation, often critically so. But whether foolish or not, it was clearly shared by Soviet leaders. Credibility as both a desired goal and an instrument was central to Khrushchev's 'meniscus strategy' of increasing tensions to compensate for military weakness,[108] it was what he sought in calling for a missile trade,[109] and throughout the crisis he continued his habit of talking about the importance of displaying his own 'nerve' and weakening Kennedy's – and did so in much cruder terms than the Americans used.

Fourth, and linked to the reasons why credibility was so important, the costs of a nuclear war were so great that neither side was willing to try to exact the last possible concession from the other at the cost of continuing a confrontation that might get out of control. Khrushchev would have withdrawn the missiles in return for a no-invasion pledge; the sweetener of the Jupiters arrangement was not needed. For his part, Kennedy was almost certainly willing to give more than that and probably would have made the trade in public if this had been necessary. Here too the missile crisis was not unique. Kennedy was willing to make major concessions over Berlin if Khrushchev had pushed harder, and the latter in turn might not have resisted if the US had dismantled the Berlin Wall in its first few days. I am not implying that the leaders were foolish or feckless; far from it, they sensibly understood that nuclear weapons required an unusual degree of prudence.[110]

Fifth, as the previous paragraph indicates, Kennedy and Khrushchev consistently had to make trade-offs between the danger of war and the cost of diplomatic concessions. This contributed to the pendulum swings between periods of détente and periods of high tension throughout the Cold War. So it is not entirely surprising that the extreme danger of the missile crisis was followed by a concerted effort to manage relations quite differently. But this effort was not automatic and took real statesmanship on the part of both leaders. Kennedy's American University speech in June 1963 reaching out to the Soviet Union was a major step toward conciliation. That it reflected the President's deep-seated convictions that were not universally shared is shown by the fact that the State and Defense departments were excluded from the process because they might have tried to undercut it.[111] Khrushchev's willingness to reciprocate should also not be taken for granted. While it was coupled with efforts to gain nuclear and political parity with the US, it was also a genuine effort to reach agreement, including the informal understanding that he would no longer try to change the status quo in Berlin. This was not the only way a leader could have responded to the crisis. Khrushchev admired Kennedy's willingness to restrain the military and believed that this showed that, contrary to his earlier beliefs, Kennedy was not only someone who could not easily be bullied, but was also a leader who one could do business with.

A final characteristic of the crisis may be less typical of the Cold War, although perhaps if we look more carefully we will find that it played a larger role than we might think. Here I am referring to the trust that Kennedy placed in Khrushchev. It was fine for the Attorney General to say that the arrangement had to be kept secret and for Dobrynin to say that it would be. But why should Kennedy have had any faith that the Chairman would live up to his word? Even in its most benign interpretation, the arrangement was discrepant from the image Kennedy was trying to project, and the fact that he demanded secrecy gave Khrushchev a hostage. As Len Scott notes, 'Khrushchev kept his silence',[112] but Kennedy was running a great risk because at any point Khrushchev could have gone public. Even though proof would have been impossible, once attention was focused on a swift withdrawal of the Jupiters, many people undoubtedly would have concluded that Kennedy had not only agreed to a trade, but had lied about it. It is only a slight exaggeration to say that Kennedy placed his fate in Khrushchev's hands. Of course if Khrushchev had revealed the secret he would have destroyed his relationship with Kennedy, but in some circumstances this might have seemed worthwhile and, in any event, Kennedy knew that Khrushchev was impulsive. What Khrushchev's intentions were in this regard is not entirely clear. Sergei Khrushchev reports that while his father 'wanted very much to get written guarantees' about the Turkish missiles, this was not vital. 'White House promises to remove the missiles would come in very handy for foreign consumption, to counter those people who would inevitably rant and rave that he had retreated under pressure from the imperialists.'[113] This obviously implies that he planned to tell the Chinese and others of the arrangement, which meant that it would almost inevitably become public.[114] How this fits with what Sergei reports was his father's desire to build a trusting relationship with Kennedy is unclear, and was probably yet another contradiction Khrushchev did not think through.

So this appears to have been an instance of unusual trust, one that is hard to explain by standard IR theories. But perhaps there was more trust in the Cold War than most of our accounts would have it. Could we have otherwise survived?

Notes

1 I am grateful for comments by Richard Immerman, Mark Kramer, Melvyn Leffler, Leopoldo Nuti, Stephen Sestanovich, Len Scott, Marc Trachtenberg, Philip Zelikow and an anonymous reviewer.
2 Kent's comment is in 'A Crucial Estimate Relived', originally published in CIA's classified *Studies in Intelligence* in 1964 and reprinted in Donald Steury (ed.), *Sherman Kent and the Board of National Estimates: Collected Essays* (Washington, DC: Center for the Study of Intelligence, Central Intelligence Agency 1994) p. 185. Although this is not the place to discuss all the sources of the US intelligence failure, central was the inability of American leaders and analysts to empathize with Khrushchev and understand the pressures on him, McGeorge Bundy, *Danger and Survival: Choices about the Bomb in the First Fifty Years* (New York: Vintage Books 1988) pp. 415–20.
3 Ernest R. May and Philip D. Zelikow (eds), *The Kennedy Tapes: Inside the White House during the Cuban Missile Crisis* (New York: W.W. Norton & Company 2002) p. 62.
4 But had they placed a higher probability on the Soviet's putting missiles in, they would not have reduced the U-2 coverage on 10 September in response to the danger that the newly emplaced anti-aircraft missiles might bring down a reconnaissance flight and trigger a politically costly situation in the run-up to the Congressional elections, David Barrett and Max Holland, *Blind over Cuba: The Photo Gap and the Missile Crisis* (College Station, TX: Texas A&M University Press 2012).
5 May and Zelikow, *Kennedy Tapes*, p. 197.
6 Ibid., p. 182.
7 Ibid., p. 332.
8 Ibid., p. 71.
9 James G. Blight and David A. Welch, *On the Brink: Americans and Soviets Reexamine the Cuban Missile Crisis* (New York: Farrar, Straus and Giroux 1990) pp. 215–16.
10 Ibid, pp. 263–4; Dobrynin's cable of 25 October 1962, *Cold War International History Project Bulletin*, 8–9 (Winter 1996–7) 288.
11 Both game theory and schools of social constructivism that stress that reality is constituted by intersubjective understandings depend on the players having stable expectations about the other and so run into difficulties in these situations. The Director of the CIA, John McCone, had predicted the Soviet action (although his reasoning was incorrect) but he refrained from bragging

and while generally taking a hard line during the crisis was not totally confident.

12 For other examples, of Kennedy and his colleagues trying to explain Khrushchev's behaviour, see May and Zelikow, *Kennedy Tapes*, pp. 42, 249, 315.

13 For the Pentagon's estimate that US troops would suffer 18,500 causalities in an invasion even if the Soviets did not use tactical nuclear weapons, see the analysis and documents on the National Security Archive: www.gwu.edu/~nsarchiv/NSAEBB/NSAEBB397/ (last accessed 27 September 2014).

14 Blight and Welch, *On the Brink*, pp. 209–12.

15 James Fearon, 'Rationalist Explanations for War', *International Organization*, 49/3 (Summer 1995) 379–414.

16 Stephen Walt, 'Rigor or Rigor Mortis? Rational Choice and Security Studies', *International Security*, 23/4 (Spring 1999) 34, note 85; Jonathan Mercer, 'Rational Signaling Revisited', in James Davis (ed.), *Psychology, Strategy and Conflict* (New York: Routledge 2013) p. 70.

17 Robert Lovett quoted in Sheldon M. Stern, *The Cuban Missile Crisis in American Memory: Myths versus Reality* (Stanford, CA: Stanford University Press 2012) p. 27.

18 John F. Kennedy, 'Foreword' to Theodore Sorensen, *Decision-making in the White House* (New York: Columbia University Press 1963) p. xi.

19 Timothy Wilson, *Strangers to Ourselves: Discovering the Adaptive Unconscious* (Cambridge, MA: Harvard University Press 2002).

20 Timothy Naftali, 'The Malin Notes: Glimpses inside the Kremlin during the Cuban Missile Crisis', *Cold War International History Project Bulletin*, 17/18 (Fall 2012) 299–301.

21 The American decision to deploy missiles to Europe was not well thought out either. See Philip Nash, *The Other Missiles of October: Eisenhower, Kennedy, and the Jupiters 1957–1963* (Chapel Hill, NC: University of North Carolina Press 1997).

22 Department of State, *Foreign Relations of the United States [FRUS], 1961–1963, Vol. VI, Kennedy–Khrushchev Exchanges* (Washington, DC: Government Printing Office 1996) p. 168. Raymond Garthoff argues that even the Soviet leaders 'recognize[d] that the initiative in precipitating the crisis, if not the responsibility and blame, resided in their decision on deploying the missiles': Garthoff, *Reflections on the Cuban Missile Crisis* (Washington, DC: The Brookings Institution 1989) p. 158.

23 I have discussed this problem in explaining President Bush's decision to invade Iraq in 'Explaining the War in Iraq', in Trevor Thrall and Jane Cramer (eds), *Why Did the United States Invade Iraq?* (New York: Routledge 2012) pp. 25–48. For a discussion of the general problem of a priori under-determination and *ex post facto* over-determination, see James Kurth, 'U.S. Policies, Latin American Politics, and Praetorian Rule', in Phillippe Schmitter (ed.), *Military Rule in Latin America* (Beverly Hills, CA: Sage 1973) pp. 244–58.

24 William Taubman, *Khrushchev: The Man and His Era* (New York: Norton 2003) p. 532; also see May and Zelikow, 'Conclusion', in May and Zelikow (eds), *Kennedy Tapes*, pp. 416–19.

25 Nikita Khrushchev, *Khrushchev Remembers*, trans. and ed. by Strobe Talbott (Boston: Little, Brown and Company 1970) p. 494; Sergei Khrushchev, *Nikita Khrushchev and the Creation of a Superpower*, trans. by Shirley Benson (University Park, PA: Pennsylvania State University Press 2000) p. 489; Janos Radvanyi, *Hungary and the Superpowers: The 1956 Revolution and Realpolitik* (Stanford: Hoover Institution Press 1972) p. 137. Interestingly enough, the remark does not appear in the Radvanyi's reporting cable summarizing Mikoyan's talk, *Cold War International History Project Bulletin*, 17/18 (Fall 2012) 445–8.

Mikoyan's son provides a different and I think strained interpretation of the latter statement, Sergo Mikoyan, *The Soviet Cuban Missile Crisis: Castro, Mikoyan, Kennedy, Khrushchev, and the Missiles of November*, ed. by Svetlana Savranskaya (Stanford CA: Stanford University Press 2012) p. 94. The Jupiter missiles in Turkey that figured in the later bargaining played at least some role in Khrushchev's decision to send missiles to Cuba. Although it is hard to say how much weight we should put on his annoyance at realizing that there were hostile missiles on the other side of his Black Sea vacation residence and his desire to give the Americans 'a little of their own medicine' (Khrushchev, *Khrushchev Remembers*, p. 494), their example stirred Khrushchev's thinking and the precedent gave him not only rhetorical justification, but a degree of legitimacy, and perhaps contributed to his sense that the US would get over its shock and accept the deployment. On the last point, see James G. Blight, Bruce J. Allyn, and David A. Welch, *Cuba on the Brink: Castro, the Missile Crisis, and the Soviet Collapse* (New York: Pantheon 1993) p. 79; Richard Ned Lebow and Janis Gross Stein, *We All Lost the Cold War* (Princeton, NJ: Princeton University Press 1994) pp. 77–8.

26 Double standards are almost universal, and the Soviet leaders certainly held their fair share of them. For a popular summary of the psychological research, see Robert Kurzban, *Why Everyone (Else) Is a Hypocrite* (Princeton, NJ: Princeton University Press 2010).

27 Blight, Allyn, and Welch, *Cuba on the Brink*, p. 79.

28 Lebow and Stein, *We All Lost the Cold War*. For general discussions of the importance of status and honour, see, for example, Donald Kagan, *On the Origins of War and the Preservation of Peace* (New York: Doubleday 1995); Richard Ned Lebow, *A Cultural Theory of International Politics* (New York: Cambridge University Press 2008). Sergei Khrushchev links status to the defense of Cuba, arguing that he believed that 'if the Soviet Union was to be recognized as a great power, it must inevitably assume responsibility for the security of its allies. Otherwise, no one would believe it to be a world leader', Khrushchev, *Nikita Khrushchev*, p. 482.

29 As Bundy perceptively remarks, 'the more "expert" men were in attending to the Berlin crisis, the stronger their disposition to read the Soviet deployment to Cuba as a move in the Berlin game', Bundy, *Danger and Survival*, p. 422. For a strong argument that Berlin was indeed central and a good canvassing of the alternatives, see Graham Allison and Philip Zelikow, *Essence of Decision: Explaining the Cuban Missile Crisis* (New York: Longman 1999) pp. 82–109.

30 For summaries of Khrushchev's belligerent remarks about Berlin in the summer of 1962, see Taubman, *Khrushchev*, pp. 539–40; Aleksandr Fursenko and Timothy Naftali, *Khrushchev's Cold War* (New York: W.W. Norton 2006) pp. 446–7, 458; May and Zelikow, 'Conclusion', in May and Zelikow, *Kennedy Tapes*, pp. 426–7. Dobrynin testifies that his conversations with Khrushchev when he was departing to assume his position of ambassador lead him to conclude that 'Khrushchev believed he had a chance to shift the status quo in his favor in Berlin', Anatoly Dobrynin, *In Confidence: Moscow's Ambassador to America's Six Cold War Presidents* (New York: Times Books 1995) p. 64; also see pp. 61–2. Khrushchev linked Cuba and Berlin in a letter to Kennedy of September 28 (i.e. after Kennedy's statement that missiles in Cuba would be unacceptable but before they were discovered): *Kennedy–Khrushchev Exchanges*, pp. 158–9, and, in an odd linkage, on July 30 Kennedy appears to have agreed to cease low-level surveillance flights over the Soviet ships heading to Cuba in return for a Soviet promise to put the Berlin issue 'on ice', Aleksandr Fursenko and Timothy Naftali, *'One Hell of a Gamble': Khrushchev, Castro, and Kennedy, 1958–1964* (New York: Norton 1997) p. 194. Taubman suggests that

we should not be too quick to take the threats to Berlin at face value: Khrushchev perhaps 'didn't … know his own mind at all, an explanation for why no one else did either', *Khrushchev*, p. 540.

31 Khrushchev, *Nikita Khrushchev*, p. 528. Sergei also says that Berlin did play a role, but only in providing an example of how a superpower could and had to protect its outpost: p. 482.

32 Fursenko and Naftali, *Khrushchev's Cold War*, chapter 17.

33 Ibid, pp. 440–3; Presidium notes, May 21, 1962: http://millercenter.org/scripps/archive/kremlin (last accessed 18 September 2014).

34 Bundy, *Danger and Survival*, p. 445.

35 Fursenko and Naftali stress another dimension of the Cuban issue. In the spring and summer of 1962 Khrushchev was very worried that Castro would switch his allegiance from the Soviets to the Chinese, Fursenko and Naftali, *'One Hell of a Gamble'*, pp. 167–70.

36 For an exception, see Fursenko and Naftali, *Khrushchev's Cold War*, p. 483. Furthermore, the record of the Presidium meetings (the 'Malin notes') are sketchy and incomplete.

37 *Cold War International History Project Bulletin*, 17/18 (Fall 2012) 307–10. The quote is from p. 307.

38 For a different reading of the Soviet deliberations, see May and Zelikow, 'Conclusion', in May and Zelikow (eds), *Kennedy Tapes*, pp. 416–17, 420–1.

39 Fursenko and Naftali, *Khrushchev's Cold War*, p. 484.

40 Sergey Radchenko, 'The Cuban Missile Crisis: Assessment of New, and Old, Russian Sources', *International Relations*, 26 (September 2012) 332–3.

41 Gromyko's cable of 20 October in *Cold War International History Project Bulletin*, 8–9 (Winter 1996–7) 280–1.

42 Quoted in Taubman, *Khrushchev*, p. 562.

43 Arnold Horelick, 'The Cuban Missile Crisis: An Analysis of Soviet Calculations and Behavior', *World Politics*, 16 /3 (April 1964) 365.

44 Adam Ulam, *Expansion and Coexistence: The History of Soviet Foreign Policy, 1917–67* (New York: Praeger 1968) pp. 670–1; Ulam, *The Rivals: America and Russia Since World War II* (New York: Viking 1971) pp. 328–30.

45 Thomas Schelling, *The Strategy of Conflict* (Cambridge, MA: Harvard University Press 1960).

46 May and Zelikow, *Kennedy Tapes*, p. 283.

47 Schelling, *Strategy of Conflict*.

48 Dobrynin's cable of 25 October, in *Cold War International History Project Bulletin*, 8–9 (Winter 1996–7) 288. Recent literature in international politics stresses the importance of the commitment to domestic audiences, which is often said to give democracies a bargaining advantage. For a summary, see the symposium 'Do Audience Costs Exist?' *Security Studies*, 21 (July–September 2012) 369–415.

49 Indeed on the first day of the crisis Kennedy said that although perhaps he should not have drawn the line in this way, once he had done so 'and then they go ahead and do it, and then we do nothing, then I would think that our risks increase', May and Zelikow, *Kennedy Tapes*, p. 62.

50 Fursenko and Naftali, *'One Hell of a Gamble'*, p. 182; Khrushchev, *Khrushchev Remembers*, pp. 493, 495–6.

51 Department of State, *FRUS, 1961–1963, Vol. V, Soviet Union* (Washington, DC: Government Printing Office 1998) p. 177.

52 *Kennedy–Khrushchev Exchanges*, p. 177.

53 Schelling, *Strategy of Conflict*, chapter 8. There were lots of ways force would escalate, and Kennedy and his colleagues had little reason to decide which of them was the most likely; McNamara, quoted in Blight and Welch, *On the*

Brink, p. 192. The extent of this kind of danger was central to defense debates in the Cold War, and remains an important topic for research. For discussion, see Robert Jervis, *The Meaning of the Nuclear Revolution: Statecraft and the Prospect of Armageddon* (Ithaca, NY: Cornell University Press 1989) pp. 84–98.

54 Zorin cable of 26 October, in *Cold War International History Project Bulletin*, 8–9 (Winter 1996–7) p. 290.

55 Len Scott, 'Intelligence and the Risk of Nuclear War', in David Gioe, Len Scott, and Christopher Andrew (eds), *An International History of the Cuban Missile Crisis: A 50-year retrospective* (Abingdon: Routledge 2014) chapter 3.

56 Khrushchev, *Nikita Khrushchev*, p. 568.

57 Ibid., p. 560.

58 For a discussion of what was happening with the submarines, see Svetlana Savranskaya, 'New Sources on the Role of Soviet Submarines in the Cuban Missile Crisis', *Journal of Strategic Studies*, 28/2 (April 2005) 233–59.

59 Nikita Khrushchev, *Khrushchev Remembers: The Glastnost Tapes*, ed. and trans. by Jerrold L. Schecter and Vyacheslav Luchkov (Boston, MA: Little, Brown and Company 1990) p. 178. For the parallel American feelings that things were getting out of control, see Bundy, *Danger and Survival*, p. 426.

60 For Castro's explanation for the letter, see Blight, Allyn, and Welch, *Cuba on the Brink*, pp. 109–12.

61 Blight and Welch, *On the Brink*, p. 264. As early as 25 October, the Presidium notes reveal Khrushchev saying that although the USSR needed to get an American promise not to invade Cuba, 'beyond that, it is not worth forcing the situation to the boiling point', *Cold War International History Bulletin*, 17/18 (Fall 2012) 309. The shooting down of the U-2 and Castro's letter showed that the situation was dangerous and might spin out of control but they did not reveal American willingness to run high risks since they were things the US had not done. In theory, even greater pressure on Khrushchev would have been exerted by actions that the Americans took knowing that they were risky. Such actions would have both increased the danger of war and revealed high levels of American resolve, but since American leaders shared Khrushchev's aversion to high risk they preferred to avoid such actions.

62 *Kennedy–Khrushchev Exchanges*, p. 187. Throughout the crisis the Americans felt time pressures generated by the continuing work on the missile sites, and in their deliberations talked about when the missiles would become operational. But much of this discussion was confused and the importance of this factor remains unclear.

63 Khrushchev, *Nikita Khrushchev*, pp. 560, 562; see also Khrushchev, *Khrushchev Remembers*, p. 497.

64 Fursenko and Naftali, *'One Hell of a Gamble'*, p. 185; Dobrynin cable of 27 October, *Cold War International History Project Bulletin*, 5 (Spring 1995) 80. Khrushchev's memory of Dobrynin's cable is much more extreme and dramatic, talking about the possibility that the military would 'overthrow [the President] and seize power', *Khrushchev Remembers*, pp. 497–8. For the discussion by Soviet and American participants concerning this discrepancy, see Blight and Welch, *On the Brink*, pp. 264–5.

65 May and Zelikow, *Kennedy Tapes*, note 2, p. 474; Blight, Allyn, and Welch, *Cuba on the Brink*, pp. 255, 261.

66 Sergei Khrushchev reports that the Presidium did get a briefing on the effects of a nuclear exchange, but 'Father listened with half an ear. The solution must be sought in diplomacy, not in military plans', *Nikita Khrushchev*, pp. 597–8. No such briefing appears in declassified Soviet records, but these are incomplete.

67 Department of State, *FRUS, 1961–1963, Vol. V, Soviet Union*, pp. 187, 192. The

notes of the Presidium meeting following McNamara's 'no cities' speech of 9 June 1962 include this strange comment: 'They are not equal, but they were saying that the forces are equal', *Cold War International History Project Bulletin*, 17/18 (Fall 2012) 304.

68 As Sergei Khrushchev puts it, 'fear has big eyes', *Nikita Khrushchev*, pp. 536, 624.

69 Mikoyan, *The Soviet Cuban Missile Crisis*, p. 230.

70 This is the term used by Barton Bernstein in his perceptive 'The Cuban Missile Crisis: Trading the Jupiters in Turkey?' *Political Science Quarterly*, 95/1 (Spring 1980) 98.

71 A good overview is Don Munton, 'The Fourth Question: Why Did John F. Kennedy Offer up the Jupiters in Turkey?' in Gioe, Scott, and Andrew, *An International History of the Cuban Missile Crisis*, chapter 13. For one version of how early reports that the American might be willing to engage in a missile trade reached Khrushchev, see Fursenko and Naftali, *'One Hell of a Gamble'*, pp. 249–50.

72 For Kennedy's annoyance, see May and Zelikow, *Kennedy Tapes* pp. 659–60; for a summary of the ExComm discussion of removing the missiles, see Nash, *The Other Missiles of October*, pp. 127–32, 146–7. Indeed, as Nash points out, the ExComm 'fully expected the Soviets to demand a missile trade', *The Other Missiles*, p. 132, and the only surprise was that it was so long in coming.

73 Dobrynin cable of 19 October 1962, *Cold War International History Project Bulletin*, 8/9 (Winter 1996–7) 279. Why Kennedy said this is unclear. I doubt if he was trying to commit himself to refusing to make such a trade because it is unlikely that he knew the talk would reach Moscow (and if he did he would have been running the risk of tipping off the Soviets to the fact that the missiles had been discovered) and, the talk being off the record, his comments were not made public. Indeed, as far as I can tell, no American record of this talk has yet been published.

74 May and Zelikow, *Kennedy Tapes*, p. 307. Indeed, it is only a slight exaggeration to say that Kennedy followed the admonition of Obama's Chief of Staff Rahm Emanuel: 'you never want a serious crisis to go to waste, and what I mean by that is an opportunity to do things that you think that you could not do before'; Chief of Staff Rahm Emanuel, 'Interview with *Wall Street Journal*', *Wall Street Journal*, 19 November 2008. An interesting counterfactual is how the crisis would have unfolded had he issued the warning earlier. Done early enough, it might have made it a bit less likely that Khrushchev would have put missiles into Cuba. But had it been done after Khrushchev's decision was made but before October, it might have complicated matters because a trade would have not been a possible way to resolve the crisis.

75 Fursenko and Naftali, *'One Hell of a Gamble'*, p. 275; also see Sergei Khrushchev, *Nikita Khrushchev*, p. 604, Nikita Khrushchev, *Khrushchev Remembers: The Last Testament*, ed. and trans. by Strobe Talbott (Boston, MA: Little, Brown and Company 1974) p. 512, and Khrushchev, *Khrushchev Remembers: The Glastnost Tapes*, p. 179. In November 1962, Mikoyan told the Warsaw Pact ambassadors that Kennedy had told him that 'the Polaris-type submarines make the bases in England, Italy, and Turkey redundant. The American party had already worked out a plan, he said, to eliminate these bases', cable from the Hungarian legation in Washington to the Hungarian Foreign Ministry, 5 December 1962, in *Cold War International History Project Bulletin*, 17/18 (Fall 2012) 447. But our knowledge of how the Soviets, and especially the Soviet military, saw the value of the Jupiters is very limited.

76 For the full story of the Jupiters in Italy from the emplacement to the withdrawal, see Leopoldo Nuti, 'Dall'operazione Deep Rock all'operazione Pot

Pie: una storia documentata dei missili SM Jupiter in Italia', *Storia delle Relazioni Internazionali*, 11/12 (1996–7) 95–138 and 105–49; see also Leonardo Campus, 'Italian Political Reactions to the Cuban Missile Crisis', in Gioe, Scott, and Andrew, *An International History of the Cuban Missile Crisis*, chapter 12. As Campus notes, in their memoirs both Robert Kennedy and Khrushchev do mention the former as including the missiles in Italy in the arrangement, Robert Kennedy, *Thirteen Days: A Memoir of the Cuban Missile Crisis* (New York: W.W. Norton 1969); Khrushchev, *Khrushchev Remembers: The Last Testament*, p. 109; Khrushchev, *Memoirs of Nikita Khrushchev, Statesman, 1953–1964* (Providence, RI: Brown University Press 2007) p. 350; Khrushchev, *Khrushchev Remembers: The Last Testament*, p. 512.

77 For a discussion, see Leopoldo Nuti, 'Italy and the Cuban Missile Crisis', *Cold War International History Project Bulletin*, 17/18 (Fall 2012) 662.

78 For the participants' discussion of the impact of responsibility during the crisis, see Blight and Welch, *On the Brink*, pp. 107–8.

79 Nash, *The Other Missiles of October*, p. 148. Dean Rusk says that many of the influential discussions were between pairs of the participants outside of the meetings: Dean Rusk as told to Richard Rusk (ed.), Daniel Papp, *As I Saw It* (New York: Norton 1990) p. 232.

80 Naftali, 'The Malin Notes', p. 302; Fursenko and Naftali, *'One Hell of a Gamble'*, p. 285.

81 Khrushchev, *Nikita Khrushchev*, p. 623.

82 Bundy, *Danger and Survival*, pp. 432–3; Rusk, *As I Saw It*, p. 240; Rusk's interview in Blight and Welch, *On the Brink*, pp. 172–4; McNamara quoted in ibid, p. 191; Dean Rusk, George Ball, Robert McNamara, and Roswell Gilpatric, 'The Lessons of the Cuban Missile Crisis,' *Time*, September 27, 1982, 85. Perhaps the most nuanced judgment is the one reached by Raymond Garthoff, a former intelligence analyst who played a supporting role in the crisis (although he was not privy to the arrangement) who later became an accomplished scholar, 'It was not a direct element of a deal, a quid pro quo, but it was raised in the negotiation and, from the Soviet standpoint, was a consideration in making the deal', Garthoff, *Reflections on the Cuban Missile Crisis*, p. 162. He also refers to the Jupiters as a 'sweetener', ibid, pp. 47, 95.

83 Dobrynin cable of 27 October, *Cold War International History Project Bulletin*, 5 (Spring 1995) 80.

84 *Cold War International History Project Bulletin*, 8–9 (Winter 1996–7) 346.

85 Robert Jervis (ed.), *The Logic of Images in International Relations* (Princeton, NJ: Princeton University Press 1970; second edn., New York: Columbia University Press 1989).

86 Isabel Kershner, 'Israel, in Shift, Lets Building Materials Cross Into Gaza', *New York Times*, 31 December 2012; for the subsequent situation, see Fares Akran and Jodi Rudoren, 'Gaza Farmers Near Fence with Israel Remain Wary', ibid., 8 June 2013.

87 Bruce J. Allyn, James G. Blight, and David A. Welch (eds), *Back to the Brink: Proceedings of the Moscow Conference on the Cuban Missile Crisis, January 27–28, 1989* (Lanham, MD: University Press of America 1992) pp. 92–3.

88 Bundy, *Danger and Survival*, pp. 432–3; Rusk, *As I Saw It*, p. 240; Rusk's interview in Blight and Welch, *On the Brink*, pp. 172–4; McNamara quoted in ibid, p. 191.

89 *Kennedy–Khrushchev Exchanges*, pp. 189–90.

90 Dobrynin cable of 30 October, *Cold War International History Project Bulletin*, 8–9 (Winter 1996–7) 304. The letter was literally returned; it is not in the American records.

91 Arthur Schlesinger Jr., *Robert Kennedy and His Times* (Boston, MA: Houghton

Mifflin 1978) p. 523. In fact, Khrushchev's letter only implicitly made the link to the withdrawal of the Soviet missiles from Cuba. Whatever the degree of linkage, the precedent had an interesting if fleeting echo. When President Nixon learned that the Soviets were constructing a submarine base at Cienfuegos in Cuba, he immediately sent a note to Kissinger including the suggestion that the US put missiles in Turkey in order to 'give us some trading stock', Henry Kissinger, *White House Years* (Boston, MA: Little, Brown and Company 1979) p. 642.

92   The fullest account is David G. Coleman, *The Fourteenth Day: JFK and the Aftermath of the Cuban Missile Crisis* (New York: W.W. Norton 2012).

93   Bundy, *Danger and Survival*, p. 431; May and Zelikow (eds), *Kennedy Tapes*, p. 308.

94   Glenn Snyder and Paul Diesing, *Conflict Among Nations* (Princeton, NJ: Princeton University Press 1977).

95   http://openvault.wgbh.org/catalog/wpna-7026ce-interview-with-denis-healey-1986-part-2-of-3 (last accessed 5 June 2014); also cited in Keith Payne, "The Future of Deterrence: The Art of Defining How Much Is Enough," *Comparative Strategy*, 29 (July 2010) 220.

96   Harold Macmillan, *At the End of the Day, 1961–1963* (New York: Harper & Row 1973) p. 217; also see pp. 187, 212–13.

97   Bertrand Badie, *Diplomacy of Connivance*, trans by Cynthia Schoch and William Snow (New York: Palgrave Macmillan 2012).

98   Khrushchev, *Khrushchev Remembers*, p. 497. For the retrospective disagreements among the American participants on whether Kennedy did or was instructed to deliver an ultimatum, see Blight and Welch, *On the Brink*, pp. 66–8. A fascinating and important issue, but one that is a digression here, is whether this was a bluff or whether President Kennedy would have ordered other measures, such as a tightening of the blockade and/or a willingness to make the trade in public rather than actually use force. I think the evidence indicates that while a strike and invasion was not to be excluded, force would not have been the next step. This would mean, however, that the US was bluffing, and would explain why McNamara later said he did not believe that Robert Kennedy's message to Dobrynin was an ultimatum, Blight and Welch, *On the Brink*, p. 189.

99   Kennedy, 'Memorandum for the Secretary of State from the Attorney General', 30 October 1962, *Cold War International History Project Bulletin*, 8–9 (Winter 1996–7) 346; Dobrynin cable of 27 October 1962, *Cold War International History Project Bulletin*, 5 (Spring 1995) 80.

100   Khrushchev, *Nikita Khrushchev*, p. 565. He presumably is using the Russian text; the version in the American records is slightly different, *Kennedy–Khrushchev Exchanges*, pp. 166–7.

101   Ibid., pp. 169–70.

102   Fursenko and Naftali, *'One Hell of a Gamble'*, p. 259; also see Bundy, *Danger and Survival*, pp. 439–45; May and Zelikow, 'Conclusion', in May and Zelikow (eds), *Kennedy Tapes*, pp. 430–8.

103   For further discussion see Jervis, *The Meaning of the Nuclear Revolution*, chapters 5–6.

104   Robert McNamara in Blight and Welch, *On the Brink*, p. 64.

105   Nash, *The Other Missiles of October*, pp. 12–26, 100–1; Lebow and Stein, *We All Lost the Cold War*, p. 45; Nur Bilge Criss, 'Strategic Nuclear Missiles in Turkey: The Jupiter Affair, 1959–1963', *Journal of Strategic Studies*, 20/3 (September 1997) 114–15.

106   Schlesinger, *Robert Kennedy*, p. 516. Whether or not Kennedy was correct remains a crucial question, as does the extent to which he was he was

motivated by domestic rather than international politics. My reading of Kennedy is that the latter dominated, and my reading of Khrushchev is that Kennedy judged his adversary correctly, but obviously proof is beyond reach.

107 Nash, *The Other Missiles of October*; Robert McMahon, 'Credibility and World Power: Exploring the Psychological Dimension in Postwar American Diplomacy', *Diplomatic History*, 15 (Fall 1991) 455–71; Robert Jervis and Jack Snyder (eds), *Dominoes and Bandwagons: Strategic Beliefs and Great Power Competition In The Eurasian Rimland* (New York: Oxford University Press 1991).

108 Fursenko and Naftali, *Khrushchev's Cold War*, chapter 17.

109 Khrushchev, *Khrushchev Remembers: The Last Testament*, p. 512.

110 Sergo Mikoyan excoriates Khrushchev for his refusal to consult experts that led him to make numerous unnecessary concessions, and while there is quite a bit to this, it is hard to deny that Khrushchev was wise in giving a priority to ending the crisis: Mikoyan, *The Soviet Cuban Missile Crisis*.

111 Ted Sorensen, *Counselor: A Life at the Edge of History* (New York: HarperCollins 2008) p. 326.

112 Len Scott, 'Eyeball to Eyeball: Blinking and Winking, Spy Planes and Secrets', *International Relations*, 26 (September 2012) 361. Khrushchev mentions but does not stress the arrangement in his memoirs: *Khrushchev Remembers*, p. 512.

113 Sergei Khrushchev, *Nikita Khrushchev*, pp. 640–1.

114 Khrushchev apparently did tell Castro, who later hinted at the arrangement but never announced it, Schlesinger, *Robert Kennedy*, p. 513.

2   Examining *The Fourteenth Day*

Studying the neglected aftermath
period of the October Cuban
missile crisis, and underscoring
missed analytical opportunities

Barton J. Bernstein

The aftermath of the Cuban missile crisis

This chapter is concerned with the so-called 'aftermath' of the Cuban
missile crisis: a vital, and yet relatively neglected dimension of the history
of the most dangerous moment of the Cold War. More precisely, it is a critique of David Coleman's 2012 book, *The Fourteenth Day: JFK and the Aftermath of the Cuban Missile Crisis*.[1] When it was published Coleman's book
appeared to represent a welcome scholarly foray into the aftermath of the
crisis focusing, as it did, on events after the 'thirteen days' of 16 to 28
October 1962. Indeed, aside from a short article published in 1979, significant scholarship on the aftermath period began only in 1987 with
Raymond Garthoff's *Reflections on the Cuban Missile Crisis*.[2] Aided by his past
life as a US diplomat, Garthoff helped break new ground in debates over
the difficult aftermath of the Cuban missile crisis – although his book
devoted only a chapter to the post-28 October era. In 1998, Garthoff published an article that contended that, during the aftermath period, 'few if
any' in Washington 'really believed 'that the Soviet tactical missiles in
Cuba had available nuclear warheads', but he did not identify the 'few',
and he loosely implied that such beliefs had been unimportant.[3] In 2003
and 2005 two more significant books were published by Sheldon M. Stern,
the former John F. Kennedy Library historian. Reaching beyond Garthoff's
account, Stern did not neglect the aftermath period and paid considerable attention to President Kennedy himself. Stern, intelligently exploiting
his own substantial expertise in using the Kennedy White House materials,
devoted about a chapter in each of his two studies to the prolonged
process of the US–USSR settlement after Premier Khrushchev publicly
backed down on the morning of 28 October 1962.[4]

Two lengthy volumes by Aleksandr Fursenko and Timothy Naftali (in
1997 and 2006) each devoted a chapter to the aftermath period. These
authors skillfully exploited privileged access to otherwise unavailable
Soviet/Russian archives.[5] Other perspectives on the aftermath period were
provided by James Hershberg, who uncovered important information on

the efforts in October–November 1962, to establish a denuclearized zone in Latin America to alleviate the problem of Soviet nuclear weapons in Cuba.[6] In 2005, Svetlana Savranskaya's useful discussion of the post-crisis role of Soviet submarines appeared,[7] while Max Holland focused on the US side, issuing in *Studies in Intelligence* a path-breaking article on the so-called 'photo gap' in pre-crisis American intelligence. The gap was a period of about 38 days, from early September to nearly mid October 1962, when US intelligence-gathering planes did not fly over and photograph the area in Cuba where the Soviet MRBMs and IRBM sites were later found. In that significant essay, Holland showed how the Kennedy administration, initially in the October crisis and then in the lengthy aftermath period, concealed its earlier decisions, which had been rooted in international-political concerns, not to conduct such air surveillance of a key part of Cuba. In his 2005 essay, and in a more extended 2007 essay, Holland disagreed, in effect, with Blight and Welch, who in a 1998 article had significantly misunderstood the reasons for the 'photo gap' and thereby, in uncritically trusting officials' history, failed to place the gap in a rich interpretive context.[8]

In 2012, Holland published a co-authored book with David Barrett (*Blind over Cuba*) that further explored the surveillance gap and the Kennedy administration's sustained cover-up of it. That valuable book, more than Holland's earlier essays, intimately linked the US government's portrayal of the gap and domestic politics, and thus helps to promote an important perspective in studying US intelligence and the US national-security state.[9] In 2006, with a sharply different focus the prominent Russian historian, Sergo Mikoyan, son of Khrushchev's Deputy Premier, Anastas Mikoyan, published a lengthy book which contained considerable insights into the aftermath period (unfortunately, it was only available in English in 2012, albeit then in a greatly revised and sharply compressed form).[10] The scholarly advances outlined above have largely resulted from US and Soviet/Russian archival releases. The Cuban government, by contrast, has generally been reluctant to provide archival materials, and thus much of the study of the aftermath period, as with the October 1962 crisis itself, focuses very heavily on US–USSR relations.[11] There is therefore a great deal of important research to be done, despite the momentous advances of the recent past.

Coleman's early pioneering work

David Coleman has been one of the few scholars seeking to deal in any depth with the aftermath of the missile crisis, publishing a brief essay in 2002, followed by a substantial article that dealt, especially, with Soviet tactical nuclear weapons in Cuba.[12] Coleman disagreed – by design – with various public claims made or implied by Robert McNamara that the top officials in the US government had not believed or even suspected during the crisis that such short-range *nuclear* weapons were in Cuba. Unfortunately, Coleman's essays did not provide any *clear* evidence, from October to December 1962, that President Kennedy or his top civilian advisers actually believed or strongly thought that such *nuclear* warheads for the tactical missiles were in Cuba. Significantly, Coleman's lengthy 2007 essay sometimes moved heavily by a peculiar oscillating combination of hedged statements and strong assertions, but not by firm evidence, on this crucial set of matters, and thus left very troubling gaps. Whether or not Coleman fully recognized those very serious evidential problems, and his oscillating use of shifting judgements, remains uncertain.

In 2006, Coleman published an essay that drew heavily on the White House meeting of 5 December 1962. That top-level, once-secret meeting, occurring about five weeks after Khrushchev's public back down of 28 October, provided arresting statements by Kennedy and others on the subjects of nuclear deterrence and the strategic-arms budget, with JFK offering some probably surprising thoughts on the relationship of deterrence to the October missile crisis.[13] That 5 December session could be the subject of a major essay on such matters, and Coleman's short article did not do much more than, in a sense, scratch the surface. His own essay might, perhaps more usefully, have been entitled, 'Camelot's Uneasy and Conflicted Nuclear Thinking', and such issues could have been pursued in depth and with greater acuity.

Coleman's *Fourteenth Day*

In late 2012, presumably seeking to exploit the rather under-explored terrain of the extended aftermath period, while seeming to disregard much of the earlier literature on that period, Coleman published *The Fourteenth Day: JFK and the Aftermath of the Cuban Missile Crisis*. Coleman's book drew substantially on parts of his 2007 essay, even using a number of sentences verbatim, but he chose – perhaps in modesty – not to cite that essay in his volume or to note his repeating its language. He also generally chose not to engage, in a clearly critical-minded way, with much of the other published literature on the aftermath period.

Coleman focuses on the US side of events, mainly on the aftermath period to February 1963. The book does devote some attention to post-February 1963, without getting into the early Johnson presidency. In focusing on the post-28 October period, Coleman apparently had only minor difficulty in separating his own work from the enthusiastic tone, the near-fawning content, and the great exuberance of the early hagiography of Kennedy by Sorensen, Schlesinger Jr., and others. Unwisely, Coleman uncritically described Kennedy (p. 20) as the true author (he was not – it was very likely Ted Sorensen) of *Profiles in Courage*, and as a man (p. 66) who reportedly read 1,200 words a minute (highly unlikely), and Coleman (p. 218) recommended the RFK's deeply flawed *Thirteen Days* as a valuable account.[14]

Fourteenth Day evoked a number of favourable reviews and articles. Coleman's rather slim volume (205 pages of text, plus endnotes) is often disappointing. It is severely – and unnecessarily – limited in multiple ways. Among the many matters minimized or neglected is the intelligence dimension. Unlike Coleman's 2007 article, *Fourteenth Day* does not even mention Roger Hilsman. Nuclear deterrence receives very limited attention in the volume, and the perceived value for JFK, and his advisers, of US nuclear weaponry and of US nuclear superiority, especially in the missile crisis and the aftermath, is not usefully examined. The difficulties in civil–military relations, especially involving the Joint Chiefs of Staff (JCS), receive inadequate attention, and some key events and substantial problems are entirely omitted. *Fourteenth Day* also largely ignores the relationship of the US in the aftermath period to the NATO allies, and especially to the UK, a significant nuclear power.

Fourteenth Day barely mentions the presence of Soviet submarines in the Cuban area after 28 October, errs (p. 36) on important detail involving Soviet submarines, and entirely omits that the Soviets on the 28th sent a submarine to the Pearl Harbor area reportedly, according to Savranskaya, to 'attack that US base' if the US–USSR issues escalated into a shooting war. That submarine, of no interest to Coleman, apparently arrived in the Pearl Harbor area on 10 November, and may have carried one nuclear-armed torpedo, staying until December. Coleman never asks what US naval intelligence knew about the various Soviet submarines, and whether there was even the slightest inkling within naval intelligence, that the four special submarines near Cuba each had a nuclear-armed torpedo. Nor does he mention the dangerous anti-submarine-warfare tactics that continued, presumably approved by McNamara, at least into the early days of the aftermath period.[15]

The ignored events of 28 October

Unfortunately, Coleman chose to *begin focusing* his emphasized research, and thus the bulk of his narrative and analysis in the book, with 29 October, the so-called 'fourteenth day'. Such an unwise strategy omitted very much that was reported – in archival materials and elsewhere – by others for Sunday, 28 October, the so-called 'thirteenth day', for the many hours on that important day *after* Khrushchev's publicly announced backdown on that Sunday morning at about 9.00 (Washington time).

By starting significantly with Monday 29 October, Coleman ignored dealing with the deep annoyance and wariness, if not the anger and outrage, apparently felt that Sunday by the four US military chiefs – General Curtis LeMay, Chief of Staff of the Air Force, Admiral George Anderson, Chief of Naval Operations, General David Shoup, Commandant of the Marine Corps, and General Earle ('Bus') Wheeler, Chief of Staff of the Army. The available summary Joint Chiefs of Staff (JCS) minutes for that Sunday morning indicate the great unhappiness of those four JCS members with Khrushchev's public offer. There was an expressed fear that the Soviets might cheat. General LeMay, for example, thus stated that: 'The Soviets may make a charade of withdrawal and keep some weapons in Cuba.'[16] On that Sunday, the four military-service chiefs submitted a significant formal recommendation to Secretary of Defense Robert McNamara. From May and Zelikow's 1997 edited volume it is clear that the written JCS recommendation asserted: 'The JCS interpret the Khrushchev statement, in conjunction with the build-up, to be efforts to delay direct action by the United States while [the Soviets are] preparing the ground for diplomatic blackmail.' In another important matter also not mentioned by Coleman, the JCS on the 28th (but in opposition to the JCS chairman, General Maxwell Taylor) urged an air attack on Cuba beginning on Monday, to be followed by an invasion, *unless* there was 'irrefutable evidence' that the Soviets were dismantling their major military equipment on the island.[17]

Had Coleman focused by starting *substantially* with the 28 October, he would have been better able to present the deep antagonism between the service chiefs and JFK. Coleman also might have avoided seriously erring on (p. 125) in his own book, by incorrectly describing LeMay in October 1962 as the head of Strategic Air Command (SAC), instead of as the formal head (the Chief of Staff) of the *entire* USAF. The difference between those two official positions in the air force was not a minor distinction, but one of major operational significance with important meaning during and after the 13-day missile crisis. By focusing thoughtfully on the 28th, Coleman would also have been able to do far more in analysing the difficult situation for General Maxwell Taylor. He was a former army chief of staff, who sometimes served, probably uneasily, that day and clearly at other times in 1962, and in 1963, between the four military-service chiefs on the one side and President Kennedy and Secretary McNamara on the other side.

Deceiving the JCS, intelligence officials and analysts

By starting in depth on 28 October, and moving slowly into the next day, Monday 29 October, Coleman, if exploiting the long-available JCS summary minutes, might well have reported that Secretary McNamara was engaged in deceiving the four military chiefs and Taylor, too, on a crucial matter, a US–Soviet missile deal. The four military chiefs and General Taylor, as now-declassified records obliquely indicate, were not to be trusted with any information, not even a hint, about that highly secret deal. There was a systematic effort by Kennedy, McNamara, and a few others at the top of the US government to keep the five military men, as well as their subordinates, entirely ignorant on this matter. That is an important part of actual civil-military arrangements under Kennedy. That strategy of systematic secrecy (with substantial deceit) on this major matter of the deal – a secret only revealed more than a quarter-century later by McNamara and others – also apparently carried over, from 27–29 October, to similar Kennedy–McNamara behaviour in carefully keeping CIA Director John McCone and his intelligence agency ignorant of the secret Turkey–Cuba missile deal. The secrecy strategy also apparently barred the recently created Defense Intelligence Agency (DIA), as well as State Department intelligence, from such important information.[18]

That meant that various post-crisis studies by the major US intelligence agencies, especially in 1962–4, in seeking to assess Soviet behaviour, were greatly handicapped in not knowing of the behind-the-scenes US–USSR arrangements. The implications – regarding, among other matters, Khrushchev and Soviet flexibility, and Soviet views of JFK's own flexibility on 27–28 October – are important, though unwisely not of any interest to Coleman in his book. Only some enterprising scholar, working through the documents of the period, and probably needing declassification of many still-closed US files, and then closely examining JCS studies and US intelligence studies, may be able to address the question of the still-hidden costs of the strategy of secrecy involving the US intelligence agencies and the US military.

Fourteenth Day: strengths and weaknesses

Fourteenth Day, despite the volume's numerous weaknesses, also has significant strengths. Most importantly, it is the first book-length study focusing heavily on the aftermath of the crisis that richly emphasizes the US side of events. The volume does so in some depth, and often with revealing archival material. The book, in sometimes offering a kind of fly-on-the-wall narrative, often draws from otherwise generally still-unpublished transcriptions (partly funded by the National Historical Publications and Records Commission) made by the Miller Center team from the tapes left by President Kennedy of his conversations and meetings in 1962 and 1963 on the missile crisis and other subjects. Those tapes became publicly available, in batches, in about 1983 and 1996–2002. The substantial use of such declassified White House materials in transcripts in the book gives readers a valuable, and sometimes rich, sense of being present in meetings with the President and his associates. That sense of immediacy may well have added to the attractiveness, for the History Book Club, of offering the volume. Many of the published transcriptions quoted, or otherwise used, in *Fourteenth Day* had not previously appeared in other books or articles, though some historians (based on their own listening) have used, in more limited ways, their own brief transcriptions from segments of the White House tapes.

In view of proved, sometimes very severe problems publicly revealed by historian Sheldon Stern with the earlier published, and much publicized, bulky volumes of transcriptions from Kennedy White House tapes, scholars may, justifiably, want to be at least slightly wary in trusting all the transcriptions in Coleman's 2012 book.[19] There may well be a need for Stern or some other recognized, independent expert to work carefully through the transcriptions and provide to the public a thoughtful, fair-minded assessment.

Whatever the possible problems in exact transcriptions, *Fourteenth Day* does usefully analyse and describe the US–USSR difficulties on agreeing on how to verify Soviet removal of the medium-range ballistic missiles and their nuclear warheads from Cuba, and the US–USSR disputes into about mid November 1962 about whether the Soviets would remove their bombers from Cuba. The volume notes, but provides less analysis on, the US decision not to push energetically on Soviet removal of MiG (Mikoyan) fighters in Cuba and of all the Soviet troops there. The book unfortunately skips past, for the most part, the still greatly under-researched, and still little-discussed, issue of the Soviet Union's interest in 1962 in basing some of its submarines in Cuba, and the 1962 dealings by the US, in the short-run aftermath of October 1962, with this troubling issue of a possible Soviet submarine base in Cuba.[20]

Had President Kennedy desired in late 1963 to make the USSR's removal of its MiGs and the remaining military forces in Cuba a political issue in domestic America, the President, as Coleman shrewdly shows (p. 206) in citing a useful public-opinion poll, would have had substantial political support – probably about three-quarters of the US electorate in September 1963. Nearly two-thirds of the US electorate, in that September 1963 poll, was willing to endorse restoration of the 1962 quarantine/blockade of Cuba if the Soviets refused to take out their troops.

Coleman loosely links Kennedy's quest for better US–Soviet relations to the President's decision in late 1963 not to exploit such get-tough attitudes in the US electorate. But Coleman makes *no effort* to consider how, if at all, the administration's post-28-October promotion of Mongoose activities – overt, normally small-scale, war-type and sabotage activities against Cuba – into that explanatory framework. Nor does Coleman consider whether, and if so, how, the administration's so-called second track – some interest in secretly seeking possible accommodation with Castro – fitted into the overall US policy.

Soviet tactical nuclear missiles

A somewhat tantalizing but rather under-developed part of Coleman's volume is the references to administration decisions and view on the Soviets' tactical, nuclear-capable missiles in Cuba. According to Coleman, JFK *et al.* decided not to worry significantly in the aftermath period about the military implications (pp. 137–45, 165–8, 195, 200–3) of the known, short-range (about 20-to-25-mile), tactical, surface-to-surface missiles (termed FROGs in the west, and Lunas by the Soviets) in Cuba. Most analysts have placed the Lunas' range at about 20 to 25 miles, though Coleman (p. 137) in apparently misreading his cited source, states that the lower number for their range was only ten miles. He basically erred by about ten miles. Nearly all analysts dealing with the Lunas have placed the explosive power of the nuclear warheads for the Lunas in Cuba at two KT,[21] but Coleman suggests (p. 137), but *without* providing any source, that the nuclear warheads might have been about 20 KT, approximately the power of the Nagasaki bomb. Such a remarkable claim, so greatly at odds with the established literature on the Lunas, should, in the effort to produce solid scholarship, have been buttressed with some very firm sourcing. It seems highly likely that *Fourteenth Day* has erred – and significantly – on this.

Quietly backing *substantially* away from very explicit 2002 and 2007 claims that top US officials had believed that there were tactical-nuclear warheads in Cuba, Coleman in *Fourteenth Day* did not assert, though he obliquely insinuated at two points (pp. 140–1, 164–5), that President Kennedy in the aftermath period deeply thought and sometimes worried about this problem. Because the nuclear warheads were never spotted, US officials apparently had to rely upon an uneasy combination of inferences and assumptions, based partly on reports by US intelligence. Unfortunately, Coleman does not make systematically clear the exact nature of the intelligence reports. Coleman, in fact, seems at some junctures rather skimpily interested in this troubling set of problems.

As Coleman correctly emphasizes, some of those tactical weapons did indeed have available nuclear warheads, though the US did not know something even more important: that there were *nuclear warheads* also for 80 other Soviet tactical missiles (known as FKRs) in Cuba; they had a greater range, apparently about 90–110 miles, and their warheads were probably about five to 12/14 KT.[22] And thus, in view of these weapons and their nuclear power, there is far more to the 'story' of US responses and judgements, and the Soviets' post-28-October dealings, involving the USSR's tactical nuclear weapons in Cuba than Coleman chose to consider in necessary depth and detail.

Coleman's disinterest in Moscow's pre-October planning for Cuba means that he failed to realize that the FKRs with their nuclear warheads were part of the *original* spring 1962 plans. Coleman erred and incorrectly stated (p. 133) that those weapons and nuclear warheads were added later. Curiously, he cited three allegedly confirming sources (p. 229), and never noted that they failed to substantiate his claim. But he did briefly state (p. 138) that the dozen Lunas and their nuclear warheads were added in later planning after spring 1962, though *Fourteenth Day* never addresses an interesting question – why? It is highly significant that the presence of tactical nuclear weapons in Cuba never became the subject after the October 1962 crisis of substantial, sustained, heated concern, publicly, in the US in

1962–3. Quite rightly, top US civilian officials, as Coleman implies (pp. 144–5), privately recognized that the tactical weapons, even with nuclear warheads, were not really a military threat to the continental US, though it seems surprising that there were not more expressed worries by such top civilian officials about the vulnerability of Guantánamo, the American military base in Cuba, to such nearby weaponry.

Piecing together JCS worries and demands, and interpretations, about those tactical weapons, and the likelihood of the tactical-nuclear warheads being in Cuba, is rather difficult. Coleman, providing only some scattered discussion on the subject, does very little with that set of interesting issues. Whether he sought far more documents, and whether (as is likely) he found that many are still classified, remains unclear in his book. My own occasional requests – more than a half-dozen – for access on this subject to more US archival materials, with the use of the Freedom of Information Act (FOIA), have generally been foiled, or minimally helped, on this still very under-explored, complicated subject of the Soviet tactical weapons.

That subject involves the closely entwined problems of: (1) What exactly was understood and wanted by the US military planners and especially by the four service chiefs and General Taylor in dealing with those tactical weapons, and what did they think, and why, about the possible presence of the nuclear warheads? (2) What was observed and interpreted, and why, and thus on what basis were conclusions reached by US intelligence in 1962–3 about the actual nuclear capability, and especially about the presence of nuclear warheads, involving those weapons? (3) Were there disputes on these important matters *within* the US intelligence system and, if so, at what levels? (4) What top-level civilian officials, besides Kennedy, McNamara, and Bundy, and a few other advisers at a 7 November meeting, were *significantly* involved in the US decision-making in dealing with the problem of the Soviet tactical weapons, and what exactly did those men think about the likelihood of tactical-nuclear warheads being in Cuba?

On that last set of questions, was Secretary of State Dean Rusk, who was at that important November meeting, very involved in that decision-making in that session and at other times on the tactical missiles, and what did he think about the presence of tactical-nuclear warheads in Cuba? Was Roger Hilsman, the head of the State Department's Intelligence and Research Bureau, who apparently was not at that November meeting, involved at other times in the top-level decision-making on those Soviet tactical weapons, and what did he think about the presence of such nuclear warheads in Cuba?[23]

In presenting that 7 November meeting, Coleman quotes (pp. 144–5) from the transcribed tape, but that short quoted segment in the book is unfortunately rather limited. Not one of the speakers, in the book's quoted segment, ever mentions nuclear warheads for the tactical missiles. In fact, there were two meetings on 7 November: the first focused on foreign aid and the Congo; the evening meeting dealt with Cuba, including on-site inspections of the missile sites, the IL-28s etc.[24] Coleman's book has nothing on President Kennedy's words. Did he not speak at that meeting on the issues of the tactical missiles? If not, why not? If he did, what did he say? Why, one might ask, did the book miss such details and address the questions outlined above, even if indirectly? McCone, though probably present at that session, may not have spoken on the issue of the FROGs. He is not mentioned by Coleman as even being at that important meeting. If McCone was absent, that seems surprising, but there is no explanation by Coleman here.

Reaching beyond the rather small group identified by Coleman as speaking at that November meeting on the tactical missiles, and considering the US intelligence system alone, there are some significant questions. They build on the problems numbered above as (2) and (3), but merit more specific phrasing here: Were there important differences within the Central Intelligence Agency itself, and directly involving its Director, John McCone, on the nature of the tactical weapons and whether there were actually nuclear warheads for those short-range missiles in Cuba? Were there fears within the CIA of those tactical weapons being used against Guantánamo, even in the absence of a US attack on Cuba? Did the analysts in the still-young Defense Intelligence Agency agree among themselves or not on this subject, and what did the agency's Director, General Joseph Carroll, a former FBI agent, think?

Ultimately, with far more information than has been declassified, a full-scale, or at least a broad, and deep, important analytical study could be produced on those significant subjects. It would thoughtfully link and probably compare the US intelligence directors, the military chiefs, and the top-level political leaders to explain their varying assessments of risk, the intellectual and experiential bases for such assessments, the shifting standards for assessing evidence, the conceptions of making judgements amid uncertainty, the understanding of uncertainty, and the uneasy balancing of purposes within the US government. Such analysis will undoubtedly benefit most from an effort by a skilful scholar accustomed to dealing with US intelligence evidence and problems, and the US intelligence bureaucracies' cultures and ways, including their relationships with the JCS and top-level political leaders, and especially JFK, McNamara, and Bundy.

How Coleman managed to decide when the Soviets finally withdrew some of their nuclear-capable, tactical-missile *launchers* from Cuba is puzzling. He claims (p. 168) that the date was 5 January 1963 for the removal of ten Luna *transporters* and even gives the name of the departing ship, but he cites as his only source Fursenko and Naftali's *'One Hell of a Gamble'* (p. 315). Contrary to Coleman, this book provides *no* date or even any discussion of that alleged withdrawal, and instead gives a different date – possibly the wrong date – for the removal of the *warheads*, not the transporters. According to Robert S. Norris and Savranskaya, based on their work in recent years, and generally agreeing with Garthoff's 1998 contention, the nuclear warheads for the tactical missiles were removed from Cuba in early December 1962. That notion, without any explicit controversy, seems to be generally accepted, though the published literature does not focus at length, or in depth, on the particular December date of the withdrawal of the FROGs/Lunas.[25]

The Soviet tactical nuclear missiles and Soviet strategic-military issues

Coleman shrewdly notes (pp. 166–7) that the Soviets, with Khrushchev speaking in Moscow to the British ambassador (Sir Frank Roberts), and then a top Soviet representative (Deputy Foreign Minister Vasily Kuznetsov) soon speaking in New York, claimed in mid November that there were no longer any nuclear warheads in Cuba – that they had all been withdrawn. Those Soviet claims were *wrong*, and dangerously deceitful. Why Khrushchev knowingly took such a peculiar risk, and why Kuznetsov offered a similar guarantee, and whether Kuznetsov honestly erred or was knowingly being deceitful, are important questions involving Soviet behaviour and US–USSR relations in the aftermath period. Neither Coleman, Sergo Mikoyan, nor any other scholar to my knowledge, addresses in print this troubling puzzle.

The most likely set of admittedly partial answers, if one focuses on Khrushchev, is the following: that somewhat before and also on 12 November (when he said all nuclear warheads had been removed), and for slightly more than a week thereafter, Khrushchev planned until about 21 November on leaving the tactical nuclear weapons in Cuba, with the likely intent of transferring them to the Cubans. But Deputy Premier Anastas Mikoyan, in his very difficult dealings with Castro, obviously became frightened by such a plan; Mikoyan then successfully persuaded Khrushchev and others in the Kremlin that safety and prudence required Soviet withdrawal of the tactical nuclear warheads. In meeting with Castro, Mikoyan had come to regard him as potentially reckless, and not a leader to be trusted with nuclear weapons – and certainly not nuclear weapons provided, and *provably provided*, by the USSR.[26]

If, as the available evidence strongly suggests, Khrushchev had planned up to about mid November to leave the tactical missiles and their nuclear warheads in Cuba, and to transfer them to the Cubans, what was Khrushchev's strategic-military conception? What, in particular, was his understanding of the deterrence value of those weapons with available nuclear warheads when held by the Cubans? Can his thinking be pieced together from available sources? In the logic of deterrence, the nuclear warheads *could* only have a deterrent value *if* their presence in Cuba was made known to the US But making their presence known to the US would necessarily have meant also revealing that Khrushchev had lied on 12 November. What would have been the political cost to the USSR of that lie becoming known to the US government, and what might then have happened to the overall effort in the aftermath period to resolve various US–USSR issues, especially those involving Soviet weapons in Cuba? Had those tactical weapons and nuclear warheads been transferred to the Cubans, and had all that been kept secret, those nuclear weapons, in the event of a US armed attack on Cuba, could – and probably would – have been used against US forces. Had Khrushchev and other top Soviet officials in November, before the withdrawal decision of about 21/22 November, considered such a scenario and its implications for plunging the Soviet Union into war? Did they think that a nuclear war in Cuba could be limited to Cuba, and not spread to Europe and the USSR itself? Coleman, alas, ignores these issues.

US intelligence; US politics

Strangely, *Fourteenth Day* does not discuss the Soviet withdrawal from Cuba of the 80 FKRs, or of the Luna missiles themselves. According to a declassified report of 5 February 1963 (in the National Security Files (NSF) in the Kennedy Library's archival holdings), the US believed then, more than three months after the October crisis, that there were still between 24 and 32 FROGs in Cuba, but that now-declassified report left unclear whether those Soviet weapons were actually deemed by US intelligence as nuclear-capable. A now-declassified US intelligence briefing paper on 'The Situation in Cuba', of 18 December 1963, written more than a year after the October 1962 crisis, but not used by Coleman in his text, reported that there were still FROGs in Cuba, though that December 1963 report, like the February 1963 one, also did not mention whether those tactical missiles were deemed by US intelligence as nuclear-capable.[27]

But because a number of US sources of 1962–3 – including the useful *ONI Review* from US naval intelligence – are reportedly still mostly classified, or otherwise (according to the US government) not readily and fully available to independent researchers, there are severe limitations on research involving US intelligence on the subject.[28] It often does not even seem possible to know in appropriate depth what US intelligence actually observed, formally reported, or seemed to understand on these matters of the withdrawal from Cuba of the nuclear-capable tactical weapons, or even of the nuclear warheads for those Soviet weapons.

My own multiple requests in recent years to the CIA for the further release of its 1962–3 materials on the FROGs (Lunas) and FKRs have produced very little added material. Despite receiving a formal FOIA request in 2013 for such materials for the period of late October 1962 to December 1963, the intelligence agency only provided nine documents (some were near-duplicates), and they were drawn only from a few weeks in autumn 1962.[29] Those materials, despite their limitations, do however allow a researcher to reach conclusions beyond Coleman's book and articles. There are, as indicated in this essay, a number of kinds of close-grained, and potentially revealing, issues involving the Lunas and FKRs that Coleman's book often avoids, either out of intention or inadvertence. In addition, he too briefly deals (p. 195) with the fact that a major US newspaper, the *New York Herald Tribune*, on 20 November 1962, featured a front-page article on the reported presence of such weapons in Cuba.[30]

Fourteenth Day never mentions that other significant American newspapers – notably, the *New York Times* and *Washington Post* – at that time printed parts of the story. But that subject of such nuclear weaponry was very soon – for some reason – lost in the US press that autumn.[31] Possibly, as Coleman suggests (pp. 195–6) JFK's announcement on 20 November that the Soviets would be removing their bombers from Cuba helped divert the attention of the US press, and thus the American public, from the Soviet tactical missiles in Cuba with likely nuclear warheads. Whether JFK's US critics, albeit unsuccessfully, sought in autumn 1962, as they did in about February 1963, to make the tactical weapons and their warheads a major political issue is unexamined by Coleman. It is an interesting subject in autumn 1962 politics that has been, for some reason, neglected in the published scholarship, though Coleman briefly notes (p. 169) the February effort. The problem for autumn 1962, if pursued, can broaden and deepen the understanding of the aftermath period in the US.

Arming US forces with nuclear weapons and planning for an invasion of Cuba

Surprisingly, in view of Coleman's own earlier published writing in nuclear history, his book shows rather limited interest, despite a brief discussion (pp. 139–40) in the still very under-explored events in late October and early November 1962 involving the JCS and McNamara, and reaching up to Kennedy, on the important subject of arming the potential US invasion force for Cuba with tactical nuclear weapons. Among the important sources is a crucial 2 November report by General Taylor to Kennedy on this subject. That paper was partly summarized in navy materials (released in the mid 1980s), and in long-available JCS materials released by the early 1990s or before, and the actual 2 November report by Taylor was initially declassified in 2000. But it seems that Coleman, who does not mention that significant 2 November paper in his 2012 book, for some reason never saw the summary or a copy of the report itself up to the time he was writing his book.[32]

Taylor's report of 2 November loosely estimated (with hedges) no more than about 18,500 US casualties in the first ten days of an invasion of Cuba – *if* no nuclear weapons were used by either side. He admitted that the situation would be *far worse* and very difficult to calculate in advance in terms of US casualties *if* nuclear weapons were used, but he did not assert that such Soviet weapons were definitely in Cuba. Taylor's paper implied that the US would respond with nuclear weapons in such an invasion if they were first used by Soviet or Cuban forces. But he left technically unclear whether he believed (as he loosely implied) that there was already formal authority, without requiring any new decision by Kennedy or McNamara, for such US nuclear retaliation in Cuba. Whether Taylor's implications about the US military having the likely authority to use nuclear weapons in retaliation upset Kennedy, Bundy, or McNamara remains uninvestigated. Whether Bundy or McNamara saw or even knew of Taylor's report is unclear. Taylor's report never clearly indicated how many tactical nuclear weapons (if any) were then believed to be in Cuba. He spoke of there being 'at least one FROG' with 'an atomic capability', but that statement did not assert anything unambiguously about the presence or non-presence of nuclear warheads in Cuba for such weapons.

Taylor did not indicate whether there were disputes by US intelligence on the issue of such warheads in Cuba, or in counting/estimating the number of FROGs on the island, nor whether there was an expectation in the US military planning of seeking to bomb and thus to destroy those tactical missiles *before* the US started the ground invasion. Whether there was another statement by Taylor to Kennedy or to McNamara at about that time on these important matters is unclear, and remains to be investigated.

If there was no such statement by Taylor, or from any of the other military chiefs, on these matters provided to Kennedy or to McNamara at about that time, such an absence of a report would be very meaningful. That absence could open many questions in the 1962 government about civil–military relations, the thinking at that time about nuclear weapons, the actual control of the US nuclear weapons, and the conceptions held by various top-level officials in the US government of nuclear-war risk in the aftermath of the 13-day Cuban missile crisis.

Taylor's report of 2 November promised ultimate US success in military action against Cuba, but apparently also misinformed Kennedy by not telling him that Admiral Robert Dennison, commander of the North Atlantic fleet and apparently of the US invasion force, had already asked – actually, only a few days before – for nuclear weapons and been turned down. Why Taylor apparently misinformed Kennedy is an interesting problem, one not even noted, and certainly not addressed, in any of the scholarly literature. In view of Taylor's apparent misinforming Kennedy about Admiral Dennison's request, it seems highly likely – but not fully provable – that the actual turning down of that request was not by President Kennedy, and probably had been made by Secretary McNamara.[33] If so, there is an important question: Did McNamara on about 29 October–2 November, or even slightly later, so inform Kennedy of both the request and the turn-down? Such questions, ideally informed by more documents, can illuminate much about high-level US nuclear-war thinking in the aftermath period in dealing with the Soviets and the Cubans on the Caribbean island. The Taylor report of 2 November underscores an important theme that Coleman ignores: namely, that Kennedy in the early aftermath period reportedly asked more questions of the US military about the key invasion plan than he had during the thirteen-day crisis in October.[34]

US intelligence and Soviet missiles

Contributing to Coleman's neglect of important matters, he does not emphasize in his text – and provides only a brief comment in an endnote on p. 232 – that the Soviets actually removed *more* MRBMs (42) than the US in late October 1962 had reportedly seen (33 MRBMs) in Cuba. Coleman never mentions that in November 1962 the US navy's own reports of the number of removed missiles – involving discrepancies about the cargoes of four of the nine departing missile-carrying freighters – differed from the Soviet reports. The data on these matters have long been mostly declassified in various US archives; the long-declassified summary ExComm minutes for 5 November 1962, available in the National Security files (NSF) at the Kennedy Library, and a mostly declassified official navy history (released by the mid 1980s), provide rather easily accessible evidence on this set of interesting, and possibly surprising, matters.[35]

If US intelligence or the military, directly or indirectly, under-counted the Soviet MRBMs in Cuba before their removal, and that seems to have been the case, were there not fears that the Soviets might be cheating and retaining some MRBMs, and their nuclear warheads, in Cuba? Is there some evidence in autumn 1962 on such matters? Did Coleman ever seek to investigate this set of problems? His book is silent on this subject – as on many significant matters – involving US top policy-makers and US intelligence.

Coleman never mentions, for example, that Deputy Secretary of Defense Roswell Gilpatric, after the publicly reported removal of 42 missiles from Cuba, warned on a national television-radio programme near mid November that there might still be more Soviet missiles in Cuba. 'Cuba Might Have Other Red Missiles, US Says', headlined one prominent American newspaper in reporting Gilpatric's statement.[36] Such a publicly expressed worry by Gilpatric, though undoubtedly not intended by him for such a frightening emphasis, risked undercutting support for President Kennedy and his handling of the aftermath issues.

In that same public interview, Gilpatric also indicated that the Soviet missiles in Cuba had not threatened the favorable US strategic-nuclear balance, or even come close to doing so. That acknowledgement seemed to undercut much of the JFK–McNamara public argument during the crisis for the US acting energetically, by establishing a quarantine, to seek to compel removal of those Soviet missiles. Whether Gilpatric had cleared his statements in advance with McNamara and others in the government seems uncertain.[37] Whether JFK himself worried, after those public statements, that he was being undercut by Gilpatric is also unclear. This is a rather small but interesting, unexplored subject, one that warrants some consideration by scholars. It might reveal much about the operations of the top levels of the Defense Department, the Gilpatric–McNamara relationship, the JFK–Gilpatric relationship, and related aspects of public relations in the sustained aftermath period.

On 14 November, in a problem entirely ignored by Coleman, Roger Hilsman, the head of State's Intelligence and Research Bureau, complained to Rusk that the bureau was not receiving the required intelligence information from other segments of the US government, and the bureau was thus impaired in its analytical efforts. That memorandum to Rusk, in the sanitized version, did not make clear which organizations Hilsman was singling out, but probably he meant other intelligence units – the CIA and DIA – in the government.[38] *Fourteenth Day* is also entirely silent on the interesting fact that Hilsman was deeply worried in mid November that there were Soviet IRBMs in Cuba. Hilsman, while actually acknowledging that there was no solid evidence that Soviet IRBMs had reached the island, emphasized to Secretary Rusk on 16 November that there was no evidence that the IRBMs had been removed or were scheduled for removal. What happened to Hilsman's mid-November concerns, and whether he backed away from such worries, is apparently still unclear.[39] Whether he was unique in having such concerns, or whether they were shared by underlings in his bureau and by other US intelligence agencies is not certain. That set of subjects is one among many on US intelligence matters that remain to be investigated in some depth, and enterprising scholars may well wonder what the other intelligence agencies stated, if they were informed of Hilsman's concerns.

Missiles in Turkey; missiles in Cuba

Surprisingly, *Fourteenth Day* does not emphasize that President Kennedy, on 27 October, had offered the Soviets a secret trade: to remove the 15 American IRBMs in Turkey. That important secret deal – which was not publicly acknowledged until 1989 – is tucked into a single sentence (p. 31) and then ignored. Most missile-crisis scholars reading the book know the basic story of that secret trade, but lay readers of the book are unlikely to be properly alerted to the significance of the secret deal and thus they are unlikely to understand much of the important context in which the aftermath negotiations, following the morning of 28 October, occurred. Coleman entirely omits that the top US officials who knew about the deal long lied about it. On 28 October, for example, Rusk lied to the British ambassador on the subject. Not surprisingly, the US also lied to Turkey, as well as in NATO, and elsewhere in international forums.[40] Coleman for some reason also chose not even to mention that Secretary McNamara lied about this secret arrangement of the Cuba–Turkey missile deal on various occasions, including in dealing with Congress. On 7 February 1963, for example, in testimony before a powerful House of Representatives sub-committee, McNamara, loyal to the President and possibly untroubled by deceiving Congressional committee members, denied that there had been such an arrangement. McNamara was actually one of only a few high-level administration members, besides the Kennedy brothers, Rusk, and Bundy, who knew about this secret deal.[41]

Such systematic deceit by McNamara raises important questions about US political culture, the standards for honesty *in* the US government, and the practices by the executive branch of employing outright mendacity to protect itself in dealing with Congress and the American people. In 2004, Eric Alterman forcefully addressed such matters,[42] but these apparently did not engage Coleman, who is uninterested in the important fact that Vice-President Lyndon Baines Johnson was – according to Bundy and McNamara – kept ignorant of the secret deal.[43] A more enterprising author than Coleman might well have chosen to discuss what it meant that Johnson was apparently still kept ignorant of that secret deal. Had Johnson been encouraged, or at least allowed, to draw the wrong lesson from the missiles crisis? Did his probably drawing the wrong lessons lead him to stick in Vietnam and seek a victory along the lines of what he presumably, but inaccurately, believed President Kennedy had done in October 1962?

What would have been the political costs to JFK, in domestic politics and in international relations, if the secret Turkey–Cuba trade had become known in the aftermath period? Such important questions – guided by useful counterfactuals – were of no apparent interest to Coleman. But pursuing them can provide a helpful interpretive under-standing generally of the aftermath period, and in particular of American political culture and of America's alliance relationships.

JFK's prestige, the missile crisis, and the 1962 mid-term elections

Coleman is fully correct that President Kennedy's prestige in the 1962–3 aftermath, and in the many years since his assassination, benefited from the widespread approval in the US, and often elsewhere, of what was generally understood as his skilful, courageous, necessary, and intelligent handling of the missile crisis. Unfortunately, that judgement omits much of how Kennedy actually did handle the crisis, and Coleman seldom seeks to correct many of the important misunderstandings undergirding the very favourable assessments. Much to the surprise of informed scholars, Coleman, in explicitly recommending four books on the missile crisis, included (p. 218), among the four, Robert Kennedy's *Thirteen Days* (1969). In view of the self-serving, heavily fictional quality of that remarkably 'creative', hagiographical volume, such a recommendation by Coleman is very puzzling. Many of the problems in that myth-making book can be indicated, as historian Sheldon Stern has intelligently shown in his books (and in his essay in the present collection), by simply comparing that RFK volume to the often contrary evidence on the ExComm tapes and in the published books (including those from the Miller Center) of published ExComm transcriptions.[44]

In the aftermath period, beyond Llewellyn Thompson, ex-ambassador to Moscow, Kennedy had little expertise in Washington available at or near the top levels of the US government to draw upon for an understanding of the Soviet Union and Khrushchev. The other two generally recognized Soviet experts, besides Thompson, were elsewhere as US ambassadors abroad: Charles ('Chip') Bohlen was in France, and Kennan was in Yugo-slavia. Harriman, with some Soviet expertise, drawn mostly from the wartime and early postwar Stalin period, was usually kept by Kennedy far on the US–USSR policy-making sidelines in Washington in October–December 1962, and only later brought into US–USSR negotiations. Whether the absence, or marginality for other reasons, of Bohlen (after 18/19 October) and of Kennan, made any difference in Kennedy's decision-making in October–December is unclear.[45] But it is a subject mer-iting consideration, though such analysis may require some counterfactual thinking. Foy Kohler, the lacklustre ambassador in Moscow, seems not to have a major role during the crisis or in the aftermath, although his role has not been significantly studied (and the State Department records (RG 59 at the National Archives) and the White House files at the Kennedy library suggest he is a minor figure). Coleman only mentions Kohler twice – and both times (pp. 28, 172) are for the pre-September 1962 period. Contrary to Coleman (pp. 27–8), Kennedy devoted very *little* time, or effort, in seeking to untangle Khrushchev's motives for placing missiles in Cuba. He spent little time consulting with his Soviet experts and, in the ExComm, Kennedy had only Thompson present.

Endorsing and uncritically drawing upon the often thoughtful but ana-lytically limited 1986 essay by Thomas G. Paterson and William Brophy on the effects of the October missile crisis on the early November 1962 congressional elections,[46] Coleman chose not to dig more deeply into that subject. A wider, and broader, study of that under-examined issue might undercut parts of the Paterson-Brophy conclusion: that there was no appreciable effect generally on those elections, and no significant added advantage for the Democrats. It would be illuminating for a scholar involved with voting behaviour and electoral returns to examine closely the survey-poll results from about mid October (before JFK's quarantine speech of the 22 October) in many races, then assume variously, in a seem-ingly plausible counterfactual interpretation, a 1, 2, or 3 per cent, a 4 per cent, and also a 5, and even 6 per cent shift in voting to GOP candidates in the election under what might be called the 'publicly do-nothing' scen-ario, and the likely fierce attacks on JFK, and then for the analyst to deter-mine what the final results for the Democrats could have been in a number of congressional races in the November election. How badly would Kennedy's party, tainted by such publicly do-nothing behaviour, have fared in November 1962? Getting such answers, in such a counterfactual scenario, could be richly enlightening and broaden and deepen the thinking by analysts of the relationship of JFK's handling in October of the missile crisis to 1962 politics, and especially to the November elections.

For added intellectual leverage on the general issues of domestic politics and the missile crisis, Coleman might wisely have tried to build in his book on the page-long, revealing memorandum of 28 October by Kennedy's advisor and confidant Theodore Sorensen. In that important memorandum, probably put together right after Khrushchev's backing down that morning, Sorensen sketched likely GOP political charges against Kennedy on missile-crisis issues, and Sorensen presented possible JFK rebuttals. For some reason, though that Sorensen document has long been in the open Sorensen files at the Kennedy Library,[47] Coleman did not use it. Whether he found it, and decided it was of no value, or did not find it, is unclear. Not to use it – if he found it – was a mistake. Not to find it could suggest serious shortcomings, underscored by other evident problems, in his archival research.

Journalists and the skewering of Adlai Stevenson

Fourteenth Day is significantly lacking in archival source materials. Coleman did not use the papers of any members of Congress, thus ignoring the papers of numerous critics of the administration. In addition, despite Coleman's stated interest in JFK's dealings with the US press, the book makes *no use* by the author of the archival papers of any journalists and publishers (such as, for example, Walter Lippmann). How an able historian-author explicitly interested in the aftermath of the October 1962 crisis, and in the related responses by the US press, could do so little with the public skewering by the noted journalists Stewart Alsop and Charles Bartlett of Kennedy's UN representative Adlai Stevenson is truly remarkable. In a widely publicized article, in the 8 December issue of the then-popular, glossy, large-circulation magazine, the *Saturday Evening Post*, those two well-known journalists, claiming (unidentified) insider knowledge from high-placed US sources, contended that Stevenson, during the October crisis, had been basically an appeaser: that he had given 'Munich'-like advice, and that he had sought to sell out US interests to gain a settlement with the Soviets.[48]

The Alsop–Bartlett article receives almost no attention (p. 55) in *Fourteenth Day*. Coleman fails to indicate that President Kennedy himself was apparently a major, and perhaps the main, source for that mean-spirited and unfair attack on Ambassador Stevenson. Apparently, Kennedy repeatedly lied publicly and privately about his important role in talking to

Bartlett, a longtime friend. By encouraging a journalistic attack on Stevenson for proposing during the thirteen-day crisis a trade of the US Jupiter missiles in Turkey for the Soviet missiles in Cuba, President Kennedy managed to help conceal that he himself had *actually* made such a secret deal to seek to end the October crisis.[49]

Coleman indicates that he is significantly interested (pp. 7–14) in President Kennedy himself, in Kennedy's conceptions of power and of the presidency, and in his capacities as both a leader and politician. Despite this, Coleman (p. 20) blithely asserts that Kennedy grew up in Boston. In fact, JFK had been raised as a privileged youngster in the Boston suburb of Brookline, before moving to New York and an exclusive school. And, contrary to Coleman (p. 24), Kennedy's 'blue-collar credentials' by 1945–6 were not simply 'weak' – they were *non-existent*, as his attendance at Choate, Princeton, Harvard, and Stanford underscored. His service in the Second World War, as a naval officer, was not a 'blue-collar' activity.[50] Coleman does not consider whether Kennedy's political need in conducting his successful 1946 congressional campaign, in seeking a seat from the general Boston area, helped further to encourage young Kennedy to learn the techniques of manufacturing and reshaping facts, involving his own past, to gain electoral success. In 1945–6, as a candidate, Kennedy was basically a 'carpet bagger', a man with no real Boston past (he had never lived there before 1945, when starting his Congressional campaign), though he had spent four years in nearby Cambridge (at Harvard) between 1936 and 1940. Alas, Coleman's assessment of Kennedy's political evolution, and the development of his thinking on crucial issues, between 1946 and 1960 is similarly sketchy and unilluminating. On the very personal level, Coleman totally ignores debates on the impact of Kennedy's very active philandering, and his personally risky sexual activities,[51] on his political decision-making in the crisis and in the aftermath (especially regarding his willingness to take risks, and his assessment of risks). In addition, deeply unsettling evidence, not made public until well after JFK's death, on the president's poor health and performance-affecting drugs is never discussed by Coleman.[52]

The 'photo gap', American politics, and presidential power in the US national-security state

A serious domestic political problem for President Kennedy was that there had been, as journalist/historian Max Holland showed, a significant intelligence gap, later called a 'photo gap', that substantially occurred for high-level administration *policy reasons* and not because of bad weather. Holland first explored that problem in an important 2005 essay, so Coleman, who does cite that essay in one endnote (p. 246), had ample time – more than a half-decade – to pursue the issues in greater depth and to do the necessary research in archival materials and in congressional hearings.

That 'photo gap' occurred roughly between 6 September and 13 October, in which US surveillance ('spy') planes in that 38-day period had not flown over western Cuba, and thereby the planes had not spotted, beginning in about mid or late September, the early available evidence of the deployment of the Soviet MRBMs on the island. Through various strategies of deceit and evasion, the JFK administration, in the aftermath of the October crisis, had cleverly managed to cover up the nature of this 'photo gap' problem. The initial evidence in Holland's 2005 article, and the rich added material that he and Barrett provided in *Blind over Cuba*, reveals the largely successful efforts by the administration, including Kennedy, Bundy, McNamara, and also McCone, to conceal the nature of that gap. Had Coleman been appropriately curious, and done the necessary work, spurred partly by Holland, and building on it, Coleman might well have reached what is a somewhat surprising but warranted conclusion: McCone, though a Republican and significantly mistrusted by the two Kennedy brothers, helped to cover up the nature of the 'photo gap', and thus actually helped protect the President and the administration from domestic political assaults on this subject.

In view of McCone's valuable assistance on this politically sensitive subject, despite his own self-serving 'leaks' on some other missile-crisis issues, a once-secret Kennedy brothers' conversation of 4 March 1963 – which was used in partial transcription by Holland in 2005 but not used by Coleman in his book – takes on added meaning. President Kennedy, in the now partly transcribed tape recording, called McCone 'a real bastard'. Robert Kennedy easily agreed.[53] It appears that the two Kennedys failed to understand how much McCone had actually protected them on a very sensitive political matter – the 'photo gap' – on which they were greatly vulnerable. Coleman thus missed a substantial opportunity to examine more deeply, and more critically, the McCone–Kennedys relationship on missile-crisis issues. Why the Kennedy brothers did not appreciate McCone's political help is possibly puzzling. It is a subject that warrants consideration, and may help further to illuminate the relationship between US intelligence and the McCone-headed CIA on one side and the two Kennedys on the other.

What Coleman also seemed not adequately to understand is that the Kennedy administration, in the aftermath of the October crisis, often skilfully used its privileged control of government information to block press and Congressional inquiries, whilst thwarting Congressional investigations into the October crisis. For the Kennedy government, somewhat like its predecessors and its successors in Washington, partisan self-defence and the use of the federal government's power came fruitfully together in the expanding national-security state. That use by Kennedy and his associates of federal government power, building on the tactics of earlier presidents, helped to shape pro-Kennedy interpretations of the October 1962 crisis, its antecedents, and its aftermath.

For Kennedy, such executive-branch power on the crisis-related history was employed mostly against enterprising, probing conservatives, including, notably, Senators Thurmond, Goldwater, and Keating, and Representative Ford.[54] Part of the 1962–3 dispute between the Kennedy stalwarts and those right-wing legislators can be interpreted in mostly partisan terms, but there were also much deeper issues – entirely neglected by Coleman – of the *basic struggle* within the US government between executive and Congressional power.

The perceived value of nuclear weapons

How, in particular, did President Kennedy and others from 28 October 1962 to mid autumn 1963 interpret the roles of US nuclear superiority and of US conventional theatre superiority in those October–November 1962 events and decisions involving the missile crisis and the aftermath settlement? For some reason, Coleman entirely omits from his book JFK's arresting 5 December statement, available on a White House tape (and partly used by Coleman in his 2006 and 2007 articles), significantly questioning the continuing large strategic-arms build-up by the US. On that December meeting tape, President Kennedy said to McNamara, in effect, 'I don't quite see why we're building as many nuclear weapons as we're building'.[55] JFK also stated, 'Even what [the Soviets in nuclear weapons] had in Cuba alone would have been a substantial deterrent to me'. Whether JFK in that comment was including, besides the Soviet MRBMs, the possibility of nuclear warheads for the tactical missiles in Cuba is unclear.

Whether JFK was sincere in December 1962, and whether his December statements about nuclear weapons were based on his thoughtful analysis, or whether they were top-of-the head comments, possibly to focus criticism on the troubling size of the expanding defence budget, is tantalizingly unclear. To make strong interpretive sense of JFK's December statements, a careful analyst would have to work through a number of the *other* JFK tapes, many of the available materials on McNamara–JFK meetings, and the various files in 1962–3 on the strategic-arms budget.

McNamara, on the tape at that same 5 December session with Kennedy, argued strongly (as Coleman notes, tantalizingly, on p. 14) for building far more weaponry than was rationally needed. The Defense Secretary asserted, at one point in the budget session, in effect, '[W]e ought to buy twice what any reasonable person [says] is required'. Whether McNamara truly believed that, or chose – partly in exasperation – to exaggerate, is also unclear. Understanding McNamara's evolving thinking after the missile crisis about nuclear strategy, the nuclear-arms build-up, the impact of US domestic politics on procurement and nuclear strategy, and the influence of the JCS's expectations is a very difficult task.

McNamara's stated concerns of 5 December about LeMay's desires for a very large strategic-arms build-up are unmentioned in *Fourteenth Day*. Yet, they raise important questions about the Kennedy administration's interpretation of the roles of overall nuclear and conventional-force theatre superiority in the October missile crisis and the aftermath. What, analysts must also consider, did JCS Chairman Taylor and the other military chiefs, besides LeMay, seem to conclude about the role of US nuclear superiority in the October crisis and in the aftermath, and in general about how much US nuclear weaponry – especially what number of American ICBMs and submarine-based strategic missiles – was 'enough'? Did JFK himself, after the October crisis, and partly because of it, start to focus more sharply on the defence-military situation in Europe involving so many short-range US nuclear weapons there? Thus, did the October missile crisis, and the important aftermath period, including various US concerns about Soviet tactical nuclear missiles in Cuba, help lead to reconsidering the problems of extended nuclear deterrence and the spread by the US of nuclear weaponry abroad? Such useful questions coming out of the missile crisis, though apparently not of concern to Coleman, can lead to very significant analyses contributing richly to nuclear history and to understanding Kennedy and his administration, and the legacy for Johnson's administration. To neglect such questions, as *Fourteenth Day* does, is to overlook valuable opportunities to illuminate the sometimes contested meanings of the missile crisis.

Some distressing errors

It is dismaying that Coleman's book makes a number of troubling errors. They often suggest surprising and distressing gaps in knowledge. That is especially disappointing for any scholar working on missile-crisis-related issues, and it is now perhaps alarming in the case of Coleman, who is overseeing the Miller Center's project of publishing post-28 October volumes of transcriptions of Kennedy-White House tapes. It is surprising that none of the four established missile-crisis scholars who lauded the book on its jacket cover – Zelikow, Allison, Naftali, and Trachtenberg – caught the errors, though possibly they caught other mistakes that were corrected prior to publication. One wonders whether the respected publisher – W.W. Norton – did any independent fact-checking or sought any outside reviewers (beyond possibly the Miller Center network) to read the manuscript prior to publication.

Contrary to *Fourteenth Day*, Secretary Dean Rusk did not meet (p. 187) with Soviet ambassador Anatoly Dobrynin on 23 October (but on 22 October) to inform him *initially* of JFK's dramatic quarantine decision and imminently forthcoming speech on the 22nd about the Soviet missiles in Cuba. In addition, the US Jupiters in Turkey (p. 31) were not medium-range ballistic missiles, but intermediate-range missiles (with a 1,750-mile range), and thus could reach far into Soviet territory with their 1.4 megaton warheads, about 1,000 times the power of the Hiroshima bomb.

Also contrary to *Fourteenth Day*, Premier Khrushchev did not specify US missiles in the UK or Italy as part of a deal in his publicly seeking on 27 October (p. 109) a public deal on removal of the Jupiters in Turkey.[56] W. Averell Harriman was not new (p. 117) to the Kennedy administration in 1963, he had in fact formally joined it in early 1961, was Assistant Secretary of State for Far Eastern Affairs in October–December 1962, and even gave advice (though probably ignored) during the missile crisis.[57] In another error in the book, John J. McCloy (pp. 41–2) was not suddenly called back from Europe by Kennedy on about 28–29 October to deal with negotiations at the UN. McCloy had been, by Kennedy's design, at the UN for nearly a week, partly to control Ambassador Stevenson. Before the 28th, McCloy even attended an ExComm meeting on the 26th, as is clear in the available White House tapes and in the published minutes, and in the related editorial commentary in the 2001-published *Presidential Recordings: Kennedy, Vol. III* (on which Coleman had been an editor).[58]

On matters involving the important subject of Soviet submarines, Coleman has very serious problems. Contrary to *Fourteenth Day* (p. 36) there is *no* available evidence that any Soviet nuclear submarine was '*in* Cuba' (my emphasis) during the 13-day crisis or during the early aftermath period, and Coleman does not seek to cite any evidence to support his claim. The only Soviet subs in the much extended general area of Cuba, according to known sources, were not nuclear (but diesel-powered), and apparently no Soviet sub to at least 29 October was 'in Cuba'. Some Soviet subs were somewhat near Cuba in that period, but none of them, according to declassified contemporary US reports, got any closer to Cuba than about 125 miles away.

In dealing (p. 59) with a US journalist (Rowland Evans Jr.) who published – on 2 November 1962 – an article on a then-secret Khrushchev-to-Kennedy letter, Coleman, without providing any evidence, states that Evans had actually seen the highly secret letter. That significant claim seems questionable. Adding to problems in *Fourteenth Day*, then Coleman also proceeds to misquote Evans' own published words in Evans' 2 November *New York Herald Tribune*.[59] Such mistakes were probably the result of carelessness, and lack of concern about both evidence and accuracy. In addition to other errors, *Fourteenth Day* also has the wrong official title in one place (p. 188) for Assistant Secretary of Defense for International Security Affairs Paul Nitze, the wrong official title in one place (p. 115) for Under Secretary of State George Ball, and the incorrect name (p. 221) for Frank Pace, a member of Kennedy's foreign-intelligence-advisory board. *Fourteenth Day* also has (p. 228) the wrong name for the important US-based scholarly journal, *Diplomatic History*, and on p. 64 the wrong title for the book, *Conversations with Kennedy* (1975), by JFK's journalist friend Benjamin Bradlee. Probably more troubling, *Fourteenth Day* contends (p. 113) that the National Security Council (NSC), which was actually established under President Truman in 1947, was a 'decades-old' organization in

1962. That particular dating error is surprising, and it may be simply an arithmetic error. Or it may be linked to Coleman's deeper problems in dealing with conceptions of the US national-security state and its history, even though on a few pages briefly noted the founding date of the NSC.

Neglected matters; sourcing and analytical problems

In *Fourteenth Day* Coleman misses opportunities to pursue issues, to use more sources, and to broaden and deepen his analysis. His unwisely self-constricted approach – of excluding questions and of handling others too quickly, and of doing so little research, is disappointing. To state that *Fourteenth Day* is significantly under-conceptualized is to emphasize, among other problems, that the book, very surprisingly, devotes only about three pages to the post-28-October period involving US–USSR differences on the Berlin problem in a 21-page chapter (chapter 14). For some unexplained reason, that chapter instead focuses very heavily on pre-28 October issues. *Fourteenth Day* generally avoids issues in NATO politics, and in the US–UK 'special relationship', in the aftermath period. Besides a single 25-word sentence (p. 182) on Kennedy and the British ambassador (David Ormsby-Gore), the US–UK 'special relationship' itself receives fewer than 50 words, not even two full sentences. There is a brief, very questionable phrase (p. 10) and a few lines in a single sentence (p. 14). Such blatant neglect by Coleman, involving probably the US's closest major partner, is peculiar. Indeed, the book never notes the continuing strain with the UK, and with other NATO nations, involving the US efforts to have them cut off their trade with Cuba. Indeed, such disputes about trade, and sanctions, are totally ignored in the volume. This suggests a very limited conception of international history, and of international relations, and he has no expressed interest in international economic matters – a subject far from his concerns.

In adding to the book's errors, in discussing US air surveillance in the pre-October period, Coleman somehow 'created' a non-existent event (p. 176): a Soviet shoot-down on 4 September 1962 of a US-piloted U-2 that had strayed over Soviet territory. How Coleman went so far awry on this significant matter is puzzling; probably he misinterpreted a Soviet *complaint* of 4 September, but *without* any shoot-down, involving a U-2 flight on 30 August reportedly over Soviet territory; or he confused a PRC shoot-down of a Taiwanese U-2 on 8 September. Of course, a Taiwanese plane was not a US plane, and the PRC was not the USSR. And the Soviet complaint on the 4th and an actual Soviet shoot-down of a US U-2 were very different events.[60] Had Coleman carefully read the two quite brief documents – they total under eight full pages – that he, himself, cites (p. 241) from the Kennedy Library files for his only evidence of the alleged Soviet shoot-down on the 4th, he could easily have avoided his strange error.

Coleman, in dealing with the troubling issues of US air surveillance of Cuba in the early weeks of the aftermath period, omits some important matters and also confuses some events. In a notable example of substantial omission, he never mentions that McCone contended, and undoubtedly believed, as McCone said on 5 November, that the surface-to-air-missiles (SAMs) were probably being left in Cuba so that the Soviets could once again station 'offensive' missiles on the island.[61] In discussing (pp. 51–2) a reported anti-aircraft shooting over Cuba at a US surveillance plane on 29 October, Coleman somehow substantially misdated in his endnote (p. 219n) his key magazine source – by three full weeks! Far worse, he claimed, dubiously, that the US plane was on a *morning* flight, but he did not recognize a crucial set of matters: that no such flights for that morning were authorized by President Kennedy or Secretary McNamara, and that the discussion at the ExComm meeting that Monday morning assumed that there were *no* such flights that morning.[62] If there was in fact such a morning flight that day, then it was important for Coleman to explain who ordered it, and how Kennedy, McNamara, and others responded to what seems, on its face, a significant violation of high-level orders or a remarkable bureaucratic mistake on a crucial matter that day.

Coleman twice relied, incorrectly, on a December 1962 article ('Intelligence Briefs') in the Naval Intelligence's *ONI Review*. Each time (pp. 230, 232) he placed the article in both the wrong month and in the wrong year: January 1963.[63] That error probably slightly obscured the date when useful intelligence information became available to some US analysts. Much worse, in periodically using an interesting, partly declassified CIA report from February 1964 ('Cuba 1962: Khrushchev's Miscalculated Risk'), Coleman repeatedly – in three endnotes on p. 230, one on 231, and at least once elsewhere (p. 246) mistakenly contended, as he did in his 2007 essay, that the report was *also* by the DIA. It *definitely* was not.[64] Somehow, Coleman, in reading the cover page and related material, managed to confuse the CIA's staff of the DD/I, the Deputy Director for Intelligence, with the Defense Intelligence Agency, which was headed by General Joseph Carroll. Such a peculiar error is far more than just misreporting a few initials in authorship; they are crucially significant initials, and such an error suggests a remarkable insensitivity to the bureaucratic struggles in the early 1960s in the US government over the 'turf' of intelligence agencies, and some lack of interest by Coleman in how the CIA itself, operating at various levels after the October 1962 crisis, interpreted the then-recent matters.

Coleman entirely avoids the issue of a CIA agent (Richard Jacob) being apprehended on 2 November in the Soviet Union, and of what Kennedy was told about this matter, and whether it had any significant effect in November–December on Kennedy's relations with Khrushchev. That Jacob case is still under-studied, and might have required considerable effort by Coleman to investigate it substantially, but fully ignoring it seems strange, even though it involved complicated, and presumably still mostly heavily classified, US–USSR intelligence/spying interactions.[65] Indeed, Coleman in his handling of a number of various US intelligence issues – whether it be in disregarding Hilsman, in failing to understand McCone and the photo gap events, in ignoring the questions of likely disputes between and within US intelligence agencies, in sometimes misusing and neglecting intelligence publications and archival sources, or in overlooking other significant issues – is too often both careless and shallow. In the aftermath period, intelligence was often crucial. How events were explained, what US intelligence agencies themselves concluded, and why, and related US–USSR strains are all important parts of the significant 'story'. That not-easy-to-penetrate 'story' for the aftermath, if properly studied, combines intelligence issues and both domestic and international political decisions by the Kennedy administration. For Coleman, too often, these intertwined matters involving US intelligence are beyond his interest – and greatly so.

Rich opportunities for further scholarship

In reading *Fourteenth Day*, one has the unhappy sense that Coleman had not thought deeply about many of the interpretive issues, or critically about much of the literature on the crisis and its aftermath. He unwisely isolates his 'story' of the aftermath from what he leaves unexplored – the rich interpretive context, provided by the published scholarship on the US national-security state. That is not a phrase – the national-security state – that Coleman ever employs. Perhaps it is a conception that he chose, albeit silently, to reject and thus to ignore.

Coleman's very limited book, albeit unintentionally, may usefully open the way for other thoughtful scholars, as they look closely at the period after 28 October, to probe more deeply, to investigate more widely, to rely more substantially on the relevant published literature, to conceptualize more broadly, and to write more carefully. Unlike the other books examined in the essays in the present volume on the missile-crisis literature, *Fourteenth Day* has not been influential into mid 2014, in a direct way, on the published missile-crisis scholarship. Unlike the notable *Essence of Decision* or even some of the other missile-crisis-related books, *Fourteenth Day* has not evoked, nor is it likely to provoke, a substantial, ongoing critical literature. The book has not proposed interesting paradigms, or indeed any paradigms, though it has sometimes shrewdly exploited the Kennedy-White House tapes on the aftermath period and also raised important questions about the Soviet tactical nuclear weapons in Cuba.

This intentionally critical-minded review essay has sought to suggest only some of the desirable work, to indicate some of the problems in the scholarship (primarily Coleman's volume), and to provide a number of guiding questions, and some forms of helpful conceptualization, in doing such scholarship. This essay has not been conceived to be an exhaustive, or even nearly exhaustive, discussion of all the published missile-crisis-related literature on the post-28-October morning period, nor on all the interesting questions that might usefully be pursued.

A thoughtful, sustained historiographical essay, focusing on the memoir, scholarly, and important journalistic literature studying the aftermath period remains to be written. Such a probing scholarly article would look closely at how major issues were presented, how important issues were sometimes lost, how evidence was used or not, or misused, how new sources emerged, what subjects were left shrouded in official secrecy, and how declassified materials have changed interpretations or should change interpretations.

Scholars could also reach beyond the brief treatment in the present essay of issues of US domestic politics, the shaping of false images involving the US's handling of the missile crisis and the aftermath, and the concealing of information by the Kennedy administration. That would mean doing far more on the aftermath period and the national-security state. After all, the Kennedy administration and especially the President himself were masterful in shaping attractive, self-promoting images and self-promoting history, and in often blocking alternative conceptions.

In the aftermath period, more than during the thirteen-day missile crisis, President Kennedy, often seemed to express considerable confidence in his own judgement and in his ability. For him, there was apparently some growth of confidence in November–December, in dealing with many of the troubling difficulties, in winding down the October crisis. In high-level meetings in Washington in the aftermath period, he did not run roughshod over top subordinates, and he generally seemed, especially, to give McNamara and Bundy ample hearings, even when they disagreed with him. But President Kennedy, as the chief executive, seemed very much in control of what were *then defined* as the important decisions on major issues in that post-28 October period. The President, as Jack Kennedy and his top-level advisers well understood, was the ultimate decision-maker.

Far more can also be written about the thinking of Soviet elites on their conception of military strategy, and the place of tactical nuclear weapons in Cuba within it, throughout the October crisis and during the aftermath period. That is a complex subject. Such analysis might also address a related set of questions: Why did not Khrushchev seek on 28 October or almost immediately thereafter, to move the Soviet submarines (Foxtrots) with torpedoes and nuclear warheads *very far* from the Cuban area? Did he realize that each of those four subs had a single torpedo with an available, powerful nuclear warhead? Did he know how poor communications had been, and might continue, with these submarines distantly at sea? And was there any dispute in the Kremlin, on the 28th, when a Soviet submarine (apparently with one nuclear torpedo and many conventional torpedoes) was sent to the Pearl Harbor area? Did Khrushchev himself know then about that decision, including apparently the nuclear-capable torpedo and warhead? When and why was that submarine, some time after reaching Pearl Harbor, ordered back to its home base? Was that a top-level Kremlin decision?

At least for a brief period after Khrushchev's backdown on the morning of 28 October, Attorney General Robert Kennedy, probably acting with his brother's approval, if not at the President's direction, sought to halt marauding activities against Cuba. On the 28 October, RFK informed the FBI that he did not want 'crackpot' organizations or individuals going to Cuba and conducting assassination efforts there or firing weapons against Cuba. That order was also passed along to the CIA.[66] Whether the Kennedys, by blocking such disruptive actions, were seeking to build, or basically not to erode, Khrushchev's trust may involve analytical distinctions too subtle, and too finely calibrated, to allow for useful answers.

In all that, it is valuable not to lose some, even perhaps deep, concern with the fundamental ethical/moral dimensions: that major nation-state leaders, and sometimes their organizations acting nearly or fully independently, almost plunged the human species into massive destruction, if not full annihilation. Who in the West, or elsewhere, in the aftermath period in 1962–3, or in the frightening October crisis itself, asked publicly or privately about whether nation-state leaders, or nation-state organizations, had such a moral/ethical *right* to take such actions? What are the appropriate moral/ethical standards for guiding and judging such perilous activities that might kill many millions and even risk ending human existence? Why did not a vigorous ethical/moral literature on such problems, inspired by the October missile crisis, emerge in the aftermath period in 1962–3?[67] Historians, and others, when studying the October crisis, and the aftermath period, might well enlarge the purview of useful scholarship by considering such important matters.

Notes

1 David G. Coleman, *The Fourteenth Day: JFK and the Aftermath of the Cuban Missile Crisis* (New York: W.W. Norton 2012).
2 Barton J. Bernstein, 'Bombers, Inspection, and the No Invasion Pledge', *Foreign Service Journal*, 56/7 (1979) 8–12; Raymond Garthoff, *Reflections on the Cuban Missile Crisis* (Washington, DC: Brookings 1987) pp. 67–95; (rev. edn 1989) pp. 94–142.
3 Raymond Garthoff, 'U.S. Intelligence in the Cuban Missile Crisis', *Intelligence and National Security* 13/3 (1998) 18–63. Quotes at p. 29.
4 Sheldon M. Stern, *Averting 'The Final Failure': John F. Kennedy and the Secret Missile Crisis Meetings* (Stanford, CA: Stanford University Press 2003) pp. 385–412; ibid., *The Week the World Stood Still: Inside the Secret Cuban Missile Crisis* (Stanford, CA: Stanford University Press 2005) pp. 94–211.
5 Aleksandr Fursenko and Timothy Naftali, *'One Hell of a Gamble': Khrushchev, Castro, and Kennedy, 1958–1964* (New York: W.W. Norton 1997) pp. 287–355;

ibid., *Khrushchev's Cold War: The Inside Story of an American Adversary* (New York: W.W. Norton 2006) pp. 492–545.

6 James Hershberg, 'The United States, Brazil, and the Cuban Missile Crisis, 1962' (parts 1 and 2), *Journal of Cold War Studies* 6/2 (2004) pp. 3–20; 6/3 (2004) 5–67.

7 Svetlana Savranskaya, 'New Sources on the Role of Soviet Submarines in the Cuban Missile Crisis', *Journal of Strategic Studies*, 28/2 (2005) 233–59.

8 Max Holland, 'The "Photo Gap" that Delayed Discovery of Missiles in Cuba', *Studies in Intelligence* 49/4 (2005) 15–29; James G. Blight and David A. Welch, 'What Can Intelligence Tell Us about the Cuban Missile Crisis, and What Can the Cuban Missile Crisis Tell Us about Intelligence?' *Intelligence and National Security* 13/3 (1998) 6.

9 David M. Barrett and Max Holland, *Blind over Cuba: The Photo Gap and the Missile Crisis* (College Station, TX: Texas A&M University Press 2012).

10 Sergo Mikoyan, *The Soviet Cuban Missile Crisis: Castro, Mikoyan, Kennedy, Khrushchev, and the Missiles of November*, ed. by Svetlana Savranskaya (Stanford, CA: Stanford University Press 2012) pp. 173–268, 271–564.

11 Of utility, here: Stephen G. Rabe,'After the Missiles of Cuba: John F. Kennedy and Cuba, November 1962 to November 1963', *Presidential Studies Quarterly*, 30/4 (December 2000) 714–26; James G. Blight, Bruce J. Allyn, and David A. Welch, *Cuba on the Brink: Castro, the Missile Crisis, and the Soviet Collapse* (New York: Pantheon 1993); James G. Blight and Philip Brenner, *Sad and Luminous Days: Cuba's Struggle with the Superpowers after the Missile Crisis* (Lanham, MD: Rowman and Littlefield 2003); Peter Kornbluh (ed.), 'Kennedy Sought Dialogue with Castro Aborted by Assassination, Declassified Documents Show', *National Security Archive Electronic Briefing Book 103* (24 November 2003), www2. gwu.edu/~nsarchiv/NSAEBB/NSAEBB103/ (last accessed 29 September 2014); Don Bohning, *The Castro Obsession: U.S. Covert Operations Against Cuba, 1959–1965* (Washington, DC: Potomac Books 2005); and Hugo Abedul and R. Gerald Hughes, 'The Commandante in His Labyrinth: Fidel Castro and His Legacy', *Intelligence and National Security*, 26/4 (2011) 531–65.

12 David G. Coleman, 'After the Cuban Missile Crisis: Why Short-Range Nuclear Weapons Delivery Systems Remained in Cuba', *Miller Center Report* 18/4 (2002) 36–9; ibid., 'The Missiles of November, December, January, February … : The Problem of Acceptable Risk in the Cuban Missile Crisis Settlement', *Journal of Cold War Studies* 9/3 (2007) 5–48.

13 David G. Coleman, 'Camelot's Nuclear Conscience', *Bulletin of the Atomic Scientists* 62/3 (2006) 40–5.

14 Herbert Parmet, *Jack: The Struggles of John F. Kennedy* (New York: Dial Press 1980) pp. 324–33. Robert Dallek, *An Unfinished Life: John F. Kennedy, 1917–1963* (Boston, MA: Little, Brown and Company 2003) pp. 198–9. On questionable claims of speed reading, see Hugh Sidey's introduction, *Prelude to Leadership: The European Diary of John F. Kennedy – Summer 1945* (Washington, DC: Regnery 1995) p. xxxvi. On *Thirteen Days* as very dubious history, see Sheldon Stern, *The Cuban Missile Crisis in American Memory: Myths Versus Reality* (Stanford, CA: Stanford University Press 2012) pp. 32–53, 134–47.

15 See, for example, Savranskaya, 'New Sources on the Role of Soviet Submarines', 243–6. Joseph Bouchard, *Command in Crisis: Four Case Studies* (New York: Columbia University Press 1991) pp. 87–137 intermittently dealt with McNamara's earlier approval during the crisis of many ASW procedures. Probably such approval (not discussed by Bouchard) carried over for some days after the 28th. When queried, McNamara, in a 2002 interview, seemed rather fuzzy on this matter of a carry-over.

16 Entry of 28 October 1962, in 'Notes Taken from Transcripts of Meetings of the

Joint Chiefs of Staff, October–November 1962, Dealing with the Cuban Missile Crisis' (handwritten notes were made in 1976 and typed in 1993), received (by me) under FOIA in 1997, from JCS History, and henceforth cited as 'Notes, Transcripts/Minutes, JCS'.

17 Ernest R. May and Philip D. Zelikow (eds), *The Kennedy Tapes: Inside the White House during the Cuban Missile Crisis* (Boston, MA: Harvard University Press 1997) p. 635; ibid., *The Presidential Recordings: John F. Kennedy: The Great Crises*, 3, *October 22–28, 1962* (New York: W.W. Norton 2001) p. 517. Coleman was one of seven associate editors on this 2001 volume. The two key documents – JCS to Kennedy, 'Recommendation for Execution of CINCLANT OPLANS 312 and 316', JCSM-844–62, 28 October 1962; and Taylor to McNamara, CM-61–62, 28 October 1962 – also obtained by me (under FOIA in about 2001) from Records of the Secretary of Defense.

18 Interviews with Bundy and McNamara, 1992–3.

19 Sheldon M. Stern, 'What JFK Really Said', *Atlantic Monthly*, 225/5 (2000) 122–8. In 2014, Stern commented: 'At the Kennedy Library conference on presidential tapes in 2003, Philip Zelikow announced that the Miller Center was adding to their website an interactive feature allowing scholars to suggest corrections to their transcriptions. When *Averting "The Final Failure"* was published later that year, it included an Appendix (pp. 427–40) citing dozens of significant errors in the 2001 Miller Center/Norton JFK transcripts. Several years passed before the Miller Center even addressed my critique and the interactive feature never appeared. David Coleman finally reviewed my transcriptions and rejected almost half of them. Several scholars who have listened to the disputed transcriptions have emailed me to say that I was right.' Sheldon Stern to Len Scott, email, 27 September 2014.

20 See *Fourteenth Day*, pp. 131, 203. For high-level US concerns about a Soviet submarine base, see, for example, ExComm minutes, 3 November and also 5 November 1962, National Security Files (henceforth: NSF), Kennedy Library (Boston, henceforth JFKL), received under FOIA, and the 5 November minutes also available in National Security Archive microfiche collection, 'The Cuban Missile Crisis' (New York: Chadwyck-Healy 1992), Doc. 01998; Kennedy to McNamara, 5 November 1962, NSF, JFKL, received under FOIA (by me), and also in microfiche collection as Doc. 02002; and W.W. Rostow to Bundy, 'Report Number Seven of the Planning Committee', 5 November 1962, NSF, JFKL, received under FOIA (by me), and also in microfiche collection as Doc. 01999.

21 See, for example, Anatoli, I. Gribkov and William Y. Smith, *Operation ANADYR: US and Soviet Generals Recount the Cuban Missile Crisis* (Chicago, IL: Edition Q 1994) p. 4; Robert S. Norris, 'The Cuban Missile Crisis: A Nuclear Order of Battle, October/November 1962', paper at Woodrow Wilson Center, 24 October 2012; and Norman Polmar and John D. Gresham, *DEFCON-2: Standing on the Brink of Nuclear War during the Cuban Missile Crisis* (Hoboken, NJ: John Wiley 2006) p. 56.

22 Norris, 'Cuban Missile Crisis: Order of Battle' states 14 KT, but most others, as in *ANADYR*, p. 4, say five to 12 KT. No significant interpretive difference rests on 12 versus 14 KT for the upper limit. But Steven J. Zaloga, *The Kremlin's Nuclear Sword: The Rise and Fall of Russia's Strategic Nuclear Forces, 1945–2000* (Washington, DC: Smithsonian Institution Press 2002) pp. 84, 269, claims a range of 50 KT–120 KT, and may be basing that on reporting from an FKR deployment in Germany.

23 Hilsman, in my 1990s correspondence with him, was circumspect, if not evasive, on the subject of US disagreements – in October–November – on the nature of the FROGs/Lunas. Suggesting general agreement in October–November 1962,

see Roger Hilsman, *The Cuban Missile Crisis: The Struggle over Policy* (Westport, CT: Praeger 1996) pp. 115–17.

24 *Averting 'The Final Failure'*, p. 406.

25 Norris, 'Cuban Missile Crisis: Order of Battle'; Savranskaya, 'Postscript' in Mikoyan, *Soviet Cuban Missile Crisis*, p. 262; and Garthoff, 'US Intelligence in the Cuban Missile Crisis', p. 61.

26 Mikoyan, *Soviet Cuban Missile Crisis*, pp. 217–28.

27 Annex A to 'Soviet Forces in Cuba', 5 February 1963, NSF, JFKL (obtained by me under FOIA); and 'Briefing Notes for DDCI: The Situation in Cuba', 18 December 1963, Doc. 731; in Department of State, *Foreign Relations of the United States* [*FRUS*], *1961–1963, Vols X–XII, American Republics; Cuba 1961–1962; Cuban Missile Crisis and Aftermath* (Washington, DC: Government Printing Office 1998), microfiche supplement.

28 Such requirements meant that FOIA requests had to be filed, as explained by the navy, in about a half-dozen cases (by me) in 2012–14 in order to obtain various *ONI Review* materials.

29 CIA to Bernstein, 12 September 2013.

30 Marguerite Higgins, *New York Herald Tribune*, 20 November 1962, A1.

31 *Washington Post*, 20 November 1962, A10; *New York Times*, 20 November 1962, A6.

32 Taylor to President, 'Evaluation of the Effect on US Operational Plans of Soviet Army Equipment Introduced Into Cuba', CM-85-62, 2 November 1962, from Taylor files, JCS Records, Record Group (RG) 218, National Archives, obtained (by me) under FOIA in about 2000–2. All statements on the Taylor report in succeeding paragraphs in this section of this essay are from the long-declassified Taylor report. In a preface to the paperback edition of *Fourteenth Day* (published in 2013) pp. 4–5, Coleman implies, incorrectly, that the Taylor report had first become available in about 2012, and incorrectly also indicates that the official 1962 estimate of 18,500 US casualties in the first ten days of an invasion had not become publicly available in any released document until about 2012. On that latter material, Coleman erred hugely – by about 25 years. The casualty estimate was, in fact, available by at least the mid 1980s in the then-partly declassified 'CINCLANT Historical Account of Cuban Crisis-1963 (U)', 55, obtained (in my copy) from the navy under FOIA in 1986; and also in the early 1990s, or earlier, in another military document, Marine Corps Emergency Action Center, 'Summary of Items of Significant Interest', 1–2 November 1962, as National Security Archive Doc. 01890.

33 McNamara loosely implied that he and JFK had made such a decision (Robert McNamara, with Brian VanDeMark, *In Retrospect: The Tragedy and Lessons of Vietnam* (New York: Vintage, 1996) p. 341). Coleman, *Fourteenth Day* (p. 140) seems mildly uneasy about that claim. In a 2002 interview, McNamara vaguely recalled that he had probably made that turn-down decision, but he did not seem firm on this matter, and thus the question seems still unresolved. The various JCS minutes ('Notes, Transcripts/Minutes, JCS', and 'JCS Chronology') and the 'CINCLANT Historical Account' leave unclear who made that decision. Bundy, in early 1990s interviews, thought McNamara had probably made the decision, but was not sure.

34 Walter S. Poole, *The Joint Chiefs of Staff and National Policy, 1961–1964* (Washington, DC: GPO 2011) p. 183.

35 ExComm minutes, 5 November 1962, NSF, JFKL; and 'CINCLANT Historical Account', p. 107.

36 *Los Angeles Times*, 12 November 1962, 1. Also see *Washington Post*, 12 November 1962, A1.

37 *Washington Post*, 12 November 1962, A7.

38 Hilsman to Rusk, 'Soviet and Cuban Indications in the Light of [rest of title security-redacted]', 14 November 1962, National Security Archive Doc. 02365.

39 Hilsman to Rusk, 16 November 1962, 'Removal of IRBMs from Cuba', Taylor files, JCS Records, received (by me) under FOIA. In November 1962, Hilsman had also feared that the Soviets would leave nuclear warheads and possibly some long-range missiles – MRBMs and IRBMs – in Cuba. Hilsman to Rusk, 'Moscow's Double Ploy: Avoiding Verification While Retaining a Base', 6 November 1962, National Security Archive Doc. 02015.

40 Memorandum of conversation (on meeting with David Ormsby-Gore), 28 October 1962, in Department of State, *FRUS, 1961–1963, Vol. XI, Cuban Missile Crisis and Aftermath* (Washington, DC: Government Printing Office 1996) pp. 288–9 and memorandum of conversation, 29 October 1962 (involving the Turkish ambassador) pp. 296–7.

41 McNamara, US House Appropriations Committee, *Department of Defense Appropriations* for 1964, 88th Cong., First Sess., part I, p. 57.

42 Eric Alterman, *When Presidents Lie: A History of Official Deception and Its Consequences* (New York: Viking 2004) pp. 90–159.

43 Various interviews in the 1990s with Bundy and McNamara. See also Max Holland and Tara Marie Egan, 'What Did LBJ Know about the Cuban Missile Crisis, and When Did He Know It?' in *Washington Decoded* (19 October 2007), www.washingtondecoded.com/site/2007/10/what-did-lbj-kn.html (last accessed 29 September 2014).

44 Stern, *Cuban Missile Crisis in American Memory*, pp. 32–53.

45 On Kennan, see his diary, October–November 1962, Kennan Papers; and Barton Bernstein, 'Considering John Lewis Gaddis's Kennan Biography: Questionable Interpretations and Unpursued Evidence and Issues', *Revue européenne des sciences sociales* 52/1 (2014) 270–1. On Bohlen, see Bohlen to Rusk, 18 October 1962, in Bohlen Papers, Library of Congress; Bohlen Oral History (1964) 22–7, JFKL.

46 Thomas G. Paterson and William Brophy, 'October Missiles and November Elections: The Cuban Missile Crisis and American Politics, 1962', *Journal of American History* 73/1 (1986) 87–119; Jeremy Pressman, 'September Statements, October Missiles, November Elections: Domestic Politics, Foreign Policy, and the Cuban Missile Crisis', *Security Studies* 10/3 (2001) 80–114.

47 Sorensen, 'G.O.P. Charges that', Sorensen Papers, box 48, JFKL.

48 Stewart Alsop and Charles Bartlett, 'In Time of Crisis', *Saturday Evening Post* 235/44 (8 December 1962) 8–12.

49 See Walter Johnson (ed.), *The Papers of Adlai E. Stevenson, Vol. VIII* (Boston, MA: Little, Brown and Company 1979) pp. 348–52.

50 Coleman, *Fourteenth Day*, p. 24, slightly retreats from the statement of p. 20 on JFK's time, prior to 1945–6, spent in Boston. On JFK's relevant background, see, for example, David Nasaw, *The Patriarch: The Remarkable Life and Turbulent Times of Joseph P. Kennedy* (New York: Penguin Press 2012) pp. 48–50, 104–6, 150–61, 239–40, 476, 594–9, and 602–4.

51 Dallek, *An Unfinished Life*, pp. 475–7; Mimi Alford, *Once Upon a Secret: My Affair with President John F. Kennedy and Its Aftermath* (New York: Random House 2012).

52 On this, see Rose McDermott, *Presidential Leadership, Illness, and Decision Making* (New York: Cambridge University Press 2008) pp. 118–56.

53 Holland, 'The "Photo Gap" that Delayed Discovery', p. 30.

54 Barrett and Holland, *Blind over Cuba*, pp. 54–117.

55 Coleman, 'Camelot's Conscience' and 'The Missiles of November, December', p. 46.

56 Khrushchev to Kennedy, 27 October 1962, in *FRUS, 1961–1963, Vol. XII, Cuban Missile Crisis and Aftermath*, pp. 257–60.

57 See, for example, Harriman, 'Memorandum on Kremlin Reactions', 22 October 1962, copies in at least three separate archives – JFKL, Ball Papers (Princeton), and Harriman Papers (Library of Congress). Somehow, Coleman apparently never saw this document, which was declassified in various copies between about the mid 1970s and the late 1980s. Also see Harriman to Ball, 26 October. 1962, National Security Archive Doc. 01414.

58 Zelikow and May, *Presidential Recordings: Kennedy, Vol. III*, pp. 285–6, 299–302, and 314–18.

59 Rowland Evans Jr., in *New York Herald Tribune*, 2 November 1962, pp. 1, 8.

60 On the actual U-2 events, see George W. Pedlow and Donald E. Weizenbach, *The CIA and the U-2 Program, 1954–1974* (Washington, DC: CIA 1988) p. 201.

61 McCone, memorandum for the record (on discussion with Bundy), 5 November 1962, in *FRUS, 1961–1963, Vol. XII, Cuban Missile Crisis and Aftermath*, pp. 375–7.

62 'Over Cuba: Flak at 11 o'clock', *Time* 80, No. 23 (7 December 1962) 15; ExComm meeting, 29 October 1962, in *FRUS, 1961–1963, Vol. XII, Cuban Missile Crisis and Aftermath*, pp. 291–33; and JCS to Secretary of State, 29 October 1962 (received 2.37 p.m.), National Security Archive Doc. 01663. Coleman, *Fourteenth Day* (p. 219) somehow erred by placing that 7 December *Time* article in the 16 November issue, and *Fourteenth Day* (pp. 51–2) uncritically believed that 7 December article's claim of a 29 October-*morning* shooting over Cuba at a US surveillance plane.

63 The correct reference, for the accurate month and year, is 'Intelligence Briefs', *ONI Review*, 17/12 (December 1962), 557, obtained (by me) under FOIA. See also, in contrast, 'Intelligence Briefs', *ONI Review*, 18/1 (January 1963) 31, obtained (by me) under FOIA.

64 CIA/ORR, DD/I Staff Study, 'Cuba 1962: Khrushchev's Miscalculated Risk', obtained (by me) under FOIA from the CIA initially in 2003, and then (again under FOIA) a slightly different redacted copy, with some added declassified pages in 2013. Coleman used a 2003-redacted version in his book and in his 2007 essay, p. 40, from the National Security Files, box 35, Lyndon B. Johnson Library, Austin, TX, and the title page on that copy in the Johnson Library is identical on specified authorship (CIA/ORR DD/I) to both my 2003 and 2013 copies.

65 Garthoff, *Reflections on the Missile Crisis* (1989) pp. 63–5, wrote briefly and rather elliptically on the subject, and then Jerrold Schechter and Peter Deriabin, *The Spy Who Saved the World: How a Soviet Colonel Changed the Course of the Cold War* (New York: Scribner's Sons 1992) pp. 337–48 partly dissented and added *far more* material, though their claims and evidence should probably be carefully checked before major details are trusted. I have made a small research effort to use FOIA to build on this subject and on related subjects of spying, but to date (mid 2014) have not received any useful materials from US agencies. Coleman never mentions the arrest of the spy Oleg Penkovsky, and the controversy about whether, and if so, what President Kennedy was told. See Schecter and Deriabin, *The Spy Who Saved the World*, pp. 346–7.

66 W. C. Sullivan to A.H. Belmont, 'Call from the Attorney General to Assistant Director Courtney Evans [FBI] on October 28, 1962', 29 October 1962, National Security Archive Doc. 01662.

67 Such ethical/moral critiques by the Harvard historian and 1962 Senate candidate H. Stuart Hughes and by Harvard sociologist Barrington Moore were discussed by them in conversations/interviews (with me) in 1962–3. Sorensen, in Robert Kennedy, *Thirteen Days: A Memoir of the Cuban Missile Crisis* (New York: W.W. Norton 1969) p. 128(n), claims that Robert Kennedy had planned to address such ethical/moral issues in *Thirteen Days*. No such material has

reportedly been found in the now-opened segments of RFK papers, at the JFKL, and no one – including Sorensen or W.W. Norton, when queried by me in the 1990s – could find the original manuscript of *Thirteen Days*. There is good reason to question the actual authorship of that book, and even to suspect that Sorensen, as with *Profiles*, was the author. For an optimistic, but uncritical, use of *Thirteen Days*, see James Blight, *The Shattered Crystal Ball: Fear and Learning in the Cuban Missile Crisis* (Savage, MD: Rowman & Littlefield 1990).

3 Prime Minister and President

Harold Macmillan's accounts of the Cuban missile crisis[1]

Peter Catterall

In October 1962 Harold Macmillan had been Prime Minister for nearly six years and had been keeping a regular diary since 1950. His contemporaneous scrawled diary references to what was described therein as 'the World Crisis' became the first account Macmillan provided of the Cuban stand-off. On 4 November 1962, with the high point of the crisis seemingly passed during the previous weekend, Macmillan then provided a second account, a lengthy entry in which he tried to order his thoughts on the causes, resolution and consequences of the Cuban missile crisis.[2] This was reproduced almost *in toto* at the close of the chapter, 'On the Brink', about Cuba in the sixth and last volume of his memoirs, *At the End of the Day*. This, covering the period 1961–3, was published on 26 September 1973 in Britain and on 9 January 1974 in the US. Highlights from the memoirs were serialised before the publication of each volume in the *Sunday Times*. Publication was also marked by a televised interview with Macmillan, with the relevant section on Cuba being broadcast on BBC1 at 9.25 p.m. on 19 September 1973. As well as a radio version, this programme was repeated on 27 October 1974 and again, following Macmillan's death in 1986, in January 1987. Furthermore, an edited transcript appeared in the BBC's *The Listener* magazine.[3] Macmillan thus retold his version of the Cuban missile crisis – and other aspects of his career – many times, in a wide range of media. In the process he also, as the BBC head of Current Affairs, John Grist, observed of an earlier broadcast interview, 'polished the words of his stories'.[4] The result was that, particularly for British audiences, Macmillan's successive accounts helped to shape public understandings of the Cuban missile crisis.

At the time of the Cuban missile crisis Macmillan was 68 and by the time his memoir of that episode appeared he was nearing his eightieth birthday. As the broadcast made clear, he nevertheless remained mentally robust, returning to manage the family publishing firm after his health-induced retirement from the Premiership in 1963.[5] This helps to explain how the autobiography of 'Mr Harold' eventually ran to 3763 pages and some 1.5 million words.

Macmillan significantly chose to start work on the memoirs on 4 August 1964, the fiftieth anniversary of the most traumatic experience of his life, the outbreak of the Great War, He set out deliberately to reflect on the dramatic changes, not least the decline of Europe and the rise of the rival empires of the Americans and the Soviets who confronted each other over Cuba, which ensued from that disaster. In the process he deliberately modelled himself on the multi-volume memoirs of his great mentor and predecessor, Winston Churchill.[6]

The work was financed by the contract for £360,000 signed between the book trust Macmillan established as the owner of his literary estate and the Thomson Organisation, including serial rights in the *Sunday Times*, 'of which £34,000 is to be paid to me in four annual instalments to write the book and pay the assistants etc.'.[7] Thomson in turn contracted the American rights with Harper & Row, while the book contract with the family firm of Macmillan & Company for the rest of the world was seemingly a more modest £45,000.[8]

Prime Minister Macmillan had prepared for his eventual memoirs by, again, copying Churchill – in this case by taking away duplicates of all possible documents for his private archive.[9] Ironically, in doing so Macmillan directly contravened his own guidelines on the writing of ministerial memoirs laid down in the Cabinet memorandum in 1961:

> I attach particular important to the point … that special difficulty arises over memoirs which are constructed on the basis of official documents and keep closely to the wording of these documents, whether by quotation or by paraphrase. For this as well as for other reasons it is specially desirable that Ministers should not retain official documents in their private possession on relinquishing office … I hope that, when the times comes, all my colleagues will be careful to comply with this rule.[10]

He also went through the million words of his diaries selecting passages to be transcribed for possible inclusion by his two secretarial assistants, who were at this stage in this process Anne Macpherson and Bunty Morley. For instance, just over 70 per cent of the diaries for 1962 were selected for transcription in this way. These voluminous materials, supplemented by books and correspondence, were piled high in the old billiard room in Birch Grove, Macmillan's country house in Sussex. At the end of 1964 Anne Glyn-Jones arrived as his archivist and was told to 'browse about a bit' through these piles. This she did, producing folders of material relevant to each chapter. From the third volume onwards she also organised into thematic chapters the structure of each instalment of the memoirs.[11]

When Glyn-Jones came to sorting the material for 'On the Brink', the diary entries from ten years earlier were mainly of use for the opening days of the crisis. Macmillan padded these out with messages from Kennedy and the British ambassador to Washington, David Ormsby-Gore, and particularly with transcripts from the telephone conversations he had with Kennedy during the crisis. This, as was no doubt intended, gives the feeling of a blow-by-blow account by a closely involved participant. The relative paucity of diary entries and the alternative material selected also inevitably privileged Prime Minister–President relations. Only a close reading of the chapter reveals how important other dimensions of the crisis – such as the role of the United Nations (UN) – were to the Prime Minister at the time. The repeated references to the Acting Secretary-General U Thant,[12] for instance, are subsumed within this dialogue with Kennedy.

U Thant was also relatively overlooked in Macmillan's contemporary diary entries. The first reference to the Cuban missile crisis in the diaries is to the message received from President Kennedy at Chequers at 10 p.m. on Sunday 21 October 1962, warning of the Soviet build-up, though in 'On the Brink' he refers obliquely to the guarded indications given to British intelligence officials in Washington two days before.[13] At the time he wrote the chapter he was not aware of the extensive debates raging in Kennedy's specially convened Executive Committee (ExComm) since 16 October. 'On the Brink' nevertheless begins with Macmillan's view of the origins of the crisis from Castro's seizure of power in Cuba in 1959. He does not recapitulate the critical comments about American policy towards this new regime in his diaries from 1960, though 'On the Brink' does reproduce the scepticism he expressed to then President Eisenhower about the likely efficacy of sanctions against the Cubans.[14] The chapter then jumps to the start of the crisis, passing over episodes like the Bay of Pigs in silence. Macmillan had been aware of planning for this attempt to overthrow Castro aided by the Americans, but never considered it likely to succeed.

Nor were the British inclined to share the Administration's anxiety to lance the Cuban boil, or the methods they selected to do so. One of Macmillan's constant refrains was the need for trade expansion, not least as a means of tying countries to the West. The embargo of all trade with Cuba except medical supplies announced by Kennedy on 3 February 1962 was a step in the opposite direction and unwelcome in London. Sanctions were seen as slow and ineffective. The British had previously refused Castro's request for jet fighters under American pressure. However, Kennedy's urging of British support for the embargo to Lord Home, the British Foreign Secretary, during the latter's Washington visit in late September 1962, as the President moved towards difficult mid-term elections, met with observations that British shipping interests could only be coerced by new legislation difficult to justify in peacetime. Macmillan concluded therefore in a note to Home of 1 October, 'there is no reason for us to help the Americans on Cuba'.[15] Such interventions, as the Minister of State at the Foreign Office, Joseph Godber, pointed out, would 'merely force Castro to depend more and more completely on the Soviet Union'.[16] Indeed, it appears that a combination of US trade pressure and military exercises suggesting imminent invasion of Cuba helped, as this view might have predicted, to create the circumstances in which the Soviet leader, Nikita Khrushchev, decided in May 1962 to send missiles to Castro.[17]

Macmillan, however, does not appear to have suspected this either in his diary entry of 4 November 1962, or at the time of writing 'On the Brink.' Instead, he speculated that Khrushchev's motive was to threaten the embattled outpost of West Berlin. Indeed, his only diary reference in 1962 to Cuba prior to the outbreak of the crisis was, in noting on Home's return from Washington his objections to a trade embargo that '[t]he Russians are clearly using Cuba as a counter-irritant to Berlin'.[18] Nor did Macmillan note at the time or subsequently the growing pressure on Kennedy from senior Republicans, particularly Senator Kenneth Keating, claiming that the Soviets were deploying missiles in Cuba,[19] even though he hints that British intelligence also suggested a build-up of some kind there.[20]

Keating's claim was publicly denied by Kennedy on 4 September 1962. Nevertheless, from August the President began to receive daily intelligence reports on Cuba. Conclusive proof both of missiles and Il-28 bombers being assembled was finally provided by a U2 over-flight on 14 October and presented to the President in Washington at 8.45 a.m. on 16 October. Thereafter Kennedy's hastily convened Executive Committee (ExComm) debated what to do, but neither Ormsby-Gore nor David Bruce, the US ambassador to London, were officially told of the crisis until 21 October,[21] earlier in the day than Macmillan.

Apparently Kennedy decided initially not to consult the British because he felt 'They'll just object' to the idea of a military response. There was agreement in ExComm that Macmillan and President de Gaulle of France should be given 24 hours' notice of action.[22] However, the Americans only moved to informing their allies of the crisis as their thinking shifted instead to a limited naval blockade,[23] to commence on 24 October. Nevertheless, Macmillan's reaction to Kennedy in their first telephone conversation of the crisis late on 22 October – only briefly mentioned in 'On the Brink'[24] – was very similar to Kennedy's own a week earlier, arguing that the President ought 'to seize Cuba and have done with it'.[25] In contrast, Macmillan was doubtful both about a blockade's legality and it speedily achieving its objectives; in which case Kennedy might find that 'he may never get rid of Cuban rockets except by trading them for Turkish, Italian or other bases'. Indeed, early in that conversation he asked 'What are you going to do with the blockade? Are you going to occupy Cuba and have done with it or is it going to just drag on?' Kennedy, however, did not want to pursue that option because it 'invites [Khrushchev] so directly into Berlin'. Furthermore, such action would require seven days to mobilise.[26] What it did not require was a similar build-up of NATO forces, with resulting public alarm. Macmillan therefore, as he recounts in 'On the Brink' rebuffed hints from Washington of the need for heightened alert levels.[27]

Apart from mentioning 'certain precautions affecting the Royal Air Force' Macmillan had nothing further to say on the subject therein.[28] This was consistent with and carried into his memoirs his contemporary concern to avoid alarming the public. At the time the Prime Minister made clear to Bomber Command, responsible for the nuclear-armed V-force bombers, the need therefore to eschew any overt preparations. There was accordingly no reference in Macmillan's memoirs to the shift on the morning of 27 October from Alert Condition 4 (with one crew at 15 minutes readiness) to Alert Condition 3, with six and then 12 aircraft at this level of preparedness. He was himself probably unaware that the entire force of some 120 bombers was then placed on cockpit readiness, within five minutes of take-off, for much of that afternoon.[29] Alert Condition 3 remained in place until 5 November.

There may be a further reason for Macmillan's reticence on this subject. He had taken the view when Foreign Secretary in 1955 that nuclear weapons had abolished war.[30] No doubt he was unwilling to emphasize in 'On the Brink' how close he came to being proved wrong on this, or the extent of his personal responsibility for preparations which would have eclipsed in their outcome even the hideousness of the Great War. His ongoing drive to negotiate a ban on nuclear tests, which Bruce saw as almost an obsession, was similarly shaped by his acute awareness of global anxieties about the military and environmental threats posed by these new and horrific weapons.

Macmillan's concern for speedy action reflected the same concern to manage public opinion, not just in Britain but around the world. His fear was that otherwise demand for a peace conference could grow, fed by European public opinion sceptical about being brought to the brink of nuclear war by Americans now having to live, as they themselves had long done, under the Russian nuclear shadow.[31] As he told Kennedy in the early hours of 23 October, 'if we are forced to a conference all the cards are in this man's hands'.[32] Indeed, Macmillan's notes in preparation for this conversation include the observation 'If you aim at a conference would it not be better to have a fait accompli first?'[33]

Macmillan's views on the risks involved in a conference can seem inconsistent with his previous record on the subject. After all, he was an inveterate enthusiast for a renewal of the East–West conversations he had participated in as Foreign Secretary in 1955, which he had tried to revive in the run-up to the abortive Paris summit of 1960.[34] Some kind of conference was therefore naturally at the forefront of his mind early in the crisis. The question was, however, what outcome could be expected from such an event? After all, as Macmillan noted to Ormsby-Gore on 22 October, such an event would provide a perfect opportunity for the Soviets to broach issues like Berlin, which the British were keen not to entangle in the Cuban crisis. This risk, and the chance that such an event would be used to 'endanger the unity of the [NATO] Alliance', was also very much the theme of the Prime Minister's remarks to the first Cabinet meeting of the crisis on 23 October.[35] A conference was therefore to be seen as a last resort option. The Prime Minister made it clear that 'I could not allow a situation in Europe or in the world to develop which looks like escalating into war without trying some action by calling a conference on my own', but this was for the ambassador's 'personal information only'. It proved unnecessary to pursue this option. Accordingly, this particular passage was not included in the extensive extract from this telegram to Ormsby-Gore reproduced in 'On the Brink'.[36] Nor was Macmillan's brief revival of the idea of some kind of limited summit later on 27 October when he feared the crisis was heading towards conflict.[37]

On the other hand, a conference which enabled progress on more general disarmament issues, not least on Macmillan's aspirations for a test ban, could certainly be desirable, if feasible. Whether the Americans might support such an idea for a general conference, with Cuba as a preliminary, was therefore raised by Home with Ormsby-Gore on 24 October. The ambassador, however, decided not to raise this with the President. It did not accord with how the Administration was trying to present the crisis: as the ambassador noted, 'for the Americans this is a clear challenge by the Soviet Union and ... Castro is a mere cypher in the game'. Home's idea was therefore a non-starter;[38] thereafter discussion of a conference dropped from British contributions to the crisis. Nor, apart from brief and isolated references (for instance on p. 212), does it feature in 'On the Brink'.

The risks of being pushed into talks from which the Soviets would be the main beneficiaries were made apparent by the groups who, in the early stages of the crisis, called for such a conference. These included the non-aligned countries supporting the Ghana/United Arab Republic (Egypt) resolution to the United Nations Security Council on 24 October. This, and the accompanying calls for an international conference from President Nkrumah of Ghana, risked presenting the crisis as occasioned by the American quarantine, rather than the placing of Soviet missiles on Cuba. A conference on such terms was clearly attractive to the Soviets; the Polish ambassador inviting himself to visit Home at the Foreign Office on the morning of 24 October to present a suggestion along these lines. He was firmly rebuffed by the Foreign Secretary, well aware that attention should be focused instead upon the missiles already in place on the island.[39] Talks along these lines were fraught with dangers.

This was made further apparent when U Thant, under non-aligned pressure, despatched to Kennedy and Khrushchev messages on the afternoon (New York time) of 24 October, calling for a standstill in both Soviet shipments and the quarantine pending talks. While Macmillan made no mention in 'On the Brink' of the Ghanaian or Polish initiatives, he made clear therein his doubts about U Thant's intervention, recording his comments in his telephone call with Kennedy that evening that 'I think that's rather tiresome of him because it looks sensible and yet it's very bad'. It was bad because, as Kennedy had just noted, it distracted from the

American goal of removing the missile sites, on which work was steadily continuing.[40] It was also, as Macmillan noted in his diary, that '[n]ow that [the] Russians have been proved blatant liars, no unpoliced agreement with them is possible'.[41]

This meant that proof of Soviet duplicity had to be provided, not least for the benefit of the British public and sceptical opinions, particularly in the non-aligned world. As Macmillan notes in 'On the Brink', his reaction to the photographic evidence of the missile sites Bruce showed him on 22 October was that they had to be widely publicized with expert interpretation. British pressure and Bruce's support led to sanitized versions of the pictures being released in London on 23 October. Macmillan in 'On the Brink' incorrectly claims that these photographs were first publicized at the Security Council on that day. There is no doubt that their presentation there by the US ambassador, Adlai Stevenson, was one of the most theatrical moments of the crisis. However, it did not happen until two days later and again was almost certainly with British encouragement.[42]

Meanwhile, on 23 October, Macmillan met with a Labour delegation who asked if he would go to Washington,[43] as Attlee had done at a similar juncture during the Korean War. Though he raised this possibility with Kennedy the following evening, in his diary the Prime Minister merely noted '[t]hey hadn't much to say'.[44] Nor did his diary entry refer to the related problems of managing the press and public opinion, despite a note from his private secretary, Tim Bligh, warning that lobby correspondents were asking if Britain had been consulted on the developing crisis.[45] Such material does not appear to have been the bundles taken from Downing Street amongst which Glyn-Jones ferreted out the background information for this chapter. Macmillan did nevertheless meet with the lobby correspondents on the evening of 25 October, noting '[t]he consumption of alcoholic refreshment was extraordinary'.[46]

Meanwhile, on 24 October at 2.00 p.m. (Greenwich Mean Time [GMT]), the quarantine around Cuba came into force. At around 11.30 p.m.[47] (British Summer Time [BST]) that evening Macmillan again spoke to Kennedy. Apart from the U Thant proposals and Kennedy's concern to make sure Macmillan had the arguments needed to counter the Opposition in the Commons debate scheduled for the following day,[48] the main item was a question from Kennedy on whether or not, if work continued on the missiles 'we then tell them that if they don't get the missiles out, ... we're going to invade Cuba?' Notwithstanding his earlier belligerence, Macmillan now asked for time to think about this. Kennedy had confirmed early in the conversation that some Soviet ships had turned around. This, U Thant's intervention and the soft answer Khrushchev gave to the Acting Secretary-General, led the Prime Minister to conclude in his response, sent on 25 October and reproduced in 'On the Brink', that 'events have gone too far'.[49] Macmillan may have been an ardent antiappeaser in the 1930s. Now, however, he felt UN inspection of the sites to ensure their immobilisation would remove the threat posed by the missiles, without the need for military action.

It is not clear at what time this document was despatched, but a handwritten note by Macmillan's foreign policy private secretary, Philip de Zulueta, suggests that it was at 10.25 a.m. (BST).[50] This idea of immobilisation, however, hardly featured when Kennedy and Macmillan had their third conversation of the crisis after 11.00 p.m. (BST) on 25 October.[51] Macmillan briefly raised it as the main objective of the Americans, but the President concentrated on naval aspects of the crisis. The Americans, however, were well aware of the significance of the missiles already on the island, knowing as they did that the Soviets were still pushing on apace with the bases under construction on Cuba. Accordingly, Kennedy observed to ExComm the following morning (26 October) – confirmed to Macmillan that evening – that additional action was needed to remove these weapons.[52] Forcible removal was the option stressed to the British, French and West German ambassadors in Washington that evening. At the same meeting the ambassadors were told the American estimation that the Soviets had intended a showdown over Berlin on completion of the Cuban bases, to coincide with Khrushchev's upcoming visit to the US.[53] That, of course, depended on completion without detection, no longer a possibility. Khrushchev also plainly failed to consult his ambassadors in Washington or at the UN in New York either about the missile deployment or the likely American reaction. Towards the end of the crisis Britain's ambassador to the Soviet Union, Sir Frank Roberts, acutely recalled 'Khrushchev's well-known proclivity for setting out courses of action without knowing where they could lead him, coupled with his undoubted talent for making the best of the resulting situation'.[54] Whether his improvisation on 26 October turned out best for him is another matter. This consisted of a first letter in which Khrushchev suggested to Kennedy the possibility of dismantling the missiles in Cuba, in return for a guarantee that Cuba would not be invaded, tightened in a second message (on 27 October) by linkage with the quid pro quo of American withdrawal of 'analogous weapons' such as the 15 Jupiter Intermediate Range Ballistic Missiles (IRBMs) installed in Turkey in 1961.

Neither Macmillan nor Kennedy was aware of this when they spoke for the fourth time during the crisis at 11.15 p.m. (BST) on 26 October,[55] though the latter mentioned some unofficial hints along similar lines from Russian officials. The President had in fact conceded the merits of such a guarantee for Cuba in ExComm earlier that day. Macmillan was not made aware of this, or of the way in which the Americans intended to use the Brazilians to float this idea.[56] Such a possibility, however, clearly piqued the Prime Minister's interest.[57] He then returned to the idea of a UN inspection team to 'ensure that these missiles were made inoperable during the period of any conference or discussion', suggesting that it be led by U Thant, before dropping into the conversation his own swop proposal, the immobilisation of the 60 Thor IRBMs deployed in Britain in 1958–9.[58] This would have been a significant gesture as normally 65 per cent of this force (39 missiles) was on 30 minutes readiness. Indeed, at 11.00 a.m. on 27 October (BST) the Prime Minister agreed a move to Alert Condition 3 for Bomber Command, which meant that 59 of the Thors were at 15 minutes readiness, remaining so until 5 November.[59] None of this, however, was mentioned at the time in Macmillan's diary, and it was only obliquely referred to in 'On the Brink'. Similarly, the fact that, despite the President's non-committal response, particularly to the Thor swop, these three schemes were then reiterated in a message to Kennedy in the early hours of 27 October (BST) was also passed over in silence.[60]

There are, indeed, no diary entries at all for Saturday 27 October. Macmillan and Home had cancelled all their weekend engagements.[61] From the diary of Macmillan's press secretary, Harold Evans, it is clear that the day was spent in great anxiety that Kennedy might have decided that there was no other way and 'was hell-bent on destroying the missile sites. This carried the strong possibility of Soviet retaliation in Berlin or elsewhere, with the prospect of escalation into nuclear war.' In these circumstances, Macmillan 'felt he must intervene' in ways which would achieve the immobilisation of the weapons without resort to US military action.[62] These anxieties would not have been assuaged by Ormsby-Gore's telegram received at 4.00 a.m. that morning. Reporting the meeting with Secretary of State Dean Rusk and his fellow ambassadors from France and West Germany the previous evening (Washington time) he noted that, '[w]hen asked what further action the United States might take if they failed to obtain a satisfactory outcome in the talks with U Thant, [the Secretary of State] indicated that they would have to consider destroying the sites by bombing'. At least Rusk confirmed that the three principal European allies would be consulted before any such eventuality occurred.[63]

On 27 October ExComm began to meet at around 10.00 a.m. Washington time, by which time it was already 3.00 p.m. in London. For Macmillan much of the day had passed. It is therefore difficult to endorse the claim of scholars such as May and Zelikow that both Macmillan and Ormsby-Gore became de facto members of ExComm during the crisis.[64] The fact that neither was physically present, and that Macmillan sometimes only received limited reports on what was transpiring in Washington from Ormsby-Gore and often had to wait for hours for detailed telegrams to come through necessarily limited his direct knowledge of events across the Atlantic. One example is the news of the shooting down of the American U2 surveillance aeroplane over Cuba, which very much exercised ExComm on the afternoon of 27 October.[65] Macmillan talked in some detail about this incident in his BBC interview in 1973. At the time, however, he was only belatedly apprised of it.[66] A telegram from the British embassy in Cuba bearing this news did not arrive until in London 6.38 a.m. on 28 October, having seemingly been nine hours in transmission.[67] Another example is that, in the ExComm discussions early on 27 October, the text arrived of Khrushchev's second message to Kennedy. In contrast, the copy of this message in the Prime Minister's files is from the news agency Reuters, a transcript of the broadcast on Radio Moscow.

Home's handwritten notes on the British copy of this message observed that the build-up goes on – a point made by Kennedy in his noon (Washington time) broadcast – whilst the US had rejected the Turkey linkage. Home's comments ended, '[s]till trying to keep it to this [Western] hemisphere'.[68] This kind of language no doubt reflected British attempts to respond to American sensitivities, tutored by the 1823 Monroe doctrine, about outside interference in their part of the world.

It is not clear when Home made these notes. However, it is apparent from the despatch Home sent to Britain's ambassador to the UN, Sir Patrick Dean, at 3 p.m. (London time) that day that various British schemes for UN involvement in immobilisation were indeed designed to keep the issue in the Western hemisphere, avoiding 'reciprocity in the European area'. Home's suggestions therefore focused on U Thant leading an inspection team to Cuba, Cuban inviolability and/or establishing a nuclear-free zone in Latin America. The reciprocity in the European area that the Thor offer undoubtedly constituted was additional, something to be used 'if it would make all the difference'.[69] A telegram sent to the Washington embassy at 2.30 p.m. asked that Rusk also be informed of these instructions.[70]

It was not until 8.07 p.m. on 27 October that Kennedy's response to Macmillan's memorandum of their previous evening's conversation arrived in London. This message is not mentioned in Harold Evans' diary, but it seems to have been the cause of the anxiety he noted. It gave Kennedy's reaction to Khrushchev's broadcast, concluding:

> This morning I authorised a release restating our position that work on the Cuban bases, which is still continuing, must stop before we can consider other proposals.
>
> I do not feel that this country should allow itself to become engaged in negotiations affecting the individual security interests of our NATO allies. Any initiatives in this respect, it seems to me, should appropriately come from Europe.
>
> I would appreciate your views on the current situation as it develops. In the meantime, I continue to believe that we must secure the actual dismantling of the missiles currently in Cuba as the first order of business.[71]

In his response – seemingly despatched an hour or so later following discussions with Home, Rab Butler, Ted Heath, Peter Thorneycroft and the Permanent Under-Secretary at the Foreign Office (and former ambassador to the US) Sir Harold Caccia[72] – Macmillan immediately indicated

'I am in full agreement with your last two paragraphs'. In particular, the penultimate paragraph was interpreted as an invitation for an initiative along the lines already broached with the President. The Prime Minister accordingly put forward a draft message to be sent to Khrushchev suggesting a standstill for negotiations during which:

1   The Soviet Government would agree to:

    (a) no further work on the missile sites in Cuba;
    (b) no imports of ballistic missiles into the island;
    (c) the existing missiles in Cuba being made inoperable (which can be done without any breach of military security).

All this under UN authority.

2   At the same time the US Government would agree to:

    (a) lift the quarantine, and
    (b) not take any physical action against Cuba during the standstill.

In a final paragraph the Thor offer was then reiterated.[73]

Seemingly it was not until after this point that a telegram from Dean arrived at 9.31 p.m. (BST) indicating U Thant's response to Home's proposals. Dean reported that in the conversation he had with U Thant at 1.00 p.m. (New York time), it was clear that the idea of following in the footsteps of his late predecessor, Dag Hammarskjöld, and actually going into the field to address problems had not occurred to the Acting UN Secretary-General. U Thant, however, considered the idea of leading an inspection team, but treated it as separate from issues such as Turkey or the inviolability of Cuba.

Dean did not pass on to his American counterparts the Thor offer idea.[74] From his telegram received at 11.22 p.m. (BST) it is not clear whether Ormsby-Gore mentioned this to the President either when he saw him that morning (Washington time). The only part of the British proposals the President appears to have responded to, from this account, is the U Thant mission idea, which Kennedy said 'could be a useful initiative', depending on timing. The rest of Ormsby-Gore's telegram was taken up with how the Americans were responding to the Khrushchev broadcast and with Kennedy's thoughts about Turkey. The President's view was reported as 'that there was little military value to be attached to the missiles in Turkey'. The issue was how the Turks would react.[75]

The Turkish ambassador to the UN made his government's displeasure apparent to Stevenson at a meeting on the evening of 27 October.[76] ExComm had meanwhile been discussing how the Americans should react to Khrushchev's linkage of Cuba and Turkey for much of the day. From a military perspective, the issue was largely symbolic. As Robert McNamara, the US Secretary of Defense pointed out, the Jupiters in Turkey were 'more obsolete than the Thor missile. The British have recognised the obsolescence of the Thor and have decided to take it out and replace it with other systems.' Clearly, as Under-Secretary of State George Ball noted, similar arrangements could be made with the Turks.[77]

The problem, as Ball earlier observed, is that once such matters were broached with the Turks this American concession 'will be all over Western Europe, and our position would have been undermined'. As Macmillan noted in 'On the Brink', if there was a deal over Turkey, '[a]ll America's allies would feel that to avoid the Cuban threat the U.S. Government had bargained away their protection'. He, however, was under the impression that 'Kennedy ... never wavered on this issue'.[78] This, indeed, was very much the impression – for exactly the reasons given by Macmillan – which the President wished to convey. As Kennedy noted at the time, this was made more problematic because the Turkey/Cuba swop had been raised publicly by Khrushchev. His approach to ExComm that day was therefore about how to respond without appearing to cave in, not least to his NATO allies.[79] US ambassadors were therefore told to avoid any Cuba/ Turkey linkage. Bruce was certainly under the impression that the Turkey option had been rejected.[80]

To reinforce this message, ExComm agreed that Thomas Finletter, the US permanent representative, should brief a NATO Council in Paris. His briefing notes were passed on to the British government at some time on 28 October. Significantly, they claimed that hopes of a solution were diminished by Khrushchev's letter of 27 October 'linking Cuban settlement to withdrawal of NATO Jupiters from Turkey, but we continue to press for solution in Cuban framework alone'. Instead, the continuing build-up of the missile sites was stressed. Allies were also warned that some ships were still heading to the quarantine zone. The NATO Council was thus informed that

> [i]n these circumstances the US Government may find it necessary within a short time in its own interest and that of its fellow nations in the Western hemisphere to take whatever military action may be necessary to remove this growing threat to the hemisphere.[81]

The US message to its allies was therefore that military action, for which preparations throughout the crisis had been taking place, may be imminent and that missile trades were not on the table. As noted in Ormsby-Gore's telegram received at 3.38 a.m. (London time) on 28 October, their line on the Thor offer was therefore that 'this w[oul]d look as though the US w[oul]d be prepared to trade the security of European nations for US security in the Western hemisphere'.[82] A similar line was also taken by the President's National Security Advisor, McGeorge Bundy, in a call to de Zulueta at 1.30 a.m. (BST).[83] They had a further conversation at 4.00 a.m. (BST) in which Bundy conveyed the essence of the Finletter briefing to the British, played down progress at the UN and suggested that the Prime Minister's Thor proposal 'is not yet right and what we would much rather have is active participation … in the North Atlantic Council' set for 10.00 a.m. on 28 October [Paris time].[84] Bundy's subsequent notes on this conversation make it clear that, while the US did not want to appear to cave in before its European allies, those same allies were being encouraged to do the caving for them. Bundy recorded that he 'tried to hint … delicately that if the UK is interested in the Jupiter proposal, it should say so in the North Atlantic Council'.[85] However, the UK was not interested in the Jupiter proposal, which was seen as positively dangerous. Throughout the crisis the British had instead been concerned to keep it confined to the western hemisphere and avoid any linkage between Cuba and anywhere else, with the possible exception of the British Thors. This aim to keep the crisis in Cuba was very much behind Home's instructions to Dean on 27 October. Not only was de Zulueta therefore not interested in taking up the Jupiter option (having been led to believe that the US were not either), but – particularly at that time in the morning – he was not even attuned to taking up the subtle hints that he should be.[86]

Bundy used alarmist language to try to push the British towards picking up his hints. It had the opposite effect to that intended. Not for the first time, Bundy misread Macmillan.[87] The Prime Minister, like his private secretary, missed the hints but was alarmed by the tone of the rest of the conversation. He was no more reassured by the President's reply to Khrushchev, responding to his offer on Cuba and ignoring Turkey, which was received in London at 1.30 a.m.[88] Subsequently in 'On the Brink' Macmillan was to credit this with successfully solving the crisis without resort to conflict, passing over very briefly his manoeuvres of that fraught weekend.[89] Yet on that Sunday morning of 28 October he clearly remained anxious. A draft message to Kennedy spoke of Macmillan's concern that U Thant was not getting anywhere. The Prime Minister wanted to contact Khrushchev directly 'when it is apparent that he is not giving way and before you are forced by his stubbornness or by the local situation to take drastic action. Can you help me on timing?' The text as actually transmitted, seemingly at 9.52 a.m. GMT, was rather more anodyne, but still contained the timing question.[90]

In 'On the Brink' Macmillan says that he then decided the timing issue himself in the absence of further communications from an early morning Washington.[91] There is certainly no evidence of an American response. The message transmitted to Moscow at around noon (and delivered by Roberts at 2.35 p.m. Moscow time), however, was rather different from the draft he had sent to Kennedy the previous day. By then Macmillan seems to have seen Dean's telegram which had arrived in London at 5.28 a.m., reporting that Castro had accepted the U Thant visit proposal.[92]

Accordingly, Macmillan's message to Khrushchev briefly touched on dealing with the missiles in Cuba through the United Nations,[93] before moving on to responding positively to the Soviet leader's own olive branch on a nuclear test ban agreement in his message to Kennedy on 27 October.[94] Evans described this as 'a mouselike message'.[95] In the absence of American approval of any other message, it however picked up on the one aspect of Khrushchev's communication that Macmillan, who had long been seeking such a test ban agreement, could legitimately address.

Bruce's view was that it was 'designed to impress [Khrushchev] with British solidarity on US Cuban policy'. Certainly there was nothing in it the US could object to. Macmillan's main regret, he told Bruce, was that he had not sent it 'several hours earlier'.[96] As it was little time had elapsed when, towards the end of Macmillan's lunch, the message came through that Khrushchev had said to Kennedy 'that the equipment on Cuba "which you call offensive" would be dismantled, packed up and returned to the Soviet Union'.[97] After all the tension the reaction of Macmillan and Home was, Bruce noted, 'mildly euphoric. Now, perhaps, a number of people immobilized during this emergency can devote future weekends to depleting the game-birds who are ravaging British agriculture.'[98]

Macmillan noted in his diary that the British message, not given to the press until 4.15 p.m. (GMT), appeared to be 'backing the horse after the race'.[99] Nevertheless, this may not have been a bad thing: as Ormsby-Gore pointed out that evening to Rusk in Washington, rather than allowing the Soviets to seize the initiative, the West must get in first with their proposals for peace, picked up in Macmillan's message.[100] Now was the time to seek the general negotiations the Prime Minister had toyed with at the start of the crisis. From Macmillan's point of view it certainly gave a fillip to his efforts for a test ban agreement and a reduction in cold war tensions. It was therefore appropriate that he ended 'On the Brink' with a quote from a letter he received from the Russian leader on 27 November 1962: 'I fully share your view, as well as that of President Kennedy, that the Cuban crisis has led to a better understanding of the need for a prompt settlement of acute international problems.'[101]

By the time Macmillan wrote this chapter both Khrushchev and Kennedy were dead. Khrushchev published some expurgated memoirs in 1971, the year of his death. However, the assassination of John Kennedy in 1963 ensured that the main Western principal in the crisis did not survive to publish memoirs. The only substantial rival account available at the time was therefore Robert Kennedy's posthumously published version, ghostwritten for him by Theodore Sorensen,[102] to which Macmillan obliquely refers briefly in his own book.[103] David Nunnerley's journalistic account, *President Kennedy and Britain* (1972) appeared too late to be noticed in the preparation of 'On the Brink'.[104]

This chapter therefore largely relied upon contemporary materials. This prompted concern from the Cabinet Office, when it came to vetting

At the End of the Day, about the plethora of verbatim quotes from classified letters, minutes and transcripts of telephone conversations. The Cabinet Secretary, Sir Burke Trend, asked if these extensive extracts could be para-phrased as 'it would be particularly embarrassing for us if verbatim quota-tions from American sources (mainly President Kennedy's messages) were published in this country'.[105] A total of 44 changes were suggested by the Cabinet Office,[106] 17 of these relating to 'On the Brink'. One was merely a correction to Macmillan's account of Cuban history. Four were deletions suggested to avoid giving offence to foreign governments who might have objected, for instance, to a diary quotation referring to the French as con-temptuous, the Germans as very frightened, the Italians as windy and the Scandinavians as sour as well as windy. This was not only undiplomatic but, certainly as far as the French were concerned, incorrect.[107]

The only deletion recommended that Macmillan jibed at – writing 'why?' in the margin – was any reference to the Thors. Presumably he was wondering why he was asked not to mention a weapon which had been decommissioned ten years earlier. He nevertheless complied with these requests, with the exception of brief passing references to the Thor offer.[108] The other 11 changes recommended were to summarise the extracts. This, however, clearly had limited effect on their preponderance in the chapter. Macmillan may have complained that Churchill's *The Hinge of Fate* (the fourth volume of his memoir *The Second World War*) contained 'too many memoranda and minutes printed verbatim. This hinders the flow of the narrative.'[109] Nevertheless, his account of the Cuban missile crisis suffered even more from this tendency. Whereas parts of Churchill's *The World Crisis* and *The Second World War* rely on such docu-ments for more than 40 per cent of the text,[110] the percentage of original documents in the text of 'On the Brink' was closer to 70–80 per cent. Cabinet Office strictures clearly had limited effect, with the publisher reluctant to comply so close to publication to requests for changes that 'would spoil the book and entail very expensive correction if we were to paraphrase them'.[111]

This probably also reflected a sense of the centrality of the Cuba section to the marketing of the book. The second paragraph of the dust jacket text proclaimed 'The British side of the Cuba crisis is told here for the first time. The continuous contact that took place, sometimes several times a day, between Prime Minister and President reveals the closeness of their personal relationship and shows how strong was British influence and support.' This clearly developed the idea of repeated calls between the two leaders, rather than the total of four telephone conversations during the height of the crisis. A similar line was also stressed in the pre-publication publicity.

The object clearly was not just to puff the book but also to engage with media and Opposition allegations at the time of the Cuban crisis that British influence with the US had been negligible. The Labour frontbencher Richard Crossman, who had worked as Macmillan's propaganda officer at Allied Forces Headquarters in North Africa during the Second World War, wrote in the *Guardian* on 26 October 1962 that these events exploded the myth of British influence.[112] This theme of lack of consultation was taken up by his party leader, Hugh Gaitskell, in the Commons debate on the Queen's Speech on 30 October 1962.[113] Amongst the Opposition there are hints from other leading figures such as Harold Wilson that this line was taken so as to justify their then argument that nuclear weapons did not buy Britain influence and therefore ought to be abandoned.[114]

Macmillan's attempts to counter this in the House on 30 October 1962 were unconvincing, not least because he was unable to go into detail on the substance of his talks with Kennedy.[115] Macmillan told the Cabinet that Kennedy and his advisers 'had shown themselves ready to ask for and to consider advice. This had been done with commitment on either side', but disclose of these talks might embarrass less-privileged European allies.[116] A key objective in 'On the Brink' was therefore, as Macmillan admitted, to dispel these accusations 'that there was no "special relationship" between London and Washington' by establishing the regularity and quality of their discussions.[117] This was achieved, for instance, by including Kennedy's message of 22 October, suggesting that the two men 'discuss the situation between ourselves by means of our private channel of communication'.[118] This channel was the KY-9 scrambler telephone, installed on 6 September 1961, supplemented by the KW-26 teleprinter. Macmillan commented in his diary on 4 November 1962 that these worked without a hitch, after a summer during which the link had been bedevilled by technical faults. This was not a universal view. *The Times* on 27 November 1962 reporting an American press briefing which belittled the Macmillan–Kennedy conversations and suggested the Prime Minister disliked this form of communication. The real problem, de Zulueta wrote to Ormsby-Gore, was that the President kept on forgetting he had to take his finger off the button to allow Macmillan to speak.[119]

The scrambler phone also distorted voices. This may account for the seemingly unenlightening nature of the transcripts. But then, as anyone who has tried to recapture the fire of a Lloyd George speech from the reproduction in *Hansard* would know, transcripts convey only a part of orality. In a passage Macmillan drafted to add to the chapter but which was not in the end included he noted '[w]e used flat and commonplace phrases of everyday life and humdrum affairs. Nevertheless, we both knew we were discussing the future, and perhaps the survival of the civilised world.'[120] In talk between two men who clearly trusted and liked each other there are always likely to be unspoken assumptions and understandings that a transcript may not capture, such as the somewhat hesitant way in which Macmillan introduced the Thor offer on 26 October. Nevertheless, Kennedy's message of 22 October warmly observed:

It is a source of great personal satisfaction to me that you and I can keep in close touch with each other by rapid and secure means at a time like this, and I intend to keep you fully informed of my thinking as the situation evolves.[121]

As it turned out, however, Macmillan was far from fully informed throughout the crisis. One example is that when writing 'On the Brink' Macmillan remained unaware of the deal the US had made with the Soviets over the Turkish missiles. Kennedy was also selective in the aspects of crisis management he sounded out the Prime Minister's views on. British influence on the conduct of the crisis did not, despite the image deliberately cultivated by the extensive edited transcripts of transatlantic telephone calls presented in 'On the Brink', emerge through such direct means.

In the past it has often been thought that the main British contributions to the management of the Cuban crisis were confined to advice from Ormsby-Gore about the breadth of the quarantine, and the pressure that led to publication of the photographs of the missile sites. Macmillan clearly believed that his ambassador did make a significant contribution to the first of these.[122] As noted above, however, Macmillan's account of the second in 'On the Brink' is inaccurate. Moreover, it understates the British role in encouraging the Americans to publicise their photographic evidence of the missiles, not least in the UN.

This may reflect Macmillan's tendency in his subsequent writings systematically to underplay the importance of the UN in his thinking at the time of the crisis. Dean is, indeed, only once mentioned in the whole of *At the End of the Day*, as having played a useful supporting role during the Cuban missile crisis to Stevenson, whom Macmillan cordially disliked.[123] 'On the Brink' similarly occluded – not least because of the Cabinet Office stipulation not to offend foreign governments – the very considerable efforts expended by the British on inter-Allied and inter-Commonwealth relations during the crisis to maintain solidarity with the Americans.

This tendency has also been replicated in later literature. Although Macmillan credited the use of the UN with the resolution of the crisis in the Cabinet of 29 October,[124] in the historiography this dimension has until recently been overshadowed by the Thor offer. However, in the same conversation that he raised the latter with Kennedy, on 26 October, he first signalled his support for the idea of Cuban inviolability and then reiterated the idea of a UN mission to ensure the missiles were inoperable. These measures would also help to head off the tendency of the increasingly assertive non-aligned countries at the UN to focus on the quarantine and not on the larger problem of the missiles.[125] As the quarantine started to bite, these became the crucial issues for Macmillan, hence his change of mind over the merits of military action. Indeed, getting a credible UN inspection regime in place was a key means of avoiding such military action, with all the risks that implied. A credible inspection regime was also, incidentally, a way of making progress on the test ban issue. The Thor offer was thus a backup, 'a third point' as Macmillan put it in the conversation of 26 October: its minor role in 'On the Brink' is accordingly appropriate.[126]

That morning Kennedy had reminded ExComm that there were three ways to remove the Soviet missiles; by negotiation, trade or invasion.[127] As the crisis developed Macmillan moved rapidly from the third option to concentrating on the first, through the auspices of the UN, with the second playing a minor role in the form of the Thor proposal. Indeed, the necessity of the first option was pointed up by the risk otherwise of a US invasion, the unpredictable consequences of which Macmillan by the end of the crisis clearly feared. UN involvement was seen as a key means of providing the reassurance necessary, given the lack of trust between the parties, to make progress on the objectives of inviolability and inspection. These two objectives reflected the ideas floated in Macmillan's conversation with the President on 26 October and formed the core of his message to Kennedy on the following evening. It is not clear what time this arrived in Washington. It certainly was not directly discussed in ExComm that afternoon. However, some hours later, Kennedy's reply to Khrushchev released about 8.00 p.m. (Washington time) on 27 October was much closer in tone to Macmillan than it was to the drafts being prepared by various members of ExComm, not least in highlighting these same themes of inviolability and inspection under the aegis of the UN.[128] This was the message that Macmillan in 'On the Brink' saw as solving the crisis.[129]

We now know that Khrushchev had decided to withdraw the missiles two days earlier. However, his problem then was how to manage this process?[130] The Turkey swop idea he raised was a means to cover this withdrawal, but one which ironically heightened tension with the Americans. Interestingly, Macmillan's speculations about Khrushchev's conduct of the crisis, written in his diary on 4 November 1962 and largely reproduced in 'On the Brink', make it clear he was aware that two sites were not comparable. 'The Turkey base is useful, but not vital. Cuba was vital.' The latter, however, was threatened by the American build-up to an invasion planned for 29 October which, as Macmillan recognised, could not be stopped by conventional military means. By withdrawal Khrushchev avoided the risk of having to use nuclear weapons, but also preserved Castro, Soviet prestige and his missiles, which were shipped home.[131] Indeed, to some extent Khrushchev was also given the credit as the peacemaker, in contrast to the bellicose Americans, in the non-aligned world.[132] Macmillan's immediate judgement of Khrushchev's decision-making was thus not without merit. What he did not know, either at the time or subsequently, was that Khrushchev also succeeded in secretly getting the American missiles out of Turkey and Italy as well.

In his comments in ExComm on 26 October Kennedy implied that the three options were alternative strategies. In practice, he pursued all simultaneously. Macmillan was never aware of this. He did not know that Bobby Kennedy had indicated to Anatoly Dobrynin, the Russian ambassador to Washington, that the Jupiters could be quietly withdrawn from Turkey within four to five months should a satisfactory arrangement on Cuba be reached. In part this was because the British seemingly did not imagine such a possibility, as being outside the Western hemisphere. But it was also because the Americans deliberately misled them, their other Allies and indeed their own ambassadors on this point. Roberts noted in his despatch on 29 October that his American counterpart fully shared his surprise at the rapid and complete Soviet climb-down.[133] Deliberate American dissimulation both distracted from the Turkey offer and ramped up as far as their allies were concerned the risk of warfare.[134] The worse example of lack of consultation from the Americans was thus not one Macmillan could try to downplay in 'On the Brink'. This was because he was not himself ever aware of it. Ironically, however, neither were those who had in 1962 complained about the lack of consultation by the Americans.

When this story did eventually come out,[135] it reinforced notions of the lack of British influence. Macmillan's government were portrayed as pursuing a Thor trade that would never shape Washington's thinking, because the Americans were already moving to the Turkey swop instead. The Thor offer was thus easily dismissed merely as reflecting, as Macmillan's own diary reference on 4 November put it, 'the frightful desire to do something'. This is despite the fact that the same sentence went on to acknowledge that 'not to do anything (except to talk to the President and keep Europe and the Commonwealth calm and firm) was prob[ably] the right answer'.[136] Indeed, the British did not do anything that they considered out of keeping with the American line. The Thor offer went unpursued. More important were their efforts to promote the UN-validated way forward which became the basis on which a solution emerged.

Before publication *The Spectator* referred to *At the End of the Day* as the most eagerly awaited volume of the memoirs.[137] This, though, was because it expected revelations not about October 1962 but about the end of Macmillan's premiership in October 1963. Cuba was not always as central to the reception of the book as the pre-publicity had assumed. Nor did it sell as well as *The Spectator* might have envisaged. At a time when respectable fiction sales were around 5,000 copies the figure reported of 20,326 non-US sales by the end of 1979 was certainly good. However, it was still way behind the sales figures for the first two volumes of the autobiography.[138] Furthermore, 'On the Brink' does not seem to have helped sales in the US. Just over two years after publication Harper & Row wrote that sales had been very slow and 'we must let the book go out of print'.[139]

In the US there was no tie-in television programme, as there was in Britain. Such a tie-in had been envisaged when the memoirs first started to appear. On 5–7 January 1966, for transmission to mark the first volume of memoirs, Macmillan was interviewed at Birch Grove over three days by John Grist, Nigel Lawson (who had been attached to Number 10 at the end of Macmillan's premiership and by then moved on to edit *The Spectator*) and Charles Collingwood (of the US broadcaster, CBS).[140] About two weeks later, CBS decided that they did not want to be tied to a trade publication.[141] The BBC nevertheless paid $5,000 for the American rights to a programme that was not broadcast there, as well as £1,000 for the British programme.[142] This was, as Grist noted, 'a quite exceptional fee'.[143] It, however, remained in place as the series was, like the memoirs, extended from the three programmes initially envisaged. The only substantial change was that from the second programme onwards the Canadian psephologist R.T. McKenzie, a professor from the London School of Economics, conducted each interview with Macmillan.

Accordingly, by the time *At the End of the Day* appeared, these BBC interviews followed a familiar and well-tested format, with broadcast on the actual day of publication. On this occasion filming took place at Birch Grove on 6–8 August 1973. After filming the producer, Margaret Douglas, would usually then edit down about five hours of rushes into a single broadcast of 50 minutes. With *At the End of the Day*, however, the BBC concluded that the material was so rich that they needed two programmes.[144] The first dealt with Europe, economic problems, the 'Night of the Long Knives' cabinet reshuffle of July 1962 and culminated with Cuba. Suitably puffed in the BBC's listing journal, the *Radio Times*,[145] it was broadcast on 19 September 1973. The second, covering security and scandals, transmitted a week later on the day of publication.

McKenzie had first interviewed Macmillan in 1954 and later wrote of his 'genuine and deep affection for the greatest living Englishman',[146] an accolade which Macmillan – who modelled himself on Churchill in so many ways – no doubt deeply relished. Unlike Churchill, Macmillan was a consummate performer on television. McKenzie's unobtrusive style provided a perfect foil. Together they developed an easy rapport which, through the medium of these programmes, as the Audience Research Report (ARR) testified, brought out Macmillan's 'qualities as a conversationalist, a person and as a politician'. As such, they also helped to develop Macmillan's final career: he came across, the ARR reported, as an elder statesman in an age of pygmies.

This was despite a limited audience share – being broadcast after the 9.00 p.m. watershed – estimated at not much more than 5 per cent of the British public.[147] Newspaper reports of the programme, however, greatly extended its reach. In particular, all picked up the assertion made in the interview (but not in 'On the Brink') that Macmillan was rung three times a day by the President. This was a considerable exaggeration, as was Macmillan's claim that he suggested publication of the photographic evidence of the missile sites. So was the statement that NATO only had two to three divisions in Western Europe at the time, facing some hundred Soviet divisions.[148] It, however, reinforced Macmillan's preceding point about the risk that Berlin would be seized if the Americans had attacked Cuba. It was in such circumstances that Macmillan thought the Turkey swop idea so dangerous for 'all credibility' – including in Berlin – 'in the American protection of Europe would have gone'. The Americans clearly agreed, hence in 1973 they continued to cover up the fact that this swop had nonetheless happened.

Macmillan's exaggerations in the broadcast built up two key impressions. The first was of the risks, not least in Europe, during the crisis. The second was of Macmillan calmly and regularly responding to the President's requests for advice. This was reinforced by McKenzie's voiceover which introduced this section of the interview in which he pointed out that the 'intimate personal link with Kennedy is one of the striking themes of Mr Macmillan's book'.[149] The journalists who reported on the programme clearly agreed, with the *Daily Mail* going so far as to headline its piece 'How I helped to stop World War Three'.[150]

In his more measured review of *At the End of the Day* Richard Crossman drew attention to the Churchillian approach adopted throughout Macmillan's memoirs. Hitherto, however, he felt that Macmillan had done so with little success: whereas Churchill 'stamped his personality on everything he wrote', Macmillan did not.

> In private conversation and, to a remarkable extent, on the television screen he has always been a very different person – debonair, adventurous, and deliciously cynical.... Unfortunately, this private personality, which comes bouncing so gaily out of the little black box, is almost entirely excluded from his writing.

For Crossman, however, *At the End of the Day* was one of the better volumes of the memoirs, and also successful in challenging Crossman's contemporary impressions. He noted:

> At the time, many of us thought that Britain hadn't been consulted. We couldn't have been more wrong. The British Prime Minister was the only non-American completely in Kennedy's confidence. So Kennedy at night ... called up his old friend to try out his ideas ... Macmillan has had to wait a long time before he could take the credit he deserves.[151]

It has been observed that Churchill's larding of his text with contemporary documents sometimes gave it a spurious authenticity.[152] In this instance, even for a sceptical reviewer like Crossman, Macmillan seems to have succeeded in doing the same. Gregg Harken suggests that a common theme of the Cold War memoir is the settling of scores,[153] and in this case

Macmillan sought to achieve this by drawing attention to his extensive contacts with the President in a way he was unable to do at the time. 'On the Brink' does not seek to offer the blow-by-blow account of how Macmillan experienced the crisis attempted in this chapter. Significant phases and themes are excluded from the narrative. Instead, the impression was conveyed – and even more so in Macmillan's skilful television performance – that Kennedy 'wanted to consult me all the time'. This was, however, more of a response to his contemporary British critics, like Crossman, than an accurate evocation of Macmillan's experience of 'that strange period';[154] in the process diverting attention from some of the key themes in the British approach to the crisis, such as the role the UN could play in managing a settlement. That in 'On the Brink' and a fortiori in his television interview with McKenzie, Macmillan was successful in responding to his contemporary critics is suggested by the comment in the *Guardian*'s review of the programme: 'The myth that Britain was left unconsulted by John Kennedy while he played poker with the fate of the world against Khrushchev over the 1962 Cuban missile crisis is finally dispelled by Harold Macmillan today.'

It is entirely appropriate that this article was entitled 'Mac and Jack' since the effect of Macmillan's successive accounts of the Cuban missile crisis was indeed to establish, with some success, a misleading view of the British side of the Cuban missile crisis as essentially the Mac and Jack show.[155]

Notes

1 I am grateful to Kevin O'Daly, Len Scott, Willie Thompson and Mark J. White for their comments on earlier drafts of this paper. This chapter was developed from Peter Catterall, 'At the End of the Day: Macmillan's Account of the Cuban Missile Crisis', *International Relations*, 26/33 (2012) 267–89. Reproduced by permission of SAGE Publications Ltd.

2 See Peter Catterall (ed.), *The Macmillan Diaries: Prime Minister and After, 1957–1966* (London: Macmillan 2011) pp. 508–18.

3 'Harold Macmillan Talks to Robert McKenzie about the Last Years of His Premiership – Part One', *The Listener*, 11 October 1973, 482–6. See also 'Harold Macmillan Talks to Robert McKenzie about the Last Years of His Premiership – Part Two', *The Listener*, 18 October 1973, 507–10.

4 BBC Written Archives Centre, Caversham [henceforward WAC]: R94/72/1, John Grist to Bush Bailey, 19 January 1966.

5 Alan Maclean, *No, I Tell a Lie, It Was the Tuesday ...* (London: Kyle Cathie 1997) chapter 13.

6 Peter Catterall, 'At the End of the Day: Macmillan's Account of the Cuban Missile Crisis', *International Relations*, 26/3 (2012) 269.

7 Catterall, *Prime Minister and After*, p. 645 (10 December 1964).

8 Macmillan & Co archives, British Library, London [henceforward M&Co]: Uncatalogued folder 'At the End of the Day 2', undated finance note. I am grateful to Alysoun Saunders and Helen Melody for access to these papers.

9 M&Co: Uncatalogued folder 'Harold Macmillan general', Macmillan to Lord Carrington, 6 August 1980.

10 The National Archives, London [henceforward TNA]: CAB 129/107, C(61)172, Harold Macmillan, 'Memoirs: Disclosure of Official Information', 30 October 1961.

11 Interview with Anne Glyn-Jones, 30 June 2014, supplemented by emails from Glyn-Jones to the author, 20 and 21 July 2014.

12 Harold Macmillan, *At the End of the Day* (London: Macmillan 1973) pp. 198, 201–2, 204–11, 215.

13 Macmillan, *At the End of the Day*, p. 180; see also David Nunnerley, *President Kennedy and Britain* (London: The Bodley Head 1972) p. 77.

14 Catterall, *Prime Minister and After*, p. 309 (17 June 1960); Macmillan, *At the End of the Day* p. 181.

15 TNA: PREM 11/3689, Macmillan to Home tel. 4223, T480/62, 1 October 1962.

16 TNA: FO 371/162347, Joseph Godber memorandum, 27 September 1962.

17 James G. Blight, Bruce J. Allyn and David A. Welch, *Cuba on the Brink: Castro, the Missile Crisis and the Soviet Collapse* (Oxford: Rowman and Littlefield 2002) p. 490.

18 Catterall, *Prime Minister and After*, p. 502 (3 October 1962), original emphasis.

19 See Max Holland, 'A Luce Connection: Senator Keating, William Pawley and the Cuban Missile Crisis' *Journal of Cold War Studies* 1/3 (1999) 139–67.

20 Macmillan, *At the End of the Day*, p. 183.

21 Nigel Ashton, *Kennedy, Macmillan and the Cold War: The Irony of Interdependence* (Basingstoke: Palgrave 2002) p. 73; Raj Roy and John W. Young (eds) *Ambassador to Sixties London: The Diaries of David Bruce 1961–1969* (Dordrecht: Republic of Letters Publishing 2009) p. 78. TNA: PREM 11/3689, Ormsby-Gore tel 2623, 20 October 1962 however makes it clear that the ambassador was aware something was afoot.

22 Ernest R. May and Philip D. Zelikow (eds) *The Kennedy Tapes: Inside the White House during the Cuban Missile Crisis* (London: Belknap Press 1997) pp. 66, 92–3.

23 L.V. Scott, *Macmillan, Kennedy and the Cuban Missile Crisis: Political, Military and Intelligence Aspects* (Basingstoke: Macmillan 1999) p. 37.

24 Macmillan, *At the End of the Day*, p. 194.

25 TNA: PREM 11/3689, record of conversation, 23 October 1962.

26 Ibid.

27 Macmillan, *At the End of the Day*, p. 190.

28 Catterall, *Prime Minister and After*, pp. 510–11 (23 October 1962); Macmillan, *At the End of the Day*, p. 190.

29 Robin Woolven, 'What Really Happened in RAF Bomber Command during the Cuban Missile Crisis?' in David Gioe, Len Scott and Christopher Andrew (eds), *An International History of the Cuban Missile Crisis: A 50-year Retrospective* (London: Routledge 2014) pp. 176–95.

30 Peter Catterall (ed.), *The Macmillan Diaries: The Cabinet Years 1950–1957* (London: Macmillan 2003) p. 459 (25 July 1955).

31 TNA: PREM 11/3689, Macmillan to Kennedy, 22 October 1962 (despatched 9.35 p.m. BST), tel. 7396, T492/62. This had, after all, been Macmillan's own initial reaction to the news, see Len Scott, ' "The Only Thing to Look Forward to's the Past": Reflection, Revision and Reinterpreting Reinterpretation', this volume.

32 TNA: PREM 11/3689, record of conversation, 23 October 1962.

33 TNA: PREM 11/3689, 'Points for President Kennedy'.

34 See Richard Aldous, *Macmillan, Eisenhower and the Cold War* (Dublin: Four Courts Press 2005).

35 TNA: CAB 128/36, CC(62)61, Cabinet Conclusions, 23 October 1962, 10.30 a.m., p. 3.

36 TNA: PREM 11/3689, Macmillan to Ormsby-Gore, 22 October 1962, tel. 7395, T.493/62; Macmillan, *At the End of the Day*, pp. 187–9.

37 Scott, *Macmillan, Kennedy and the Cuban Missile Crisis*, pp. 168–9.

38 TNA: PREM11/3690, Home tel 7457, 24 October 1962, Ormsby-Gore tel. 2667, 24 October 1962; Scott, *Macmillan, Kennedy and the Cuban Missile Crisis*, p. 95.

39 Peter Catterall, 'Modifying "a Very Dangerous Message": Britain, the Non-aligned and the UN during the Cuban Missile Crisis', in David Gioe, Len Scott and Christopher Andrew (eds), *An International History of the Cuban Missile Crisis: A 50-year Retrospective* (London: Routledge 2014) pp. 82–3; TNA: PREM 11/3690, Nkrumah to Macmillan, 25 October 1962.

40 Macmillan, *At the End of the Day*, p. 201.

41 Catterall, *Prime Minister and After*, pp. 511–12 (24 October 1962).

42 Catterall, 'Modifying "a Very Dangerous Message"', pp. 81–3; Macmillan, *At the End of the Day*, p. 196.

43 TNA: PREM11/3689, record of a meeting at Admiralty House, 23 October 1962, 5.00 p.m.

44 May and Zelikow, *The Kennedy Tapes*, p. 389; Department of Western Manuscripts, Bodleian Library, Oxford: Harold Macmillan Diaries: 23 October 1962.

45 TNA: PREM11/3689, Bligh to Macmillan, 23 October 1962.

46 Catterall, *Prime Minister and After*, p. 512 (25 October 1962).

47 According to the cover note: TNA: PREM11/3690, de Zulueta to Ormsby-Gore, 25 October 1962. Macmillan, *At the End of the Day*, p. 198 puts the conversation at 11 p.m.

48 Macmillan did not receive the U Thant message from Sir Patrick Dean at the British delegation to the UN in New York until the following morning: TNA: PREM11/3689, Dean, tel 1741, 25 October 1962 (received 6.55 a.m.).

49 Macmillan, *At the End of the Day*, pp. 198–204.

50 TNA: PREM11/3690, Macmillan to Kennedy, T505/62, 25 October 1962.

51 May and Zelikow, *The Kennedy Tapes*, pp. 427–30; Macmillan, *At the End of the Day*, pp. 205–8; TNA: PREM 11/3690, record of conversation, 25 October 1962.

52 Scott, *Macmillan, Kennedy and the Cuban Missile Crisis*, p. 153.

53 TNA: PREM 11/3690, Ormsby-Gore tel. 2690, 26 October 1962. See also Aleksandr Fursenko and Timothy Naftali, *Khrushchev's Cold War: The Inside Story of an American Adversary* (New York: W.W. Norton 2006) p. 441.

54 TNA: PREM11/3691, Roberts tel. 2077, 28 October 1962 (received 1.59 a.m.).

55 Macmillan, *At the End of the Day* (pp. 209–12) follows his contemporary diary in referring to two conversations on 26 October, but there was only one that evening. It is possible Macmillan conflated that with the previous one which had run into the early hours of that morning.

56 James G. Hershberg, 'The United States, Brazil and the Cuban Missile Crisis (Part 2)', *Journal of Cold War Studies* 6/3 (2004) 26–30.

57 U Thant had raised this point on the day before as a means of reassuring the Cubans they did not need the Russian arms: TNA: PREM11/3690, Marchant tel. 464, 25 October 1962.

58 May and Zelikow, *The Kennedy Tapes*, pp. 481–2; Macmillan, *At the End of the Day*, pp. 209–12; TNA: PREM 11/3690, record of conversation, 26 October 1962.

59 Stephen Twigge and Len Scott, 'The Other Other Missiles of October: The Thor IRBMs and the Cuban Missile Crisis', *Electronic Journal of International History* 3 (2000) pp. 3–4. http://sas-space.sas.ac.uk/3387/ (last accessed 12 September 2014).

60 TNA: PREM11/3690, Macmillan to Kennedy, T513/62, 27 October 1962.
61 As had Ambassador Bruce: Roy and Young, *Ambassador to Sixties London*, p. 81 (27 October 1962).
62 Harold Evans, *Downing Street Diary: The Macmillan Years 1957/63* (London: Hodder and Stoughton 1981) p. 225 (28 October 1962).
63 TNA: PREM11/3690, Ormsby-Gore tel. 2697, 26 October 1962.
64 May and Zelikow, *The Kennedy Tapes*, p. 692.
65 May and Zelikow, *The Kennedy Tapes*, pp. 520–1.
66 McKenzie, 'Part One', p. 483.
67 TNA: PREM 11/3691, Merchant tel. 477, 27 October 1962.
68 TNA: PREM11/3691, full text of Mr Khrushchev's message to President Kennedy, 27 October 1962.
69 TNA: PREM11/3691, Home tel. 4200, 27 October 1962.
70 TNA: PREM11/3691, FO tel. 7580 to Washington, 27 October 1962.
71 TNA: PREM11/3691, Kennedy to Macmillan, 27 October 1962, CAP5507/62.
72 Evans, *Downing Street Diary*, p. 225.
73 TNA: PREM11/3691, Macmillan to Kennedy, 27 October 1962, T518/62.
74 TNA: PREM11/3691, Dean, tel. 1800, 27 October 1962.
75 TNA: PREM11/3691, Ormsby-Gore, tel. 2701, 27 October 1962.
76 TNA: PREM11/3691, Dean tel. 1801, 27 October 1962 (received 2.14 a.m. on 28 October 1962).
77 May and Zelikow, *The Kennedy Tapes*, pp. 568, 583. A Polaris submarine was indeed subsequently deployed off Turkey: Nasuh Uslu, *The Turkish–American Relationship between 1947 and 2003* (New York: Nova 2003) p. 159.
78 Macmillan, *At the End of the Day*, pp. 212–13.
79 May and Zelikow, *The Kennedy Tapes*, pp. 500–1, 528, 564.
80 Blight, Allyn, Welch, *Cuba on the Brink*, p. 498; Roy and Young, *Ambassador to Sixties London*, p. 81 (27 October 1962).
81 TNA: PREM11/3691, briefing note for Finletter enclosed with Bligh to Samuel, 28 October 1962.
82 TNA: PREM11/3691, Ormsby-Gore tel. 2707, 27 October 1962.
83 TNA: PREM11/3691, record of conversation, 28 October 1962 (1.30 a.m.).
84 TNA: PREM11/3691, record of conversation, 28 October 1962 (4.00 a.m.).
85 John F. Kennedy Library, Boston [henceforward JFKL]: National Security Files [henceforward NSF], Box 170A, Memorandum for the record by McGeorge Bundy, 27 October 1962.
86 Ashton, *Kennedy, Macmillan and the Cold War*, p. 83.
87 Peter Catterall, 'Identity and Integration: Macmillan, "Britishness" and the Turn towards Europe', in Gilbert Millat (ed.) *Angleterre ou Albion entre fascination et répulsion* (Lille: Presses de l'Université Charles de Gaulle – Lille 3, 2006) p. 162.
88 TNA: PREM11/3691, teleprinter message, 28 October 1962 (1.30 a.m.).
89 Macmillan, *At the End of the Day*, p. 214.
90 TNA: PREM11/3691, Macmillan to Kennedy, T520/62, 28 October 1962. Daylight saving changed in both countries, with the clocks going back one hour, at 2.00 a.m. on 28 October 1962.
91 Macmillan, *At the End of the Day*, p. 214.
92 TNA: PREM11/3691, Dean tel. 1803, 28 October 1962.
93 TNA: PREM11/3691, message to all Commonwealth Prime Ministers, T522/62, 28 October 1962.
94 May and Zelikow, *The Kennedy Tapes*, p. 507.
95 Evans, *Downing Street Diary*, p. 226.
96 JFKL: NSF173, Bruce to Rusk, 28 October 1962 (8.00 p.m., GMT).
97 TNA: PREM11/3691, teleprinter message, 28 October 1962 (1.15 p.m., GMT).

98   JFKL: NSF173, Bruce to Rusk, 28 October 1962 (8.00 p.m., GMT). Bruce, like Macmillan and Home, was a keen shot.

99   Macmillan, *At the End of the Day*, p. 216.

100 TNA: PREM11/3691, Ormsby-Gore tel. 2709, 28 October 1962 (received 7.03 p.m.).

101 Macmillan, *At the End of the Day*, p. 220.

102 Robert Kennedy, *Thirteen Days: A Memoir of the Cuban Missile Crisis* (New York: W.W. Norton 1971).

103 Macmillan, *At the End of the Day*, p. 214.

104 Email from Anne Glyn-Jones, 21 July 2014.

105 M&Co: Uncatalogued folder, 'At the End of the Day 2', Trend to Macmillan, 2 March 1973.

106 In contrast, Buckingham Palace only asked for three changes to the text, none relating to 'On the Brink': M&Co: Uncatalogued folder, 'At the End of the Day 2', Martin Charteris to Macmillan, 20 March 1973.

107 Catterall, *Prime Minister and After*, pp. 514–15 (4 November 1962); Scott, *Macmillan, Kennedy and the Cuban Missile Crisis*, p. 181; Nunnerley, *President Kennedy and Britain*, p. 80.

108 Macmillan, *At the End of the Day*, pp. 210, 212.

109 Cited in Catterall, *The Cabinet Years*, p. xvii.

110 See Robin Prior, *Churchill's World Crisis as History* (Beckenham: Croom Helm, 1983), pp. 277–9.

111 M&Co: Uncatalogued folder, 'At the End of the Day 2', unnamed to Macmillan, 7 March 1973.

112 Nunnerley, *President Kennedy and Britain*, p. 75.

113 *House of Commons Debates*, 5th ser., vol. 666, col. 19 (30 October 1962).

114 *House of Commons Debates*, 5th ser., vol. 666, cols 161–2 (31 October 1962).

115 *House of Commons Debates*, 5th ser., vol. 666, cols 35–44 (30 October 1962).

116 TNA: CAB 128/36, CC(62)63, Cabinet Conclusions, 29 October 1962, 10.30 a.m., p. 2.

117 Macmillan, *At the End of the Day*, p. 198.

118 Cited in Macmillan, *At the End of the Day*, p. 186.

119 Ashton, *Kennedy, Macmillan and the Cold War*, pp. 86–7; Macmillan, *At the End of the Day*, p. 220.

120 M&Co: Uncatalogued folder, 'At the End of the Day 2', suggested amendment to p. 220.

121 Cited in Macmillan, *At the End of the Day*, p. 186.

122 Macmillan, *At the End of the Day*, p. 197.

123 Macmillan, *At the End of the Day*, p. 219. Macmillan excluded the rude remark about Stevenson reproduced in Catterall, *Prime Minister and After*, p. 517 (4 November 1962).

124 TNA: CAB 128/36, CC(62)63, Cabinet Conclusions, 29 October 1962, 10.30 a.m., p. 2.

125 Catterall, 'Modifying "a Very Dangerous Message"', p. 87.

126 Macmillan, *At the End of the Day*, p. 210.

127 May and Zelikow, *The Kennedy Tapes*, pp. 463–5.

128 May and Zelikow, *The Kennedy Tapes*, pp. 603–4.

129 Macmillan, *At the End of the Day*, p. 214.

130 Aleksandr Fursenko and Timothy Naftali, *'One Hell of a Gamble': Khrushchev, Castro and Kennedy 1958–1964* (London: John Murray 1997) pp. 256–60, 283–7; Fursenko and Naftali, *Khrushchev's Cold War*, pp. 483–5.

131 Macmillan, *At the End of the Day*, pp. 217–18.

132 Catterall, 'Modifying "a Very Dangerous Message"', p. 92.

133 TNA: PREM11/3691, Roberts tel. 2081, 29 October 1962.

134 McGeorge Bundy, *Danger and Survival: Choices about the Bomb in the First Fifty Years* (New York: Vintage 1988) p. 434.
135 On the emergence of this story see Benoît Pelopidas's chapter in this volume.
136 Macmillan, *At the End of the Day*, p. 216.
137 *The Spectator*, 7 July 1973.
138 M&Co: Uncatalogued folder, 'Harold Macmillan General', David Ballheimer to Maclean, 22 November 1979; note to Macmillan, 26 February 1980. By this point *Winds of Change* had sold 40,453 copies, *Blast of War* 33,052, *Tides of Fortune* 18,676, *Riding the Storm* 16,310 and *Pointing the Way* 11,981.
139 M&Co: Uncatalogued folder, 'Past Masters 1', Doris Karfinkel to Garnett, 27 April 1976.
140 WAC: R94/72/1, Bush Bailey to Graham Watson, 30 December 1965, Bailey to Assistant Head of Programme Contracts, 29 December 1965; Catterall, *Prime Minister and After*, p. 675 (9 January 1966).
141 WAC: R94/72/1, G. del Strother to Bailey, 19 January 1966.
142 WAC: R94/72/1, F. L. Hetley to Macmillan, 3 March 1966.
143 WAC: R94/72/1, Grist to Bailey, 1 February 1966.
144 M&Co: Uncatalogued folder 'At the End of the Day 2', Richard Garnett to Macmillan, 31 July 1973.
145 *Radio Times*, 13 September 1973.
146 'McKenzie on Macmillan', *Radio Times*, 6 February 1979.
147 Unfortunately no copy of the Audience Research Report for the Cuban broadcast has survived in the BBC Written Archives. These references come from the report for the sister programme broadcast a week later (WAC: T67/166/1, Audience Research Report, 15 October 1973).
148 The *Daily Telegraph* report on 19 September 1973 further exaggerated this to 250 Soviet divisions.
149 WAC: T67/166/1, Transcript of broadcast, 19 September 1973, pp. 15–19.
150 *Daily Mail*, 19 September 1973.
151 Richard Crossman, 'Macmillan Bows Out', *The Listener*, 27 September 1973 422–3.
152 Prior, *Churchill's World Crisis as History*, p. 279; John Ramsden, *Man of the Century: Winston Churchill and his Legend since 1945* (London: HarperCollins 2002) chapter 4.
153 Gregg Harken, review of Thomas C. Reed, *At the Abyss: An Insider's History of the Cold War* (New York: Ballantine 2004) in *Journal of Cold War Studies*, 9/2 (2007) 148.
154 McKenzie, 'Part One', 483.
155 Philip Jordan, 'Mac and Jack', *Guardian*, 19 September 1973.

4   Reform or revolution?

Scott Sagan's *Limits of Safety* and its contemporary implications[1]

Campbell Craig

On several occasions during the two-week-long Cuban missile crisis,[2] American military personnel and officials made mistakes that, as Scott Sagan shows in *The Limits of Safety*, could quite plausibly have triggered an accidental nuclear detonation, or incorrectly led US leaders to believe that a Soviet attack had just commenced, or led the USSR to believe that an American one had just been launched.[3] During the three day period 25–28 October 1962, when the political showdown between the US and the USSR was surely at its most severe, the following took place:

The 25 October: at a missile detection centre in Duluth, Minnesota, a guard spotted an intruder trying to scale a fence into the compound.[4] Warned that Soviet operatives had been deployed in the US to sabotage the American warning network before a Soviet attack, the guard shot at the intruder. This set off an alarm in a nearby US Air Force (USAF) base in Wisconsin, but the alarm erroneously indicated not a security breach but that war may have actually begun. Pilots scrambled to their aircraft before an official drove onto the runway to stop them: it had been a false alarm. The intruder shot at in Minnesota had been a bear.

The 26/27 October: the US had deployed high-altitude U-2 aircraft to collect radioactive samples from Soviet nuclear tests since the late 1950s.[5] For some reason, no one had thought to cancel the flights during the crisis. And on this day, when relations between Washington and Moscow had become extremely tense, a U-2 pilot strayed and descended to relatively low altitude over Siberian air space. Soviet fighter jets scrambled to intercept the U-2, and USAF fighters, armed with low-yield nuclear missiles, came to its aid. Somehow, the two sides avoided a clash, and the U-2 returned to neutral air space.

The 27 October: US destroyers, despite being in international waters, dropped practice depth charges on the Soviet nuclear-armed *Foxtrot* submarine B-59. Commanders aboard the submarine, having lost contact with Moscow, had every reason to assume that the attack indicated that a hot war had begun, could have launched a nuclear torpedo against their assailants. At one point the Captain, Valentin Savitsky, announced he intended to do, but was apparently dissuaded by a senior officer, Vasili Arkhipov.

Thomas Blanton, director of the National Security Archive, said in 2002 that Arkhipov was 'the guy who saved the world'.[6]

The 28 October: early in the morning of this day, with Kennedy and Khrushchev 'eyeball to eyeball', perhaps the most alarming accident of the entire crisis occurred.[7] A US radar facility in Alabama detected a satellite in the vicinity of Cuba just as someone inserted a test tape announcing an imminent Soviet attack. In other words, just as an official in the radar facility spotted what he thought was a Soviet missile en route to Florida, a simulation tape came on confirming that an attack was in progress. Strategic Air Command (SAC) in Colorado was informed that an attack was on; only after it became clear no nuclear detonation had actually happened did officials on the scene realise what went wrong.[8]

These incidents, documented comprehensively by Sagan (and others) after years of research and the dogged pursuit of classified evidence, tell us one key thing about the Cuban missile crisis. Even though the two superpowers were, by 1962, stable and secure regimes wielding vast geopolitical power, confronting one another over an issue not absolutely central to either of their basic security interests, and, most important, led by statesmen determined to find some way to avoid war, a nuclear holocaust came close to occurring anyway, simply because of mundane accidents. Sagan uses this worrisome fact to develop two scholarly arguments.

The first can be addressed quickly. One of his goals is to use evidence from the missile crisis (and a couple of later episodes, which will not be discussed here) to evaluate 'Accident theory', a branch of organizational theory that is employed regularly by military, industrial, and other institutions for which accidents can have catastrophic effects. 'High reliability' theory takes an optimistic view of its subject: modern, professional institutions are able to deploy straightforward systems which minimize, if not effectively eliminate, the chances of severe accidents; 'normal' theory argues, to the contrary, that in the real world of political pressures, bureaucratic blame-avoidance, and liberal societies that tend not to accept authoritarian institutions, accidents are likely to occur regularly, often as the result of 'bizarre and often banal failures' (p. 33) that are impossible to anticipate.[9]

Good social science evaluates theories by subjecting them to tough tests, in other words by attempting to show that the theory holds even in a case where the theory's predicted outcome is logically unlikely. As Sagan argues, there is (or certainly ought to be) no tougher test of organizational accident theory than US nuclear command and control: avoiding an accident is of the highest political priority; everyone, not just scapegoated underlings, suffers if things go wrong; 'suffer' in this case, means experiencing not an industrial meltdown or even an environmental disaster but rather a megatonne thermonuclear exchange; and nuclear command and control is subject to rigid, authoritarian military-style organisation, in which officials are isolated from the wider liberal culture, intensively trained to be disciplined and obedient, and committed to the military ethos.[10]

We are all here, of course, because 'normal' accident theory has not been confirmed by the actual accidental outbreak of a major nuclear war. In a sense, normal theory will always remain speculative on this question, because if it is ever tangibly verified there may well be no one around to note its success. Sagan's argument, however, is that the near-misses of the Cuban crisis, and other episodes he analyses, represent effective disconfirmations of high reliability theory. He maintains, and I would concur, that war was avoided in the above examples not so much because the system worked, that it decisively stopped potential accidents before they could happen, but because of individual common sense, factors outside the organization and, most important, plain luck.[11] What is more, Sagan points out that had any of the accidents mentioned above (along with a few others he discusses) led to an initial US or Soviet strike, it likely would have cascaded into a general war, as the 'fog' created by one nuclear detonation would probably have caused further overreactions and accidents. In the nuclear age, not only are the stakes of one accident spectacularly high; so is the likelihood that the initial one would, given the unprecedented chaos and uncertainty a nuclear explosion would foment, escalate toward a total nuclear exchange.

The second point of Sagan's work is the far more obvious one – to demonstrate that accidental nuclear war was, and is, quite possible. This point speaks of course not to organizational theorists but to historians and IR scholars interested in basic questions of nuclear war and peace. It demonstrates that the story of the missile crisis as one of a war averted is, in some ways, misleading; and it shows that present optimism about the absence of nuclear danger is also unwarranted. For if the reader of his book accepts that any one of the mistakes mentioned above could plausibly have triggered a nuclear war, then it follows that in a similar crisis today or tomorrow we might not be so lucky as the world was in October 1962. What larger implications can we draw from this second point? This essay will discuss two of them, and then make some concluding remarks.

Deterrence is not really the issue

During the Cold War, and particularly during the 1950s and 1960s, scholars and military officials in the West (though mainly in the US) engaged in a substantial debate about the durability of nuclear deterrence. Many of them argued that the American deterrent was either fragile or incredible – that the massive nuclear triad and warning system President Eisenhower installed in the second half of the 1950s was actually vulnerable to a Soviet first strike, that it made US commitments to allies in Europe and Asia unsustainable, or both.[12] Other figures, such as Eisenhower's Secretary of State, John Foster Dulles, also questioned the

morality of threatening total nuclear war in the first place. All of these criticisms were voiced by Democratic Party leaders in the run-up to the 1960
election, including the eventual nominee John F. Kennedy. When he
became President himself in 1961, Kennedy initially tried to replace Eisenhower's reliance on general nuclear deterrence with a new military
strategy that envisioned limited nuclear war, though this was soon abandoned. During the crisis itself, as well as the Berlin Wall showdown of the
previous year, Kennedy shied away from cold-blooded considerations of
political manipulation and limited nuclear war, preferring instead to cut
tacit deals with the USSR – an approach already perfected by Eisenhower
in the late 1950s (and one that Kennedy, as candidate, had bitterly
attacked).[13]

After the Cuban crisis, the idea that nuclear deterrence was difficult to
sustain or did not work moved to the fringes of discourse in the West,
though it would stage a brief revival in the 1980s.[14] The premise that
rational political leaders would not initiate a war that would likely, or even
possibly, lead to nuclear retaliation against their nation became commonplace; the response, so popular during the 1950s, that political leaders, or
at least Soviet political leaders, would blithely run such a risk in their quest
for global supremacy became ridiculous, an extremist view easily carica-
tured, for example, in Stanley Kubrick's *Dr Strangelove*. Nuclear deterrence
worked during the great Cold War crises of 1958–62; political leaders (if
not all of their military and civilian subordinates) on both sides were clearly
quite averse to going to war for fear of a nuclear holocaust. There are few
subjects in Cold War history which are less debated than this.[15]

Some scholars argue nevertheless that both the US and the USSR were
not content with deterrence and the condition of Mutual Assured Destruction (MAD), because military establishments on both sides planned for
limited nuclear war and deployed weapons systems to that end. This is an
odd interpretation, however, because it elevates military strategies and
weapons acquisition over the actual behaviour of political leaders when
they faced the prospect of nuclear war. When evaluating the salience of
any foreign policy, one must distinguish between what lower-level officials
say (and plan for) and what political decision-makers actually do. Leaders
of both the US and the USSR from the mid 1950s onwards accepted the
reality of nuclear deterrence, even if both nations' military bureaucracies,
and some of their allies, for their own reasons, sometimes resisted it: and
for the quarter-century after the Cuban crisis, neither Washington nor
Moscow dared to upend the condition of MAD by initiating a showdown
over basic Cold War stakes.[16] Since the end of the Cold War, the pattern
has continued: the major nuclear powers have avoided direct conflict, and
none of them so far, not even the preponderant United States, has sought
to challenge the condition of nuclear deterrence among them.

The success of deterrence during the last 50 years gives us good reason
to conclude that national leaders have accepted the main lesson of the

nuclear revolution: that the deliberate waging of major nuclear war is an act of suicide. What Sagan's thesis in *The Limits of Safety* suggests, therefore, is that if such a war occurs in the future, it is much less likely to happen because political leaders have become unafraid of nuclear war or unconvinced by the deterrent power of nuclear weapons, and more because of an accident along the lines of the many that occurred during the Cuban crisis.

It is here that the application of 'normal' accident theory over time becomes quite central to theoretical considerations of great power politics in the future. Sheer statistical logic suggests that as long as interstate anarchical politics continue, some kind of confrontation involving states with nuclear weapons will eventually happen, even if neither side seeks it, and that in one of these confrontations, despite the wishes of the political leadership on both sides, an accident will trigger not a false alarm or narrowly averted unauthorised strike, but an actual nuclear attack which could well cascade into a general war. It is extremely difficult to imagine how a replay of indefinite 'Cuban' crises in future international orders would not once see an accident (or miscalculation) spiralling out of control. It was for this reason, of course, that American and Soviet officials established direct lines of communication after 1962 and tightened up command and control procedures; they had no wish to experience that again.

This conclusion speaks directly to the argument put forward by some international relations theorists – especially neorealists – that the contemporary unipolar order is likely, or certain, to revert to multipolarity in the foreseeable future. Interstate realist theory argues that international politics tends toward a balance of power, and that sooner or later one or more large states will build up their economic and military capabilities in order to 'balance' against the US much as the Soviet Union did after the Second World War.[17] Indeed, some of these theorists have suggested that such balancing is likely to stabilize great-power politics; that a new Cold War between, say, China, the European Union, or some other nation and the United States would be more conducive to long-term peace than the continuation of the unbalanced unipolar order we see today.[18]

Sagan's organizational theorizing about the Cuban crisis provides us with one of the most powerful reasons to reject this neorealist argument. Even if future American leaders, along with future Chinese, or European, or Indian ones, remain deterred by the prospect of nuclear war, and even if they develop effective military organisations designed to prevent the unauthorised or inadvertent outbreak of war, the advent of a new multipolar system composed of nuclear great powers competing bitterly for global sway, as did the US and the USSR during the Cold War, must increase, not diminish, the danger of a general nuclear war. Indeed, if great-power balancing is an eternal condition of international politics, a tragic premise logically central to neorealist thinking, then it is difficult to see how such realists can deny that the world they postulate will eventually suffer a general nuclear war. The only way around this is to claim that Cold Wars will recur forever without once going hot, a view quite at odds with the pessimistic political understanding associated with all forms of realism, not to mention basic common sense. This problem constitutes in itself a powerful objection to balance-of-power inevitability that most realists have not reckoned with.

Anarchical multipolarity means nuclear war, someday. What about unipolarity? The absence of balancing over the past two decades, since the collapse of the USSR in 1991, suggests to other international relations theorists that the United States is destined to remain the world's sole superpower over the indefinite future, and that we are hence unlikely to see the rise of new Cold Wars and the geopolitical crises that accompany them.[19] Is this a way to get around Sagan's pessimistic concerns about major nuclear war?

Unfortunately, normal accident theory comes logically into play in a unipolar condition as well. A key argument Sagan makes in *The Limits of Safety* deals with the durability of tight-coupled and complex systems. Such systems require ongoing determined authority, particularly in liberal political orders. They require committed leaders, highly disciplined employees, and a steady flow of generous funding to maintain redundant safety mechanisms and high-tech maintenance. Sagan shows how SAC spared no expense to achieve this during the Cold War.[20]

The problem here is that it may become difficult to sustain the political and institutional will to maintain such a system over the long term, especially in the absence of great-power rivalries and crises. SAC was able to command elite leaders and ample funding because during the Cold War the possibility of an accident leading to catastrophe in a major crisis remained quite real, even in the calmer period after 1962. But as the pressure of traditional geopolitical danger ebbs, organisations naturally cut corners, relax rules, and lose funding as the urgency of system perfection diminishes over time – as has been seen recently in several highly publicised fiascos within the US nuclear establishment. This suggests that while a unipolar order will not, by definition, witness great-power showdowns à la the Cuban crisis, it may see a minor confrontation with a lesser power lead to an accident as organisational authority over the US nuclear complex inevitably relaxes. The ensuing cascade would not result in a possible general nuclear war between two superpowers, as in 1962, but in an age of thermonuclear weaponry, this is cold comfort. Whether or not China or Russia qualifies as a great power in our contemporary environment, if an accidental nuclear war involving one of these nations spiralled out of control, it would be hardly less catastrophic than the one that could have happened 50 years ago; and even an accidental war with a smaller nuclear power (such as Pakistan) would lead to the deaths of tens of millions.[21]

Sagan's organisational analysis of the Cuban missile crisis, then, gives us reason to believe that a nuclear war could well occur over the foreseeable future even if one accepts that the leaders of all major nuclear states will always buy into the logic of deterrence, and even if the world remains unipolar over the *longue durée*. The crux of his argument is that the problem is, in the end, *apolitical*. If deterrence means that any leader, no matter how acute his or her ideology, dissatisfaction with the international status quo, or territorial ambition may be, will want to avoid nuclear war, accident theory suggests that organisations will eventually permit an error that leads to such a war, irrespective of the nature of the regime in charge. A large swath of international relations theory argues that the rise of certain kinds of powers to international preponderance is likely to lead to peace.[22] Sagan's interesting rejoinder is that even a world full of liberal democracies would run the risk of nuclear war, for the simple reason that all of them use organisations.

The dangers of proliferation

If nuclear deterrence works, reasoned the late pioneering IR theorist Kenneth Waltz, then it should work among all nations, not just the two Cold War superpowers. In 1980 Waltz wrote an enormously influential and controversial paper, titled *The Spread of Nuclear Weapons: More May be Better*, in which he argued that the acquisition of the bomb by small states would contribute to international stability and hence was 'more to be welcomed than to be feared'.[23] The argument was straightforward: when a state acquires a basic retaliatory nuclear arsenal, no rational state will try to conquer it. The security nuclear weapons provide will make states less paranoid about their enemies, reducing one source of tension; it will dissuade these enemies from contemplating attack, reducing another; moreover, if nuclear deterrence stops small states from going to war, the chances of a regional war escalating to the superpower level diminish correspondingly.

Waltz's essay delivered a broadside to the non-proliferation regime, a collection of international organisations and institutes dedicated to enforcing the Nuclear Non-Proliferation Treaty of 1968, which sought to prevent the spread of the bomb to small states and encourage the larger nuclear powers to disarm.[24] For many in the so-called 'international community', non-proliferation had long been seen as an unquestioned good, as debatable a project as, say, literacy programmes or drought prevention. Lurking behind this international consensus was the widespread, if normally unsaid, conviction that the basic requirements of nuclear deterrence – government competence and rationality – was evident among the existing nuclear states but perhaps not so much among some of those seeking a bomb. Waltz's rebuttal was that the leader of any state can be expected to want his or her regime and society to survive, and the one sure-fire way to threaten that survival is to use one's nuclear weapons aggressively. He further asked why governments would spend billions and devote decades to obtain a bomb only to blithely use it in an act of suicide. Finally, he also raised the possibility that some of those making this tacit non-proliferation argument were guilty of ethnocentric or even racist presumptions.[25] It is a debate that has not gone away.

Sagan's response to Waltz's thesis, published in a 1995 book (*The Spread of Nuclear Weapons: A Debate* – revised editions in 2003 and 2012) remains perhaps the strongest argument for nonproliferation in print. Much as his application of accident theory to great-power behaviour avoids distinguishing between political regime-types or ascribing nuclear aggressiveness to certain types of leaders, so his assessment of the dangers of nuclear proliferation to smaller states avoids the ethnocentrism that Waltz identifies in the non-proliferation regime. Simply put, Sagan argues that the problems nuclear organisations face in large powers are likely to be even worse in small ones. He identifies three key reasons for this.

First, small states seeking to acquire a basic arsenal (such as North Korea, Iraq in the 1990s, or perhaps Iran today) will have to dedicate a large proportion of their resources to the simple act of building a working bomb, particularly in the face of international sanctions and boycotts. This will leave them with much less money to develop a sophisticated command and control system, and to build in the redundancies and fail-safe technologies necessary to avoid an accidental or unauthorised launch. Waltz counters that small regimes will have far fewer bombs to worry about – there is no comparison between, say North Korea's arsenal today and the American arsenal of around 1960 – and that political leaders in small states will be exceptionally motivated to protect their bombs, given how much they have gone through to acquire them. Sagan allows these points, but insists that simple material realities overcome them. A small state will have less money and access to the most modern technologies. It will have a smaller population from which to choose capable military and civilian commanders. It will be less familiar with organisational techniques for avoiding accidents and unauthorised use. What is more, small nuclear states (such as Pakistan) can find themselves in turbulent regional environments where the danger of infiltration and sabotage is far greater than in large states with well-guarded borders and friendly neighbours. Normal accident theory is not necessarily more likely to apply to small states, Sagan argues, countering Waltz's charge of ethnocentrism: but it would make no sense to presume that they are less vulnerable to the problem. That a poor person may be less capable of protecting his or her possessions than an affluent one is not a castigation of him or her – it is just a reasonable statement.

Furthermore, many of the poorer states that have sought a bomb over the past twenty years do not possess the tradition of clear civil authority over the military that one finds in wealthier and more established states.

Civilian leaders, wary of antagonizing powerful military officials, may be reluctant to insist upon the unglamorous business of establishing acceptable command and control systems or to punish them for substandard work in this field. In a crisis, military officials on the scene may feel less constrained by civilian pressure to remain cool, not to take matters into their own hands. In *The Limits of Safety*, Sagan stresses how vigorously the Kennedy administration sought to ensure absolute civilian control over the military during the Cuban crisis, and how nevertheless officials at the operational level took matters into their own hands on several occasions. How would a civilian government with less authority cope in a similar episode?

Finally, and of most interest, Sagan points to a problem far more relevant to small states than to large ones: the spectre of preventive war. Though the US toyed with the idea of waging a preventive war during the crisis, by launching a major attack on the Cuban installations with the hope of eliminating all of them before they could be used, this had to be weighed against the possibility that the USSR would have responded with its strategic forces deployed elsewhere.

For a small state in possession of only a handful of bombs, preventive or pre-emptive war becomes a far greater risk, a problem particularly relevant today. A large nuclear state may come to believe that it can launch an attack that can take out the entire arsenal of its adversary. The logic of deterrence would suggest that it would not do so, and Sagan is a bit inconsistent here, but his larger point holds: the simple knowledge that one's total arsenal may be vulnerable to enemy pre-emption will encourage riskier tactics at the operational level. Eager to ensure that a few missiles will get off before such an attack, a small state government may relax redundancies (such as the 'two-man' doctrine) or delegate launch authorisation powers to military officials on the ground. In such conditions (which may now obtain in Pakistan), normal accident theory magnifies radically in importance.

The debate between Sagan and Waltz highlights a basic theoretical disagreement between these two scholars that cuts to the core of international relations scholarship. For Waltz, structural incentives push states toward policies that enhance their survival, and there is no more vivid incentive than to stay out of a nuclear war. The lessons of the missile crisis are political: when confronted with the possibility of nuclear war, leaders become extremely cautious and seek above all to avoid hostilities. Because states are going to pursue that end irrespective of their political make-up, one can essentially ignore what is going on inside of them and assume that they will become war-avoiders. The conclusion to Waltz's argument is obvious: the more states that get nuclear weapons, the more peaceful international relations will become. A world in which all states had nuclear weapons, then, would be a world of perpetual peace, a kind of utopia.

The theory Sagan develops in *The Limits of Safety* and deploys in his debates with Waltz arrives at precisely the opposite conclusions. If Waltz ignores the internal nature of the state, if he 'black boxes' it, Sagan in a sense 'black boxes' the international system. For him, political outcomes are shaped by the fact that all governments by necessity use organisations, and all organisations are vulnerable to accidents, no matter what kind of regime is in charge of them, and – crucially – no matter what kind of international conditions prevail. As long as states possess nuclear weapons, one will eventually go off, and the more states that possess them, the sooner it will happen. A world in which all states had nuclear weapons, in other words, would be a world on the imminent brink of catastrophic war, one started by a faulty warning system, drowsy pilot, or panicky base commander. It would be a dystopia, for the short period it lasted.

The Limits of Safety and the contemporary politics of non-proliferation

Sagan's examination of near-misses during the Cuban missile crisis provides a cogent and persuasive case that nuclear war was more likely than commonly perceived during the last two weeks of October 1962. On pure historical grounds, it is an extremely important argument, and one that has remained compelling even as much new documentation on both the US and Soviet sides has been released over the past two decades and important new accounts of the crisis have appeared.

The major objective of the book, however – together with his extension of the argument in his debates with Waltz – is not to provide a simple historical account, but to show that nuclear war remains a constant possibility because of the existence of organisations in control of nuclear weapons and the fact that accidents happen within even the most effective of them. The likelihood that an accidental nuclear attack during an international crisis would cascade into general war, due to the unprecedented chaos and panic the explosion of any nuclear weapon would create, makes this problem one of supreme importance. His final analysis is simple: a nuclear accident is going to happen, sometime; when it happens, it could well escalate into an interstate war; and the more nations that have nuclear arsenals, the sooner such a disaster will occur. It is a deeply pessimistic story.

What should be done? Sagan makes two overarching suggestions. First, he calls upon the US (and presumably all nuclear states) to develop more effective systems of command and control over their nuclear arsenals. The argument here is essentially technocratic. The US should modernise its nuclear organisations, eliminate as much of its offensive and battlefield nuclear weaponry as possible, and rigorously apply normal accident theory (and not high-reliability theory) in its training of personnel and development of new weapon systems. It should systematically study cases of accidents and near-misses of the past in order to troubleshoot existing defects, undertake war-game exercises based upon an initial accidental detonation, and it should indoctrinate all civilian and military personnel associated with the nuclear establishment in the terrifying lessons of the Cuban and other crises.

Moreover, Sagan urges US and international agencies to assist other existing nuclear states with their own command and control techniques – which, at the time of his writing, meant above all the new states of Russia and other former Soviet republics with nuclear weapons on their soil. Applied to the present day, Sagan's advice could well apply to India, Pakistan, and even, if implausibly, North Korea.

Sagan's second argument is simply to oppose the spread of nuclear weapons to other states, and especially smaller and less technologically advanced ones. He stresses that in supporting non-proliferation he is advocating not so much aggressive actions to prevent states eager for a bomb from getting one, but rather to create an environment in which few states are interested in going nuclear. In the debate with Waltz, Sagan writes that the real challenge 'is to create a future in which government leaders, the organizations under them, and the citizens of nonnuclear states around the globe believe that it is in their interests to remain non-nuclear states'.[26]

Sagan recognizes the limitations of these two recommendations, and acknowledges that the pessimistic, almost fatalistic, implications of his foregoing argument would seem to imply more dramatic action, such as the abolition of nuclear weapons entirely. In a very short section, however, he iterates the familiar reasons why abolition is unworkable – namely, the ease of building and deploying weapons surreptitiously – and concludes that such an objective is simply too utopian to consider seriously. Indeed, he makes the very important point that a programme of abolition which did not reliably prevent surreptitious rearmament could well be much more dangerous than the current order.[27]

Both of Sagan's recommendations are quite sensible. Who could argue with the idea that nuclear weapons organisation sought to be rigorously modernised and improved to prevent accidents, or that we should try to promote an international order in which nations have no desire to acquire the bomb? Nevertheless, to conclude this essay I will try to show how these two objectives are contradictory, and how Sagan's moderate suggestions may make the problem worse rather than better.

According to Sagan, as long as the international system of interstate anarchy persists, an eventual nuclear war is in the cards. He accepts this, but argues that radical change to prevent this outcome is impossible or at least highly unrealistic. Thus he supports modernisation of existing arsenals and non-proliferation efforts, especially those which aim to create an international environment in which states eschew the bomb, as shorter-term, practical steps to avoid nuclear danger over the foreseeable future.[28] Sometimes, however, the practical becomes the enemy of the necessary. For Sagan's two central policy recommendations, when taken together, will do nothing other than solidify the nuclear status quo that portends eventual war.

By modernising their nuclear systems, by spending billions of dollars or pounds or euros on technical and organizational improvements to their large arsenals, the major nuclear states will certainly diminish the likelihood of an accidental war, but they will at the same time signal to the rest of the world that they intend to deploy thermonuclear weaponry over the indefinite future. This was certainly the message conveyed by President Obama's announcement of an $85 billion upgrade of the US nuclear arsenal in 2010, and of the similar Russian declaration in early 2012.

From the point of view of accident theory, the US and Russian decisions make perfect sense. In the world of international politics, however, they have different effects. What these moves indicate to other states, and especially the non-nuclear states Sagan wants to dissuade from wanting a bomb, is that the major nuclear powers have no interest in changing the existing order, and are perfectly content with an international system divided between nuclear 'haves' and nuclear 'have-nots'. They may talk about a world without nuclear weapons, as President Obama did in Prague in 2009, but their actions say otherwise.

This hypocrisy matters, because the non-proliferation treaty, originally signed in 1968, stipulated quite clearly, in Article VI, that the major nuclear states were obligated to disarm just as other states were to eschew the bomb. Otherwise, non-nuclear states would have been agreeing to lock themselves into a condition of permanent military inferiority. Some 40 years later, none of the major nuclear powers appear anywhere close to disarmament. States that gave up their projects to build a bomb under international pressure, such as Brazil, are infuriated by the complete disregard by the major nuclear states of Article VI. Other states, such as Iran, point to the brazen hypocrisy of nations like the US when seeking to justify their nascent projects.[29]

By concentrating upon the apolitical problems of accidents and organisational cultures, in other words, Sagan does not acknowledge how his two recommendations work at cross-purposes. There are many ways to create an international order in which states will be less likely to seek nuclear arsenals, but the one sure way of undermining such a project is to endorse the permanent nuclearisation of the major powers. Not only will this encourage some aggrieved states to get their own bomb; it also demoralises other states who have long been committed to nuclear disarmament and non-proliferation. What is more, it does nothing about the deeper problem of nuclear anarchy. Sagan is surely correct that the modernisation of existing nuclear arsenals will reduce the chances of an accidental war over the near-term, but if he is saying anything in *The Limits of Safety*, it is that the very nature of organisations make such a war certain over the long term in any event.

Indeed, there is a deeper problem with Sagan's support for practical improvements in nuclear safety. By advocating the modernisation of existing nuclear organizations and supporting non-proliferation policies, he pushes to the fringes the only serious long-term solution to nuclear danger, which is the abolition, not necessarily of all nuclear weapons, but of the interstate system which permits the possibility of their being used in an international war. Sagan is correct that the abolition of nuclear weapons is inviable, and indeed more dangerous than doing nothing, if states are able to build them again surreptitiously. But the solution to that is to construct a global entity powerful enough to prevent that from happening, which is to say, a world government. Proliferation optimists like Waltz can consistently claim that the dangers of a world state, and/or the impossibility of building one, is so evident that the spread of nuclear weapons to more and more states is the least bad of all possible outcomes – that we have to hope that the logic of deterrence will work forever. But everything that Sagan argues in *The Limits of Safety* runs counter to Waltz's reasoning. In a condition of eternal interstate anarchy, a nuclear war will someday happen in the real world of accidents, panic, and organisational breakdown.

Sagan has put forward the most compelling critique of Waltz's deterrence optimism, by using the Cuban missile crisis as a historical case to show, irrefutably in my opinion, that an international order dependent upon eternal deterrence will be eventually undermined by the 'banal and often bizarre failures' that occur in the actual world of international politics. But his solution to this problem also avoids the actual world of international politics. It does not contend with the impossibility of maintaining non-proliferation when the main nuclear powers refuse to disarm, nor with the likelihood of a war among them in any event. Indeed, the ameliorative solutions Sagan proposes to forestall this disaster are likely to create a political impasse which will make things worse. As many politicians and scholars argued after the bombings of Hiroshima and Nagasaki, and again after the missile crisis, the radical dangers of the nuclear revolution can only be solved by correspondingly radical changes to the international order. Sagan masterfully reveals to us how these radical dangers were even worse than anyone then imagined, yet his moderate solutions to the problem are incommensurate with that story.

Notes

1 This chapter was developed from Campbell Craig, 'Testing Organisation Man: The Cuban Missile Crisis and *The Limits of Safety*', *International Relations*, 26/3 (2012) 291–303. Reproduced by permission of SAGE Publications Ltd.
2 Some scholars argue that the crisis began, in effect, well earlier than the conventional starting date of 16 October 1962, that it continued in key respects until well into November, and that the 'Thirteen Days' duration is hindsighted or even historically incorrect. This essay would reply that while it is difficult to

pinpoint the exact beginning and end of any historical episode, and that certainly key participants did not realise at the time that the crisis was definitely over on 28 October, it was only during this period that leaders of the two sides were seriously reckoning with the possibility of imminent war.

3 Scott D. Sagan, *The Limits of Safety: Organisations, Accidents, and Nuclear Weapons* (Princeton, NJ: Princeton University Press, 1993).

4 Ibid., pp. 99–100.

5 Ibid., pp. 135–8.

6 See William Burr and Thomas S. Blanton (eds), *The Submarines of October: National Security Archive Electronic Briefing Book No. 75*, 31 October 2002. www2.gwu.edu/~nsarchiv/NSAEBB/NSAEBB75/ (last accessed 19 September 2014).

7 Sagan, *Limits of Safety*, pp. 130–1.

8 Sagan's accounts of these incidents are in Sagan, *Limits of Safety*, chapters 2–3. Further discussion of accidents during the crisis can be found in Aleksandr Fursenko and Timothy Naftali, '*One Hell of a Gamble: Khrushchev, Castro Kennedy and the Cuban Missile Crisis 1958–1964* (London: John Murray 1997) and Michael Dobbs, *One Minute to Midnight: Kennedy, Khrushchev and Castro on the Brink of Nuclear War* (London: Hutchinson 2008).

9 Sagan, *Limits of Safety*, pp. 11–52.

10 Ibid., pp. 49–51.

11 On this point, see Benoît Pelopidas, 'Bad Luck: How Nuclear Experts Stopped Taking Nuclear Accidents Seriously', unpublished manuscript.

12 See, for example, Henry Kissinger, *Nuclear Weapons and Foreign Policy* (New York: Council on Foreign Relations 1957) and Albert Wohlstetter, 'The Delicate Balance of Terror', *Foreign Affairs* 37/1 (January 1959) 211–34.

13 See Campbell Craig, *Destroying the Village: Eisenhower and Thermonuclear War* (Columbia University Press, 1998). On Kennedy's initial alarmism, see Christopher Preble, *Kennedy and the Missile Gap* (DeKalb, Il: Northern Illinois Press 2004); for its effect on Soviet perceptions of the US, see Aleksandr Fursenko and Timothy Naftali, *Khrushchev's Cold War: The Inside Story of an American Adversary* (London: W.W. Norton 2006).

14 The classic case for reviving the possibility of winnable nuclear war is Keith Payne and Colin Gray, 'Victory is Possible', *Foreign Policy*, 39 (Summer 1980) 14–27. Acute criticism of this way of thinking can be found in Robert Jervis, *The Illogic of American Nuclear Strategy* (Ithaca, NY: Cornell University Press 1984) and George Kennan, *The Nuclear Delusion* (New York: Pantheon 1983).

15 Though see John Mueller, *Atomic Obsession: Nuclear Alarmism from Hiroshima to al Qaeda* (Oxford: Oxford University Press 2009). Mueller, in making a strong case that the threats of nuclear terrorism and proliferation are seriously exaggerated, also advances an interesting, but historically untenable, argument that nuclear fear played only a small role in the Cold War. For a recent argument that nuclear superiority played a role in determining the victor in Cold War crises, see Matthew Kroenig, 'Nuclear Superiority and the Balance of Revolve: Explaining Nuclear Crisis Outcomes', *International Organization* 67/1 (January 2013) 141–71. This article produced a very interesting debate on the H-Diplo website; see Francis Gavin *et al.*, 'What We Talk About When We Talk About Nuclear Weapons.' H-Diplo/ISSF forum, http://issforum.org/ISSF/PDF/ISSF-Forum-2.pdf. (last accessed 19 August 2014).

16 Campbell Craig, 'The Nuclear Revolution: A Product of the Cold War, or Something More?' in Richard Immerman and Petra Goedde (eds), *Oxford Handbook of the Cold War* (Oxford: Oxford University Press 2013) 360–76. On the Soviet side, also see Naftali and Fursenko, *Khrushchev's Cold War*. The two superpowers did find themselves in a kind of nuclear showdown in the Able Archer crisis of 1983. But this, unlike the crises of the late 1950s/early 1960s,

was quite clearly not triggered by either side over a contested geopolitical stake, and therefore did not require either side to back down, as happened in Berlin and Cuba.

17 The classic argument is John Mearsheimer, *The Tragedy of Great Power Politics* (New York: W.W. Norton 2001); also see Charles Glaser, 'Will China's Rise Lead to War?' *Foreign Affairs*, 90/2, (March/April 2011) 80–91. For a recent rebuttal, see William Wohlforth and Stephen Brooks, 'Assessing the Balance', *Cambridge Review of International Affairs*, 24/2 (2011) 2–19.

18 For a formidable new study that rejects the inevitability of a balance-of-power system, see Nuno Monteiro, *Theory of Unipolar Politics* (Cambridge: Cambridge University Press 2014).

19 See G. John Ikenberry, William Wohlforth, and Michael Mastanduno, *International Relations Theory and the Consequences of Unipolarity* (Cambridge: Cambridge University Press 2011).

20 A thorough journalistic account of attempts to prevent nuclear accidents throughout the Cold War and up to the present is Eric Schlosser, *Command and Control: Nuclear Weapons, the Damascus Accident, and the Illusion of Safety* (New York: Penguin 2013). Schlosser gives many military commanders, above all Curtis LeMay, credit for installing massive fail-safe procedures, yet describes how again and again these came close to failing due to banal organisational or political errors.

21 See Gregory Koblentz, 'Command and Combust', review of Schlosser, *Command and Control*, in *Foreign Affairs*, 93/1 (January/February 2014) 167–72.

22 A clear trend in the study of International Relations is the abandonment of purely structural models in favour of hybrid works which emphasise the central role of regime type and political agency. For democratic peace, neoliberal, and defensive realist cases for an enduring peace based upon the particular nature of major powers, see, respectively, Bruce Russett and John Oneal, *Triangulating Peace* (New York: W.W. Norton 2001); G. John Ikenberry, *Liberal Leviathan* (Princeton NJ: Princeton University Press 2011); and Charles L. Glaser, *Rational Theory of International Politics* (Princeton, NJ: Princeton University Press 2010).

23 Kenneth Waltz, *The Spread of Nuclear Weapons: More May be Better*, Adelphi Papers No. 171 (London: International Institute for Strategic Studies 1981).

24 The non-proliferation regime has been under severe pressure on several fronts. For the argument that it has become essentially a tool of great-power interest, see Campbell Craig and Jan Ruzicka, 'The Nonproliferation Complex', *Ethics and International Affairs* 27/3 (Fall 2013) 329–48.

25 Mueller also criticises the implicit elitism of non-proliferation policies; see *Atomic Obsession*, chapter 10.

26 Scott D. Sagan and Kenneth N. Waltz, *The Spread of Nuclear Weapons: A Debate* (London: W.W. Norton, 1995) p. 133.

27 This problem was perceived by American and Soviet officials at the outset of the atomic age. See Campbell Craig and Sergey Radchenko, *The Atomic Bomb and the Origins of the Cold War* (New Haven, CT: Yale University Press 2008) chapters 5–6.

28 Sagan has reiterated these points in recent writings. See Scott D. Sagan, 'The Case for No First Use', *Survival*, 51/3 (June–July 2009) 163–82 and especially ibid., 'Shared Responsibilities for Nuclear Disarmament', *Daedalus*, 138/4 (Fall 2009) 157–68, in which Sagan stresses in particular the responsibility of *non-nuclear* states to further the non-proliferation cause. In neither article does Sagan suggest that more substantial reform is necessary to achieve an enduring nuclear peace.

29 On this point, see Craig and Ruzicka, 'The Nonproliferation Complex'.

5 'The best and the brightest'

The Cuban missile crisis, the Kennedy administration and the lessons of history

R. Gerald Hughes

He may live long, he may do much. But here is the summit. He can never exceed what he does this day.
>   (Edmund Burke's eulogy of Charles James Fox for his attack on the
>   East India Company, House of Commons, 1 December 1783)[1]

The first thing one does to evaluate a ruler's prudence is to look at men he has around him.
>   (Niccolò Machiavelli)[2]

History and memory

Since 1962, the narrative, analysis and lessons of the Cuban missile crisis have been constantly reappraised, reinterpreted and reimagined. This process has involved policy-makers, intelligence officers, journalists, historians, political scientists and others. This catholic constituency has produced a rich field of historical study, with many of the most influential accounts being the reminiscences of certain of the participants in the Cuban missile crisis.[3] A number of these were written by former members of Kennedy's unofficial missile crisis 'war cabinet', the Executive Committee of the National Security Council (ExComm). Much of this body was composed of the Kennedy-appointed makers of US national security policy, individuals often termed 'the best and the brightest'.[4] And, if we follow Machiavelli's advice and scrutinise Kennedy's advisors we can learn a great deal about the President and his times. ExComm-ite accounts of the missile crisis[5] are, nevertheless, inherently problematic. As Dean Acheson observed, nobody ever looked second best in his own record of a conversation.[6] Ted Sorensen, JFK's special counsel, himself conceded 'the hazards of memory, inevitably influenced by selectivity and hindsight'.[7] Yet, the opinions of such figures are of such importance that their omission from the historical record would be a sin of the highest order. One author thus asserts that National Security Adviser McGeorge Bundy's recollections of the Cuban missile crisis are as valuable a source as Henry L. Stimson's memoir treatment of Hiroshima.[8]

The notion that statesmen learn from history is almost always dismissed as a chimera. Hegel wrote that

> Rulers, Statesmen, Nations, are wont to be emphatically commended to the teaching which experience offers in history. But what experience and history teach is this – that peoples and governments never have learned anything from history, or acted on principles deduced from it.[9]

This does not mean that history is not endlessly mined for *presentist* purposes. Michael Howard warned that the 'trouble is that there is no such thing as "history". History is what historians write, and historians are part of the process they are writing about.'[10] This is certainly the case with the Cuban missile crisis given the prominence of participant-memoirists in its historiography.

1914 and all that

In 1986, Richard Neustadt and Ernest May observed that 'the uses made of history appear to have contributed, demonstrably, to the high quality of analysis and management apparent during the missile crisis'.[11] The most obvious manifestation of this is the notion that the lessons of 1914, partly extracted from Barbara Tuchman's *Guns of August*, helped determine Kennedy's policy choices. 1914 was superimposed onto 1962 when Sorensen, Schlesinger and RFK alluded to it in print.[12] Sorensen says that Kennedy's fascination with 1914 pre-dated Tuchman's book and went back to a course he had taken at Harvard. A favourite Kennedy word was 'miscalculation' and his studies at Harvard had caused him to realise 'how quickly countries which were comparatively uninvolved were taken, in the space of a few days, into war'.[13] Prime Minister Harold Macmillan, a veteran of the First World War, also read Tuchman's book and, having drawn similar conclusions to JFK, offered sympathetic counsel to the President during the crisis.[14] JFK urged his senior national security officials to read Tuchman's (recently published) book,[15] and littered his discussions with historical allusions to how 'the Germans, the Austrians, the French and the British ... somehow seemed to tumble into war'. Kennedy was determined not to have to face the question that had confronted Germany's Chancellor, Bethmann-Hollweg, after he had failed to prevent war in 1914: 'How did it all happen?' (The German had supposedly responded: 'Ah, if only we knew').[16] Kennedy was nevertheless acutely aware that the Superpowers in 1962, like the Great Powers in 1914, had core national interests upon which they could not compromise. As Henry Kissinger argued a month after the crisis: JFK had little option but to respond firmly to the deployment of Soviet missiles. To do otherwise would 'embolden' opponents and diminish US 'credibility'.[17]

Secretary of Defense Robert McNamara later recalled the influence of Tuchman's book in October 1962 representing, as it did, 'a powerful indictment of the European leaders who allowed the crisis of July 1914 … to escalate into World War I'. At the ExComm meeting of the morning of 18 October 1962, Secretary of State Dean Rusk essentially parroted Tuchman's argument, stating: 'We all, of course, remember the guns of August where certain events brought about a general situation which at the time none of the governments involved really wanted. And this precedent, I think, is something that is pretty important.'[18] Not all of the ExComm-ites were convinced of the utility of analogy, however. Arthur Schlesinger, special assistant to the White House and a historian by profession, later asked whether, or not, 'the history invoked [in a given situation was] really the source of policies, or is it the source of arguments designed to vindicate policies adopted for antecedent reasons?' After all, such patterns of thought were dangerously seductive: 'Once a statesman begins to identify the present with the past, he may in time be carried further than he intends by the bewitchment of analogy.'[19]

Bewitched or not, Tuchman's book caused JFK to fear that he might share the fate of the leaders of Europe in 1914. Robert Kennedy was fully aware that his brother's legacy, and his own political career, could only benefit from portraying JFK's conduct during the missile crisis within a heroic historical narrative. RFK thus claimed that his brother had stated that 'I don't ever want to be in that position. We are not going to bungle into a war',[20] vowing that 'I am not going to follow a course which will allow anyone to write a comparable book about this time, *The Missiles of October*'.[21] JFK was especially keen to avoid the 'misunderstandings' that had arisen between the powers in 1914 out of the myriad 'personal complexes of inferiority and grandeur'.[22] Interestingly, Tuchman herself acknowledged the influence of the written word upon policy-makers, asserting that but for Wilhelm II's having read Alfred Thayer Mahan's 1890 work, *The Influence of Sea Power on History*, he might never have embarked upon the programme of naval expansion that made an enemy of the British Empire. Indeed, 'there might have been no world war'.[23]

John Keegan noted that *The Guns of August* proffered 'important advice: leave the subordinates to deal with the telegrams while the boss keeps a clear head to decide for peace or war'. Alas, he then bought into RFK's version of the past with alacrity, believing the missile crisis 'produced a book still eminently valuable to a statesman in crisis, Robert Kennedy's *Thirteen Days*. It tells how Bobby … spared his brother Jack the confusions that helped to drive Europe into the First World War'.[24] One author has suggested that, since Tuchman's thesis is now accepted by historians as being 'wrong', JFK had based his policy on false premises.[25] This is an odd proposition. The lesson that JFK had taken from Tuchman's book – that policy-makers must retain control of events – was not synonymous with the central thesis advanced in *The Guns of August* (which was that Europe had blundered into war in 1914, a line that came under sustained attack after the formulation of the so-called 'Fischer thesis' in the 1960s).[26] But it is simply not true to imply that Fischer's views have been accepted either uncritically or universally.[27] In any case, while historiographical nuance is essential for the study of 1914, the conclusions JFK drew from Tuchman in 1962 were perfectly sound.

While 1914 fascinated him, it was the countdown to the Second World War that had dominated Kennedy's formative years. Thomas Powers wrote that

> October 1962 was not August 1914 because John Kennedy had learned the lessons of Munich, which may be summarised as follows: get angry in private, think before you speak, say what you want, make clear what you're prepared to do, ignore bluster, repeat yourself as often as necessary and keep the pressure on.[28]

JFK never forgot that his father, Joseph P. Kennedy, had been, especially when ambassador to Britain, a defeatist and an outspoken supporter of Appeasement.[29] In 1940, having just graduated from Harvard with a dissertation on Britain and Appeasement (published as *Why England Slept*),[30] JFK was asked by his father how to go about refuting the widespread charges of appeasement made against him in the US. Jack duly obliged and advised his father that many Americans 'are guilty of throwing around the term [appeasement] when they might never have stopped to think exactly what they mean'. JFK felt it necessary to challenge this imprecision 'because no one – be they isolationist, pacifist, etc. ... likes to be called an appeaser'.[31] JFK came to be an admirer of the British historian A.J.P. Taylor and, from his work, drew the lesson that 'Hitler thought that he could seize Poland, that the British might not fight [or] ... after the defeat of Poland, might not continue to fight'.[32] That said, the Munich analogy – which consistently discouraged conciliation in foreign policy – was challenged in the missile crisis by a comparison of the contemporary situation with Pearl Harbor.[33] At an ExComm meeting on 18 October, Under Secretary of State George Ball warned that a surprise attack on Cuba would resemble Pearl Harbor: 'it's the kind of conduct that's such that one might expect of the Soviet Union. It is not conduct that one expects of the United States.'[34] A (previously and subsequently belligerent) RFK concurred, supposedly adding: 'For 175 years we had not been that kind of country.'[35] Summing up, Sorensen wrote that a 'fundamental objection' to any US surprise air attack on Cuba was that it would represent a 'Pearl Harbor in reverse', an attack 'on a small nation ... [that] history could neither understand nor forget'.[36] RFK feared that the President might be compared to Japan's wartime premier, Hideki Tōjō, if he attacked Cuba without warning.[37] That he, nevertheless, continued to adopt a hawkish stance in the ExComm (repeatedly advocating measures that would have led to war) indicates that his concerns with striking Cuba without warning were concerned more with his brother's reputation, rather than with any moral squeamishness.[38] But, in the popular histories of the crisis the lesson is hardly so nuanced: the narrative there being that RFK opposed airstrikes because he rejected a first strike as being immoral. In sum, in terms of the lessons of history, the Kennedy administration came out looking very well in the dominant narratives of the crisis. It had avoided the diplomatic blunders of 1914; rejected the craven appeasement that had led to Munich; and spurned the reckless aggression of Pearl Harbor.

Innenpolitik und Außenpolitik

Domestic policy can only defeat us; foreign policy can kill us.

(John F. Kennedy)[39]

In all of the foreign policy crises discussed above, excessive attention has been directed at external pressures on the state under scrutiny, as opposed to the dynamics of domestic policy. Bundy's *Danger and Survival* downplayed the fact that domestic politics were driving JFK's policy during the crisis: 'Indeed, Bundy raised to the level of statesmanship Kennedy's vulnerability to domestic political attacks. The assumption was that given the expectations of the American people, the president had no choice but to engage in brinkmanship.'[40] In fact, policy towards Latin America had long been driven by domestic factors and the Monroe Doctrine of 1823 had itself had been the product of such forces.[41] This had long seemed a settled state of affairs, but the emergence of a nuclear-armed Soviet Union had significant potential to threaten US hegemony over the Western hemisphere. On 31 August 1962, Senator Kenneth Keating (R-NY), with an eye on the upcoming mid-term elections,[42] told the Senate that the Kennedy administration was blind to the possibility of the Soviet Union deploying missiles in Cuba.[43] Kennedy stated on 4 September 1962 that 'the presence of offensive ground-to-ground missiles ... [would mean] the gravest issues would arise'.[44] Kennedy was nonetheless reassured by CIA reports that judged it unlikely that the Soviets would deploy missiles in Cuba.[45] The fact that the Soviet Union did so meant that, in the words of John Kenneth Galbraith, US ambassador to India in 1962, the 'political needs of the Kennedy administration [caused] it to take almost any risk to get them out'.[46] It was this combination of high-risk nuclear diplomacy and volatile electoral political consideration that made the Cuban missile crisis so dangerous.

Schlesinger and Sorensen defended Kennedy over the April 1961 Bay of Pigs disaster with typical verve.[47] Schlesinger later said that the affair showed that JFK 'was quite prepared to cut his losses and never felt that he had to prove his manhood by irrational bellicosity'.[48] Sorensen portrayed the President as a naïve innocent who privately lamented: 'How could I have been so stupid, as to [have] let them go ahead?'[49] Publicly, although JFK declared: 'I'm the responsible officer of the government and that is quite obvious', he also mobilised his formidable propaganda and 'dirty tricks' machinery to place the blame elsewhere.[50] Hedley Donovan recalled that

> Kennedy ... was getting preposterous praise – and amazingly high ratings in the polls – for simply stating the inescapable constitutional fact that he was 'responsible'. Which did not stop him from telling scores of friends, senators, journalists ... that his mistake was to pay attention to the CIA and the military brass.[51]

Kennedy's success here caused the main scapegoat for the Bay of Pigs, DCI Allen Dulles, to imply criticism of the President by asserting that 'I know of no [intelligence] estimate that [asserted that] a spontaneous rising would be touched off by the landing'.[52] Despite a long history of such correctives, many authors continue to exonerate Kennedy from blame for the Bay of Pigs disaster to this day.[53] This is, of course, rarely the case with conservatives and, in 1990, Ronald Reagan lamented Kennedy's 'tragic error' in abandoning 'the Cuban freedom fighters' at the Bay of Pigs: 'If he hadn't done so, perhaps history would have been much different in Central America.'[54]

After April 1961 the Kennedys hated Castro all the more, convinced that Havana was intent on exporting revolution to the Americas.[55] This has led to suggestions that JFK was planning to invade Cuba before any missiles were discovered there,[56] a claim angrily rebutted by Schlesinger.[57] One should nevertheless not underestimate the contemporary domestic pressure on Kennedy, given Cuba's special place in the history of US foreign relations.[58] George Ball recalled that Castro's alliance with Moscow confronted Washington

> with a patent violation of a revered item of our national credo: the Monroe Doctrine. That doctrine forbade European powers from intrusion into the Western Hemisphere, which we regarded – though we avoided stating it in those terms – as our exclusive sphere of interest and influence.[59]

In this spirit, the Taylor Commission's report into the Bay of Pigs advocated an active policy.

> [Castro's] continued presence within the hemispheric community as a dangerously effective exponent of communism and anti-Americanism constitutes a real menace capable of eventually overthrowing the elected governments in any one or more of the weak Latin American

republics. There are only two ways to view this threat; either to hope that time and internal discontent will eventually end it, or to take active measures to force its removal.[60]

Hostility towards Castro was derived from an impulse to dominate Cuba, although any number of authors have peddled the discredited line that JFK only had some vague notion of administration plots against Castro.[61] In fact, JFK authorised RFK to embark on a programme of terrorism against Cuba (Operation Mongoose), which called for the assassination of the Cuban leadership.[62] The declassified minutes of an October 1962 meeting of the Mongoose planning group (which included RFK), record that 'General Lansdale said that another attempt will be made against the major target [Castro] which has been the object of three unsuccessful missions, and that approximately six new ones are in the planning stage'.[63] Following his brother's assassination Bobby Kennedy continued to insist that there had been no plot to assassinate Castro. And, years later, Schlesinger asserted that even if any such thing had existed it was all a secret CIA plot, of which the Kennedys had no knowledge.[64]

Castro later asserted that JFK had suspended Mongoose, and might have normalised relations with Cuba had he not been assassinated.[65] Although there had been intimations that the Kennedy administration had sought a rapprochement with Cuba,[66] on the very day that the President died in Dallas, CIA officers met with a treacherous Cuban official, Rolando Cubela Secades, in Paris to provide him with a poison-tipped ballpoint pen with which to assassinate Castro.[67] McNamara, incredibly, concluded of Mongoose:

> covert operations always convey to those on the receiving end more hostile intent than is meant or available ... the Cubans, however, believed that [Mongoose] was a forerunner to an invasion ... [leading] them to seek assistance from the Soviets, which in turn led to the Cuban Missile Crisis.

McNamara opined that 'We in Washington' shared the view that such planning was simply what Bundy later termed (in 1987) as 'psychological salve for inaction'.[68] This dishonest conclusion ignores the fact that planning for the ousting of Castro resumed as soon as the missile crisis had ended. Indeed, at the end of November 1962, Bundy himself had told the ExComm that 'Our ultimate objective with respect to Cuba remains the overthrow of the Castro regime and its replacement by one sharing the aims of the Free World'.[69] Bundy was on message here. In truth, Kennedy was a prisoner of his own Cold War assumptions and failed to see the connection between his covert war against Castro and Khrushchev's decision to send nuclear weapons to protect Cuba from invasion.[70]

Establishing the heroic narrative

> [Kennedy has shown] not only the courage of a warrior, which is to take the risks that are necessary, but also the wisdom of the statesman, which is to use power with restraint.
>
> (Walter Lippmann, 13 November 1962)[71]

> All history becomes subjective; in other words, there is properly no History, only Biography.
>
> (Ralph Waldo Emerson)[72]

As the threat of war receded, the Kennedy White House, and its numerous partisans in the media, successfully constructed the crisis as heroic narrative.[73] It is probable that no president has ever enjoyed the adulation directed at Kennedy after the Cuban missile crisis. *Newsweek* declared that Americans now had 'a sense of deep confidence in their president and the team he had working with him'.[74] The Soviet leader, Nikita Khrushchev, never recovered domestically from the humiliation of the withdrawal the missiles from Cuba, and this contributed to his being forced from power in 1964. Kennedy's martyrdom on 22 November did much to secure his place in history as the saviour of peace and, additionally, caused many to absolve him of any blame attached to the US adventure in Vietnam.[75]

Following JFK's assassination, the overwhelmingly positive popular vision of his White House court as a modern day Camelot was further institutionalised by Kennedy's former courtiers. Schlesinger enthused that Kennedy's 'combination of toughness and restraint, of will, nerve and wisdom, so brilliantly controlled, so matchlessly calibrated, [had] dazzled the world'.[76] Hans J. Morgenthau termed Schlesinger and Sorensen's biographies of JFK 'monuments' to what they saw as the dead President's 'greatness'.[77] Given this, Kennedy's memoirist-aides would surely – if they were honest – have subscribed to Churchill's quip that 'History will be kind to me, for I intend to write it'.[78] Emerson's point about history may appear to suggest that all such works, being written from someone's *unique* position, are necessarily subjective – and so no more or no better than biography. In fact, he was instead arguing that it was in the interplay between the historical text and the reader that meaning was established. According to this logic, the 'monumental' qualities as have been ascribed to biographies of Kennedy and the 'greatness' attached to their subject were established by socially conditioned readers at least as much as the authors of the panegyrics.

Kennedy was less than frank on the issue of the agreement to remove the Jupiters from Turkey (just as he and his adherents were similarly economical with the truth over a series of other key events in October 1962).[79] As Bundy later noted: 'we misled our colleagues, our countrymen, our successors, and our allies'.[80] On 28 October 1962, Schlesinger recorded his fear that opponents would soon start sniping at the recent settlement.

Indeed, he went so far as to wonder whether, or not, 'it might have been more acceptable politically if we had traded the Turkish bases (which McNamara wants to get rid of anyway) instead of committing ourselves to tacit recognition of the Castro regime in Cuba'.[81]

The official version of the resolution of the crisis only had a limited shelf life, as archival release policy would, eventually, let the cat out of the bag.[82] In 1969, Robert Kennedy's *Thirteen Days* revealed that he had told Anatoly Dobrynin, the Soviet ambassador in Washington, on 27 October that the President planned to remove the Jupiters anyway – but he insisted there was no trade.[83] In 1978 Arthur Schlesinger's biography of RFK went so far as to state that 'the Kennedys [had] made a personal, but not official, pledge that the Turkish missiles would go'.[84] The full truth came out when, in *Time* in 1982, a number of Kennedy's advisors revealed (at Bundy's suggestion) the existence of the Turkish deal. This confession was crafted to minimise the impact of the deal over the Jupiters which, they added, Kennedy had already decided to remove from Turkey. They then immediately contradicted themselves by admitting that the secrecy surrounding the Jupiter part of the deal was necessary because any leak 'would have had explosive and destructive effects on the security of the U.S. and its allies'.[85] Sorensen later testified that Rusk had suggested that the USSR be requested to keep any Jupiters deal secret. When Robert Kennedy's book revealed the secret deal, Sorensen, as editor, removed any references to the deal.[86]

The ExComm myth

> The Senators are good men, but the Senate is an evil beast.
>
> (Roman maxim)

The Kennedy administration's national security policy was determined in a very specific environment, what French sociologist Pierre Bourdieu termed the *habitus* (the social networks where a given world view translates knowledge into cognition by means of a particular mind set).[87] This, on occasion, lends itself to the phenomenon known as *Groupthink*. In the Kennedy administration, the *habitus* of the policy-making elite was constructed from the socio-political architecture of Cold War America: Ivy League schools, West Point, the national security state, think tanks, and the US Congress. In this environment the decision-making processes of the leaders of Washington's Cold War strategy was formulated and implemented.[88] The men JFK recruited as 'the best and the brightest' were the human products of an intellectual military-industrial complex of the mind. As Michael Howard noted of one of ExComm's notables:

> Bundy writes as an insider; one close to the Truman administration, intimately involved with the Kennedy and Johnson administrations,

a trusted consultant to President Carter. He observed decision-making at close hand – not just during the Cuban missile crisis – and though he never obtrudes his own experience, he clearly has a visceral understanding of what is involved, which gives his work peculiar authority.[89]

In addition to never losing sight of *who* exactly is writing any given piece of history, it is important to understand the nature of the evidence being presented. In 1953, Harold Macmillan (then a government minister) noted of Cabinet minutes:

> Historians reading this fifty or a hundred years hence will get a totally false picture … [finding] the Cabinet … so intellectually disciplined that they argued each issue methodically and intellectually through to a set of neat and precise conclusions. It isn't like that at all.[90]

This was precisely the impression that one gets, however, if one reads Sorensen and Schlesinger's accounts of ExComm meetings, where Camelot's Knights of the Round Table deployed their collective wisdom. RFK made ExComm sound like an Ivy League history seminar, claiming that the President had selected 'people who raised questions, who criticized, on whose judgment he could rely, who presented an intelligent point of view, regardless of their rank or viewpoint'.[91] McNamara later identified the ExComm as crucial to avoiding war,[92] but the depiction of the ExComm by many of its former members was not wholly accurate. Powers found the discussions banal and pedestrian with 'none of the intellectual rigour of proper debate'. The 'alleged brilliance of these men David Halberstam once called "the best and the brightest" is rarely in evidence'.[93]

'The best and the brightest' sought to portray themselves as voices of sanity, faced with military hawks eager for the initiation of a nuclear war by timetable.[94] But the ExComm tapes revealed that 'the best and the brightest' were, almost without exception, readier than their President to risk nuclear war. General Maxwell Taylor, Chairman of the Joint Chiefs in 1962, later expressed the view that

> during the EXCOM discussions, I never heard an expression of fear of nuclear escalation on the part of any of my colleagues. If at any time we were sitting in the edge of Armageddon, as nonparticipants have sometimes alleged, we were too unobservant to notice it.[95]

Those members of ExComm who favoured a hard line against the Soviets typified the political elite in Washington at this time. After the President had briefed Congressional leaders about the Soviet missiles in Cuba he told Schlesinger: 'when you get a group of senators together, they are always dominated by the man who takes the boldest and strongest line.'

This observation caused Morgenthau to recall the salience of the Roman maxim which held that '[t]he Senators are good men, but the Senate is an evil beast'.[96]

In the face of persistent intransigence from ExComm members, Kennedy eventually imposed his will because he recognised that any military action could easily escalate to a full nuclear exchange.[97] In demonstrating the President's moderation in the ExComm, the archival record partly accords with the accounts of Sorensen and Schlesinger. But the authors of the 1982 'confession' omitted one detail: most of the ExComm had opposed the Jupiters' deal (especially RFK, Bundy and McNamara).[98] The ExComm tapes make it abundantly clear that RFK's attempt to portray himself as the dove par excellence was a dishonest historical invention. Indeed, even if he confessed to a fear of JFK being cast as another Tōjō, RFK demonstrated considerable ingenuity in seeking a pretext to attack Cuba, asking if there was 'some other way we can get involved ... through Guantánamo Bay or ... some ship ... [and possibly even] sink the *Maine* again'.[99] In spite of such outbursts, the myth of RFK as a dove was repeatedly endorsed over an extended period by the influential figure of Arthur Schlesinger.[100] In truth, Adlai Stevenson, US ambassador to the United Nations, was alone in consistently pursuing a 'dove-ish' line in the ExComm although JFK, with typical ruthlessness, encouraged his friends in the press to portray Stevenson as an 'appeaser' who wanted to secure another 'Munich' by trading the Cuban for the Turkish missiles.[101]

Between 1987 and 1992, the historiography of the crisis was driven forward by critical oral history conferences. While these provided a number of new insights, certain of their participants were able to reinforce the narratives established by the first wave of informed assessments of the crisis (often comprising their own writings). On occasion participants were obliged to revise their versions of the past, but such dramatic shifts were rare. After the first conference in Hawk's Cay, Florida, in 1987, Schlesinger recorded that he was 'struck ... with special force [by] JFK's absolute determination to avoid a military confrontation'.[102] McNamara's public insistence that there was not going to be war in 1962 was challenged by historians who deployed McNamara's own words from the ExComm against him. McNamara nevertheless stood his ground.[103] During the Moscow conference in 1989, McNamara continued to downplay the risk of war in October 1962 and found support for his position from Sorensen and Bundy. This caused another participant, Pierre Salinger (Kennedy's press secretary), to write of his 'disappointment [that] ... some of the participants seemed to judge the events of 1962 from the perspective of the cooled political climate of 1989 détente'.[104] McNamara himself recalls that, by 1989, it was clear that misinformation and misperception meant that the crisis had been very dangerous indeed. Naturally, that was in line with what he (and the President) had thought at the time. When, at the 1992 Havana conference it was revealed that the Soviets had a large number of operational nuclear weapons in Cuba, McNamara was alarmed after Castro confirmed that, had the US invaded, 'I believe [the Soviets] would have used tactical nuclear weapons'. From this, McNamara derived what he later termed the 'most important substantive lesson' of the crisis: 'The indefinite combination of human fallibility and nuclear weapons carries a very high risk of potential nuclear catastrophe.'[105]

Camelot's critics

I think that no episode, perhaps, in modern history has been more misleading than that of the Munich conference. It has given many people the idea that never must one attempt to make any sort of polit- ical accommodation in any circumstances.

(George Kennan)[106]

Force is the only thing the Russians understand.

(President Harry S. Truman)[107]

Kennedy's opponents, naturally, rejected the heroic version of events over Cuba peddled by the White House's propaganda machine. The notion that Khrushchev had out-manoeuvred Kennedy in October 1962, rapidly became a conservative article of faith. US military superiority, especially in nuclear armaments, meant that Moscow would have backed down if only Kennedy had kept his nerve. In 1972 Richard M. Nixon opined that during 'the Cuban missile crisis, [a war] would have been "no contest", because we had a ten to one superiority [in nuclear weapons]'.[108] General Alexander Haig, later Nixon's White House Chief of Staff, believed that: 'The legend of the eyeball to eyeball confrontation invented by Kennedy's men paid a handsome political dividend. But the Kennedy-Khrushchev deal was a deplorable error resulting in political havoc and human suffer- ing through the Americas.'[109] For Haig, the

loss of the Jupiters represented a significant reduction in Turkish national security – not only in terms of the missiles themselves, but because their disassembly symbolized a loss of American will to defend a NATO ally.... The removal of the Jupiters, which protected Europe, in return for the removal of the Soviet missiles in Cuba, which pro- tected the U.S., would certainly be seen as proof that Washington ... put the safety of its own people above that of its allies.[110]

Senator Barry Goldwater (R-AZ), later crushed by Lyndon Johnson in the 1964 presidential election, charged that Kennedy had deliberately engineered the crisis so as to gain advantage in the mid-term elections of November 1962.[111] The defeated Republican candidate in California's gubernatorial election, Richard Nixon, stated that the missile crisis had lost him the election.[112] Goldwater lamented that 'We locked Castro's communism into Latin America and threw away the key to its removal' as Kennedy engaged in 'appeasement' and 'surrender[ed]' to Soviet 'blackmail'. William F. Buckley, the doyen of all right-thinking Americans, complained that Kennedy had killed the Monroe Doctrine of 1823 stone dead.[113] And, from within the administration itself, Assistant Secretary of Defense Paul Nitze thought that Kennedy should have used the missile crisis to get Moscow 'to give up its efforts to establish Soviet influence in this hemisphere'.[114]

On 19 October 1962 USAF Chief of Staff, Curtis LeMay, had stormed: 'This blockade and political action I see leading into war. I don't see any other solution for it. It will lead right into war. This is almost as bad as the appeasement at Munich.'[115] Even after Khrushchev accepted Kennedy's proposals on 28 October, LeMay stated: 'The Soviets may make a charade of withdrawal and keep some weapons in Cuba.'[116] When the crisis was over LeMay told a stunned Kennedy to his face that: 'We have been had. It's the greatest defeat in our history. We should invade today.'[117] In short, LeMay's view echoed Churchill's verdict on Munich: too much had been sacrificed to buy a short-term peace.

Lessons?

In 2012, on the fiftieth anniversary of the crisis, Graham Allison reflected

> that history does not repeat itself, but it does sometimes rhyme ... the Cuban missile crisis stands not just as a pivotal moment in the history of the Cold War but also as a guide for how to make sound decisions about foreign policy.[118]

If we accept that the formulation of any theory involves the extraction of the *universal* from the *specific*, does the Cuban missile crisis provide any real guide for the twenty-first century? If it does is this because it acts as a guide to statesmanship or to the diplomatic-strategic art of crisis management?[119] Clausewitz advised that:

> Theory exists so that one need not start afresh each time sorting out the material and plowing through it, but will find it ready to hand and in good order. It is meant to educate the mind of the future commander, or, more accurately, to guide him in his self-education, not to accompany him to the battlefield; just as a wise teacher guides and stimulates a young man's intellectual development, but is careful not to lead him by the hand for the rest of his life.[120]

When assessing the events of October 1962 it is difficult to disagree with Barton Bernstein:

> there is serious reason to doubt whether generalizations from that crisis period would fit more normal times and situations in ... efforts to construct conceptual frameworks to understand decision making. The missile crisis embodied an important uniqueness: the concentrated period, and the sense of peril and possible disaster.[121]

The notion of learning from history is difficult (and dangerous when it comes to nuclear crisis management). Bundy insisted that the best way forward 'was not how to [avoid war] and "manage" a grave crisis, but how important it is not to have one [in the first place]'.[122] Alas, the necessity of avoiding confrontation became overshadowed by an insistence on standing tall during periods of tension. This notion of Kennedy having prevailed by virtue of a policy of strength embedded itself in policy-making processes and in political discourses generally. It persists to this day: recently with regard to the Iranian nuclear threat.[123] (Although Kennedy often employed the rhetoric of unyielding resolution to mask uncertainty or caution).[124] Michael Dobbs has noted the damaging effect of the legend of the President facing down Khrushchev.

> The 'eyeball to eyeball' imagery made for great drama (it features in the 2000 movie '13 Days'), but it has contributed to some of our most disastrous foreign policy decisions, from ... the Vietnam War under Johnson to the invasion of Iraq under George W. Bush. If this were merely an academic debate, it would not matter very much. Unfortunately, the myth has become a touchstone of toughness by which presidents are measured.[125]

Schlesinger sought to issue correctives to the image of Kennedy as hardliner. In 1995, he wrote that

> Noam Chomsky seems to have the idea that Kennedy was a macho, victory-at-any-cost type. In fact, he was cautious and not inclined to make heavy investments in lost causes. His presidency was marked precisely by his capacity to *refuse* escalation – as in Laos, the Bay of Pigs, the Berlin Crisis of 1961, and the Cuban missile crisis.[126]

Lyndon Johnson's aides, alas, embraced the propaganda about crisis management and strategy – with disastrous results in Vietnam. Clark M. Clifford, who succeeded McNamara in 1968, noted that Bundy *et al.* were 'possessed [of] a misplaced belief that American power could not be successfully challenged, no matter what the circumstances, anywhere in the world'.[127] The real lesson of the Cuban missile crisis was that nuclear superiority was of limited utility. As Kenneth Waltz noted, power, in whatever form, did not mean that one can get one's way all of the time.[128] Elite opinion in Washington and Moscow thus (gradually) embraced détente from 1962 onwards.[129] The new stability in the international system in Europe was born of a new Superpower community of interest over Berlin, Germany and the nuclear issue.[130] The catalyst for this development was the crisis in Cuba.

Historical truth and political legend

> Every generation needs to know that without JFK the world might no longer exist as a result of a nuclear holocaust stemming from the Cuban Missile Crisis.
>
> (Theodore C. Sorensen)[131]

> Churchill once said that the politician always thinks only of the next election, but that the statesman thinks of the next generation. Dr Adenauer is a great politician.
>
> (Thomas Dehler)[132]

Kennedy was a politician who wanted to look like a statesman in order to be a more successful politician. He was not exceptional in this regard. The traditional view of the crisis in Cuba made Kennedy a historical giant, a 'great man' in Thomas Carlyle's now discredited term.[133] Acheson was closer to the truth when he attributed the outcome of the crisis to 'plain, dumb luck'.[134] Kennedy himself feared that his reputation would be tarnished through scholarly revelation and Ben Bradlee later recalled that, soon after the crisis, Kennedy denounced historians as 'bastards ... always there with their pencils out'. Nevertheless, as Sheldon Stern asserts, the ExComm tapes demonstrate that Kennedy had 'succeeded to a remarkable degree – although not without some "help" from Khrushchev and some genuine luck'.[135] Luck was given less prominence in ExComm-ite memoirs. George Ball asserted that, regardless of

> the views of the academic second-guessers as to how the affair should have been handled – and they have not been reticent – I ... [think] that under John F. Kennedy's firm leadership we gave a superior performance ... arguing out all available courses of action in an intellectual interchange that was the most objective I [have] ever witnessed in government.

McNamara meanwhile opined that the Cuban missile crisis was 'the "best managed" crisis of the last half of the century, but we were very lucky as well'.[136] Stern is of the opinion that if 'the crisis could have been "rerun," say 100 times, nuclear war would surely have occurred in many of those reruns. Nobody really "managed" the Cuban missile crisis. That's the greatest myth of all.'[137]

Powers notes that, in the first week of the crisis, Kennedy made only two substantive decisions. But they were vital. First, the Soviet missiles in Cuba were intolerable. Second, he would state this publicly before taking any action. 'If Kennedy had blustered but done nothing, or if he had blown the missiles and their Soviet crews sky-high in a sneak attack, all sorts of horrors might have followed.' Instead, his actions provide a 'salutary example of intelligent statesmanship'.

> Kennedy did not live to write his account of the lessons learned from the Cuban missile crisis, but it would probably have sounded very much like the sort of thing marriage counsellors say every day to marriage partners at the breaking point: leave your anger in the office, decide what you want, if you want to make up, say so; if it's over, say that; draw the line and make it clear, set your limits, stick to your guns – all those common-sense things.[138]

In February 1989, Pierre Salinger trenchantly observed that:

> One thing is clear. Neither side "won" the Cuban missile crisis. Rather, two leaders reached an understanding that nuclear war was unthinkable. And the rapid evolution of relations after the crisis demonstrates that both leaders wanted to work toward a better understanding.[139]

That neither the crisis in Cuba nor the confrontation in Berlin (the latter judged by some to be the more dangerous)[140] did not lead to war was more down to good fortune rather than the crisis management of the Superpowers.[141] Indeed, the underestimate of Soviet forces in Cuba in 1962, allied to the pressures for a military solution, meant that the US was far closer to war with the USSR than the Kennedy administration knew at the time.[142] The very real possibility of nuclear war had, nevertheless, been manifestly obvious to all. This prompted demands for a fundamental reappraisal of the perils of the nuclear age. In 1963, Walter Lippmann wrote:

> There are a good many people in the West who do not understand the nuclear age, and they are forever charging us with appeasement because we do not brandish the nuclear bomb in all our controversies with the Soviet Union. But prudence in seeking not to drive your opponent into a corner is not weakness and softness and appeasement. It is sanity and common sense and a due regard for human life.[143]

The crisis demonstrated to McNamara that US nuclear superiority was 'not such that it could be translated into usable military power to support political objectives' while Rusk observed: 'The simple fact is that nuclear power does not translate into usable political influence.'[144] Given that Kennedy, in January 1963, had told Congressional leaders that '[a]ny action they take in Berlin we can take … in Cuba',[145] it seemed that the only option was to pursue the path of negotiation. By this juncture, as Robert Jervis has noted, the fear of being labelled an 'appeaser' was increasingly being offset by fears of nuclear war.[146] The pursuit of détente, so Kennedy's admirers insist, would surely have been the Holy Grail of Kennedy's second term. This was reflected in his rhetoric: 'in the final analysis, our most basic common link is that we all inhabit this small planet. We all breathe the same air. We all cherish our children's future.'[147] Early in 1963, Schlesinger asserted that 'one main reason why the world has changed and we seem in some respects to have moved beyond the Cold War is precisely because of the initiatives JFK took after the missile crisis'.[148] The Cuban missile crisis stands as Kennedy's monument in history, a reminder to the world that, in the international politics of the nuclear age, what doesn't kill you makes you stronger.

In the years following Kennedy's assassination, the ExComm memoirists performed an explicitly political role through their construction of the recent past. This was designed to bolster the Kennedy legend and, as such, was not unprecedented. Julius Caesar's account of the conquest of Gaul,[149] and Churchill's memoir of the Second World War were both written with an explicit agenda. In the case of the latter, this was especially true of Churchill's first volume of memoirs, *The Gathering Storm*, which mounted a robust assault on the Appeasement of the 1930s.[150] Scholarly nuances were overlooked and the popular view that Churchill had been right about Appeasement, just as Kennedy had been right about the missiles in Cuba, swept all before them as these respective narratives instantly established hegemonic status. In the missile crisis, Sorensen opined that Kennedy had demonstrated 'forethought, precision, [and] subtlety', while Schlesinger hailed a performance that 'dazzled the world' and Robert Kennedy saluted his brother's 'purposefulness and strength'.[151] Such hyperbole had the desired impact. Through their accounts of the Cuban missile crisis, Kennedy's policy-maker/memoirists had successfully constructed a dominant historical narrative. In an interview given on 29 November 1963, the recently widowed Jackie Kennedy told the historian Theodore H. White: 'There'll be great Presidents again … but there'll never be another Camelot.' An emotional White affirmed this, concluding: 'For one brief shining moment there was Camelot.'[152] The insider accounts of the events of October 1962 were hugely influential in perpetuating the image of the Kennedy White House as a modern-day Arthurian court. Quoting W.H. Auden, Sorensen stated of the dead president: 'What he was he was; what he is slated to become depends on us.'[153] Through their construction of the past, Sorensen, Schlesinger, Robert Kennedy *et al.* ensured that the myth of Camelot endures to this day.

Notes

1 John F. Kennedy, *Profiles in Courage* (London: Hamish Hamilton 1965), p. 8.
2 Niccolò Machiavelli, *The Prince*, trans. Peter Bondanella (Oxford: Oxford University Press 2005 [1532]) p. 79.
3 These being either memoirs (*mémoire, memoria*: translated as memory or reminiscence) or autobiography. Memoirs are composed of an individual's writings about moments or events, public and private, from a life. Autobiography tells the story of a life.
4 David Halberstam, *The Best and the Brightest* (New York: Harper & Row 1972).
5 The main books under consideration here being: Arthur M. Schlesinger Jr., *A Thousand Days: John F. Kennedy in the White House* (Boston, MA: Houghton Mifflin Company 1965); Theodore C. Sorensen, *Kennedy* (New York: Harper & Row 1965); Robert F. Kennedy, *Thirteen Days: A Memoir of the Cuban Missile Crisis* (New York: W.W. Norton 1969); McGeorge Bundy, *Danger and Survival: Choices about the Bomb in the First Fifty Years* (New York: Random House 1988).
6 Michael R. Beschloss, *Taking Charge: The Johnson White House Tapes, 1963–1964* (New York: Touchstone 1997) p. 553n.
7 Ted Sorensen, *Counselor: A Life at the Edge of History* (New York: Harper Perennial 2009) p. xvi.
8 Kai Bird, *The Color of Truth, McGeorge and William Bundy: Brothers in Arms* (New York: Touchstone 2000) pp. 245–6.
9 Georg W.F. Hegel, *The Philosophy of History* (New York: Dover 1956 [1837]) p. 6.
10 Michael Howard, 'The Lessons of History', *The History Teacher*, 15/4 (1982) 492.
11 Richard E. Neustadt and Ernest R. May, *Thinking in Time: The Uses of History for Decision Makers* (New York: Free Press 1986) p. 16.
12 Sorensen, *Kennedy*, p. 513; Schlesinger Jr., *A Thousand Days*, p. 832; Kennedy, *Thirteen Days*, p. 62.
13 Sorensen, *Kennedy*, p. 513.
14 Alastair Horne, *Macmillan 1957–1986, Vol. II of the Official Biography* (London: Macmillan 1989) p. 383.
15 Robert S. McNamara, James Blight, Robert K. Brigham with Thomas J. Biersteker, Col. Herbert Schandler, *Argument Without End: In Search of Answers to the Vietnam Tragedy* (New York: Public Affairs 1999) p. 153.
16 Robert Dallek, *Camelot's Court: Inside the Kennedy White House* (New York: Harper 2013) p. 320.
17 Walter Isaacson, *Kissinger: A Biography* (London: Faber and Faber 1992) pp. 115–16.
18 McNamara *et al.*, *Argument Without End*, p. 153; ExComm meeting, 11.10 a.m., 18 October 1962. Ernest R. May and Philip D. Zelikow (eds), *The Kennedy Tapes: Inside the White House during the Cuban Missile Crisis* (New York: W.W. Norton 2002) p. 79.
19 Arthur Schlesinger Jr., 'On the Inscrutability of History', *Encounter*, 27/5 (1966) 13.
20 Robert S. McNamara, with Brian VanDeMark, *In Retrospect: The Tragedy and Lessons of Vietnam* (New York: Vintage 1996) p. 96.
21 Kennedy, *Thirteen Days*, p. 105; Schlesinger Jr., *A Thousand Days*, pp. 711–12; McNamara, *In Retrospect*, p. 96; McNamara *et al.*, *Argument Without End*, p. 153.
22 Kennedy, *Thirteen Days*, p. 30.
23 Barbara Tuchman, *The Guns of August* (London: Robinson 2000 [1962]) p. 321. The book which supposedly inspired Wilhelm II was originally published as A.T. Mahan, *The Influence of Sea Power upon History: 1660–1783* (Boston, MA: Little, Brown and Company 1890).

24 John Keegan, 'Servant of a Theory', *The Spectator*, 16 November 2002.

25 Jordan Michael Smith, 'Did a Mistake Save the World?' *Boston Globe*, 21 October 2012.

26 Fritz Fischer, *Griff nach der Weltmacht: Die Kriegzielpolitik des kaiserlichen Deutsch-land 1914–1918* (Düsseldorf: Droste 1961). This book, arguing for German war guilt, was published in English in 1967.

27 Marc Trachtenberg, *History and Strategy* (Princeton, NJ: Princeton University Press 1991) p. 50.

28 Thomas Powers, 'And after We've Struck Cuba?' (1997) in *Intelligence Wars: American Secret History from Hitler to Al-Qaeda* (New York: New York Review Books 2004) p. 171.

29 Andrew L. Johns, *Vietnam's Second Front: Domestic Politics, the Republican Party, and the War* (Lexington, KY: University Press of Kentucky 2012) p. 21.

30 John F. Kennedy, *Why England Slept* (London: Hutchinson 1940).

31 JFK to Joseph P. Kennedy, 5 December 1940. Martin W. Sandler (ed.), *The Letters of John F. Kennedy* (London: Bloomsbury 2013) p. 15.

32 Kennedy, television and radio interview, 17 December 1962. Sorensen, *Kennedy*, p. 513.

33 Dominic Tierney, ' "Pearl Harbor in Reverse": Moral Analogies in the Cuban Missile Crisis', *Journal of Cold War Studies*, 9/3 (2007) 49–77. On the post-war memory of Munich, see R. Gerald Hughes, 'The Ghosts of Appeasement: Britain and the Legacy of the Munich Agreement', *Journal of Contemporary History*, 48/4 (2013) 688–716.

34 Sheldon M. Stern, *Averting 'The Final Failure': John F. Kennedy and the Secret Cuban Missile Crisis Meetings* (Stanford, CA: Stanford University Press 2003) p. 104.

35 Tierney, ' "Pearl Harbor in Reverse" ', 67.

36 John F. Kennedy Library (JFKL), Boston, MA: Sorensen Papers, box 48. Mem-orandum (TCSPP-048-011), 20 October 1962.

37 Eric Alterman, *When Presidents Lie: A History of Official Deception and Its Con-sequences* (New York: Viking 2005) p. 109.

38 Dean Rusk, by contrast, warned that the manner in which the British, French and Israelis had brushed legal considerations aside over Suez in 1956 had greatly undermined their cause. The US had done the same over the Bay of Pigs in 1961. For Rusk: 'The legal case was very important.' Dean Rusk, as told to Richard Rusk, *As I Saw It* (London: Penguin 1991) p. 233. Bobby Kennedy later dismissed Rusk's role in the crisis, stating: 'he would leave these important meetings deciding whether the world was going to blow up ... to meet with some ambassador or tend to some other function or go to dinner.... He really took the easy course.' JFKL: Boston, MA: Oral History Program (OHP): RFK (8), interview by Arthur Schlesinger Jr., Washington, DC, 27 February 1965, pp. 605–6. Rusk later noted: 'The emotion [of the ExComm] portrayed by Bobby Kennedy in his book *The Thirteen Days* [*sic*] ... was unique to Bobby.' Rusk, *As I Saw It*, p. 231.

39 Schlesinger Jr., *A Thousand Days*, p. 380.

40 Bird, *The Color of Truth*, p. 246.

41 Ernest R. May, *The Making of the Monroe Doctrine* (Cambridge, MA: Harvard University Press 1975).

42 Rhodri Jeffreys-Jones, *The CIA and American Democracy* (New Haven, CT: Yale University Press 1989) p. 136.

43 Stern, *Averting 'The Final Failure'*, p. 26.

44 Department of State, *Bulletin*, XLVII/1213, 24 September 1962, 450. Read to news correspondents on 4 September by Pierre Salinger, White House Press Secretary.

45 The CIA intelligence estimate of 19 September judged it very unlikely that the

Soviets would introduce offensive weapons into Cuba. 'The Military Buildup in Cuba', CIA SNIE 85-3-62, 19 September 1962.

46 Russell D. Buhite, 'From Kennedy to Nixon: the end of consensus' in Gordon Martel (ed.), *American Foreign Relations Reconsidered: 1890–1993* (London: Routledge 2002) p. 131.

47 Schlesinger Jr., *A Thousand Days*, pp. 211–41; Sorensen, *Kennedy*, pp. 324–44. Sorensen noted that while Kennedy had got a 'political black eye' over the Bay of Pigs, failure on 27 October 1962 would have 'far graver consequences.' Sorensen, *Counselor*, p. 5.

48 Letter to Joseph S. Clark, 5 January 1971. Arthur Schlesinger Jr., *The Letters of Arthur Schlesinger, Jr.*, edited by Andrew and Stephen Schlesinger (New York: Random House 2013) p. 403.

49 Sorensen, *Kennedy*, p. 309.

50 Seymour M. Hersh, *The Dark Side of Camelot* (London: HarperCollins 1998) p. 208.

51 Hedley Donovan, *Roosevelt to Reagan: A Reporter's Encounters with Nine Presidents* (New York: Harper & Row 1985) p. 77.

52 Allen Dulles, *The Craft of Intelligence* (London: Weidenfeld and Nicolson 1963) p. 167.

53 A recent example being Tim Weiner's appalling *Legacy of Ashes: The History of the CIA* (New York: Doubleday 2008) pp. 217–39.

54 Ronald Reagan, *An American Life* (New York: Simon and Schuster 1990) p. 472.

55 Michael Grow, *US Presidents and Latin American Interventions: Pursuing Regime Change in the Cold War* (Lawrence, KS: University of Kansas Press 2008) p. 42; Howard Jones, *The Bay of Pigs* (Oxford/New York: Oxford University Press 2008) p. 129; Richard M. Bissell Jr., *Reflections of a Cold Warrior: From Yalta to the Bay of Pigs* (New Haven, CT: Yale University Press 1996) p. 201.

56 James G. Hershberg, 'Before "The Missiles of October": Did Kennedy Plan a Military Strike against Cuba?', *Diplomatic History*, 14/2 (1990) 163–98.

57 Richard J. Aldrich, 'CIA History as a Cold War Battleground: The Forgotten First Wave of Agency Narratives' in Christopher Moran and Christopher Murphy (eds), *Framing Intelligence History: The Historiography of British and American Secret Services since 1945* (Edinburgh: Edinburgh University Press 2012) p. 36. Schlesinger insisted that any 'contingency planning' emanated from the Pentagon, not the White House.

58 José M. Hernández, *Cuba and the United States: Intervention and Militarism, 1868–1933* (Austin, TX: University of Texas Press 1993); Louis A. Pérez Jr., *Cuba in the American Imagination: Metaphor and the Imperial Ethos* (Chapel Hill, NC: University of North Carolina Press 2008).

59 George W. Ball, *The Past Has Another Pattern: Memoirs* (New York: W.W. Norton 1982) p. 177.

60 Memorandum No. 4, Cuba Study Group to President Kennedy, 13 June 1961. Department of State, *Foreign Relations of the United States [FRUS], 1961–1963, Vol. X, Cuba, 1961–1962*, www.state.gov/www/about_state/history/frusX/226_235.html (last accessed 27 September 2014).

61 Powers, 'And after We've Struck Cuba?' pp. 228–9. For a lenient view of the Kennedys here, see Lawrence Freedman, *Kennedy's Wars: Berlin, Cuba, Laos and Vietnam* (Oxford: Oxford University Press 2000) pp. 150–2.

62 Christopher Andrew and Vasili Mitrokhin, *The World Was Going Our Way: The KGB and the Battle for the Third World* (New York: Basic 2005) pp. 18, 30.

63 Gerald R. Ford Library, Ann Arbor, MI: 'Minutes of Meeting of the Special Group (Augmented) on Operation MONGOOSE', 4 October 1962. This document was provided to the Ford administration as part of the President's commission on CIA activities in 1975. It was declassified in 1997.

64 Letters to John McCone, 7 January 1976 and Bill Moyers, 5 July 1977. *The Letters of Arthur Schlesinger, Jr.*, pp. 436–7, 450–2.

65 Fidel Castro, with Ignacio Ramonet (trans. Andrew Hurley), *My Life* (London: Allen Lane 2007) pp. 591–2, 709n.

66 On the secret negotiations between JFK and Castro, see William M. LeoGrande and Peter Kornbluh, *Back Channel to Cuba: The Hidden History of Negotiations between Washington and Havana* (Chapel Hill, NC: University of North Carolina Press 2014) pp. 42–78.

67 Stephen G. Rabe, 'John F. Kennedy and the World' in James N. Giglio and Stephen G. Rabe, *Debating the Kennedy Presidency* (Lanham, MD: Rowman & Littlefield 2003) p. 45.

68 McNamara *et al.*, *Argument Without End*, p. 215. Bundy reiterates his point in *Danger and Survival*, p. 416.

69 JFKL: Sorensen Papers, Box 49. TCSPP-049–002. Bundy, Memo for JFK, 'Future Policy toward Cuba', 30 November 1962 (circulated to ExComm).

70 Sheldon M. Stern: personal email exchange with the author, 17 September 2014.

71 Ronald Steel, *Walter Lippmann and the American Century* (Boston, MA: Atlantic Monthly Press/Little, Brown 1980) p. 536.

72 Olaf Hansen, *Aesthetic Individualism and Practical Intellect: American Allegory in Emerson, Thoreau, Adams, and James* (Princeton, NJ: Princeton University Press 1990) p. 87.

73 Sheldon M. Stern, *The Cuban Missile Crisis in American Memory: Myths versus Reality* (Stanford, CA: Stanford University Press 2012) p. 4.

74 Peter J. Ling, *John F. Kennedy* (London: Routledge 2013) p. 147.

75 R. Gerald Hughes, ' "In the Final Analysis, It Is Their War": Britain, the United States and South Vietnam in 1963' in R. Gerald Hughes, Peter Jackson and Len Scott (eds), *Exploring Intelligence Archives: Enquiries into the Secret State* (London: Routledge 2008) pp. 204–6. For a refutation of JFK mythology, see Diane Kunz, 'Camelot Continued: What if John F. Kennedy had lived?' in Niall Ferguson (ed.), *Virtual History: Alternatives and Counterfactuals* (London: Picador 1997) pp. 368–91.

76 Schlesinger Jr., *A Thousand Days*, p. 716.

77 Hans J. Morgenthau, 'Monuments to the Late President' (January 1966), in *Truth and Power: Essays of a Decade* (New York: Praeger 1970) p. 157.

78 Devin O. Pendas, 'Testimony' in Miriam Dobson and Benjamin Ziemann (eds), *Reading Primary Sources: The Interpretation of Texts from Nineteenth- and Twentieth-century History* (London: Routledge 2009) p. 227.

79 Alterman, *When Presidents Lie*, pp. 90–159.

80 *Bundy, Danger and Survival*, p. 434. Bundy also misled his readers by ignoring his own opposition to the missile trade.

81 Journal entry for 28 October 1962. Arthur Schlesinger Jr., *Journals: 1952–2000*, edited by Andrew and Stephen Schlesinger (New York: Penguin 2007) p. 177.

82 The Freedom of Information Act (FOIA) was signed into law by LBJ on 4 July 1966. R. Gerald Hughes and Len Scott, ' "Knowledge Is Never Too Dear": Exploring Intelligence Archives' in Hughes, Jackson and Scott (eds), *Exploring Intelligence Archives*, p. 18.

83 Alterman, *When Presidents Lie*, pp. 101–2.

84 Arthur M. Schlesinger Jr., *Robert Kennedy and His Times* (London: Futura 1979 [1978]) p. 564.

85 Dean Rusk, Robert McNamara, George W. Ball, Roswell L. Gilpatric, Theodore Sorensen and McGeorge Bundy, 'The Lessons of the Cuban Missile Crisis', *Time*, 27 September 1982.

86 Bruce J. Allyn, James G. Blight and David A. Welch (eds), *Back to the Brink:*

Proceedings of the Moscow Conference on the Cuban Missile Crisis, January 27–28, 1989 (Lanham, MD: University Press of America 1992) pp. 92–3.

87 Pierre Bourdieu with Loïc Wacquant, *Réponses: Pour une anthropologie réflexive* (Paris: Seuil 1992) p. 103. On culture and Bourdieu as an explanatory tool, see Peter Jackson, 'Pierre Bourdieu, the "Cultural Turn" and the Practice of International History', *Review of International Studies*, 34/1 (2008) 155–81. See also Akira Iriye, 'Culture and International History' in Michael J. Hogan and Thomas G. Paterson (eds), *Explaining the History of American Foreign Relations*, second edn (Cambridge: Cambridge University Press 2004) pp. 241–56.

88 On the institutional and historical roots of the ExComm, see David R. Gibson, *Talk at the Brink: Deliberation and Decision during the Cuban Missile Crisis* (Princeton, NJ: Princeton University Press 2012) pp. 49–53.

89 Michael Howard, 'Nuclear Danger and Nuclear History', *International Security*, 14/1 (1989) 176–7.

90 Hughes and Scott, ' "Knowledge Is Never Too Dear" ', p. 26. On Macmillan and the use and abuse of history, see Peter Catterall, 'Prime Minster and President: Harold Macmillan's Accounts of the Cuban Missile Crisis', this volume.

91 Kennedy, *Thirteen Days*, p. 117.

92 McNamara *et al.*, *Argument Without End*, p. 396.

93 Powers, 'And after We've Struck Cuba?' p. 178

94 Gen. Maxwell D. Taylor, *Swords and Plowshares: A Memoir* (New York: Da Capo 1972) pp. 268–9.

95 Maxwell D. Taylor, 'Reflections on a Grim October', *The Washington Post*, 5 October 1982.

96 Morgenthau, 'Monuments to the Late President', pp. 158–9.

97 See, for example, Kennedy's altercation with Nitze over the issue of ensuring that the JCS had briefed US personnel in Turkey not to fire the Jupiter missiles, even if attacked, without a direct presidential order. Stern, *Averting 'The Final Failure'*, pp. 144–6.

98 Ironically, JFK's main allies here were LBJ and McCone – hardly his close friends. Barton J. Bernstein, 'Understanding Decisionmaking, U.S. Foreign Policy, and the Cuban Missile Crisis', *International Security*, 25/1 (2000) 159–60.

99 ExComm meeting 6.30 p.m., 16 October 1962. May and Zelikow (eds), *The Kennedy Tapes*, p. 68. The mysterious explosion that sank the battleship USS *Maine* in Havana harbour on 15 February 1898 had a decisively negative impact on US public opinion of Spain. Ivan Musicant, *Empire by Default: The Spanish-American War and the Dawn of the American Century* (New York: Henry Holt 1998) pp. 151–2.

100 Stern, *The Cuban Missile Crisis in American Memory*, pp. 32–53; letters to the *New York Times*, 29 August 1964 and the *New Republic*, 29 September 1964. *The Letters of Arthur Schlesinger, Jr.*, pp. 278, 286; Schlesinger Jr., *Robert Kennedy and His Times*, p. 573; journal entry for 13 November 1983. Schlesinger Jr., *Journals*, p. 557.

101 David Kaiser, *American Tragedy: Kennedy, Johnson, and the Origins of the Vietnam War* (Cambridge, MA: Harvard University Press 2000) p. 148.

102 Schlesinger Jr., journal entry for 24 March 1987. *Journals*, p. 631.

103 Deborah Shapley, *Promise and Power: The Life and Times of Robert McNamara* (Boston: MA: Little, Brown and Company 1993) pp. 183–5.

104 Pierre Salinger, 'Gaps in the Cuban Missile Crisis Story', *New York Times*, 5 February 1989.

105 McNamara *et al.*, *Argument Without End*, pp. 9–11. Quotes at p. 11.

106 Yuen Foong Khong, *Analogies at War: Korea, Munich, Dien Bien Phu, and the Vietnam Decisions of 1965* (Princeton, NJ: Princeton University Press 1992) p. 174.

107 G.W. Sand (ed.), *Defending the West: The Truman-Churchill Correspondence, 1945–1960* (Westport, CT: Praeger 2004) p. 152.

108 Francis J. Gavin, *Nuclear Statecraft: History and Strategy in America's Atomic Age* (Ithaca, NY/London: Cornell University Press 2012) p. 111.

109 Humberto Fontova, *Fidel: Hollywood's Favorite Tyrant* (Washington DC: Regnery Publishing 2005) p. 26.

110 Alexander M. Haig Jr., with Charles McCarry, *Inner Circles: How America Changed the World* (New York: Warner 1992) pp. 102–3.

111 Larry J. Sabato, *The Kennedy Half-Century: The Presidency, Assassination, and Lasting Legacy of John F. Kennedy* (New York: Bloomsbury 2013) p. 273.

112 Matt Lait, 'Looking Back at the 1962 Gubernatorial Race', *Los Angeles Times*, 22 March 1992.

113 Jon Wiener, *How We Forgot The Cold War: A Historical Journey Across America* (Oakland, CA: University of California Press 2012) pp. 220–1.

114 Paul H. Nitze, *From Hiroshima to Glasnost: At the Center of Decision – A Memoir* (London: Weidenfeld and Nicolson 1990) p. 237.

115 JFK meeting with the Joint Chiefs of Staff, 9.45 a.m., 19 October 1962. May and Zelikow (eds), *The Kennedy Tapes*, p. 113; Stern, *The Cuban Missile Crisis in American Memory*, p. 163; Theodore C. Sorensen, 'The Leader Who Led', *New York Times*, 18 October 1997.

116 Aleksandr Fursenko and Timothy Naftali, *'One Hell of a Gamble': Khrushchev, Castro Kennedy, and the Cuban Missile Crisis, 1958–1964* (New York: W.W. Norton 1999) p. 287.

117 Michael R. Beschloss, *The Crisis Years: Kennedy and Khrushchev, 1960–1963* (New York: HarperCollins 1991) pp. 543–4.

118 Graham Allison, 'At 50, the Cuban Missile Crisis as Guide', *New York Times*, 15 June 2012.

119 On crisis management during the Cuban missile crisis, see Gordon A. Craig and Alexander L. George, *Force and Statecraft: Diplomatic Problems of Our Time*, third edn (New York/Oxford: Oxford University Press 1995) pp. 112–15, 202–5, 214–16.

120 Carl von Clausewitz, *On War*, ed. and trans. Michael Howard and Peter Paret (Princeton, NJ: Princeton University Press 1984 [1832]) p. 141.

121 Bernstein, 'Understanding Decisionmaking', p. 144. For similar, with specific reference to diplomacy, see David A. Welch, 'The Cuban Missile Crisis', in Andrew E. Cooper, Jorge Heine and Ramesh Thakur (eds), *The Oxford Handbook of Modern Diplomacy* (Oxford: Oxford University Press 2013) p. 836.

122 Bundy, *Danger and Survival*, p. 462.

123 Bernd Kaussler, *Iran's Nuclear Diplomacy: Power Politics and Conflict Resolution* (Abingdon: Routledge 2014) pp. 2–3, 5.

124 Denise M. Bostdorff and Steven R. Goldzwig, 'Idealism and Pragmatism in American Foreign Policy Rhetoric: The Case of John F. Kennedy and Vietnam', *Presidential Studies Quarterly*, 'Conduct of Foreign Policy', 24/3 (1994) 515–30.

125 Michael Dobbs, 'The Price of a 50-Year Myth', *New York Times*, 15 October 2012.

126 Letter to Herbert Kriedman, 15 May 1995. *The Letters of Arthur Schlesinger, Jr.*, p. 555. Italics in the original. For similar, see Schlesinger's journal entry for 22 November 1988. *Journals*, p. 663.

127 Robert Mann, *A Grand Delusion: America's Descent into Vietnam* (New York: Basic 2001) p. 453.

128 Kenneth Waltz, *Theory of International Politics* (Reading, MA: Addison-Wesley 1979) pp. 191–2.

129 Bundy, *Danger and Survival*, p. 542; Jussi M. Hanhimäki, *The Rise and Fall of*

Détente: American Foreign Policy and the Transformation of the Cold War (Washington, DC: Potomac 2013) pp. 5–10.

130 Andreas Wenger, 'Der lange Weg zur Stabilität: Kennedy, Chruschtschow und das gemeinsame Interesse der Supermächte am Status quo in Europa', *Vierteljahrshefte für Zeitgeschichte*, 46/1 (1998) 69–99.

131 Sorensen, 22 October 2010. Quoted in Sabato, *The Kennedy Half-Century*, p. 422.

132 'Zitate', *Der Spiegel* 25, 20 June 1956.

133 On agents and structures, see Philip Pomper, 'Historians and Individual Agency', *History and Theory*, 35/3 (1996) 281–308.

134 Dean Acheson, 'Homage to Plain Dumb Luck' in Robert A. Devine (ed.), *The Cuban Missile Crisis* (Chicago, IL: Quadrangle 1971) pp. 197–8.

135 Benjamin C. Bradlee, *Conversations with Kennedy* (New York: W.W. Norton 1975) pp. 127–8; Stern, *The Cuban Missile Crisis in American Memory*, p. 158.

136 Ball, *The Past Has Another Pattern*, p. 309; McNamara *et al.*, *Argument Without End*, p. 151.

137 Sheldon M. Stern: personal email exchange with the author, 17 September 2014. On luck, see Benoît Pelopidas, 'We All Lost the "Cuban Missile Crisis": Revisiting Richard Ned Lebow and Janice Gross Stein's Landmark Analysis in *We All Lost the Cold War*', this volume.

138 Powers, 'And after We've Struck Cuba?' pp. 183–4.

139 Salinger, 'Gaps in the Cuban Missile Crisis Story'. For a similar line of argument, see Eckart Conze, 'Konfrontation und Détente: Überlegungen zur historischen Analyse des Ost-West-Konflikts', *Vierteljahrshefte für Zeitgeschichte*, 46/2 (1998) 280.

140 Nitze, *From Hiroshima to Glasnost*, p. 205.

141 Christof Münger, *Die Berliner Mauer, Kennedy und die Kubakrise: Die westliche Allianz in der Zerreißprobe 1961–1963* (Paderborn: Schöningh 2003).

142 Branislav L. Slantchev, *Military Threats: The Costs of Coercion and the Price of Peace* (Cambridge: Cambridge University Press 2011) p. 39.

143 Walter Lippmann, 'Cuba and the Nuclear Risk', *The Atlantic*, 211/2 (1963), 57.

144 Trachtenberg, *History and Strategy*, p. 235.

145 David G. Coleman, *The Fourteenth Day: JFK and the Aftermath of the Cuban Missile Crisis* (New York: W.W. Norton 2012) p. 191.

146 Robert Jervis, *Perception and Misperception in International Politics* (Princeton, NJ: Princeton University Press 1976) p. 224.

147 JFK Commencement Address at American University, 10 June 1963. Jason K. Duncan, *John F. Kennedy: The Spirit of Cold War Liberalism* (New York: Routledge 2014) p. 199. RFK later wrote that, during the crisis, JFK had been preoccupied with the possibility that millions of children would die in the event of war. Robert F. Kennedy, 'Foreword' to John F. Kennedy, *Profiles in Courage*, p. 12.

148 Schlesinger Jr., journal entry for 15 January 1963, *Journals*, p. 334.

149 *Commentarii de Bello Gallico*: Julius Caesar, *The Gallic War: Seven Commentaries on The Gallic War with an Eighth Commentary by Aulus Hirtius*, trans. Carolyn Hammond (Oxford: Oxford University Press 2008). On this, see Josiah Osgood, 'The Pen and the Sword: Writing and Conquest in Caesar's Gaul', *Classical Antiquity*, 28/2 (2009) 328–58.

150 Winston S. Churchill, *The Gathering Storm: The Second World War: Vol. I* (London: Cassell 1948). On this, see R. Gerald Hughes, *The Postwar Legacy of Appeasement: British Foreign Policy since 1945* (London: Bloomsbury 2014) pp. 5–7, 12, 15, 18–19; David Reynolds, *In Command of History: Churchill Fighting and Writing the Second World War* (London: Allen Lane 2004) pp. 67–144;

idem, 'Churchill's Writing of History: Appeasement, Autobiography and *The Gathering Storm*', *Transactions of the Royal Historical Society*, Sixth Series, volume 11 (2001) pp. 221–48.

151 Alterman, *When Presidents Lie*, p. 90.

152 Theodore H. White, 'For President Kennedy: An Epilogue', *Life*, 55/23, 6 December 1963. White later wrote that his words had been intended to comfort Jackie Kennedy and that his piece had resulted from a 'misreading of history'. In truth, White conceded, '[t]he magic Camelot of John F. Kennedy never existed'. Theodore H. White, *In Search of History: A Personal Adventure* (New York: Harper & Row 1978) p. 524.

153 Sorensen, *Counselor*, p. 372.

6 The three puzzles

Essence of Decision and the missile crisis[1]

Don Munton

The 1962 Cuban missile crisis – the most dangerous great power confrontation in human history – is now more than a half-century old. The best-known book on the crisis, Graham Allison's 1971 *Essence of Decision: Explaining the Cuban Missile Crisis* has passed its own fortieth birthday. The book has had an impact few academic books ever have. It is thus an opportune time to assess this pioneering work's contribution to understanding its chosen event.

Essence in essence

Essence of Decision was as provocative as it was praised.[2] From the beginning, it was both an intellectual and popular hit. So universally known is *Essence of Decision* that its very title is regularly punned by other missile crisis writings and by non-missile-crisis books, sometimes without any felt need to cite the original.[3] To place its hit status in perspective, this is a book first published not only 'b4' Amazon.com and Twitter but 'b4' personal computers and the internet. And it sells still.

A striking paradox about *Essence of Decision* (or *Essence*) is that its fame has less to do with what it had to say about the missile crisis itself than with the set of theoretical models used to explain the crisis. The book's organization reflects its emphasis on exploring alternative explanatory theories. It developed three now-familiar models of decision-making – the rational actor, organizational process and governmental (or bureaucratic) politics models. It devotes a chapter to each model (chapters 1, 3 and 5). It is for these models that *Essence* has become universally known and widely cited across the social sciences.

The remaining chapters each examine three 'central puzzles' of the missile crisis: (1) Why did the USSR deploy nuclear missiles to Cuba? (2) Why did the US blockade Cuba? and (3) Why did the USSR withdraw its missiles? In this now-famous mating of models with missiles, exploring the models takes pride of place over telling the story. The even-numbered, substantive chapters (2, 4 and 6) each apply one model to answer all three questions, rather than each chapter focusing on a particular puzzle.

Unlike conventional histories, therefore, it provides largely scattered and brief narratives of crisis events. In the pages of *Essence*, the history of the crisis thus unfolds in bits and starts.

A second paradox concerns the explanatory models in *Essence of Decision*. Allison argues generally that analysts must venture beyond the familiar rational-actor model and employ the organizational and bureaucratic models to arrive at an adequate understanding of events like the Cuban missile crisis.[4] The general argument that the models in our heads influence the conclusions we come to remains unassailable. The utility of the organizational and bureaucratic models, on the other hand, has come into dispute. For these models, the passage of time has been unkind. Familiarity has bred contention. Even sympathetic critics have severely questioned the original models and interpretations.[5] Mounting historical evidence has tended not to bolster the once innovative, even sexy, organizational and bureaucratic models (2 and 3) – as many analysts had expected further evidence would. Rather, evidence on the missile crisis has tended to reinforce the traditional rational-actor model (1). The more we learn about the crisis, in other words, the less support emerges for *Essence's* argument about the value-added quality of the latter two models.[6] What made the book famous has brought it the most controversy.[7]

Many existing appraisals of *Essence of Decision*, even those by historians, emphasize the three models.[8] What follows is therefore a somewhat unconventional treatment.[9] My focus here is on the explanatory puzzles and the answers *Essence* provides to those puzzles, rather than on the famous models. This focus on explanations of the crisis and conclusions about its events will involve confronting the changing interpretations of crisis events and exploring the interaction between established notions and recently discovered facts.

One of the most central of contemporary missile crisis debates concerns the agreement John Kennedy and Nikita Khrushchev reached in resolving the missile crisis and the role of a secret concession the President made to withdraw American Jupiter missiles from Turkey. About both the agreement and the concession much more will be said here. I also raise some additional questions about the missile crisis beyond *Essence's* now-holy trinity of puzzles.

The 1999 second edition of *Essence of Decision*, co-authored by Allison and Philip Zelikow (hereafter *Essence2*), employs the same three models, addresses the same three puzzles and follows the same basic format as the original (with one significant exception).[10] The answers to all three puzzles in *Essence2*, however, differ in some respects from those of the first edition. Moreover, the changes do not all always parallel the evolution of the literature.

The present chapter focuses on the substantive conclusions of both editions – on the historical accounts and explanations provided. It is nevertheless not a direct or point-by-point comparison of the two editions.[11]

I assume readers have some familiarity with both the crisis and at least one edition of the book.

Historiographical stages

It helps contextualize both editions of *Essence of Decision* if we identify four more-or-less consecutive but overlapping stages of missile crisis research. The first consisted largely of 1960s memoirs and popular history, broadly defined, all of them American voices. The most prominent of these were Robert F. Kennedy's *Thirteen Days*, Theodore Sorensen's *Kennedy*, Roger Hilsman's *To Move a Nation*, Arthur Schlesinger's *A Thousand Days*,[12] and journalist Elie Abel's *The Missile Crisis*.[13]

The 1971 publication of *Essence of Decision* (hereafter *Essence*1) opened the second stage, one of serious scholarly research. Allison based his missile crisis chapters on the secondary literature (for example, both the RFK and Abel books) and extensive, apparently confidential, interviews (not individually referenced). *Essence*1 established a new orthodoxy on the crisis but soon prompted some critics. Two of these, Donald Hafner and Barton Bernstein, focussed on the same issue, the Jupiter missiles in Turkey, an issue to which Allison refers but one he does not emphasize.[14]

A surging tide of declassified documents, the release of secret White House tape recordings, and a series of participant-expert observer conferences marked the third stage.[15] The John F. Kennedy Presidential Library (JFKL) began releasing material in the late 1970s and continued that process apace through the 1980s and 1990s.[16] Of particular interest, it released fully 22 hours of hitherto secret White House tape recordings relating to the missile crisis – albeit slowly, over 14 years.[17] The US National Archives, the Central Intelligence Agency and the British National Archives (as it is now known) followed suit with documents.[18] The private National Security Archive secured release of many US materials. The Cold War International History Project provided a key outlet.[19]

The fourth and most recent stage is heavily represented by international (i.e. non-US) perspectives and by re-evaluations and refinements, based partly on stage three disclosures. The volumes here include important contributions from Soviet, Cuban, British and European as well as American analysts, as well as the second edition of *Essence of Decision*.[20] The current scene is, in short, a more varied and crowded one than when the original edition of *Essence* emerged, but one from which a significant consensus has emerged on many key issues.

In *Essence*2, Allison and Zelikow themselves state they make use 'of *all* information in the public record' (p. xiii, emphasis added). On most subjects, that would normally pose a challenge. On this subject, at this point in time, given the now vast and detailed missile crisis literature, it is an unrealistic claim.

Deploying the missiles: going for advantage in Berlin?

As Robert McNamara later asked, in effect rephrasing the first of *Essence's* three puzzles, 'What in God's name did Khrushchev think he was doing?'[21] Early analysts and missile crisis participants alike, implicitly engaging in rational-actor analysis, commonly inferred three Soviet motives for sending ballistic missiles to Cuba: (1) to narrow the US advantage in long-range strategic missiles, (2) to use the missiles in Cuba to strengthen the Soviet position in a divided Berlin, and (3) to help defend Cuba.

Allison and Zelikow argue Khrushchev deployed medium range R-12 ballistic missiles to Cuba, and tried to deploy intermediate-range R-14 missiles, to bolster Soviet strategic capability and to gain leverage for a favourable solution on Berlin (*Essence2*, p. 107). Virtually all experts accept the former explanation as one goal if not the primary goal. Virtually none subscribes to the supposed Berlin motive, as described.[22]

In the early 1960s Washington and Moscow both perceived Berlin as a key Cold War problem. In 1961 the Soviets and East Germans had begun constructing the soon-to-be-famous wall to seal off West Berlin. In October, amidst rising tensions, Soviet and US forces directly confronted each other at 'Checkpoint Charlie', the major crossing-point between east and west. The forces involved were conventional although they included armed battle tanks. The stand-off ended after a few days and without shots fired. The wall would survive for almost another three decades without another similar confrontation.

Berlin was thus in the minds of US officials pondering Moscow's moves and motives in October 1962. But Washington suspicions do not prove a Kremlin motive. As logical as perceived links seemed at the time, only circumstantial evidence suggests Berlin was a motive in the Cuba deployment.[23] A half-century on, that's 'slim pickens'. On the other hand, key Soviet participants in the oral history conferences argued Moscow decision-makers made no such link.[24]

Having said that, a case can be made that there might still have been an indirect connection. A successful deployment of missiles to Cuba, one which the US was forced to accept, would have greatly enhanced Soviet prestige globally and dealt a significant blow to American prestige. In that sense, it would have better positioned Nikita Khrushchev to force a resolution of the Berlin problem more favourable to the USSR. Thus, while such a breakthrough on Berlin was not Khrushchev's main goal in deploying missiles to Cuba, the two situations could have been linked, had the deployment been successful.[25]

Deploying the missiles: defence of Cuba

Allison and Zelikow acknowledge Khrushchev was worried about losing communist Cuba (*Essence2*, p. 84) and had 'ample basis for suspicion' that the US would invade the island and overthrow Castro (*Essence*2, pp. 84–5). Indeed, they allow that this threat was always 'in the background'. Nevertheless, they still insist defending Cuba was not a significant Soviet motive for the deployment.

The authors of *Essence*2 mount various arguments against the defence of Cuba idea. All seem unpersuasive. They make much of two facts: that President John Kennedy (hereafter also JFK) told Soviet Foreign Minister Andrei Gromyko during a mid-October 1962 meeting that the United States was not planning to invade Cuba, and that Gromyko did not report Kennedy's assurances to Moscow (*Essence*2, p. 108). Gromyko's oversight, such as it was, however, does not prove Cuba's fate was unimportant to Nikita Khrushchev.

Two considerations lessen the significance of JFK's comment to Gromyko. The President had already made a similar statement in September. Moreover, when he repeated it in October, he immediately retracted any implied promise. The situation had changed, he told Gromyko, because the Soviets were now building up Cuba's military capability.[26] The President's statement was thus actually more threat than assurance. More importantly, no Kennedy assurance in October could have alleviated Soviet concerns about Cuba's security at the time Khrushchev ordered the missile deployment – fully six months earlier.

*Essence*2 also argues that the defence of Cuba explanation is inconsistent with the nature and number of missiles sent. Nuclear missiles were not 'necessary', say Allison and Zelikow, and certainly not so many of them (*Essence*2, pp. 86–8, 108–9). No metric exists however to calculate the forces 'required' to ensure deterrence. Moreover, whether or not a chosen action is 'optimal' is 'completely irrelevant' to explaining decisions.[27]

Allison and Zelikow further argue that the Soviet deployment of short-range, tactical nuclear weapons would not and could not have deterred an American invasion because Washington was unaware they were in Cuba (*Essence*2, p. 209). Hence, Cuban security was not Moscow's concern. The logic here is simply invalid. Had the crisis unfolded as Khrushchev hoped, had the USSR completed and announced the full deployments in November as planned, then the tactical missiles might very well have helped deter an American invasion. Moscow's original motives cannot be assessed *ex post facto*, according to the way events unexpectedly unfolded months later.

Various critics of the 'defence of Cuba' theme also argue that, however much ballistic missiles might have deterred a US attack, they would not have helped 'defend' Cuba. This general deterrence argument assumes, incorrectly, that Soviet thinking then rested on the deterrence–defence distinction as much as did American strategic thought.[28] The same argument does not apply at all to the tactical nuclear weapons. Their capability militarily was defensive, as was that of Soviet ground troops sent to Cuba.

Defending Cuba is widely and reasonably now regarded as a primary Khrushchev goal for the deployment.[29] Support for this motive grew in recent decades as evidence emerged on extensive US planning for an invasion of Cuba and covert CIA operations against Fidel Castro.[30] Whatever Washington's true intentions, Cuban and Soviet concerns about Cuba's security were more than reasonable.

Blockading Cuba: 'Take 'em out' or 'Talk 'em out'?

The second of the three central questions is 'Why did the United States blockade Cuba?' The rational-actor approach explained Kennedy's decision to blockade Cuba as a compromise response to the missile deployment between two extremes: doing nothing, which would have been politically untenable, and attacking the missile sites or invading Cuba, both of which would have dangerously escalated the conflict.[31] *Essence*1 shows that Kennedy's so-called Executive Committee, or ExComm, came to focus increasingly during the first crisis week on the blockade ('force 'em out') rather than on the air strike ('take 'em out') or full scale invasion ('go in and get 'em out') options.[32]

In a highly interesting and useful departure, Allison and Zelikow argue that the ExComm did not in the end pose establishing a blockade and using or threatening military force as dichotomous alternatives. Rather, the group constructed a more complex set of options: a blockade *and* an ultimatum, on the one hand, versus a blockade *and* negotiating, on the other hand (pp. 119–20).[33] Allison and Zelikow clearly believe the ultimate US response was the former combination, not the latter. Arguably, however, Kennedy's actual response was imposing a blockade, issuing an ultimatum *and* negotiating an agreement.

Most early analyses suggested the negotiating ('talk 'em out') option got short shrift.[34] In fact, negotiating a deal involving the Jupiters in Turkey was neither overlooked nor an afterthought. Nor did it only enter the picture late when Khrushchev raised it on 27 October. The 'friggin' missiles in Turkey figured early and figured often in US crisis thinking. Allison and Zelikow correctly note they were matters of 'constant discussion' (*Essence*2, p. 241). And, contrary to Dean Rusk's claim (*Essence*2, p. 127), the Kennedy administration did not actually reject Khrushchev's proposal regarding the Jupiters on October 27; it only deferred its answer by a day.[35]

*Essence*2 poses the same blockade question as *Essence*1. But it also provides an answer that changes the question itself. The appropriate puzzle to be pursued is not why the President chose a 'blockade' but why he chose the combination of responses he did. Making that conceptual shift, in turn, raises the question of how negotiation played out as part of the combination of responses.

Withdrawing the missiles: caving in to threat?

Why did the Soviet Union withdraw the missiles? (*Essence*2, p. 78). According to Allison and Zelikow, 'the blockade did not change Khrushchev's mind. Only when coupled with the threat of further action ... did it succeed in *forcing* Soviet withdrawal of the missiles.' In actual fact, the necessary factor was 'the *threat of the air strike or invasion*' (*Essence*2, p. 128, emphases added). One might quibble with the wording here – John Kennedy did not specifically make any threats, publicly or even privately to the Soviets, about possible air strikes or an invasion. But the American military preparations were not hidden and the Soviets presumably used their imaginations as to the further action Kennedy might take. The thrust of the *Essence*2 argument, however, is that US threats, per se, more or less alone, *forced* Khrushchev to withdraw the missiles from Cuba.

That explanation is at least debatable. First of all, the blockade itself was not irrelevant. It did affect Khrushchev's thinking. When he learned Kennedy had scheduled a televised address for 22 October, the Soviet leader initially feared the President might order an immediate military attack. The announced blockade signalled American resolve and made clear to Khrushchev he had misjudged Washington's reaction to the missiles, but also suggested to him that the US might be willing to deal. Moreover, the effective naval blockade, coupled with the interception of all Soviet submarines in the area, underscored the US conventional military advantage in the Atlantic and Caribbean.[36] The blockade also stopped the entire shipment of intermediate-range R-14 missiles. This was arguably the point in time at which Khrushchev began to realize there was no real alternative to withdrawal, short of risking Cuba and nuclear war. Realizing one has to change one's position is distinct from changing it, but is a critical start psychologically. Arguably, then, the blockade *did begin* to change Khrushchev's mind.

Second, there is little evidence that Khrushchev himself dwelt as much on the specific possibilities of an air strike or invasion as on other, broader consequences. There is an abundance of evidence that he thought deeply about and feared an uncontrolled escalation and a resulting nuclear war (e.g. *Essence*2, pp. 355, 362). Khrushchev, to be sure, had dramatic evidence of possible escalation: a 27 October attack on an American U-2 spy plane, Cuban forces firing on low-level unarmed US reconnaissance aircraft, other US planes violating Soviet airspace, and Castro apparently urging a pre-emptive nuclear strike. The fact that unauthorized action by Khrushchev's own troops brought down the U-2 only emphasized the dangers. Beyond specific threats to Cuba therefore was the threat of nuclear catastrophe, arguably his overriding concern.

Forty years ago, Graham Allison suggested that both Kennedy and Khrushchev sought a peaceful solution, recognizing the need to avoid 'the final failure', as the American President called it.[37] 'This nuclear crisis',

Allison observed, 'seems to have magnified both rulers' conceptions of the consequences of nuclear war, and each man's awareness of his responsibility for these consequences' (*Essence*1, p. 212). Allison's analysis would later be confirmed by documentary evidence and oral testimony. The two men felt accountable 'to humanity as a whole, not solely to their respective national interests [or] personal political fortunes'.[38] Their mutual sense of personal responsibility was eloquently summed up by Khrushchev. 'We don't have the right to take risks', he told an associate at the height of the crisis. 'We now have a common cause, to save the world from those pushing us toward war.'[39]

To be sure, Khrushchev's own thinking shifted during 1962, from wanting, as he said, to 'drop a hedgehog' down the Americans' pants to extending a helping hand. The shift is reflected in another comment he made, about his ally, Castro. Fidel was 'a very hot-tempered person', Khrushchev said, one who 'failed to think through the obvious consequences of a proposal that placed the planet on the brink of extinction'.[40] The same could be said of Khrushchev himself, before 22 October 1962. He then saw the quicksand into which he was walking, reconsidered his poorly conceived deployment decision, and backed out before becoming stuck. John Kennedy's thinking also shifted dramatically during late October, from assuming he had no choice but attacking Cuba to making a politically dangerous deal.

Arguably, then, the missile crisis did not end by military threat alone. Khrushchev, boxed in, needed a formula for retreat with which he could live. If he had not received acceptable terms, things might well have ended differently. Kennedy brandished the stick *and* offered a carrot (*Essence*2, p. 385). His response to the deployment was not just a blockade and threats of further action but also informal negotiation. An agreement was negotiated rapidly, only partially put to paper, and never signed, let alone ratified. It was an agreement nevertheless. Its written part was Kennedy's conditional pledge to end the blockade and eschew an invasion of Cuba. Khrushchev publicly promised to withdraw the missiles and later the IL-28 bombers. The secret part was a Kennedy concession on the Jupiter missiles. The so-called 'missile trade' was really a mutual missile withdrawal pact. Our understanding of this accord has evolved and deepened, as some background will show.

Ordering the Jupiter missiles removed from Turkey

According to Elie Abel, Kennedy was surprised during the missile crisis to discover that American Jupiter missiles were still in Turkey. He 'distinctly remembered' ordering them removed. Robert Kennedy's *Thirteen Days* made a similar but slightly more nuanced claim.[41] In *Essence*1, Graham Allison hypothesized that Washington bureaucracies must have frustrated the president's removal order.[42] Later writers picked up this version of events. For those seeking evidence of bureaucratic politics, it was a veritable Krupp Diamond.

Only it was not. Within a few years, and before official documents became available, Donald Hafner brilliantly shredded this myth.[43] Based on public material and the secondary literature, Hafner used Kennedy's own words and actions to show the president knew very well before and during the missile crisis that the Jupiters remained in Turkey as of October 1962. Hafner also inferred there had been no withdrawal order (prior to October); he was correct but lacked direct evidence on this point and his reasoning was debatable.[44]

We know now that there was in fact no pre-crisis presidential directive. And thus no bureaucratic politics obstructed a presidential directive. Take that, Model 3. To be sure, Kennedy had directed his officials to explore ways to remove the Jupiters, and he did 'want them gone'.[45] He did not however explicitly *order* the missiles withdrawn – at least not before 28 October 1962.[46]

The Jupiter directive myth has proven difficult to shake off, and to see for what it was. Did some White House aides, including Robert Kennedy, 'forget' and 'garble' the story (*Essence2*, pp. 252–3, n. 116)? Perhaps, but that is surely being too kind. While some aides may have honestly believed that story, others who knew the truth consciously sought to spin history, including RFK. President Kennedy's men were hardly the first in history to spin events for political reasons – or the last.

A deal or not a deal? That was the question

Even as the missile crisis dust was still settling, public speculation arose that its abrupt and unexpected end suggested some sort of secret deal with the Soviet devil.[47] The New Frontiersmen denied this rumour with all the 'vigah' they could muster. Jack Kennedy, they insisted, had done no such thing. Dean Rusk and Robert McNamara so testified under oath to Congress.[48] US officials also told NATO allies the same story. They were, for the most part, believed.

The fact Robert Kennedy and Soviet ambassador Anatoly Dobrynin held secret discussions during the missile crisis become public knowledge in 1966 from Abel's book. That volume however makes no mention of the Jupiters being discussed. Cracks in the storyline nevertheless soon appeared with the posthumous publication in 1969 of RFK's *Thirteen Days*.

Washington observers could not help but notice it showed Bobby telling Dobrynin during their now famous meeting of 27 October that the President would remove the Jupiters from Turkey. Prior to the release of *Thirteen Days*, 'both admirers and critics [had] assumed that President Kennedy had been wholly unresponsive on the Turkish missiles'.[49] RFK's account thus surprised both groups. For different reasons, the account challenged fundamental beliefs. For admirers, it undermined the image of

JFK's 'unwavering firmness'. For critics, it shook their conviction that he had engaged in 'unforgivable risk taking'.

In retrospect, a most interesting but overlooked feature of the 1971 edition of *Essence of Decision* was its treatment of the Jupiter issue. Allison notes RFK's claim that he told Dobrynin 'there could be no *quid pro quo*', no deal involving the Jupiters of the sort Khrushchev proposed earlier that day. But Allison also argues that *Thirteen Days* 'discloses important, confirming evidence' of such a deal; indeed, it '*could not have been plainer*' (*Essence*1, 229–30; emphasis added). In effect, there *was* a quid pro quo. The Kennedy brothers offered up the Jupiters for the R-12s.

Allison's speculation here was sound. In *Thirteen Days*, RFK assures Dobrynin that JFK wanted the missiles removed, and soon after the crisis, 'those missiles *would be gone*'.[50] If this were all RFK had actually said to Dobrynin, it would still have conveyed a clear message: assuming Khrushchev withdrew his ballistic missiles, the President of the United States was committing himself to removing the Jupiters.

The first edition of Nikita Khrushchev's memoirs, published in the US in 1970, was silent on the Jupiter concession. The 1974 edition, published posthumously, briefly describes the deal.[51] This edition garnered less attention, however; Khrushchev's revelation was largely ignored. Andrei Gromyko similarly wrote about the arrangement, citing *Thirteen Days*.[52] Before that the allies broke the silence. Fidel Castro spoke about the deal in the late 1960s and Turkey's Prime Minister publicly acknowledged it in 1970.[53]

In 1980, historian Barton Bernstein argued the case for an explicit Kennedy–Khrushchev agreement. Based on some declassified JFKL documents he concluded the President 'privately offered a hedged promise … to withdraw the Jupiter missiles'.[54]

Two years later, on the twentieth anniversary of the missile crisis, six high-level Kennedy administration officials revised the record. But only modestly. They acknowledged that RFK indeed gave the Soviets an 'explicit' (not implicit), private 'assurance': the President would remove the Jupiters. They nevertheless insisted he had made no 'deal' involving 'our missiles in Turkey for theirs in Cuba'.[55] This is, frankly, political semantics: what American officials may have seen as merely an 'explicit assurance' was for the Soviets, and unbiased observers, an important offer that became part of an agreement.

In 1989, Theodore Sorensen made a 'confession' to the Moscow oral history conference.[56] The *Thirteen Days* account, he said, did not faithfully render the Kennedy–Dobrynin meeting. Indeed, it was not how Robert Kennedy himself had described the discussion. As the book's ghost 'editor', Sorensen had taken it upon himself to alter RFK's wording.[57] The original notes were 'very explicit' said Sorensen. Removing the missiles 'was part of the *deal*'.[58]

Dobrynin himself recalled that RFK had portrayed the Jupiters as a significant concession.[59] Sorensen's revised version matches closely

Dobrynin's telegram to Moscow that fateful evening (and corroborates Khrushchev and Gromyko). The ambassador's account is widely considered reliable.

Whatever the value added in Sorensen's confession, it was a significant reversal of the public position traditionally taken by Kennedy administration officials. All had long remained loyal to a common pledge to maintain the secret. As McGeorge Bundy eventually acknowledged: 'We denied in every forum that there was any deal ... we misled our colleagues, our countrymen [*sic*], our successors, and our allies.'[60]

Despite these revelations, *Essence*2 offers a decidedly more ambivalent take on the Jupiter issue than the 1971 edition, a view at variance with the mounting evidence.[61] Allison and Zelikow accept that RFK made an 'offer' (*Essence*2, pp. 129, 361) but simultaneously cast doubt by referring to 'the offer on the Jupiters, *such as it was* ...' (*Essence*2, p. 129, emphasis added). They also quote and seem to accept McGeorge Bundy's 1988 version of the RFK–Dobrynin meeting – one that describes something less than a clear offer.[62] They oddly refer to John Kennedy's 27 October 'Trollope Ploy' letter, which ignored Khrushchev's Jupiter proposal, as the President's 'final move' (*Essence*2, p. 363), thereby relegating to a sort of limbo Kennedy's later response on the Jupiters. *Essence*2 also misleadingly suggests the Jupiter matter was handled subsequent to the crisis 'through NATO' (pp. 365–6). In fact, the NATO Council eschewed a formal decision on withdrawal of the Jupiters from Turkey and Italy on the grounds that the countries concerned had already settled the matter. More generally, *Essence*2 plays down both the public and secret offers as factors in resolving the crisis (e.g. p. 242). I return to this latter point below.

Allison and Zelikow make little to nothing of the two fall-back options Kennedy initiated in the event Khrushchev rejected the secret Jupiter offer. One option was to arrange a public trade under the auspices of the United Nations Acting Secretary General.[63] The other, less well formed, was to call a NATO meeting for Monday 29 October to discuss the Jupiters.[64] Since neither back-up plan proved necessary, their historical importance is easily overlooked. These plans, however, are highly significant. They demonstrate President Kennedy's commitment to including the Jupiters in the overall agreement and his willingness to take large political risks to do so.

The conventional wisdom has always been that obtaining Turkey's agreement to decommissioning the Jupiters during the crisis would have been extremely difficult, if not politically impossible (*Essence*2, pp. 242, 352). New evidence suggests otherwise: at least some Turkish officials were amenable in late October 1962 to such a withdrawal. Space constraints here prohibit details, but a senior Turkish foreign ministry figure informed a NATO ally directly on 25 October that the government could probably accept a Jupiter deal.[65] Moreover, some Kennedy administration officials likely obtained this information by 27 October, before Robert

Kennedy left for his fateful meeting with Dobrynin. If so, it was perhaps a key factor behind the secret offer. A change in Turkish thinking also may help explain aspects of the ExComm discussion that day and explain why Ankara so quickly and readily accepted the US Jupiter decommissioning post-crisis.[66]

Assessments commonly note that the Cuban crisis led directly to the so-called 'Hot Line' agreement and to the partial nuclear test ban. Observers disagree on whether the causal factor was a crisis-reinforced fear of nuclear confrontation or a crisis-induced sense of possible Superpower cooperation. It was likely both. What most assessments overlook is that the crisis also led to, indeed featured, its own arms agreement.[67] This pact comprised both a limited mutual withdrawal from allied territory of offensive nuclear missiles, and an implicit understanding eschewing future deployments. So thoroughly overlooked is this pact that it lacks a name.[68] It was nevertheless the first-ever nuclear arms reduction agreement.

Withdrawing the missiles: making the other Berlin connection

Where did the idea originate for a secret Jupiter side-agreement? Some observers point to a telegram from the US ambassador in Ankara (*Essence*2, p. 252, note 114). But there was an earlier historical precedent – a secret Kennedy–Khrushchev agreement that resolved the 1961 Berlin tank stand-off.

In October 1961 President Kennedy asked his brother to pass to Moscow a secret message about the Berlin tank stand-off, using a back-channel contact at the Soviet embassy in Washington. JFK proposed a mutual and staged withdrawal of the tanks facing each other at the Wall.[69] If Khrushchev would remove his tanks, US forces would follow. Khrushchev agreed, the tanks pulled back, and the crisis quickly evaporated. By extraordinary coincidence, John Kennedy made this proposal exactly a year to the day before he asked Robert to convey another message – the secret offer to withdraw US missiles in Turkey.

The Checkpoint Charlie deal and the Jupiter part of the missile crisis agreement have some striking parallels. Both aimed to defuse tense East–West confrontations, both comprised mutual arrangements with an initial Soviet withdrawal followed by an American one, both employed informal channels and oral rather than written assurances and, tellingly, both were done secretly. The 1961 agreement, really a 'tank withdrawal' accord, was thus a precedent for the 1962 agreement on withdrawing missiles from Cuba and Turkey. Did the earlier accord consciously serve as a model for the Kennedy brothers and Nikita Khrushchev in October 1962? The parallels would have been hard to miss.

Withdrawing the missiles: the role of the Jupiters

However ambivalent *Essence2* is on the nature of the Jupiter 'offer' (or promise, or assurance), the book is crystal clear on the impact the offer had. According to *Essence2*, it had none. Dobrynin's overnight cable arrived on 28 October after Khrushchev had already told the Presidium meeting they should withdraw the missiles and accept Kennedy's non-invasion pledge (*Essence2*, pp. 129, 349, 363).[70] Kennedy's offer therefore came too late to influence Khrushchev's 'decision' to dismantle and 'crate' the R-12s.[71]

It is tempting to dismiss Kennedy's Jupiter offer simply because of this timing – but too easy to do so. The offer may well have affected the Presidium meeting and its formal decision. And it was not unimportant to Soviet policy-makers.

To begin with, Khrushchev first told his Presidium colleagues he was willing to dismantle the missiles in Cuba not on 28 October but on 25 October (*Essence2*, p. 349), three days prior. In what sense, then, had Khrushchev 'decided'?

As his letters to Kennedy suggest, Khrushchev changed his mind more than once during the three day interim, not about withdrawal per se, but about the conditions under which he would withdraw.[72] If he had by then made an unconditional decision to withdraw, he could have simply, unilaterally, announced that decision. The fact he did not simply order a retreat on 25, 26 or 27 October suggests he was still deciding what US commitments would comprise an acceptable bargain. He had heard the US threats. But he had also discerned in Kennedy's letters an American willingness to talk. Khrushchev's behaviour during those days was that of a man in search of a deal; he was trying to 'haggle'.[73]

Events on Saturday 27 October certainly deeply worried Khrushchev, in particular the anti-aircraft missile attack on the unarmed U-2 spy plane. His own forces had fired first, contrary to orders. So far, surprisingly, the US had not retaliated. It was time to call off the haggling and cut the best deal possible. Khrushchev was nevertheless quite willing to receive an improved offer.

Second, the Presidium did know about the Dobrynin telegram, containing both RFK's warning and the Jupiter offer, before making its final decision. Allison and Zelikow say Dobrynin's telegram affected the mood of the meeting (*Essence2*, p. 362) but still insist the secret offer had no impact.[74] McGeorge Bundy, who had opposed any such Jupiter offer, up to the end, and who thus has every reason to minimize its importance, acknowledges that 'no one can say for certain that this additional concession, so small in one sense, did not have its own importance in the speed and clarity of Khrushchev's final and best decision'.[75]

Third, can we simply assume that the actual R-12 missile withdrawal, let alone Moscow's later withdrawal of tactical nuclear weapons, would have necessarily proceeded as they did in the absence of an agreement the terms of which were acceptable to Khrushchev and his colleagues? Many observers did not expect Khrushchev to live up to his promise, and it was perhaps as surprising that he had immediately implemented the promise as that he made the promise itself. Successful negotiations are those that not only 'get to yes' but also get implemented by both sides. And policy decisions do not always lead directly to implementing actions – as we know from a considerable literature, including both editions of *Essence.*

Whatever its influence on Soviet decision-making on 28 October, Kennedy's offer on the Jupiters and their actual withdrawal became integral to the deal – for both sides. For its part, Washington proceeded to dismantle, indeed destroy, the obsolete Jupiter missiles with considerable dispatch, even uncharacteristic zeal.[76] Khrushchev too, of course, quickly withdrew not only the MRBMs but also, more secretly, his nuclear-armed, short-range missiles. The political value of the deal to Khrushchev was obvious, allowing him to declare victory of sorts.[77] His letter to Kennedy the following day highlighted the secret provision quite deliberately. In the 1970s and then again at the 1989 Moscow conference, Andrei Gromyko indicated Moscow always regarded the Jupiter withdrawal as key to the crisis resolution.[78] And the Soviets never re-deployed land-based nuclear missiles to Cuba.[79]

Posing other questions

Consider the timing of *Essence*'s three puzzles: Khrushchev's deployment decision came in April 1962 with the deployment itself occurring May–October 1962; Kennedy and the ExComm debated the blockade decision from 16 to 21 October; and Moscow approved the R-12 withdrawal on 28 October. The 'blockade' is the only American decision here; none of the puzzles deals with US decisions during the entire second week of October – a crucial period. Nor do any of the puzzles relate to decisions during subsequent weeks and months.

We cannot understand the crisis fully without understanding the two leaders' decisions to negotiate and conclude the agreement that resolved the crisis. As John Lewis Gaddis emphasizes, Kennedy as well as Khrushchev 'made some big concessions in the interests of peace'.[80] That some parts of their agreement were public and one part was kept secret only increases the intrinsic importance of at least one additional puzzle: *Why did the leaders negotiate the agreement they did?* That question has of course been at least partly addressed in the discussion here.

Other questions arise from perhaps the most sacred of missile crisis-related historical cows – the lingering but wrong-headed notion that the crisis lasted but thirteen days. This framing of events began with the administration and publication of RFK's *Thirteen Days* itself and continued in the more recent movie of the same title. The notion that the crisis ended on or around 28 October is implicit in the term Cubans still use the 'October crisis' and the phrase 'the missiles of October'. The thirteen-days idea is still found in recent writings.[81] And it remains a feature of *Essence*2, from page 1 ('those thirteen days of October 1962'), to its reproduction of the October 1962 calendar, to later references (*Essence*2, pp. 77, 327, 366). This myth was challenged long ago; it is time to discard it fully.[82]

Conceptualizing the crisis as lasting thirteen days blinkers us to important questions about events before 16 October as well as events in November and beyond. One question concerns the so-called 'photo gap' – why there was a dangerous delay in obtaining hard intelligence on the missile sites under construction in Cuba.[83] If we extend the crisis period into November and December we might well ask: *Why did Khrushchev withdraw Soviet tactical nuclear weapons from Cuba?* Whether or not American threats explain his decision to withdraw the MRBMs (a point debated earlier) in late October, such threats cannot explain the much later withdrawal of the tactical nuclear missiles. The US intelligence community was late identifying the tactical weapons in Cuba and never confirmed their nuclear capability.[84] By the time Khrushchev quietly ordered them out, in December, Kennedy's threats of late October were no more. Khrushchev's removal of these missiles therefore makes more sense in terms of complying fully with the spirit as well as letter of his agreement with Kennedy.

Another puzzle: *Why was Kennedy willing to permit a substantial (but conventional) Soviet military presence in post-crisis Cuba?* Essentially this is a question about the largely domestic political risks of having both nuclear-capable fighter-bombers and large numbers of Soviet troops remain in Cuba. It also includes the continued presence of advanced surface to air missiles (SAMs), which posed a military threat to American U2 flights in the months after the missile crisis. This puzzle is largely neglected and not yet well explained.[85]

Conclusion

The early literature on the Cuban missile crisis includes Eli Abel's *The Missile Crisis* and Robert Kennedy's *Thirteen Days* as well as the first edition of *Essence of Decision*. The myths about the crisis that emerged from this early literature were numerous and some quite profound.

Longstanding myths about the missile crisis include the idea that Kennedy had ordered US missiles withdrawn from Turkey prior to the crisis, that threats of force and superior American military capabilities 'forced' Soviet missiles out of Cuba, that 'talking 'em out' (negotiating with Khrushchev) was never a serious consideration, and that Kennedy made no deal to end the crisis. *Essence*1 and *Thirteen Days* helped propagate and perpetuate these myths. More recent contributions such as *'One Hell of a Gamble'* helped to dispel some of these myths.

The 1971 edition of *Essence* also argued strongly for examining the crisis from the organizational and bureaucratic politics perspectives as well as, if not more than, from the rational-actor perspective. The considerable historical evidence compiled in stages two and three of missile crisis research has generally not supported the idea that intra-governmental factors influenced missile crisis decisions. Indeed, the evidence has pointed elsewhere. (*Essence2* simply omitted the discussion from *Essence1*, which had applied bureaucratic politics to explaining the first puzzle – the Soviet missile deployment; but little or no evidence had emerged since 1971 to substantiate what had been an engaging but speculative discussion).[86] To be sure, the missile crisis qua crisis was arguably strongly biased against the organizational process and bureaucratic politics models.

The bulk of more recent evidence emphasizes the role of leaders and their calculations in answering the three famous puzzles. I thus question aspects of *Essence2*'s conclusions on all three central puzzles: its emphasis on a supposed 'Berlin' motive for the missile deployment and its rejection of the 'defence of Cuba' motive; its reformulation of the US response to the deployment; and its inattention to the Khrushchev–Kennedy agreement as a factor in resolving the crisis.

The two leaders did trade threats, but then traded offers. Kennedy made a significant concession, to dismantle the Jupiters. The agreement he and Khrushchev constructed in the end was informal but vital, and is still often overlooked. The Jupiter concession was kept secret, although arguably not kept as secret for as long as scholars often assume. Resolution of the crisis was 'much more of a draw than a US victory'.[87]

Essence2 does not so much dispute these points as betray a decided ambivalence toward them, or at least some of them. It surely does not – as claimed – consider 'all' of the available evidence. More importantly, it does not adequately incorporate certain now well-accepted, key facts. In particular, it relegates the secret Jupiter concession and the Kennedy–Khrushchev agreement to near irrelevance.

The missile crisis was not only a tough case for the organizational and bureaucratic models but a much less than perfect fit for the Realist form of the rational-actor model. Both Khrushchev and Kennedy pursued objectives that were neither concrete nor in the lasting national interest, and certainly not all objectively given ones. The available evidence makes clear that both leaders reformulated their perceptions and goals during October 1962, did so fundamentally, and did so in ways that departed from the preferences of close advisors. The two leaders had fears but also listened, learned and changed. Where does that observation lead? Suffice it to say here, the missile crisis may be a rewarding and rich case for a fruitful marriage of rational-actor, cognitive and constructivist approaches.

What if John Kennedy had publicly revealed and then defended the *entire* missile crisis agreement with Nikita Khrushchev, including the Jupiter concession? Had he done so, Kennedy would have challenged and might have dented a core Western belief – that the Cold War must be waged by arming heavily and 'standing up to the communist threat'. Keeping the concession secret facilitated the myths that there had been 'no deal' and that the US had simply forced Moscow to back down. These myths bolstered Kennedy's presidency but also powerfully reinforced that core belief about waging the Cold War.

Whatever the actual impact of the Kennedy–Khrushchev agreement on the crisis's outcome, the mere fact they were able to reach an agreement amidst those tensions is highly significant. That fact, and the accord's viability, both illustrate that surviving the Cold War was not ultimately about ideology or threats or military power, let alone nuclear weapons. It was about empathizing and about constructing common interests. To their credit, both leaders soon followed up – Khrushchev advocating Superpower arms control even as the crisis was winding down and Kennedy advocating 'a strategy of peace' in a June 1963 commencement address. By then, however, neither man had much time left to pursue the new vision.

Notes

1 This chapter is a revised version of an article originally published in *International Relations* in 2012: developed from 'Hits and Myths: The Essence, the Puzzles and the Missile Crisis', *International Relations*, 26/3 (2012) 305–25. Reproduced by permission of Sage Publications Ltd. My debts in this work go back far and extend to many, especially Denis Stairs, Kim Richard Nossal, Len Scott, David Welch and countless former students who suffered class exposure to missile crisis fever. I am also indebted to Miriam Matejova, for her perceptive comments on a draft.

2 Graham Allison, *Essence of Decision: Explaining the Cuban Missile Crisis* (Boston: Little, Brown and Company 1971) [henceforth *Essence*].

3 Bruce J. Allyn, James G. Blight and David A. Welch, 'Essence of Revision: Moscow, Havana, and the Cuban Missile Crisis', *International Security*, 14/3 (Winter 1989–1990) 136–72; David Patrick Houghton, 'Essence of Excision: A Critique of the New Version of *Essence of Decision*', *Security Studies*, 10/1 (Fall 2000) 151–78; Patricia McMahon, *Essence of Indecision* (Kingston and Montreal: McGill-Queens 2009).

4 For the authors' own summary conclusions on the three models, see Graham Allison and Philip Zelikow, *Essence of Decision: Explaining the Cuban Missile Crisis* (New York: Longman 1999). [henceforth *Essence2*] pp. 380–3, 387.

5 See, for example, David A. Welch, 'The Organizational Process and Bureaucratic Politics Paradigms: Retrospect and Prospect', *International Security*, 17/2 (Fall 1992) 112–46.

6 Ibid; Len Scott and Steve Smith, 'Lessons of October: Historians, Political Scientists, Policy-Makers and the Missile Crisis', *International Affairs*, 70/4 (October 1994) 659–84; Houghton, 'Essence of Excision'.

7 To be fair, the missile crisis was an extraordinarily tough case for showing off the impact of intra-government forces. Crises tend to centralize decision-making, to push leaders to the forefront, and the 1962 crisis did so more than most. Thus, the decks were stacked very substantially against models 2 and 3.

8 For example, Barton J. Bernstein, 'Understanding Decisionmaking, U.S. Foreign Policy, and the Cuban Missile Crisis', *International Security*, 25/1

(Summer 2000) 134–64; Houghton's excellent review focuses on the models and factual errors of *Essence*1, but not much on the 'critical puzzles' per se.

9 The present evaluation is similar in purpose to Allyn, Blight and Welch, 'Essence of Revision'; they focus on key findings of the oral history conferences while the focus here is to answer anew the *Essence* puzzles.

10 Allison and Zelikow, *Essence of Decision.* This version omits applying Model 3 to the first puzzle, the missile deployment.

11 The review article by Houghton, 'Essence of Excision' is such a point-by-point comparison.

12 Robert F. Kennedy (hereafter also RFK or 'Bobby'), *Thirteen Days: A Memoir of the Cuban Missile Crisis* (New York: Norton, 1969); Theodore C. Sorensen, *Kennedy* (New York: Harper and Row 1965); Roger Hilsman, *To Move a Nation* (New York: Doubleday 1967); and Arthur M. Schlesinger Jr., *A Thousand Days* (New York: Fawcett Premier Books 1965).

13 Elie Abel, *The Missile Crisis* (Philadelphia, PA: Lippincott 1966). Abel used extensive interviews and had indirect access to a primary document. RFK personally read to him from a 'black binder' of missile crisis period 'notes'. Sorensen's book also makes use of his own notes of meetings.

14 Donald L. Hafner, 'Bureaucratic Politics and "Those Frigging Missiles"; JFK, Cuba, and U.S. Missiles in Turkey', *Orbis*, 21/2 (Summer 1977) 307–33; Barton J. Bernstein, 'The Cuban Missile Crisis: Trading the Jupiters in Turkey?' *Political Science Quarterly*, 95/1 (Spring 1980) 97–125. See also Barton J. Bernstein, 'Reconsidering the Missile Crisis: Dealing with the Problems of the American Jupiters in Turkey', in James Nathan (ed.) *The Cuban Missile Crisis Revisited* (New York: St Martin's Press 1992) pp. 55–129.

15 James G. Blight and David A. Welch, *On the Brink: Americans and Soviets Reexamine the Cuban Missile Crisis* (New York: Hill and Wang 1989; second edn: Noonday 1990); Bruce J. Allyn, James G. Blight and David A. Welch, *Back to the Brink: Proceedings of the Moscow Conference on the Cuban Missile Crisis, January 27–28, 1989 (Boston,* MA: University Press of America 1992) and James G. Blight, Bruce J. Allyn and David A. Welch, *Cuba on the Brink: Castro, the Missile Crisis and the Soviet Collapse* (New York: Pantheon 1993).

16 Bernstein's article and another by Jocelyn Maynard Ghent ('Canada, the United States, and the Cuban Missile Crisis', *Pacific Historical Review*, 48/2 (May 1979) 159–84) were among the first published studies to use declassified JFKL documents. A survey of JFKL missile-crisis-related files conducted by the present author in 2009 suggested many documents still classified in the 1980s to early 1990s had by then been declassified.

17 Ernest R. May and Philip D. Zelikow (eds), *The Kennedy Tapes: Inside the White House During the Cuban Missile Crisis* (Cambridge, MA: Harvard University Press 1997); Sheldon Stern, *Averting 'The Final Failure': John F. Kennedy and the Secret Cuban Missile Crisis Meetings* (Stanford, CA: Stanford University Press 2003). Stern says the JFKL only acknowledged existence of the Kennedy tapes after the Watergate scandal unearthed Nixon-era White House tapes.

18 Mary S. McAuliffe, *CIA Documents on the Cuban Missile Crisis, 1962* (Washington DC: Central Intelligence Agency 1992); Jane Priestland, *British Archives on the Cuban Missile Crisis 1962* (London: Archival Publications International 2001). Other archives, particularly Canada's National Archive, have been much slower to release relevant material. The documents are, after all, only a half-century old.

19 Laurence Chang and Peter Kornbluh, *The Cuban Missile Crisis, 1962* (New York: The New Press 1992) and *Cold War International History Project Bulletin*, Issue 5 (Spring 1995), www.wilsoncenter.org/publication-series/cwihp-bulletin (last accessed, 4 April 2012).

20 See, for example, Aleksandr Fursenko and Timothy Naftali, *'One Hell of a Gamble': Khrushchev, Castro, and Kennedy, 1958–64* (New York: W.W. Norton 1997); General Anatoli I. Gribkov and General William Y. Smith, *Operation Anadyr: US and Soviet Generals Recount the Cuban Missile Crisis* (Chicago, IL: Edition Q 1994); Anatoli Dobrynin, *In Confidence: Moscow's Ambassador to America's Six Cold War Presidents* (New York: Random House 1995); Carlos Lechuga, *In the Eye of the Storm: Castro, Khrushchev, Kennedy and the Missile Crisis* (Melbourne: Ocean Press 1995); L.V. Scott, *Macmillan, Kennedy and the Cuban Missile Crisis* (London: Macmillan 1999); Philip Nash, *The Other Missiles of October* (Chapel Hill, NC: University of North Carolina Press 1997); Jutta Weldes, *Constructing National Interests: The United States and the Cuban Missile Crisis* (Minneapolis, MN: University of Minnesota Press 1999).

21 Blight and Welch, *On the Brink*, p. 352, n. 3.

22 For what is now the conventional view, see Fursenko and Naftali, *'One Hell of a Gamble'*; John Lewis Gaddis, *We Now Know, Rethinking the Cold War* (Oxford: Oxford University of Press 1997) among others. *Essence*1 also discarded this motive, finding it 'not tenable', p. 46.

23 For an alternative view, albeit one not well supported by evidence, see Jonathan Haslam, *Russia's Cold War* (New Haven, CT: Yale University Press 2010).

24 Blight and Welch, *On the Brink*, p. 327.

25 I am grateful here for comments from Len Scott.

26 Memorandum of Conversation, meeting with Gromyko, Washington, 18 October 1962, #29, *Foreign Relations of the United States [FRUS], 1961–1963, Vol. XI*, https://history.state.gov/historicaldocuments/frus1961-63v11/d29 (last accessed 16 December 2014). For Kennedy's statement in September see *Essence*2, p. 79.

27 Jonathan Bendor and Thomas H. Hammond, 'Rethinking Allison's Models', *American Political Science Review*, 86/2 (June 1992) 306.

28 As General Anatoli Gribkov observes, 'arcane theories of nuclear deterrence mattered less to us' (*Essence*2, p. 99). *Essence*2 does not always maintain the deterrence–defence distinction; for example, it refers to US Polaris submarines being 'committed to Turkey's defense', *Essence*2, p. 114.

29 For a relatively early statement, see Thomas Paterson, 'Commentary: The Defense of Cuba Theme and the Missile Crisis', *Diplomatic History*, 14/2 (Spring 1990) 249–57. An unexplained feature of *Essence*1 is repeated reference (in chapter titles but not in the text) to the missile crisis as 'Cuba II'. The Bay of Pigs invasion was 'Cuba I', p. 47. Linking the 1962 crisis to the 1961 invasion arguably points, at least implicitly, to a continuing invasion threat.

30 James Hershberg, 'Before the "Missiles of October": Did Kennedy Plan a Military Strike against Cuba', *Diplomatic History*, 14/2 (Spring 1990) 163–98; Fursenko and Naftali, *'One Hell of a Gamble'*, chapter 7.

31 Allison never succumbed in *Essence*1 to the common tendency to refer to the 'quarantine', a term coined for the crisis by the State Department legal advisor and widely adopted at the time. The term has not since entered into common usage by other states nor become accepted. The dominant legal opinion now is that the October 1962 blockade was not legal under international law, Don Munton and Elizabeth Rennie, 'The Cuban Missile Crisis', in Rüdiger Wolfrum (ed.) *Max Planck Encyclopedia of Public International Law* (Oxford: Oxford University Press 2011). Allison and Zelikow refer to Soviet ships 'carrying outlawed contraband' (*Essence*2, p. 122). It was the 'quarantine' that was arguably illegal, not the cargo on the ships.

32 Some of this terminology is John Kennedy's own, Sheldon Stern, *The Week the World Stood Still: Inside the Secret Cuban Missile Crisis* (Stanford, CA: Stanford University Press 2005) p. 140. On a minor point, *Essence*2 spells the abbreviation of the group name as 'ExCom' rather than 'ExComm', which has become the

common form and is used here. On a non-serious note, I recall a student in the 1980s being puzzled about a lecture of mine on the missile crisis in which I referred to the option of a US 'air strike'; she bravely and rightly asked why it would have mattered at the time if any airlines had gone on strike.

33 *Essence*2 itself reverts, on occasion, to referring simply to a 'blockade', for example, p. 329.

34 For Allison and Zelikow's summary of the pros and cons of the six alternatives, see *Essence*2, pp. 111–20.

35 Hafner, 'Bureaucratic Politics and "Those Frigging Missiles"'; McGeorge Bundy, *Danger and Survival: Choices about the Bomb in the First Fifty Years* (New York: Random House 1988) p. 445.

36 This is a point made elsewhere in *Essence*2, for example, p. 380.

37 Stern, *Averting 'The Final Failure'*; the 1997 edition of Ernest R. May and Philip D. Zelikow (eds), *The Kennedy Tapes: Inside the White House during the Cuban Missile Crisis* (Cambridge, MA: Harvard University Press 1997), incorrectly transcribed this phrase as 'the prime failure'.

38 Welch, 'The Organizational Process', p. 136. See Blight and Welch, *On the Brink*, especially pp. 319–21.

39 Stern, *The Week the World Stood Still*, p. 195.

40 Quoted by Gaddis, *We Now Know*, p. 277.

41 Abel, *The Missile Crisis*, pp. 191–2. RFK was undoubtedly Abel's source here. In *Thirteen Days*, RFK was actually more careful with his words than later accounts imply: he (or Sorensen as editor) states the President assumed his 'wishes' (not his 'order') regarding the Jupiters would be carried out. RFK also says he told Anatoli Dobrynin his brother 'had ordered their removal some time ago', pp. 108–9. If he did (which Dobrynin disputes) then the statement was surely misleading, unless 'some time ago' could mean earlier that evening when JFK and a few aides agreed to make the Jupiter offer. On the claims of Kennedy aides, see Hafner, 'Bureaucratic Politics and "Those Frigging Missiles"', 309–14. The political advantage to be gained by the myth was to defend the President against domestic political attack by downplaying the importance of telling the Soviets about the Jupiters.

42 Allison is unambiguous: Kennedy 'had twice ordered their withdrawal', *Essence*1, pp. 101, 209, 225. Allison also claimed the US Navy did not follow the President's orders about where to position the blockade line, a separate myth. This notion has also been disproven, see Joseph Bouchard, *Command in Crisis* (New York: Columbia University Press 1991) pp. 111–12. *Essence*2 provides a different account, pp. 232–3.

43 Hafner, 'Bureaucratic Politics and "Those Frigging Missiles"'.

44 Hafner incorrectly assumed that, if Kennedy knew the missiles were in Turkey, he *therefore* could not have ordered them removed. In theory, Kennedy could have directed their removal (but did not) and the bureaucracy might have failed to implement it (as Allison claimed, albeit incorrectly).

45 Kennedy ordered the Pentagon to examine 'what actions can be taken to get the Jupiter missiles out of Turkey', National Security Action Memorandum, 181, 23 August 1962, Department of State, *Foreign Relations of the United States* [*FRUS*], *1961–1963, Vol . X, Cuba 1961–1962* (Washington, DC: United States Government Printing Office, 1997) p. 957.

46 The missiles themselves had legally become Turkish property. While their warheads were technically under American custody, they were in practice often mated with the missiles for lengthy periods and thus ready to fire.

47 Speculations there had been a secret deal are noted by: Bundy, *Danger and Survival*, pp. 434, 447; Nash, *The Other Missiles of October*, pp. 159, 161, 167; Fursenko and Naftali, *'One Hell of A Gamble'*, p. 321.

48 For McNamara's denial, see Bundy, *Danger and Survival*, p. 447.
49 Ibid., p. 434.
50 Kennedy, *Thirteen Days*, p. 108, emphasis added
51 See Strobe Talbott, *Khrushchev Remembers* (Boston, MA: Little Brown, 1970), pp. 498–9; Strobe Talbott (ed.), *Khrushchev Remembers: The Last Testament* (Boston, MA: Little, Brown and Company, 1974) p. 512; and Strobe Talbott, Jerrold Schecter and Vyacheslav Luchkov, *Khrushchev Remembers: The Glasnost Tapes* (Boston, MA: Little, Brown and Company 1990) p. 179.
52 Andrei Gromyko, 'U.S. Manipulations Leading to the Cuban Missile Crisis', *USSR International Affairs*, 7 September 1971, and 'The Caribbean Crisis', in V.V. Zhurkin and Ye.M. Primakov (eds), *Mezhdunarodnye konflikty* (Moscow: Mezhdunarodnye Otnoshenya 1972). 70–95, both cited by Bernstein, 'The Cuban Missile Crisis'.
53 Nash, *The Other Missiles*, p. 160 and Süleyman Seydi, 'Turkish–American Relations and the Cuban Missile Crisis, 1957–63', *Middle Eastern Studies*, 46/3 (May 2010) p. 451. Turkey likely knew about or suspected the secret concession in October 1962; if so, *Thirteen Days* would have confirmed their suspicions.
54 Bernstein, 'The Cuban Missile Crisis', 98.
55 Dean Rusk, Robert McNamara, George Ball, Roswell Gilpatric, Theodore Sorensen and McGeorge Bundy, 'The Lessons of the Cuban Missile Crisis', *Time*, 27 September 1982, 31
56 Sorensen, in Allyn, Blight and Welch, *Back to the Brink*, p. 93.
57 Allison suggests in *Essence*1 that, had Robert Kennedy lived, he would have edited out of *Thirteen Days* the information about the Jupiter offer and the truth about this meeting would never have surfaced.
58 Other Kennedy advisors, including McGeorge Bundy, supported Sorensen's account of events.
59 Dobrynin, *In Confidence*, pp. 87–8 [see text above]
60 Bundy, *Danger and Survival*, p. 434.
61 See, among others, Gribkov and Smith, *Operation Anadyr*, p. 144; Stern, *The Week the World Stood Still*; Richard Ned Lebow and Janice Gross Stein, *We All Lost the Cold War* (Princeton, N.J.: Princeton University Press 1994); James N. Giglio, *The Presidency of John F Kennedy* (Lawrence, KS: University Press of Kansas 1991). See also the contributions by Aleksandr Fursenko and Timothy Naftali, Raymond Garthoff and James Hershberg to the *Cold War History Project Bulletin*, Issue 5 (Spring 1995); and James Hershberg, 'More on Bobby and the Cuban Missile Crisis', Issue 8–9 (Winter 1996–7).
62 Bundy, *Danger and Survival*, pp. 432–3.
63 On the 'Cordier ploy' see Blight and Welch, *On The Brink*, pp. 83–4; Bundy *Danger and Survival*, pp. 435–6, and Nash, *The Other Missiles of October*, pp. 144–5
64 Stern, *The Week the World Stood Still*, p. 193.
65 Telegram #139, Canadian embassy Ankara to External Affairs, 25 October 1962, 'Turkish Reactions to the Cuban Crisis', Library and Archives Canada, RG25, 4184, 2444–40, part 11. Canada's Washington embassy received a copy of the telegram the same day, and almost certainly passed this appreciation to the State Department by 26 October. For a more detailed discussion of this message, see Don Munton, 'The Fourth Question: Why Did John Kennedy Offer up the Jupiters in Turkey?' in David Gioe, Len Scott and Christopher Andrew (eds), *An International History of the Cuban Missile Crisis* (Abingdon: Routledge 2014) 258–78.
66 If the Canadian Ankara report reached senior US officials by October 27, it helps explain why the Kennedy brothers began talking that day in the ExComm meeting about sending an emissary to Turkey and requesting an emergency NATO meeting for the 29th. Such plans would have been politically dangerous

in the extreme if the Turkish government had in fact remained strongly opposed to a Jupiter withdrawal.

67 The only exception is Nash, *The Other Missiles of October*, p. 149.

68 The 'Mutual Missile Withdrawal Agreement' of October 1962 seems an appropriate name. International law has ample precedents for unwritten and un-ratified inter-state agreements.

69 Raymond Garthoff published the fullest version of this story the same year *Essence*2 came out, 'The US–Soviet Tank Confrontation at Checkpoint Charlie', in Stephen Cimbala (ed.), *Mysteries of the Cold War* (London: Ashgate, 1999). Garthoff, however, first brought the secret agreement to light eight years earlier, ibid., 'Berlin 1961: The Record Corrected', *Foreign Policy*, 84 (Fall 1991) 142–56.

70 The documentary evidence is from Fursenko and Naftali, *'One Hell of a Gamble'*, pp. 284–6. *Essence*2 also strongly implies a disconnection between the resolution of the crisis and the Jupiter issue, see p. 242.

71 *Essence*2 does not attempt to specify precisely when Khrushchev ultimately 'decided' to withdraw the missiles, but implies it was between 27 October and the Presidium meeting on the 28th (see especially p. 385). Perhaps we need to distinguish between his decision (taken by 25 October) to withdraw the R-12s in principle; a decision (on 27 or 28 October) to accept Kennedy's public offer (to end the blockade and not invade Cuba), that preceded news of Kennedy's Jupiter offer, and the formal decision (made and announced on 28 October).

72 Khrushchev's position at the 28 October Presidium meeting represented 'another about-face', *Essence*2, p. 128.

73 Bundy, *Danger and Survival*, p. 445.

74 It is unclear what if any evidence substantiates *Essence*2's claim that the 'signal' of Kennedy's offer 'was overwhelmed in the general tone of threat and urgency' of the Presidium meeting (p. 129).

75 Bundy, *Danger and Survival*, p. 445. Bundy had opposed any Jupiter offer and thus has every reason to minimize its importance. To determine how 'small' the Jupiter concession actually was, consider the fact that the majority of the ExComm had consistently found it a totally unacceptable concession.

76 The process, from start to finish, took six-months, less than implied by the phrase 'the grinding of the machinery in Washington ... led to actual withdrawal', *Essence*2, p. 242.

77 Khrushchev could save himself 'from the shipwreck of his bold venture', Bundy, *Danger and Survival*, p. 441.

78 Blight and Welch, *On the Brink*, p. 341.

79 In the early 1970s, Washington confronted Moscow on the building of a base off Cienfuegos, Cuba, potentially for Soviet missile submarines. See Raymond Garthoff, 'Handling the Cienfuegos Crisis', *International Security*, 8/1 (Summer 1983) 46–66.

80 Gaddis, *We Now Know*, p. 278.

81 See, for example, Michael Dobbs, *One Minute to Midnight: Khrushchev, and Castro on the Brink of Nuclear War* (London: Knopf 2008) p. xiii

82 Chang and Kornbluh, *The Cuban Missile Crisis*, pp. xvii and 233. Allison and Zelikow do briefly note the problem of the Soviet IL-28 bombers in Cuba, *Essence*2, pp. 364–5.

83 For a thorough examination of this see David M. Barrett and Max Holland, *Blind over Cuba: The Photo Gap and the Missile Crisis* (College Station, TX: Texas A&M University Press, 2012).

84 Allison and Zelikow claim the US knew about tactical nuclear weapons 'late in the crisis' (*Essence*2, p. 216). This claim is unsubstantiated and likely incorrect. It may fail to distinguish the delivery systems from their warheads. American

intelligence discovered some types, but not all, of the tactical missiles in Cuba. American experts knew that some of these missiles were potentially nuclear capable, but assumed they were all conventional. Some were. They also assumed none had come with nuclear warheads. But some did.

85 Allison and Zelikow mention in passing the Corona satellite system that by 1961 was replacing or augmenting the vulnerable U-2 spy plane. They do not however explore the open question of why the Corona satellites were not employed to obtain photo intelligence from Cuba even thought they were fully operating during the fall of 1962. David G. Coleman, 'The Missiles of November, December, January, February', *Journal of Cold War Studies*, 9/3 (Summer 2007) 5–48, raises this question, but personally I find the answers not entirely convincing.

86 Houghton, 'Essence of Excision', p. 163.

87 Scott and Smith, 'Lessons of October', p. 680.

7 We all lost the 'Cuban missile crisis'

Revisiting Richard Ned Lebow and Janice Gross Stein's landmark analysis in *We All Lost the Cold War*

Benoît Pelopidas

Richard Ned Lebow and Janice Gross Stein's *We All Lost the Cold War* remains an important and widely quoted contribution in the fields of political science and political psychology twenty years after its publication.[1] As opposed to other classics on the so-called 'Cuban missile crisis', which are also analysed in this edited volume, this book is not exclusively focused on this crisis. It is recognized as 'the most acute confrontation of the Cold War' (p. 5) and is one of the two case studies in the book, the other one being the 1973 Middle Eastern crisis. These case studies support the conclusion that the end of the Cold War was delayed rather than caused by the strategy of nuclear deterrence.[2] As is abundantly clear from the title of the book, its main target is American Cold War triumphalism, of which victorious nuclear crisis management through strength and resolve is just one aspect. The limitations of this important book only constitute a powerful invitation to build upon its main argumentation. I will suggest avenues for doing so in the last part of this chapter.

When this book was first published, in January 1994, the scholarship on the Cuban missile crisis was in the process of experiencing a revolution. With glasnost, the Soviet archives were slowly opening and since 1987, Bruce Allyn, David Welch and James Blight had been organising a series of conferences bringing together US and Soviet participants in the crisis, giving a voice to the Soviet side and, to a lesser extent, to the Cuban side,[3] in a historiography which was almost exclusively US and elite-centred.[4] Alongside those oral history interviews, an additional volume of Khrushchev's memoirs was published by his son Sergei in the autumn of 1990, almost two decades after two earlier volumes.[5] Even on the American side, McGeorge Bundy, President Kennedy's special assistant for National Security Affairs at the time of the crisis, published his account of the American nuclear age in 1988, devoting 72 pages to the Cuban missile crisis and Secretary of State Dean Rusk, who had kept a low profile on the issue for decades, published his memoirs in 1990 as a long interview with his son Richard.[6]

The 1990s have arguably produced the most influential books on the Cuban missile crisis written by political scientists and international relations scholars: Scott Sagan's *The Limits of Safety* in 1993 from the perspective of organizational theory,[7] Jutta Weldes' *Constructing National Interest*, a critical constructivist take on the construction of US national interests during the crisis[8] and the second edition of Graham Allison's foundational book *The Essence of Decision*, co-authored with Philip Zelikow, in 1999.[9]

This essay will neither recount the whole argument of Lebow and Stein in detail, nor will it assess all their claims about the contribution the book was intended to make.[10] Instead, it will argue that *We All Lost the Cold War* made three major contributions to the scholarship about the Cuban missile crisis which invite us to continue the effort.

First, the book brought new empirical material to the study of the crisis through oral history interviews (p. x) on the US and Soviet sides as well as archival research. Second, it developed the perspective of political psychology in the study of the crisis, which allowed for a critique of the strategy of deterrence as contributing to the creation of the crisis, not just its resolution. By strategy of deterrence, they meant deliberate attempts at signalling intent to use nuclear weapons and other capabilities if specific red lines are crossed in order to deter the supposed enemy from attacking first. They contrasted this 'strategy of deterrence' with the 'fact of deterrence' which described the effect on the supposed enemy of the mere possession of nuclear weapons.[11] In other words, they argued that threats intended to deter the other party did not only bring the crisis to a successful resolution, they had the adverse effect of contributing to its origin. To make that argument, they used psychology and the evidence that had just been made available on the case of the Cuban missile crisis, within the framework of the 'third wave of deterrence theory'.[12] The first wave is usually understood as the attempts by theorists in the very first years of the nuclear age to introduce the concept of deterrence in the discussion of the consequences of the invention of nuclear weapons; the second wave of deterrence theory is considered to have started in the late 1950s with the use of game theoretic models to better understand actors' tactics, while not providing empirical evidence for their claims. The so-called third wave, starting in the 1970s, engaged with this particular problem. The modified deterrence theory that would follow from this empirical research program would have to account for different attitudes towards risk-taking, to reconceptualise rewards and probabilities and to reconsider the problems of misperceptions as well as domestic and bureaucratic politics. Lebow and Stein are emblematic representatives of this wave. Third, this book was and remains a powerful case for the disputed interpretation that the US did not win the Cuban missile crisis because no one did. Incidentally, this provides the reader with a powerful critique of nuclear superiority as a decisive factor in crisis management, and of nuclear crisis management itself. This essay will conclude by underlining how the limitations of the book suggest ways for contemporary analysts to approach the puzzles of the 'Cuban missile crisis'.

New documents and oral history

Lebow and Stein's book contributed to the trend of uncovering Soviet documentation and accounting for the Soviet experience of the crisis: their book revealed the English version of the telegram of Anatoly Dobrynin, which was sent on 27 October 1962 and had only recently been declassified (pp. 524–6; see also pp. 122–3 for the analysis of the 'secret deal'). It makes clear that the deal to trade the Turkish Jupiter missiles against the Soviet missiles in Cuba was made explicit by President Kennedy, and exposes a couple of his reasons for asking to keep it secret: not jeopardising NATO's unity or the US position in it.[13]

> 'And what about Turkey?' I [Anatoli Dobrynin] asked R. Kennedy.
> 'If that is the only obstacle to achieving the regulation I mentioned earlier, then the president doesn't see any unsurmountable difficulties in resolving this issue', replied R. Kennedy. 'The greatest difficulty for the president is the public discussion of the issue of Turkey. Formally the deployment of missile bases in Turkey was done by a special decision of the NATO Council. To announce now a unilateral decision by the president of the USA to withdraw missile bases from Turkey – this would damage the entire structure of NATO and the US position as the leader of NATO, where, as the Soviet government knows very well, there are many arguments. In short, if such a decision were announced now it would seriously tear apart NATO.'[14]

Of course, a fair assessment of the novelty of this evidence has to take into account that two or three former members of the Executive Committee, Ted Sorensen, Dean Rusk and possibly McGeorge Bundy (depending how you read his statement), admitted that there had been a deal to trade Turkish missiles against Soviet missiles in Cuba. In *Danger and Survival* published in 1988, Bundy wrote that: 'By keeping to ourselves the assurances on the Jupiters, we misled our colleagues, our countrymen, our successors, and our allies.'[15] As Barton Bernstein rightly noted, Bundy's words are slightly more ambiguous than our retrospective assessment suggests. Let's read Bundy:

> The other part of the oral message [to Dobrynin] was proposed by Dean Rusk: that we should tell Khrushchev that while there could be no deal over the Turkish missiles, the president was determined to get them out and would do so once the Cuban crisis was resolved. The proposal was quickly supported by the rest of us [...]. Concerned as we all were by the cost of a public bargain struck under pressure at the apparent expense of the Turks, and aware as we were from the day's discussion that for some, even in our own closest councils, even this *unilateral private assurance* might appear to betray an ally, we agreed

> without hesitation that no one not in the room was to be informed of this additional message. Robert Kennedy was instructed to make it plain to Dobrynin that the same secrecy must be observed on the other side, and that any Soviet reference to our assurance would simply make it null and void.[16]

Bundy did not actually write about a 'deal'. Instead, he still granted the high ground to the Kennedy administration by euphemising it as a unilateral private assurance.[17] But Ambassador Dobrynin complained about this account at the Moscow conference and, as a result, in January 1989, Theodore Sorensen publicly acknowledged that he had redacted the missile deal out of Robert Kennedy's *Thirteen Days* and, contrary to Bundy, explicitly acknowledged a 'deal'.[18] Finally, after decades of silence, Dean Rusk made a similar confession to his son in his memoirs.

These confessions were published a few years before the book by Lebow and Stein and are acknowledged in it (p. 144). Given that it was not in their interest to make such confessions which, to a certain extent, might have been damaging to McGeorge Bundy, this made the claim very plausible. However, documentary evidence in English was now provided for the first time. This could not have happened earlier as Dobrynin had remained the Soviet ambassador to Washington until 1986 and the practice of publishing revelatory exposes was uncommon, to say the least, among Soviet diplomats, before the time of glasnost.

Lebow and Stein's interviews also tended to confirm that the American U-2 plane which had been shot down over Cuba on 27 October 1962, as reported at the 4.00 p.m. Ex-Comm meeting on that day, resulted from a 'violation of [...] standard orders' (pp. 9, 302–3). In any case, Lebow and Stein's analysis is definitely an important contribution to this effort to restore the multiple voices that made the crisis through archival research as well as oral history interviews.[19]

Deepening the psychological critique of rational deterrence theory and the strategy of deterrence

Beyond this new evidence, Lebow and Stein built upon their previous work to elaborate a psychological critique of rational nuclear deterrence theory which led them to formulate a critique of the strategy of deterrence in the context of the Cuban missile crisis. Of course, the critique of the adverse effects of nuclear deterrence did not start with this book.[20] However, it was framed as a psychological critique of the implicit assumptions of rational deterrence theory, following a line of argument they had suggested a decade earlier in a 1985 co-authored volume on *Psychology and Deterrence*.[21] The arguments developed in this earlier volume were a clear prelude to the so-called third wave of deterrence theory outlined above.[22] Their purpose was to combine historical research[23] with a concern with psychological factors in nuclear decision-making in order to challenge the rationalistic assumptions of existing deterrence theory at the time and, as a consequence, call into question the supposed successes of nuclear deterrence as a policy practice. This challenge was theoretical, methodological as well as empirical and *We All Lost the Cold War* is the culmination of almost fifteen years of work on the issue, partly jointly, partly separately.[24] In 1985, in their first collaboration, Lebow was very clear about this research program. He wrote that:

> the unifying theme of this volume is disenchantment with deterrence both as a theory of state behaviour and as a strategy of conflict management. [...] while deterrence may sometimes succeed in discouraging the use of force, it may also be instrumental in provoking it.[25]

They developed the theoretical[26] and methodological aspects[27] of their critique in three joint journal publications and a few separate publications between the 1985 book and *We All Lost the Cold War*.[28] At the theoretical level, their core contention has to do with the limits of validity of deterrence theory regarding the preferences of the other party and the theory's inability to predict them. As a consequence, the most important aspects of the explanation of crisis behaviour are excluded from deterrence theory.[29] Methodologically, the assessment of deterrence suffers from two main flaws at different stages of the analysis, which have opposite consequences: a selection bias which is in favour of deterrence failure first, because the successes of deterrence leave hardly any trace of the intent to challenge the status quo and second, an operationalisation bias which retrospectively overestimates deterrence successes due to a retrospective assignment of the roles of challenger and defender. In other words, a systematic empirical assessment of deterrence will most likely take the absence of behavioural evidence of intent to attack on the part of the deterree as sufficient to exclude a given case from the analysis. As a result, the universe of cases might not include all valid cases of successful deterrence. However, the second mistake produces the opposite effect. It consists in assigning the roles of challenger and defender a posteriori, based on how a given situation unfolded. A challenger is retrospectively designated as opposed to a defender whose identity is determined by the outcome of the crisis. Such an assignment of the role of challenger might not adequately reflect the situation at the beginning of the crisis under study; it is likely to overestimate deterrence successes because it does not require a high standard of evidence to identify the challenger and its intention to attack.

Empirically, the 1985 volume only anecdotally referred to the Cuban missile crisis[30] but, in the nine years between its publication and that of *We All Lost the Cold War*, the two authors have intensively published on the case.[31] As early as 1987, they characterized the crisis as a case of 'deterrence failure' and provided a short case study[32] which explicitly intended to show the counterproductive effects of a deterrence policy, both in terms of general deterrence (chapter 2 and 3), in which armed forces are maintained to regulate the relationship between two opposing states without any of them 'mounting an attack' and immediate deterrence, which describes 'the relationship between opposing states where at least one side is seriously considering an attack while the other is mounting a threat of retaliation in order to prevent it' (chapter 4).[33]

Lebow and Stein described the logic leading from a threat intended to deter to its adverse effects in the following way:

> deterrers provoke the kind of behaviour they have sought to prevent because of the unexpected effect of their intervention on the cost-benefit calculus of a challenger. They differ, of course, in that the calculations involved are conscious and political, not unconscious and psychological. Perhaps the best contemporary example is the Cuban missile crisis.[34]

They were not the only ones pursuing that line of empirical argument at the time.[35]

In the study presented in *We All Lost the Cold War*, this culminated at two levels: the distinction between the fact of deterrence and the strategy of deterrence (both in terms of immediate and general deterrence), and a reinterpretation of the causes and outcome of the crisis through this lens. This distinction led them to observe the tension between the two, labelled 'the ultimate irony of nuclear deterrence' and defined as 'the way in which the strategy of deterrence undercut much of the political stability the reality of deterrence should have created' (p. 367). The confidence analysts had – and often still have – in their ability to identify who is the defender and who is the challenger before assessing the success of a strategy of deterrence made it harder to realize that 'American and Soviet leaders alike saw themselves as the defender and their adversary as the challenger' (p. 310). This is due to psychologically identifiable dynamics which make it hard to cope with deterrence failure in a crisis when your strategy and your mode of understanding your relationship with the relevant other was deterrence. One of the most obvious effects of this understanding is the creation of exaggerated threat assessments which become counterproductive (pp. 328–31).

Through mechanisms cognitive psychologists call the attribution error, people overestimate the role of the other's intent as a cause of an undesirable outcome over situational constraints they faced; at the same time, they expect the other to understand that this outcome is less due to their intent than to the situational constraints they face; if you combine this bias with the proportionality bias, which consists in assuming that the importance the other places in a given goal is proportionate to the costs the other is willing to pay in order to achieve this goal, you understand why the crisis escalated after the first failure of American deterrence, i.e. when the Soviets placed missiles in Cuba. The Americans interpreted their warnings before the crisis and the quarantine as defensive moves dictated by the situation and expected the Soviets to understand them in the same way; on the contrary, they interpreted the Soviet attempt at deploying the missiles in secret as a sign of their aggressive intentions and underestimated the role of situational constraints on their end. Due to the proportionality bias, the Americans saw the Soviet willingness to risk a war as a sign that they expected a massive reward from the outcome of this crisis.

These are just two examples of how Lebow and Stein grounded the notion of the security dilemma in cognitive psychology at the individual level in order to interpret the crisis. The security dilemma describes the constraints under which policy-makers have to make decisions about security policy: they cannot be certain of the other party's intentions, nor can they be sure of the exact extent of their capabilities. As a consequence, it remains extremely difficult to anticipate how he/she will interpret and respond to a particular policy, which might prove to be counterproductive.[36] The set of psychological biases they identify leads them to show that: 'deterrence can impede early warning, lead to exaggerated threat assessments, contribute to stress, increase the domestic and allied pressures to stand firm, and exacerbate the problem of loss of control' (p. 325). As a consequence, the US strategy of nuclear deterrence is interpreted as partly responsible for Khrushchev's decision to place missiles in Cuba when the fact of nuclear deterrence, i.e. the mutual fear of nuclear war, is supposed to have induced caution on both sides. This point deserves a long quote:

> The origins of the missile crisis indicate that general deterrence was provocative rather than preventive. Soviet officials testified that the American strategic build-up, deployment of missiles in Turkey, and assertions of nuclear superiority, made them increasingly insecure. The President viewed these measures as prudent, defensive precautions against perceived Soviet threats. His actions had the unanticipated consequence of convincing Khrushchev of the need to protect the Soviet Union and Cuba from American military and political challenges.
>
> (p. 49)

So Lebow and Stein used cognitive psychology to make the provocative claim that both the optimistic reading of nuclear deterrence as the peacemaker and the critical reading of the weapons as sources of escalation are only half true and do not capture the entirety of the relationship between the two leaders during the crisis. From their perspective, the fact and strategy of deterrence acted both as sources of escalation and sources of restraint at different times.

Reassessing the outcome of the crisis: not a US victory

To this day, the Cuban missile crisis remains perceived as an overall American victory, even if the size of the victory has been revised.[37] The common interpretation underlines the success of a policy of resolve backed by nuclear superiority.[38] In 1992, Soviet scholar Fedor Burlatskiy provided testimony that argued against such an interpretation[39] and Lebow and Stein's provocative argument followed this line of enquiry; it engaged with the two above-mentioned aspects of the claim for victory: the winning strategy was nuclear coercion backed by presidential resolve and this was made possible by the US military superiority. This discussion matters all the more where the merits of nuclear coercion and nuclear superiority are still debated in the International Relations scholarship, as I will show below. Even more importantly, the memory of the crisis might have shaped or at least contributed to justifying the use of coercive policies and the pursuit of nuclear superiority by several US administrations. Two prominent cases among those would be Johnson's support for escalation in Vietnam and Nixon and Kissinger's use of nuclear brinkmanship and support of nuclear superiority where they thought it possible to regain it. All of this can be related to their specific reading of the outcome of the crisis and what caused it.[40]

Lebow and Stein's argument was based on the idea that both sides compromised: 'The Kennedy-Dobrynin meeting and the Kennedy-Khrushchev exchange of letters [...] allowed the two leaders to work out an accommodation that safeguarded the interests of both and permitted Khrushchev to retreat with minimal loss of face' (p. 313). They added: 'although the administration had ruled out an invasion of Cuba, Khrushchev considered Kennedy's pledge not to invade an extremely important concession' (p. 362), on top of a 'second, important concession', i.e. 'to remove the American Jupiter missiles from Turkey at a decent interval after the crisis' (p. 363). Soviet documents which have become available after the publication of the book suggest that the first of those two concessions actually played no role in Khrushchev's decision to remove Soviet missiles from Cuba.[41] Even if one accepts that the first concession mattered, one has to recognise that the United States came out of the crisis much better off than the Soviet Union and that the American leader could present this outcome as his victory when the Soviet leader had to face humiliation.

Those arguments were almost immediately controversial. Less than a year after the publication of *We All Lost the Cold War*, Eric Herring published his dissertation in which he accepted most of Lebow and Stein's argument except the denial of a US victory. In other words, he agreed that 'US nuclear superiority was not responsible for the outcome of the Cuban missile crisis', that 'the existence of that superiority helped to provoke the Soviet Union into deploying missiles in the first place' and that

Khrushchev acted the way he did because he believed him to be resolute'
but still characterised the outcome of the crisis as 'not a total victory for the
United States, but an outcome which favoured it, even if it had to make
limited concessions'.[42] Similarly, as recently as January 2013, in an article
on 'Nuclear Superiority and the Balance of Resolve: Explaining Nuclear
Crisis Outcomes', Matthew Kroenig still coded the Cuban missile crisis as a
US victory.[43] He bypassed Lebow and Stein and referred to Richard Betts'
earlier work arguing that 'it is hard to avoid the conclusion that the imbalance of nuclear power – US superiority – was an influence'.[44]

Lebow and Stein were actually more nuanced than it seems in their
claims and sound contradictory when they recognise that '[Khrushchev's]
capitulation in the face of American military pressure was a humiliating
defeat for the Soviet Union and its leader. Soviet officials confirm that it
was one factor in his removal from power a year later' (p. 352). This
remains a slight problem but becomes much less of a contradiction once
we connect this point with the arguments evoked earlier that reliance on
deterrence before a given crisis will create an incentive to use its assumptions to explain its failure (p. 331). In that respect, the continued reliance
on deterrence is an overall loss for both parties in Lebow and Stein's argument because it extended the duration of the Cold War (postscript). The
point here is not to adjudicate on this last argument but to explain why
the apparent contradiction noted above becomes a simple tension within
their analytical framework. As I will elaborate in the concluding section,
engaging further with the role of luck in the outcome of the crisis might
have solved this tension.

Conclusion: a research programme inspired by Lebow and Stein's contribution

After twenty years, *We All Lost the Cold War* should be remembered as providing the English translation of a key document confirming the confessions or half-confessions by Bundy, Sorensen and Rusk that Robert
Kennedy had, with the approval of the President, offered a secret deal to
Soviet Ambassador Dobrynin, which consisted in trading the Soviet missiles in Cuba against American missiles in Turkey; analysts and policy-
makers should remember its detailed discussion of the adverse effects of
deterrence as a strategy due to psychological biases; the idea that a nuclear
crisis such as the one taking place in 1962 cannot be considered as a US
victory appears as one of the most important arguments of the book, and
one which calls for further elaboration. I will only start this effort here by
suggesting avenues for future research.

In view of a research programme, this book calls for a renewed engagement with the role of luck in the nuclear age. Reviewing the recent literature on the crisis in the autumn of 1994, Len Scott and Steve Smith aptly
wrote that:

there is now ample evidence that the fact that the crisis did not lead to nuclear war was due, in large part, to good luck. In our view this is a most important finding since it undermines the claims of those who think that nuclear crises can be safely managed and that command and control systems will work as they are meant to work.[45]

This renewed engagement with luck is all the more important as Lebow and Stein's excessive efforts to position themselves against a revisionist interpretation of Cold War history (p. ix), which is described as granting an explanatory role to 'American good luck' (p. 95), unfortunately lead to an inconsistency in their treatment of luck.[46] Indeed, if one does not recognise the share of luck in the outcome of the crisis, then one is forced to conclude, against Lebow and Stein, that the Soviets lost more than the United States in the end: their leader lost face worldwide and the crisis was widely recognised as an American victory and they ultimately did not get a formal non-invasion pledge of Cuba until the Nixon administration.

Further elaboration on this notion would provide Lebow and Stein with more consistent arguments on two fronts: first, accounting for luck would strengthen considerably their diagnosis that no one won the Cuban missile crisis; second it would complement their awareness that a strategy of deterrence can aggravate the problem of loss of control and Lebow's earlier argument that the management of nuclear crisis is nothing more than a dangerous illusion.[47] However, their conclusion that 'nuclear deterrence is robust when leaders on both sides fear war and are aware of each other's fears' (p. 366), suggests that there is a way to make nuclear deterrence controllable or that the theory cannot account for luck (a similar impression appears on pp. 110–11 where their multilevel analysis used to account for the outcome of the crisis does not identify luck). This neglect of the role of luck is demonstrated further by the fact that Lebow and Stein do not engage much with Scott Sagan's *Limits of Safety* (quoted on p. ii of the preface) who reviewed the record of American nuclear weapons-related accidents and concluded that: 'it was less good design than good fortune that prevented many of those accidents from escalating out of control'[48] or with Bruce Blair's book on *The Logic of Accidental Nuclear War*.[49]

So, Lebow and Stein's argument calls for a deeper engagement with luck in social sciences, nuclear history and in the case of the Cuban missile crisis in particular.[50] Conceptually, in the social sciences, a better understanding of the role of luck which cannot be reduced to a manageable quantity called risk requires further analysis, distinguishing between risk and uncertainty. The notion of luck defended here as uncertainty and uncontrollability, or impossibility to know, predict and control would exclude all the episodes of near-misses which might be due to nuclear deterrence operating at the individual level. The discussion among the commanding officers in the Soviet submarine B-59 which lost contact with headquarters and came under attack on 27 October 1962 is a case in point. If it turns out that Captain Arkhipov persuaded Captain Savitsky not to fire his nuclear torpedo and that he did so because he was afraid of the consequences of launching a nuclear projectile at the enemy, then this might then qualify as an illustration of existential deterrence.[51] Adjudicating this particular case would require more detailed research and might not even be feasible. However, the moments when Kennedy and Khrushchev took the right decisions out of false information or lack of information appears as hard-to-dispute cases of luck. For instance, Kennedy's resisting the pressure to invade or bomb Cuba and impose a quarantine owes something to his *erroneous* belief that nuclear warheads are not on the island yet.

The framing of the crisis in terms of risk gives the false impression that it accounts for the role of luck when it actually mischaracterises it. To paraphrase Mary Douglas, 'risk is not a thing, it is a way of thinking' that relies on probabilistic logic and language. It is driven by a desire for control and a faith in that control, which ends up denying the specificity of luck by reducing it to a knowable and quantifiable factor in social life.[52] On the contrary, taking luck seriously would force analysts to reconsider the decisions made at the time from a political and ethical perspective, which has been significantly lacking from the scholarship on the crisis. If luck was necessary to save us all, and 'good management' was not the only cause of the happy ending, many essential political and ethical questions open up.

Contrary to the common but misguided idea that recognising the role of luck leads to relinquishing responsibility,[53] it opens the possibility of a critical engagement with the allocation of responsibility and its ethical and political justification. It simply denaturalises the existing socio-political order and makes visible the possibility of alternatives to be imagined and acted upon. As defined above, risk creates a specific form of accountability and blame based on the expectation of control[54] and this is obviously not the only possible one.

Recognising the role of luck would allow analysts to allocate responsibility in a radically different manner. How to allocate it once it is established that complete control is impossible? In the specific context of Cuba, once one recognises that those weapon systems were not perfectly controllable, given their destructiveness and the absence of effective defence against a nuclear (retaliatory) strike, the political authorities cannot take full credit for this success any longer and, given the scope of the consequences of a negative outcome, have to account for why they did let the crisis escalate to that level in the first place. Of course, the issue of allocation of responsibility relies on counterfactuals of all the other possible worlds.

That in turn opens a much deeper question: would the events in Cuba have turned critical in the absence of nuclear weapons? This counterfactual definitely has to feature in our assessment of their role in the crisis. More profoundly, was the public aware of the limits of safety and command and control at the time? Beyond the moral paradox of nuclear deterrence,[55] acknowledging the role of luck and the existence of uncertainty allows the analyst to see the possibility of an unauthorized/inadvertent nuclear strike. Did the American public know that it is vulnerable to a retaliatory strike caused by a launch which might be accidental?[56] Those are variations of the same basic question: under which circumstances does the American public accept the possibility of failure of nuclear deterrence? Which likelihood of failure is acceptable to them and in the name of what are they willing to expose their lives? Those questions are worth asking for the part of the world population which would have potentially been affected by the consequences of nuclear use.

Another series of questions follows: politically, how does this uncertainty affect the role of security institutions, the meaning of alliance commitments and the possibility of neutrality? Of course, any social logic involves luck as uncertainty and contingency to a degree, so I do not mean to say that there is anything special with the logic of this chain of events. All I am arguing here is that this common role of luck becomes exceptionally consequential in this particular context.

Therefore, a meaningful extension of Lebow and Stein's contribution to a broader effort of giving a voice to the other side of the crisis would be to analyse the perceptions of the crisis as a global event, rather than a purely bipolar crisis.[57] The pressing questions following the shift to the global level, the acceptance of the role of luck and the diagnosis by Lebow and Stein that everyone lost the Cuban missile crisis, are that of the awareness of nuclear vulnerability which existed in different parts of the world, and how it came into being.[58]

We All Lost the Cold War already asked sophisticated counterfactual questions and this is an avenue still worth pursuing. For example, this is one of the few books which investigate why those events were indeed a crisis (chapter 5) and why they turned out the way they did. Similarly, the authors allude, although only briefly, to the rapprochement between Khrushchev and Kennedy as a result of the crisis, considered in that instance as a shared learning experience. They even venture to wonder whether, had Kennedy not been assassinated and Khrushchev not removed from office in October 1964, the Cold War could have been shortened by the cooperation between those two men (p. 145).[59]

Historically, an important puzzle is why no one in the ExComm grasped the importance of taking into account the possibility of catastrophic error in assessing the US response to the Soviet missiles. This is a very important puzzle indeed because even the contemporary experiences of Secretary of Defense McNamara with Admiral George Anderson, Chief of Naval Operations during the crisis, who reportedly wanted to sink Soviet ships in spite of the President's orders to enforce the quarantine,[60] were not enough to remove the sense that the crisis was manageable and would be managed.[61] The psychological perspective elaborated by Lebow and Stein already suggested hypotheses to account for this persisting sense of controllability.[62] In particular, cognitive psychology has developed a lot of insights about over-confidence and the illusion of control, which seem to go hand in hand with Lebow and Stein's angle.[63] Beyond the over-confidence at the time of the crisis, Lebow and Stein's argument calls for a broader investigation on how it persisted over time. How did the creation of the crisis as a reference point from which policy lessons were meant to be learnt coexist with the perpetuation of a sense of over-confidence? This essay only suggests the possible role of a misunderstanding of uncertainty and luck or its reduction to risk in this dynamic. Combining cognitive psychology, sociological investigation and historical critique to understand why we seem to have learned the wrong lessons from 1962 appears as one of the strongest reasons to argue that we all lost the Cuban missile crisis.

Notes

1 It was chosen by *Choice*, the journal of American Library Association devoted to reviewing published works, as one of their outstanding academic titles for 1994.
2 Richard Ned Lebow and Janice Gross Stein, *We All Lost the Cold War* (Princeton, NJ: Princeton University 1994) p. 5 and postscript.
3 James G. Blight and David A. Welch, *On the Brink: Americans and Soviets Reexamine the Cuban Missile Crisis* (New York: Hill and Wang 1989); Bruce J. Allyn, James G. Blight and David A. Welch, *Back to the Brink: Proceedings of the Moscow Conference on the Cuban Missile Crisis, January 27–28, 1989* (Lanham, MD: University Press of America 1992); James G. Blight, Bruce J. Allyn and David A. Welch, *Cuba on the Brink: Castro, the Missile Crisis and the Soviet Collapse* (New York: Rowman and Littlefield 2002 [revised edition]).
4 Among many books, the classic accounts remain: Graham Allison and Philip Zelikow, *The Essence of Decision: Explaining the Cuban Missile Crisis* (New York: Pearson 1999); Jutta Weldes, *Constructing National Interest: The United States and the Cuban Missile Crisis* (Minneapolis, MN: University of Minnesota Press 1999); and the three studies by Sheldon M. Stern, *The Cuban Missile Crisis in American Memory: Myths and Realities* (Palo Alto, CA: Stanford University Press 2012); *The Week the World Stood Still: Inside the Secret Cuban Missile Crisis* (Palo Alto, CA: Stanford University Press 2005) and *Averting 'The Final Failure': JFK and the Secret Cuban Missile Crisis* (Palo Alto, CA: Stanford University Press 2003). See also: David G. Coleman, *The Fourteenth Day: JFK and the Aftermath of the Cuban Missile Crisis* (New York: W.W. Norton 2012) and David R. Gibson, *Talk at the Brink: Deliberation and Decision during the Cuban Missile Crisis* (Princeton, NJ: Princeton University Press 2012). James Hershberg's chapter on 'the Cuban missile crisis' in the second volume of the *Cambridge History of the Cold War* (Cambridge: Cambridge University Press 2010) remains mostly focused on the showdown between the Kennedy and Khrushchev administrations.
5 Nikita S. Khrushchev, *Khrushchev Remembers: The Glasnost Tapes* (Boston, MA: Little Brown and Company 1990; translated and edited by Jerrold L. Schecter with Vyacheslav V. Luchkov); the earlier volumes, both translated and edited by Strobe Talbott, were *Khrushchev Remembers* (Boston, MA: Little Brown and Company, 1970), and *Khrushchev Remembers: The Last Testament* (Boston, MA: Little Brown and Company 1974). Khrushchev's son also published a book in June 1990: *Khrushchev on Khrushchev: An Inside Account of the Man and His Era, by*

His Son, Sergei Khrushchev (Boston, MA: Little Brown and Company 1990) but the book does not include much regarding the Cuban missile crisis.

6 McGeorge Bundy, *Danger and Survival: Choices about the Bomb in the first Fifty Years* (New York: Random House 1988), chapter 9: 'the Cuban Missile Crisis'; Dean Rusk, *As I Saw It*, edited by Richard Rusk and Daniel S. Papp (New York: W.W. Norton 1990). For a critical assessment, see Stern, *The Cuban Missile Crisis in American History and Memory*, chapters 5 and 7: 'The Forgotten Voice of Dean Rusk' and 'the Selective Memory of McGeorge Bundy'.

7 See Campbell Craig's essay in this volume.

8 Weldes, *Constructing National Interests*.

9 Lebow and Stein clearly positioned themselves against the original *Essence of Decision* in the introduction to their volume when they described it as 'for fifteen years considered the standard account of the crisis' (p. 13). For an analysis of Allison and Zelikow's essay in the historiography of the crisis, see Don Munton's chapter in this volume.

10 Regarding the relationship between Kennedy and Khrushchev, Lebow and Stein disputed the prevailing interpretation at the time and showed that the Soviet leader did not take the risk to place missiles in Cuba because he felt his American counterpart lacked resolve, but rather for the opposite reason. This claim is actually very hard to prove or disprove based on the available documents even today, so this essay will not pretend to assess it. As a consequence of this claim, Lebow and Stein rejected the idea that Khrushchev did not place missiles in Cuba because he thought Kennedy would not do anything against it, but rather, because he 'indulged in wishful thinking' (p. 67; see more broadly chapter 2).

11 What they call the 'fact of deterrence' seems to correspond to what is commonly referred to as existential deterrence.

12 Robert Jervis, 'Deterrence Theory Revisited', *World Politics* 31/2 (1979) 289–324.

13 This was immediately perceived as a major contribution by Len Scott and Steve Smith, 'Lessons of October: Historians, Political Scientists, Policy-Makers and the Cuban Missile Crisis', *International Affairs*, 70/4 (October 1994) 669.

14 Telegram by Soviet Ambassador Anatoly Dobrynin reporting on his last meeting with US Attorney General Robert Kennedy on 27 October 1962.

15 Bundy, *Danger and Survival*, p. 434.

16 Ibid., pp. 432–41.

17 On this very issue, see Barton J. Bernstein, 'Reconsidering the Missile Crisis. Dealing with the Problems of the American Jupiters in Turkey', in James A. Nathan (ed.), *The Cuban Missile Crisis Revisited* (New York: St Martin's Press 1992) 94–6.

18 'Ambassador Dobrynin felt that Robert Kennedy's book did not adequately express that the "deal" on the Turkish missiles was part of the resolution of the crisis. And here I have a confession to make to my colleagues on the American side, as well as to others who are present. I was the editor of Robert Kennedy's book. It was, in fact, a diary of those 13 days. And his diary was very explicit that this was part of the deal; but at that time it was still a secret even on the American side, except for the six of us who had been present at that meeting. So I took it upon myself to edit that out of his diaries, and that is why the Ambassador is somewhat justified in saying that the diaries are not as explicit as his conversation.' Sorensen's comments, in Allyn, Blight and Welch, *Back to the Brink*, pp. 92–3.

19 This is clearly based on the appreciation of the fathers of this effort, Allyn, Blight and Welch, for Lebow and Stein's book. They wrote that: 'For a good summary discussion of the Cuban missile crisis in the context of the Cold War

and its end, see Richard Ned Lebow and Janice Gross Stein, *We All Lost the Cold War* (Princeton, N.J.: Princeton University Press, 1994)'; Bruce J. Allyn, James G. Blight, and David A. Welch, afterword from *Cuba on the Brink*, revised edition, n. iv. For a more detailed appreciation of the controversy around the telegram by Anatoly Dobrynin, see Jim Hershberg, 'Anatomy of a Controversy. Anatoly F. Dobrynin's Meeting with Robert F. Kennedy, Saturday, 27 October 1962', *Cold War International History Project Bulletin* 5, (Spring) 1995, available at www2.gwu.edu/~nsarchiv/nsa/cuba_mis_cri/moment.htm (last accessed 19 February 2014).

20 Among many other important titles, one should quote Michael McGwire, 'Deterrence: the Problem Not the Solution', *SAIS Review*, 5/2 (Summer/ Autumn 1985) 105–24.

21 Robert Jervis, Richard Ned Lebow and Janice Gross Stein, *Psychology and Deterrence*, with contributions from Patrick M. Morgan and Jack L. Snyder (Baltimore, MD: Johns Hopkins University Press 1985). The authors themselves acknowledge the continuity in their joint work and trace it back to this specific volume in the preface to *We All Lost the Cold War*, p. xi.

22 Amir Lepovici, 'The Emerging Fourth Wave of Deterrence Theory – Toward a New Research Agenda', *International Studies Quarterly*, 54/3 (2010) 707.

23 In his introduction to the volume which inaugurated the third wave of deterrence research, *Psychology and Deterrence*, in 1985, Robert Jervis noted that 'until recently we did not even have many case studies of deterrence attempts and deterrence failures'. Introduction: Approach and Assumptions', p. 1.

24 It is significant that when asked by the *Journal of Strategic Studies* to review Lawrence Freedman's book on deterrence in 2005, Lebow chose to refer almost exclusively to *We All Lost the Cold War* and not to his previous work. See Richard Ned Lebow, 'Deterrence, Then and Now', *Journal of Strategic Studies* 28/5 (2005) pp. 765–73, n. 4, 8, 9 and 12.

25 Richard Ned Lebow, 'Conclusions', *in Psychology and Deterrence*, pp. 203, 217.

26 Richard Ned Lebow and Janice Gross Stein, 'Beyond Deterrence', *Journal of Social Issues* 434 (1987) 5–71; ibid., 'Rational Deterrence Theory: I Think, Therefore I Deter', *World Politics* 42/2 (1989) 208–24.

27 Ibid., 'The Elusive Dependent Variable', *World Politics* 42/3 (1990) 336–69; Ibid., *When Does Deterrence Succeed and How Do We Know?* (Ottawa: Canadian Institute for International Peace and Security 1990).

28 Janice Gross Stein, 'Deterrence and Reassurance', in Philip Tetlock *et al.* (eds), *Behavior, Society and Nuclear War, Vol. II* (New York: Oxford University Press 1991).

29 Lebow and Stein, 'Rational Deterrence Theory: I Think, Therefore I Deter', 215–17.

30 Lebow and Stein, *Psychology and Deterrence*, pp. 10, 15, 139, 181, 189, 230–1.

31 Lebow did so on his own first in at least six publications, including two books, one of which was published before he started working with Stein: Richard Ned Lebow, *Between War and Peace: The Nature of International Crises* (Baltimore, MD: Johns Hopkins University Press 1981); ibid., 'The Cuban Missile Crisis: Reading the Lessons Correctly', *Political Science Quarterly*, 98/3 (Fall 1983) 431–58; ibid., *Nuclear Crisis Management: A Dangerous Illusion* (Ithaca. NY: Cornell University Press 1987) – this book noticeably showed how the memory of the Cuban missile crisis as a successfully managed nuclear crisis kept alive the idea that managing a nuclear crisis was possible; Raymond L. Garthoff, 'Was Khrushchev Bluffing in Cuba? No', *Bulletin of the Atomic Scientists*, 5/6 (July–August 1988) 41–4; Richard Ned Lebow, 'A Rejoinder: The Case Is Not Closed', *Bulletin of the Atomic Scientists*, 5/6 (July–August 1988) 44; ibid., 'The Traditional and Revisionist Interpretations Reevaluated: Why Was Cuba a Crisis?' in Nathan, *The*

Cuban Missile Crisis Revisited pp. 161–86. The continuity of the research pro-
gramme and of the core arguments is visible in Lebow's question to Sergei
Mikoyan during the 1987 conference about the counterproductive effect of the
American threat intended to deter. Blight and Welch, *On the Brink*, p. 243.

32 Lebow and Stein, 'Beyond Deterrence', 19–23.

33 The distinction between general and immediate deterrence was first proposed
by Patrick Morgan in *Deterrence: A Conceptual Analysis* (Beverly Hills, CA: Sage
1983, second edn) p. 30.

34 Lebow and Stein, 'Beyond Deterrence', 19.

35 For another argument that US nuclear superiority and/or strategy of nuclear
deterrence contributed to incentivise the Soviets to place the missiles in Cuba
rather than prevented the crisis, see Raymond L. Garthoff, *Reflections on the
Cuban Missile Crisis* (Washington, DC: The Brookings Institution 1989) p. 188.

36 On this notion, see Ken Booth and Nicholas J. Wheeler, *The Security Dilemma:
Fear, Cooperation and Trust in World Politics* (Basingstoke: Palgrave 2008) introduction and chapter 2.

37 Interestingly enough, Daniel Ellsberg, who has become a strong opponent of
nuclear weapons over the years, told me that he would still call the Cuban
missile crisis an American victory. Interview with Daniel Ellsberg, Kensington,
CA, 2 July 2014. Gabriel Robin wrote a short book in 1984 to develop the argument that the Soviet Union was not the real loser of the crisis but it was written
in French, has never been translated, and has not got any echo either in the
scholarly or policy world in France. Gabriel Robin, *La Crise de Cuba: du mythe à
l'histoire* [*The Cuban Crisis: From Myth to History*] (Paris: IFRI/Economica 1984)
p. 137. The argument is of course more developed but on this particular page,
Gabriel Robin explicitly argued that Khrushchev had not lost the Cuban missile
crisis. Interview with Gabriel Robin, 18 July 2014.

38 As a matter of fact, the most recent assessment confirmed the massive nuclear
superiority of the US side. Hans M. Kristensen and Robert S. Norris, 'The
Cuban Missile Crisis: A Nuclear Order of Battle, October and November 1962',
Bulletin of the Atomic Scientists, 68/6 (2012) 85–91.

39 Fedor Burlatskiy, 'The Lessons of Personal Diplomacy', *Problems of Communism*,
41 (Spring 1992) 8–13. It is interesting to note that while Lebow and Stein
agreed with Burlatskiy on that point and developed his interpretation, they
named him as one of the key Soviet sources of the interpretation of the relationship between Kennedy and Khrushchev they rejected. This interpretation
focused on the aftermath of the Vienna Summit of June 1961 where the two
leaders had first met. Khrushchev would then have felt that Kennedy was weak
and would not oppose the deployment of missiles in Cuba. Lebow and Stein
saw this as the a result of an echo/contamination phenomenon in which Soviet
actors and academics well versed in Western scholarship about those issues can
actually repeat Western theses back to their authors, giving them the illusion of
authenticity, (p. 12).

40 On Johnson: Stern, *The Cuban Missile Crisis in American History and Memory*,
chapter 10: 'Lyndon Johnson and the Missile Crisis: An Unanticipated Consequence?'; on Nixon and Kissinger, Francis J. Gavin, *Nuclear Statecraft: History
and Strategy in America's Atomic Age* (Ithaca, NY: Cornell University Press 2012)
pp. 105, 111, 119.

41 See Sergey Radchenko's chapter in this volume and James Hershberg, 'The
Cuban Missile Crisis', in Melvyn Leffler and Odd Arne Westad (eds), *Cambridge
History of the Cold War, Vol. II* (Cambridge: Cambridge University Press 2010) p. 83.

42 Eric Herring, *Danger and Opportunity: Explaining International Crisis Outcomes*
(Manchester: University of Manchester Press 1995) pp. 168–70. See chapter 8
on those issues.

43 Matthew Kroenig, 'Nuclear Superiority and the Balance of Resolve: Explaining Nuclear Crisis Outcomes', *International Organization*, 67/1 (January 2013) 154. For a convincing critique of the methodology of this article, see Matthew Fuhrmann and Todd Sechser, 'Debating the Benefits of Nuclear Superiority for Crisis Bargaining, Part II', *The Ducks of Minerva*, March 2013, available at www.whiteoliphaunt.com/duckofminerva/2013/03/debating-the-benefits-of-nuclear-superiority-for-crisis-bargaining-part-ii.html (last accessed 22 September 2014).

44 Kroenig, 'Nuclear Superiority and the Balance of Resolve', 151.

45 Scott and Smith, 'Lessons of October', 683.

46 The only other instance in which the book refers to luck is the verbatim quote of the assessment of the causes of the outcome of the crisis by Dean Acheson, i.e. 'plain dumb luck.' (p. 295)

47 Lebow, *Nuclear Crisis Management*. This absence is all the more surprising as Lebow outlines multiple paths to unintended war in this book. A significant part of the analysis, published in 1987, relied upon the idea that the First World War was an accidental war, which has become highly debatable, but the point remains that Lebow was sensitive to the multiple possibilities of unintended war in this earlier single-authored book.

48 Scott D. Sagan, *The Limits of Safety: Organizations, Accidents and Nuclear Weapons* (Princeton, NJ: Princeton University Press 1993) p. 267.

49 Bruce Blair, *The Logic of Accidental Nuclear War* (Washington, DC: The Brookings Institution 1993). This might be due to the pacing of publication, given that the two books above were published a year before *We All Lost the Cold War*. Scott Sagan confirmed that he had not interacted with Lebow and Stein about their research for the book before it was published. Correspondence with Scott Sagan, July 2014.

50 This is particularly important to better understand and, possibly, learn from, cases of near use of nuclear weapons which peaceful outcome cannot be explained by deterrence. For recent accounts of such cases see Eric Schlosser, *Command and Control: Nuclear Weapons, the Damascus Accident and the Illusion of Safety* (New York: Allen Lane 2013) and Patricia Lewis, Heather Williams, Benoît Pelopidas and Sasan Aghlani, *Too Close for Comfort: Cases of Near Nuclear Use and Options for Policy* (London: Chatham House 2014). www.chathamhouse. org/sites/files/chathamhouse/home/chatham/public_html/sites/default/files/20140428TooCloseforComfortNuclearUseLewisWilliamsPelopidasAghlan i.pdf. (Last accessed 29 September 2014). Regarding the issue of how close we came to the brink in the Cuban missile crisis, see Sergey Radchenko's essay in this volume.

51 Esther Eidinow aptly summarises the problem when she notes that: 'the concept of risk, which flourished particularly during the latter part of the twentieth century, although at first sight chiefly concerned with the vagaries of chance, is revealed as a language of control, and faith in that control.' *Luck, Fate and Fortune: Antiquity and Its Legacy* (Oxford: Oxford University Press, 2011), p. 158. For more on Savitsky and Arkhipov, see Sergey Radchenko's chapter in this volume.

52 Mary Douglas, 'Risk and Danger', in *Risk and Blame* (London: Routledge 1992) p. 46; Eidinow, *Luck, Fate and Fortune*, p. 157.

53 Douglas, *Risk and Blame*, p. 46.

54 Ibid.

55 For a deterrent threat to possibly have that effect, the party issuing the threat has to be prepared to use the weapons, and this intent has to be communicated to the adversary. Therefore, in a deontological approach in which the intent has the same moral value as the perpetration of the act itself, such a (hopefully) self-negating intent is paradoxical.

56 Alice George's research noted a decline in support for civil defence after the crisis and interpreted it as a sign of rising awareness in the vulnerability of the American homeland. Alice George, *Awaiting Armageddon: How Americans Faced the Cuban Missile Crisis* (Chapel Hill, NC: The University of North Carolina Press 2003) 161–9.

57 A promising first attempt in that direction is David Gioe, Len Scott and Christopher Andrew (eds), *An International History of the Cuban Missile Crisis: A 50-year Retrospective* (London: Routledge 2014).

58 All those aspects are developed conceptually and empirically in Benoît Pelopidas (ed.), *Global Nuclear Vulnerability* (edited collection in preparation).

59 This is based on the testimony of two of Khrushchev's former collaborators: Ned Lebow has consistently argued in favour of a careful use of counterfactuals in international relations: "What's So Different about a Counterfactual?", *World Politics* 52(4), July 2000, pp. 550–85; with Philip Tetlock, 'Poking Counterfactual Holes in Covering Laws: Cognitive Styles and Historical Reasoning', *American Political Science Review*, 95/4 (December 2001) 829–43 and *Forbidden Fruit: Counterfactuals and International Relations* (Princeton: Princeton University Press 2010).

60 Stern, *The Cuban Missile Crisis in American History and Memory*, p. 55. JFK told the story back to McNamara in those terms, before asking him to confirm, and McNamara did.

61 Robert McNamara, who later on spoke eloquently about the role of luck in the outcome of the Cuban missile crisis and shaped his legacy as a dove in the ExComm, actually conveyed a sense of perfect control at the time; he even advocated taking major risks at key moments in the crisis. On 27 October 1962, he said, 'you really need to escalate this'. Quoted in Sheldon M. Stern, *The Cuban Missile Crisis in American History and Memory*, p. 54 and, more broadly, chapter 4: 'The Mythmaking of Robert McNamara'.

62 This would elaborate on the famous line Kennedy gave to John Kenneth Galbraith after the crisis: 'Ken, you have no idea how much bad advice I received in those days.' John Kenneth Galbraith, *Name-Dropping: From FDR On* (Boston, MA: Houghton Mifflin 1999), p. 105.

63 For an excellent summary of this intellectual tradition and its contribution, see Daniel Kahneman, *Thinking Fast and Slow* (New York: Penguin 2011), part 3. This is all the more relevant as Lebow and Stein referred to his earlier works with Amos Tversky in the book. See among other references, chapter 13, n. 25 and 27.

8 On hedgehogs and passions

History, hearsay, and hotchpotch in the writing of the Cuban missile crisis[1]

Sergey Radchenko

The Cuban missile crisis has become one of the most-written-about events in the history of the twentieth century, a subject of seemingly endless scrutiny in scholarly accounts of widely varying quality, in memoirs and fiction and in documentaries and Hollywood blockbusters. But while the factual basis for understanding the events of October 1962 has dramatically expanded, in particular in the last twenty or so years, we are as far as ever from definitive answers about key aspects of the crisis. This observation applies especially to the Soviet side. Denied the luxury of taped discussions – a treasure trove for historians and political scientists of America's 'thirteen days' – students of Soviet decision-making are left to piece together a plausible narrative from fragmentary notes, often self-serving memoirs and hearsay. Fifty years on, despite the best achievements of Kremlinology – that Cold War art of educated guessing about Soviet policy and decision-making – and despite the more recent archival revelations, we are largely at a loss when it comes to accounting for the key Soviet decisions prior to and during the crisis. As a result most historians resort to the safety of multi-causality to paper over the uncertainties born of the glaring gaps in the record.

A revolutionary hedgehog

The first port of call for the Soviet side of the story concerns Khrushchev's decision to send nuclear missiles to Cuba: what was he thinking? It was one of the first questions John F. Kennedy put to the participants of the inaugural ExComm meeting on 16 October 1962. When, six days later, JFK went on air to announce the US naval 'quarantine' against Cuba, Moscow offered several explanations including: the missiles were there to defend Cuba against a US invasion – something many a Kremlinologist refused to accept as a valid reason rather than a mere ploy of Soviet propaganda. Alternative answers included the 'quick fix' proposition – that is, that Moscow made up for its inferiority in InterContinental Ballistic Missiles (ICBMs) by putting shorter-range missiles right off the US coast – as well as the idea of a calculated gambit, designed to trade Cuban missiles for US Jupiter missiles in Turkey, or at least for concessions in Berlin. All of these possible explanations were broached at that first ExComm meeting, and were soon accepted as the must-mentions of informed public discussion of the subject.

Nearly ten years passed before any serious new evidence emerged on the Soviet role in the crisis. It came in the form of Nikita Khrushchev's memoirs, smuggled to the West and published in multiple volumes beginning in 1971. Khrushchev's confused ramblings, while on the whole supportive of the 'defence of Cuba' line of argument, contained claims that could substantiate a wide variety of interpretations of Soviet decision-making, including notions of Soviet 'prestige' (read: Khrushchev's own prestige), even credibility ('if Cuba fell, other Latin American countries would reject us ...'), whilst addressing the balance of power ('we'd be doing nothing more than giving them [the Americans] a little of their own medicine').[2] *Khrushchev Remembers* and its successor, *Khrushchev Remembers: The Last Testament* (1974), became about all there was on the Soviet side of the story for over 15 years, even though it was impossible to surmise, as indeed with any memoir, the accuracy of what Khrushchev remembered, and where he misremembered, and to what extent he engaged, consciously or unconsciously, in after-the-fact rationalizations.[3]

With the end of the Cold War, the paucity of sources yielded to fabulous wealth. Soviet veterans of the crisis hastened to tell their stories for the first time, reshaping and informing this nascent historiography.[4] Much of the new testimony confirmed the weathered Soviet claim about defending Cuba as a socialist bridgehead, with strategic concerns (in the sense of the nuclear balance) trailing far behind.[5] The notable exception to the change of emphasis was General Dmitrii Volkogonov's path-breaking book, *Sem' Vozhdei*, which leaned to the side of the strategic imperative. Volkogonov's most memorable contribution was the unreferenced anecdote about Khrushchev allegedly telling the Soviet Defence Minister, Rodion Malinovsky, that it would not be a bad idea to 'throw our hedgehog in the Americans' pants'.[6] This anecdote later made its way to the English-language literature and, occasionally furnished with imagined historical detail, now appears in a dozen books on the subject as 'evidence' in support of the strategic character of Khrushchev's decision.[7] Even so, the calculating, strategic-minded Khrushchev of old has practically vanished from scholarly accounts. He has been replaced by a new Khrushchev, the passionate believer in Communism, the defender of the Cuban revolution.

Among Russian historians who did the most to advertise the 'new' Khrushchev was the late Sergo Mikoyan, the son of Khrushchev's close confidant and Cuba trouble-shooter Anastas Mikoyan. Mikoyan Jr. became one of the favourite commentators on the crisis for Western audiences. In 1990 Bernd Greiner, writing in *Diplomatic History*, claimed he had a 'detailed knowledge of the discussions and decisions in the [Soviet] Presidium' and an interview with Mikoyan was advertised under the ambitious title: 'The Cuban Missile Crisis Reconsidered: *The* Soviet View.'[8] In that interview, as in many subsequent interviews, Mikoyan staunchly defended the argument that Khrushchev sent missiles to Cuba to defend the island against a US invasion. His views to this effect have been cited by a large number of Western scholars, notably those of the revisionist streak.[9] For, if Mikoyan was right about Khrushchev's motives (and – in the words of Thomas Paterson – he was 'well-positioned to know') then one could conceivably blame the US for causing the Cuban missile crisis by resorting to covert and overt actions to destabilize Castro's regime. Patterson (in his commentary on Mikoyan's interview) continues: 'Khrushchev would never have had the opportunity to install dangerous missiles in the Caribbean if the United States had not been attempting to overthrow the Cuban government.'[10]

Just how 'well positioned' was Mikoyan to know what was happening behind the scenes in 1962? In the early 1990s, when the history of the Cuban missile crisis was being rewritten thanks to new revelations on the Soviet side, no one could answer this question with any degree of certainty. Now we can, however, thanks to the publication of Sergo Mikoyan's own seminal work on the Cuban missile crisis, *The Soviet Cuban Missile Crisis.*[11] Mikoyan argues in somewhat unequivocal terms that Khrushchev's main motive for sending missiles was to save Cuba from invasion. Fortunately, he provides detailed references for his claims so that rather than assuming his insider knowledge (as was the case with earlier studies of the crisis in the West) we can try to understand how Mikoyan became so convinced of the correctness of his position, and whether his sources truly justify such conviction.

Most of the evidence apparently comes from Sergo Mikoyan's notes of conversations with his father, all of which postdate the crisis – we are not told by how much. Thus, Anastas Mikoyan recalled:

> Even before his trip to Bulgaria, [May 1962] he [Khrushchev] told me [about] his concerns about possible aggression from the United States. I shared his concerns completely. There was no specific plan of action in place at that point. Upon his arrival from Bulgaria in May, Khrushchev told me that he was constantly thinking about possible options of defending Cuba from an invasion.[12]

This is no smoking gun; reservations that apply to Khrushchev's memoirs may equally apply here including selective memory, and *ex post facto* rationalization. The full context of Anastas Mikoyan's remarks is also missing.

The second piece of evidence is Mikoyan Sr.'s statement before Soviet officers on 21 November 1962:

> And if they [the Americans] had done that [invaded], there would have been no revolutionary Cuba. That would have been a great blow

to the entire world Communist movement, to all socialist countries, to everything progressive. That would have thrown back the struggle of the peoples of Latin America, which is itself in the very early stages, and not only Latin America, but Africa too.[13]

This was said in the context of explaining to the Soviet officers why the Soviet government decided to prevent the Americans from strangling Cuba. However, one would expect Mikoyan to confirm to the Soviet officers the truthfulness of the Soviet propaganda about defending Cuba and scoring a great victory as a result of Kennedy's non-invasion pledge. Presumably, he would not be telling Soviet officers that Moscow sent missiles to Cuba to redress the Soviet strategic inferiority vis-à-vis the United States. In this context, how could one depict the decision to withdraw as a victory for the USSR?

The same reservations may apply to Sergo Mikoyan's third piece of evidence – Nikita Khrushchev's cables to Mikoyan in November 1962 while the latter was in Cuba struggling to explain Moscow's about-face to the very unhappy Cuban leadership. According to the now available cables, which were intended as Khrushchev's guidance for Mikoyan in his talks with the Cubans, the Soviet leader argued:

> We sent our people to Cuba when an invasion was expected. We knew that if there was an invasion the blood of both the Cuban and Soviet peoples would be spilled. We did that. We did that for Cuba, for the Cuban people.[14]

'We undertook a great risk', Khrushchev further claimed, 'and we knew that we were taking a great risk, because the danger of unleashing thermonuclear war really did emerge at the most intense moment.... All this is being done primarily for Cuba and not for us.'[15] Mikoyan followed this line of argument in his own heated discussions with Castro and other Cuban leaders.[16] However, we would not really expect Khrushchev or Mikoyan to tell Castro – who was already furious over becoming a trading chip in Soviet–American relations – that the rationale for placing missiles to Cuba was to close the missile gap with the US.

The last important piece of evidence cited by Sergo Mikoyan is something he would have not known in the early 1990s, as it came to light only recently. Yet it happens to offer the best support for his line of argument about defending Cuba. The evidence is the fragmentary record of the Presidium meetings, the so-called Malin notes (published in full in 2003 in Russia, and now also accessible, in translation, on the Miller Center's Kremlin Decision-Making Project website).[17] The first fragment is that of the meeting on 21 May 1962, where Khrushchev first broached the question of sending missiles to Cuba. The fragment reads: 'On aid to Cuba. How to help Cuba, so that it holds on (Khrushchev).'[18] We also now have

Khrushchev's unclear comments at the 22 October 1962 meeting: 'The thing is that we do not want to unleash a war; he wanted to scare, to deter the USA in relation to Cuba.'[19] It is difficult to draw sweeping conclusions from just a couple of lines of text. This evidence, when tallied with the other information assembled in Mikoyan's book, would warrant the conclusion that defending Cuba was one of the concerns on Khrushchev's mind but it would not support the unequivocal interpretation that it was the only or even necessarily the primary concern. More likely, this concern and strategic arguments were so tightly connected and interrelated in Khrushchev's mind that he would not be able to distinguish one from the other – as he did not in his memoirs.

In this connection, it is helpful to cite from the recollections of the deputy commander of the Soviet forces in Cuba, Leonid Garbuz, who reports on Khrushchev's remarks at a meeting on 7 June 1962: 'Khrushchev began his talk with a phrase: "we in the C[entral] C[ommittee] have decided to throw a 'hedgehog' to the Americans: to place our rockets in Cuba so that America is not able to swallow the Island of Freedom.".'[20] Thus, the hedgehog hypothesis became conveniently married to the idea of defending Cuba from US invasion.[21] Was the 'hedgehog' meant to protect Cuba, or was Cuba meant to offer convenient quarters for the 'hedgehog'? This is not something we can answer with confidence. It is instructive that Mikoyan, after his many statements in defense of Khrushchev the romantic, yields to the brute logic of the evidence by stating towards the end of his analysis that he finds the 'compromise' interpretation (which emphasizes both the defence-of-Cuba theme and Khrushchev's strategic imperatives) 'more or less acceptable'.[22] As James Hershberg argues, Khrushchev's decision 'defies mono-causal explanation; like Harry S. Truman's dropping of the atom bomb on Japan… it had overlapping objectives'.[23]

One thing that one can say with confidence is that with the proliferation of Soviet oral history on the Cuban missile crisis, it is no longer safe to claim that Khrushchev was motivated strictly by strategic considerations – indeed, no one does so. What one sees in recent years, however, is the increasing prevalence of the opposite point of view – the line of argument that emphasizes Khrushchev's irrationality, his romanticism and idealism. This has happened despite the fact that, as demonstrated above, there is no real evidence for making unequivocal statements to this effect. Interestingly, some of the new Cold War historiography does not necessarily go as far as to investigate the existing evidence to the fullest.

An example of this tendency is the highly influential work by Vladislav Zubok and Constantine Pleshakov, *Inside the Kremlin's Cold War*. The authors argue:

> It was not the temptation to use the Cuban Revolution as a chance
> to improve the Soviet position in the strategic balance of the

superpowers that brought the Soviet missiles to San Cristobal, Cuba; rather, it was a new strategic capability that emboldened Khrushchev to launch an overseas operation to save the Cuban Revolution.[24]

What about the evidence? If we check the reference to this particular statement we see that it is merely a 1993 interview with the former Soviet diplomat Oleg Troyanovskii. Ironically, Troyanovskii later published memoirs, in which he gave equal weight to Khrushchev's preoccupation with strategic balance).[25] Interestingly, Zubok softened the 'revolutionary' side of his revolutionary-imperial paradigm with the recent book, *The Soviet Union and the Cold War from Stalin to Gorbachev*. This more nuanced view also draws on Oleg Troyanovskii for evidence – a good example of how the same kind of evidence may be used to support opposite interpretations.[26]

Where Zubok has moved away from 'revolutionary' explanations of the Soviet missile deployment then John Lewis Gaddis, by contrast, has come to emphasize Khrushchev's 'ideological romanticism'. In his 1997 account of the Cold War, *We Now Know*, Gaddis judged the Soviet leader to have acted out of 'desperation' – a view that inspired unforgiving criticism on the part of Sergo Mikoyan who said in no uncertain terms: 'J. Gaddis is far from understanding the psychology and the method of thinking of the Soviet leaders.'[27] If Mikoyan had read his later book, *The Cold War*, he would come away with a more sympathetic impression, for Gaddis now claims that Khrushchev, far from being desperate,

> intended his missile deployment chiefly as an effort, improbably as this might seem, to spread revolution throughout Latin America. He and his advisers had been surprised, but then excited, and finally exhilarated when a Marxist-Leninist insurgency seized power in Cuba on its own.

Khrushchev, Gaddis adds, 'was like a petulant child playing with a loaded gun'.[28]

There is not much in Gaddis' account to substantiate this provocative imagery, with the possible exception of one remark about Fidel Castro, which Mikoyan is said to have made after meeting the Cuban leader: 'Completely like us. I felt as though I had returned to my childhood.'[29] This remark – cited in *'One Hell of a Gamble'* – was probably mistranslated (by Fursenko and Naftali, not Gaddis). It seems that Mikoyan actually said 'I had a feeling that my youth [as opposed to 'childhood' – SR] has returned' – a very minor point, true, though a youth with a gun, for better or worse, is not exactly a child with a gun of Gaddis' imagery.[30] The important issue here is that one somewhat mistranslated remark by Mikoyan (not Khrushchev), made in a context that is far from clear, has appeared time and again in the literature as evidence for the Soviet leader's 'ideological romanticism', becoming almost a must-mention and a counterpart to Volkogonov's hedgehog anecdote.

There is an epistemological problem here. The shift in the existing historiography of the Cuban missile crisis towards greater emphasis on Soviet 'romanticism' – something that we have clearly witnessed since the mid 1990s, and, indeed, something this author has enthusiastically embraced[31] – is not grounded in indisputable, unequivocal evidence but, for the most part, in selective citations from studies that (in turn) selectively cited from other studies that drew on materials which are often still not freely available to researchers interested in the examination of the evidence. For example, the aforementioned remark by Mikoyan has been cited time and again in the emerging literature to provide a very interesting effect. David Priestland, for instance, mentions Mikoyan's 'childhood' moment to argue that the Soviet leaders sought to 'infuse some youthful spirit into the ageing body of Soviet Communism'.[32] The same remark appears in Odd Arne Westad's highly acclaimed *Global Cold War*,[33] citing from Piero Gleijeses, who cites in turn from Fursenko and Naftali,[34] who cite from a cable sent by the Soviet intelligence agent in Havana, Aleksei Alekseev, on 10 February 1960. The cable itself is at the archive of the Russian Service of External Intelligence (SVR), inaccessible to scholars, so that we simply cannot know why Alekseev would report, via intelligence channels, on the comments Mikoyan – then arguably the number two man in the leadership – made to other members of his own delegation. Whatever the reasons, Mikoyan's chance remark has come to signify for many the strength of Soviet ideological commitment to Cuba.

Another piece of evidence that is extensively used to support the above argument is a further remark by Mikoyan, this time to Dean Rusk: 'You Americans must realize what Cuba means to us Old Bolsheviks. We have been waiting all our lives for a country to go Communist without the Red Army, and it happened in Cuba. It makes us feel like boys again!' First cited in Schoenbaum's *Waging Peace and War* in 1988, this statement had since appeared in dozens of books and articles on the Cuban missile crisis. For instance, Hal Brands cites it to support his argument that the Soviets were 'thrilled' by the Cuban revolution 'in an ideological sense'.[35] Lebow and Stein use the same snippet to emphasize Mikoyan's 'sentimental attachment' to Cuba.[36] Mervyn Bain resorts to Mikoyan's remark to argue that Khrushchev had a 'close personal affinity' with Castro.[37] The point here is not at all to argue that Mikoyan was lying to Rusk, or to his close associates (if anything, the coincidence suggests that he was saying about the same thing to both the friend and the foe) but to point out that we have come to depend heavily on such snippets of information to paint a picture of the Soviet involvement in the Cuban missile crisis as heavily coloured by ideological imperatives.

Indeed, a renewed interest in ideology has increasingly characterized scholarship on the Cold War as a whole. As Westad has argued, '[an] increasing number of historians and international relations experts in the West ... believe that their materials tell them that the Cold War was more about ideas and beliefs than about anything else'.[38] This is certainly plausible, yet one may also ask why is it that they believe so, and is it not true that they are encouraged to believe so by the existence of influential and mutually supporting studies by key Cold War scholars that emphasize ideology as the primary motivation for Cold War decision-makers? The Cuban missile crisis serves as merely one of the case studies for illustrating the role of ideology in Soviet policy-making. But it is an important one. If we say that there is no compelling evidence that Khrushchev was motivated by 'revolutionary romanticism' – even if there is also no real evidence to the contrary – where does it leave us with regard to the centrality of ideology in New Cold War scholarship? There are, no doubt, other case studies to draw upon but one should certainly be aware of the potential pitfalls in over-reliance on uncertain scraps of evidence, for fear of building too lofty a castle upon a foundation of sand. Alas, the bottom line is: we do not know precisely why Khrushchev sent missiles to Cuba. More than 50 years on, we are still struggling with this essential and perhaps impossible question. This of course makes it difficult to draw sweeping conclusions from the existing literature.

Khrushchev withdraws

The second important question that has multiple answers in the existing literature of the Soviet side of the crisis is how – and why – Khrushchev, after taking the gamble to secretly deploy MRBMs and IRBMs to Cuba, decided to withdraw those same missiles from the island. Historians and political scientists have had difficulty making sense of the decision-making process behind three letters Khrushchev sent to Kennedy as the crisis climaxed: one, a private one, on 26 October, and two letters on 27 and 28 October, respectively, which were broadcast by Radio Moscow. In the first letter, Khrushchev proposed – although arguably only implicitly and in somewhat vague terms – that the Soviet Union would withdraw missiles from Cuba in return for Kennedy's non-invasion pledge. In the second (public) letter Khrushchev upped the ante by asking for a quid pro quo: removal of Soviet missiles from Cuba in return for the US withdrawal of Jupiter missiles from Turkey. Finally, on 28 October, the Soviet leader agreed, unequivocally, to take the 'weapons which you regard as offensive' (i.e. the R-12 and R-14 missiles, though not the tactical nuclear weapons, of which Kennedy was not aware) out of Cuba. These twists and turns of policy within the space of two days can now be understood much better, because of the release of key documentation on the Russian side.

The most important development was the declassification of the Malin notes for October 1962. These were first introduced (in a somewhat cursory manner) in Fursenko and Naftali's *'One Hell of a Gamble'*, though it was not until the publication of *Khrushchev's Cold War*, by the same authors, that this evidence was utilized in full.[39] The Malin notes are quite fragmentary, missing (amongst other things), the records of the Presidium discussion on 23 October. Sergo Mikoyan fills the gap here with notes of his father's (naturally) self-centred recollections (also borrowed by Fursenko and Naftali).[40] We do have the records for the 25 October meeting, and these show that Khrushchev agreed to the idea of dismantling missile sites if Kennedy undertook 'not to touch Cuba'.[41] This perfectly explains his first letter to Kennedy, although Fursenko and Naftali also highlight secondary factors, for instance, that Khrushchev became scared after he had learned about Kennedy's alleged determination to get rid of Castro through Warren Rogers, an American journalist, who had been overheard to this effect by a bartender/KGB informant at the National Press Club and then confirmed the troubling news to a Soviet diplomat Georgii Kornienko. This story is de-emphasized in Fursenko and Naftali's later account, and for a good reason: it probably had very little, if any, impact on Khrushchev's decision to send that 26 October letter. The decision had by then been made.

In general, the sub-plots of the various secret meetings and backchannels have animated accounts of the Cuban missile crisis since the 1960s. Perhaps the most famous story concerns contacts between the KGB *rezident* in Washington, Aleksandr Feklisov, and the ABC journalist John Scali at the height of the crisis – known for many years and long understood to have played a crucial role in brokering a peaceful settlement of the crisis. Feklisov (then using the cover name Fomin) and Scali met on 26 October, and either the former or the latter proposed the withdrawal/non-invasion pledge compromise. Kennedy had assumed that the proposal came directly from Khrushchev, and it seemed to square with, and complement, in more concrete terms, his 26 October letter. However, some documentation emerged in the 1990s, which suggests that Feklisov may have been acting on his own initiative.[42] Until now, this question has not been settled, although it could presumably be cleared up when the cable traffic between the KGB and Feklisov is declassified in full, which one hopes will not require another 50 years. For now, one issue that we can at least say with certainty is that the Feklisov/Scali exchange was basically irrelevant to Khrushchev's decision-making between 25 October and 28 October. It certainly does not explain why Khrushchev changed his mind and added Jupiters into the settlement formula on 27 October.

Fursenko and Naftali explain this change of mind by invoking Walter Lippmann who had just proposed the Turkey/Cuba exchange in a newspaper column on Thursday 25 October – an article Khrushchev is said to have read.[43] Khrushchev's comments at the Presidium on 27 October show that he thought that it was possible that the US would agree to the 'liquidation' of their bases in Turkey, as well as Pakistan – which would make the Soviet Union 'the winner' but also that he was already resigned to scaling back these demands in case the White House refused to give way. 'I think that we should not be stubborn' was how Khrushchev explained his position before the Presidium voted on the text of the letter to Kennedy, which was broadcast on the radio later that day.[44]

In addition, it has now become clear from the Russian record that the one concession, which scholars believed had swayed Khrushchev into agreeing to withdraw missiles – Kennedy's private promise, made through Robert Kennedy via Ambassador Anatolii Dobrynin – that Jupiters would be withdrawn eventually, played no role in Khrushchev's capitulation on 28 October.[45] Khrushchev simply panicked in reaction to what appeared to be indications of an imminent US attack on Cuba. He was also greatly exercised by a letter from Fidel Castro that appeared to call for a first strike on the United States. 'Only a person who has no idea what nuclear war means, or who has been so blinded, for instance, like Castro, by revolutionary passion, can talk like that', Khrushchev complained several days later.[46] Indeed, when faced with the prospect of escalation, the Soviet leader preferred to back down and cut his losses. For him, this included the loss of Cuban trust. Mikoyan was promptly dispatched to Havana to salvage the wreck of the Soviet–Cuban alliance. Transcripts of his talks, now fully declassified, show the depth of the Cubans' resentment of having become a plaything of Khrushchev's nuclear brinksmanship.[47] The Chinese exploited the rift to the full, unleashing a propaganda campaign to discredit the embattled Soviet leader in the eyes of the Cuban and the Third World audience.[48] Release of new documentation on the Russian side shows that Khrushchev could not stomach a confrontation with the United States and the politico-military risks this entailed.

How close?

The third tantalizing question about the Soviet side of the story in the Cuban missile crisis – the subject also broached in Campbell Craig's chapter – relates to estimates of a nuclear confrontation: just how close did the world come to the brink? The emergence of new Soviet evidence on this question in the late 1980s and early 1990s gave the Western audience a powerful jolt. In the words of a *New York Times* columnist, Flora Lewis, the crisis was 'worse than we knew'.[49] Lewis was talking about the revelation, at the January 1989 Moscow oral history conference, that Soviet nuclear warheads had reached Cuba (something the Kennedy Administration could not detect but safely assumed) and 'orders could have been given at any moment' to fire them.[50] At a subsequent 'critical oral history' conference of US, Soviet (now Russian), and Cuban veterans of the affair (above all Fidel Castro himself), in Havana in January 1992, new troubling details seeped into the public domain. It turned out that the Soviet force on the island had been equipped with tactical nuclear weapons, and – it was even said – the general in charge, Issa Pliev, had pre-delegated authority on their use in case of a US invasion and loss of communications with Moscow.[51] This claim gave added weight to the argument that the chief danger of the Cuban missile crisis was not in what Kennedy or Khrushchev did or did not do but in how far they actually controlled the action on the ground. The prospect of a nuclear Armageddon as an unexpected, indeed, accidental, consequence of a US invasion of Cuba, appeared more possible in retrospect.

In 1992 the question of whether General Pliev had the authority to use nuclear weapons in Cuba prompted a lively discussion among historians, most memorably in a rather intense and at times testy exchange between Mark Kramer, on the one hand, and James Blight, Bruce Allyn, and David Welch, on the other.[52] The evidence was patchy then, and Mark Kramer argued that it was wrong to claim that the crisis was 'more dangerous than it actually was', and he insisted that Khrushchev in fact expressly forbade the use of nuclear weapons in case of a confrontation with the Americans.[53] In the twenty or so years that had passed since those early debates, we know both more and less but there is a certain degree of clarity concerning key documents.

Thus, we know that Khrushchev never approved the instruction prepared by the Ministry of Defence in early September 1962 which would have given Pliev the authority to use tactical nuclear weapons in case of a US invasion and if he could not contact Moscow. Khrushchev withheld his authorization even as he approved the shipment of additional tactical nukes to Cuba on 7 September.[54] Indeed, Gribkov retreated from his previous sensationalist claims in his book *Operation Anadyr*, co-authored with US General William Smith.[55] On the other hand, the same Gribkov claimed a few years later, in a different publication, that when Khrushchev saw Pliev before the latter's departure for Cuba, the Soviet leader,

> after thinking about it for some time ... gave the right to the commander of the Group [of forces] to use the Luna rockets as he deems fit when defending the island.... This right is given to him in case of the lack of communications with Moscow.[56]

Sergo Mikoyan cited Gribkov as telling him privately in Havana (in 1992) that the Soviet forces in Cuba would no doubt use tactical nukes against an invading force. 'There can be hardly any doubt that this would have happened', argues Mikoyan, without, however, supplying any concrete evidence, except for references to the logic of military action.[57]

We know, however, that at the outset of the acute phase of the crisis, on 22 October, Khrushchev (through the Minister of Defence Rodion Malinovsky) ordered Pliev not to resort to the 'weapons of Statsenko's and of all Beloborodov's cargo', which is understood to refer to all – including tactical – nuclear weapons.[58] Further conflicting evidence appears in the Presidium notes for 22 October (prior to the dispatch of Malinovsky's cable). Khrushchev supposedly said: 'Give the instruction to Pliev – to bring all forces to full battle readiness. Try his best at first not to use the atomic [weapons].' The fragment continues: 'If there is a landing – [use?] tactical atomic weapons, and the strategic – [wait?] until the instruction (excluding the use of the means in Statsenko's care).'[59] If this fragment is compared with Malinovsky's cable, one possible conclusion is that while Khrushchev was at first inclined to delegate the authority to use the tactical weapons to Pliev in case of a landing, he evidently had second thoughts at the last moment, and withheld authorization. The order to refrain from any use of nuclear weapons was restated 'categorically' in another cable from Malinovsky to Pliev on 27 October.[60] But if Pliev was clear about his orders after 22 October, it is still impossible to tell whether he had the authority, implied or explicit, to use tactical nuclear weapons before that date.

Even if Pliev had no authority to use tactical, or strategic, nuclear missiles, the question remains whether he, or officers under his command, could have used them nonetheless, for instance, in the heat of battle. Michael Dobbs, in a recent book on the Cuban missile crisis, emphasized that the main danger actually lay in inadvertent escalation of hostilities as a result of a 'sonofabitch moment' – that is, someone, somewhere along the command line, not following orders or making a mistake of some sort.[61] This version of events has been particularly popular since the revelation that it was a Soviet officer who ordered to shoot down a U-2 over Cuba on 27 October 1962 – without any authorization from Khrushchev, the general staff in Moscow, or even Pliev in Cuba. Sensationalist media has of course hijacked the story for their purposes. For instance, one John C. Wohlstetter, in a review of Dobbs' book, recently argued that the U-2 was shot down on Castro's orders (this has long been proven otherwise) – and how this should warn today's policy-makers in the West about the dangers of an 'Islamic Castro'. Speaking of incorrect analogies, it is truly astounding what nonsense one continues to read about the Cuban missile crisis these days![62] This seems to multiply with every passing anniversary.

Just when we thought we had heard enough of the Soviet tactical nuclear weapons in Cuba, Sergo Mikoyan unveiled new interesting evidence: these weapons – which the US basically knew nothing about – could well have stayed in Cuba were it not for Mikoyan Sr.'s eleventh hour insistence on bringing them back. Castro reportedly took it for granted that the tactical nukes – including FKR-1 and Luna rockets – would be left behind, and that the Cubans would be trained in their use. To cite the relevant passage from the book,

> the Soviets initially decided that after they withdrew the strategic missiles, the Cubans could keep the other weapons already deployed in Cuba as a kind of a 'consolation prize' in order to preserve Moscow's strategic and ideological ally in the Western Hemisphere.[63]

But Mikoyan – in view of the Cubans' evident nuclear irresponsibility and their 'passionately independent spirit', decided to pull the plug on the idea, even citing a non-existent law, which prohibited the transfer of nuclear weapons to third powers. All of this, the author contends, shows Mikoyan's foresight and brings him the accolades of the man who saved the world from the prospect of a nuclear-armed Cuba.[64]

Sergo Mikoyan first made these revelations in 2002, later detailing them in the Russian version of his book.[65] Yet, it was their wide dissemination in the translation that gave impetus to commentary to the effect that 'the scariest moment was even scarier than we thought'.[66] The difficulty here is drawing the boundaries between the Cuban aspiration and the Soviet intentions. It is one thing that Castro wanted the weapons. But could Moscow consciously agree to their transfer to a client regime? The one and only precedent was the Soviets' agreement, in 1957, to supply China with a prototype atomic bomb. But this decision was rescinded in 1959, when Khrushchev realized the dangers of such proliferation. Mao had actively sought nuclear weapons, and Khrushchev's initial (and very reluctant) agreement to help China in this respect was a consequence of repeated Chinese requests, and a reflection of Moscow's commitment to building a deeper relationship with what was at the time its most important foreign ally. If Mao had been denied a sample bomb, is it conceivable that Castro would get his hands, as if by default, on nearly a hundred nuclear warheads?

The evidence – including that presented in Mikoyan's book – is uncertain.[67] First, we have Mikoyan's telegram to Moscow, dated 8 November 1962, in which he requests permission to tell Castro that the Soviets would be willing to hand over control of 'all the Soviet weapons remaining in Cuba' and even leave experts 'in special areas' to help the Cubans in their operation.[68] Moscow agreed to this proposition on the following day. The second piece of evidence is Mikoyan's assurances to Castro on 13 November that the Soviets would leave Cuba with 'very powerful defense weapons ... incomparably more powerful than any equipment Cuba currently has ... the most advanced weapons Comrade Pavlov [Issa Pliev] currently has'.[69] Could these statements refer to tactical nuclear weapons? This is not completely clear. Yet what *is* clear is that when the issue of the Cuban possession of these weapons was explicitly raised, Khrushchev made the only possible response: 'these weapons belong to us, and are to be kept in our hands only, we never transferred them to anyone, and we do not intend to transfer them to anyone.'[70]

There were other dangerous moments throughout the crisis, most notably, the accidental overflight of Soviet territory in the Far East by another American U-2 plane, also on 27 October, due to a navigational error.[71] This incident, Dobbs and others speculate, could have been misinterpreted by the Soviets as an intelligence mission before a first strike, or even the first strike itself. But – and here is where we run into a wall on the

Russian side – very little evidence has surfaced that would shed light on the Soviet reaction to the misdirected U-2, so it is difficult to make any conclusions as to how the military – or Khrushchev – interpreted these developments, and whether the moment was as dangerous as Dobbs would make us believe, or as Khrushchev claimed in his letter to Kennedy.[72] Yet again, the paucity of evidence has hardly proved to be a barrier for journalists. The *Globe and Mail*, for instance, in reviewing Dobbs' book, confidently stated that the U-2 was not shot down by Soviet MiGs, *because* they could not reach the required altitude.[73] And so, just as we learn more about the Cuban missile crisis with every new revelation, new myths are being born and the old myths are resuscitated.

It is actually difficult to argue, just on the basis of the shooting down of U-2 over Cuba, that the Soviet chain of command over tactical, much less strategic, nukes was in danger of a breakdown. By the same token, while it is certainly interesting to have learned, from Dobbs' carefully assembled evidence, that the Soviets deployed nuclear-tipped cruise missiles to the vicinity of the Guantánamo base, and were poised to strike the base in case hostilities broke out, Dobbs himself notes that the order to strike would have had to come 'from the general staff in Moscow' – something we have long known.[74] It should be said that most of his evidence on the Soviet side – certainly useful in many ways – is basically hearsay. Documents that would shed more light on the misadventures of the Soviet tactical nuclear weapons remain classified in the Russian archives, including the precise date and manner of their removal from Cuba.

There is more evidence that has come to light in the last decade or so that has strengthened the hand of those who argue that the world came closer to the brink than most people realized. The key development here was the elaboration of the story of the four Soviet submarines on a mission to protect these Soviet shipments to Cuba. The revelation first came to light in Russia in a 1995 article by Aleksandr Mozgovoi who later authored a study, based mainly on extensive interviews with crew members of the four submarines dispatched to the vicinity of Cuba in the run-up to the crisis.[75] The most exciting passage of the book was a recollection by Vadim Orlov, head of the radio intercept team aboard one of the submarines, the B-59. Orlov claimed that the captain of the submarine Valentin Savitskii – who was 'totally exhausted' from days of US anti-submarine warfare harassment – decided to use a nuclear torpedo against his American pursuers, and was only dissuaded from doing so at the last moment, having been persuaded by the Second Captain, Vasilii Arkhipov.[76] The Americans had no idea that this submarine or the other hunter-killers, were equipped with nuclear-tipped torpedoes, and dropped practice depth charges to make them surface.

These revelations caused further controversy in the West, when they were picked up by scholars and journalists in 2002. Although it had earlier become known to scholars that the four submarines had been equipped with nuclear-tipped torpedoes, the new evidence suggested that these could well have been used without authorization. Subsequent investigations by Svetlana Savranskaya, based primarily on oral testimony, were inconclusive as to whether or not such authorization had been given, with some of the submarine captains claiming to have been told that they could strike back if attacked by the Americans.[77] Recently, Dobbs drew on the same testimony in making the argument that the world had come close to the brink. Both Savranskaya and Dobbs add a caveat to the effect that many details in this story are unclear. It is especially difficult to corroborate Orlov's story, seeing that Savitskii, Arkhipov and other key witnesses are already dead. All the same, Vasilii Arkhipov has now entered the literature as the 'guy who saved the world'.[78] There is even a Wikipedia article devoted to this important if, for all intents and purposes, undocumented feat.

Conclusions

Since the end of the Cold War we have come to learn a great deal about the Soviet side of the story of the Cuban missile crisis. Important details have come to light through increasing declassification and oral history; in particular through the efforts of individual scholars noted here and scholarly enterprises such as the Cold War International History Project (CWIHP) and the National Security Archive, among others. But it is fair to say that we have still only seen the tip of the iceberg. Key documentation remains inaccessible to this day in the archives of the Russian Ministry of Defence, and of the Navy, in the Presidential Archive, in the archives of the intelligence services (in particular, the External Intelligence Service, the SVR), and the Foreign Ministry Archive. Though Fidel Castro has released a smattering of materials, mostly in connection with the international oral history conferences he hosted in Havana in 1992 and 2001–2, Cuban documents remain mostly sealed off. The CWIHP has continued its efforts to obtain, and translate, new documents on the crisis, most recently those of the Chinese.[79] This effort is not attracting as much attention or funding as it once did in the 1990s. The gloss of novelty has worn off. It seems that we have learned so much about the crisis – what else do we need to know? Moreover, it is not even clear that new evidence could help us answer the three most vexing questions: why did Khrushchev send missiles to Cuba, why did he withdraw them and how close did the world come to thermonuclear Armageddon?

On the other hand, there is much that we have learned about the Cuban missile crisis since the Soviet side of the story began to emerge. We know that it was Khrushchev personally – not a 'collective leadership' of any kind – that committed to sending missiles to Cuba and forced the idea through the Presidium practically without any resistance. It was also Khrushchev who made the decision, at the eleventh hour, to withdraw missiles from Cuba. Earlier Kremlinological analyses tended to ponder the role of various factions within the leadership and bureaucratic and institutional interests. We have learned, thanks to disclosures on the Soviet side, that such pressures were evidently not a serious determinant of Khrushchev's actions. On the other hand, it has become clear that one cannot understand how Soviet foreign policy was made without taking into account the role of personality. With a confused personality like Khrushchev – flamboyant and romantic here, calculating and rational there – it has proven difficult to understand the twists and turns of Moscow's policy towards Cuba, and, for this matter, its foreign and defence policy in general. Hence, the new literature on the Cold War has come to emphasize irrationality and emotions, which coloured perceptions and influenced policy-making on the Soviet side. Indeed, we have seen that scholars have embraced this new, 'ideological', aspect of the Soviet Cold War experience with remarkable zeal.

Yet no amount of zeal, occasionally born of suspect evidence, has served to undermine the longtime argument that Khrushchev stepped back 'from the brink' because he was afraid of a nuclear war. His revolutionary spirit, his love of Castro, and so on – none of that sufficed to bolster Khrushchev's willingness to stand firm in the face of US pressure. Indeed, new evidence has shown that Khrushchev had blinked even earlier than it seemed at the time. Now, what exactly that means in terms of historical lessons is less clear. One could either argue that it proves that containment worked and, just as George Kennan would have predicted, the Soviet Union retreated when faced with superior force. Or, it may prove nothing, except that Khrushchev personally did not have the nerve for toughing out a stand-off with the Americans. The strong personal and subjective element in Soviet/Russian decision-making suggests that it is just as likely that Stalin, Brezhnev, or Putin would have acted the same way as that they would have acted differently. Some of the same reservations also apply to US decision-making during the crisis but, comparatively speaking, Soviet/ Russian foreign policy has proved more likely to suffer from zigzags and unexpected reversals, often due to the absence of strong institutional constraints.

Further, we have learned a lot about the details of the Soviet operation in Cuba – the logistical arrangements, the nature of military plans, and so on – including the startling revelation of the tactical nuclear weapons, deployed both in Cuba and aboard the submarines, which caused, and continue to cause, controversy among scholars and the general public. Disclosure of these sensational details over the last twenty years has not produced great clarity as to whether these weapons could, and would, have been used. The 'brink' theory has won plenty of adherents, from Allyn, Blight, and Welch in the early 1990s, to Michael Dobbs most recently. Voices of sceptics have not been heard quite as loudly, although the evidence has been anything but unequivocal, especially in the case with the submarines incident. It has become fashionable, on the basis of the new Russian literature on the Cuban missile crisis, to argue that the world had come very close to a nuclear war and that the main danger was not even in what Kennedy or Khrushchev thought or did, but in the inadvertent escalation of hostilities. Khrushchev was apprehensive about the prospects of an accidental nuclear war, and did his best to keep control of the 'red button', figuratively speaking. But, problematically, there was no 'red button' that Khrushchev could have resorted to. The command and control structure was not well integrated, and much dependent on the actions of individual commanders who decided for themselves how to interpret instructions from Moscow.

The Soviet account of the missile crisis has been presented in the West through a number of books. Some have been more successful than others. Clearly, *'One Hell of a Gamble'* and *Khrushchev's Cold War* by Fursenko and Naftali and, more recently, *Anatomi'ia Karibskogo Krizisa* by Sergo Mikoyan, have advanced our knowledge to a considerable degree. Scholarly debates have raged intermittently in conferences and in print. Few of the big debates of the early 1990s have been satisfactorily resolved. Michael Dobbs, in *One Minute to Midnight*, remarks that he was greatly surprised how much more new evidence he had been able to unearth. Even so, his book has served as another reminder of how many things he – and others – have not been able to unearth. A lot hinges on the declassification process in Russia, which has now slowed down to a crawl. New evidence continues to emerge year after year but the crucial pieces of the puzzle are still missing. The 50-year anniversary of the crisis serves to remind us that we have only just scratched the surface.

Notes

1 The author would like to thank Len Scott, Kristan Stoddart, James Hershberg, and two anonymous reviewers for comments on the early draft of this article. This chapter was developed from Sergey Radchenko, 'The Cuban Missile Crisis: Assessment of New, and Old, Russian Sources', *International Relations*, 26/3 (2012) 327–43. Reproduced by permission of Sage Publications Ltd.

2 Nikita Sergeevich Khrushchev, Edward Crankshaw, and Strobe Talbott, *Khrushchev Remembers* (Boston, MA: Little, Brown and Company 1970) pp. 493–4.

3 Another irreplaceable source was only indirectly 'Soviet' – an account by the Hungarian defector Janos Radvanyi, *Hungary and the Superpowers: The 1956 Revolution and Realpolitik* (Stanford, CA: Hoover Institution Press 1972) p. 137.

4 See, in the first instance, Bruce J. Allyn, James G. Blight, and David A. Welch, 'Essence of Revision: Moscow, Havana, and the Cuban Missile Crisis', *International Security*, 14/3 (Winter 1989–90) 136–72. This should be read with Mark Kramer's cautionary remarks on the use and abuse of CMC oral history, 'Remembering the Cuban Missile Crisis: Should We Swallow Oral History?' *International Security*, 15/1 (Summer 1990) 212–18.

5 Allyn, Blight, and Welch, 'Essence of Revision', pp. 138–44.

6 Dmitrii Volkogonov, *Sem' Vozhdei*, Vol. II (Moscow: Novosti 1995) p. 420. The English version is: Dmitrii Volkogonov and Harold Shukman, *Autopsy for an*

Empire: The Seven Leaders Who Built the Soviet Regime (New York: Free Press 1998) p. 236.

7 For instance, Don Munton and David A. Welch add 'a twinkle' in Khrushchev's eye to the anecdote. See *The Cuban Missile Crisis: A Concise History* (Oxford: Oxford University Press 2008) p. 26. See also Ernest R. May and Philip D. Zelikow, *The Kennedy Tapes* (Cambridge, MA: Harvard University 2000) p. 674; also, David Reynolds, *Summits: Six Meetings That Shaped the Twentieth Century* (Philadelphia, PA: Basic Books 2009) p. 216; John Lewis Gaddis, *The Cold War: A New History* (London: Penguin 2005) p. 75; William Taubman, *Khrushchev: The Man and his Era* (London: W.W. Norton 2004) p. 541, et seq. Most of these references made their way into the literature via Aleksandr Fursenko and Timothy Naftali, *'One Hell of a Gamble': Khrushchev, Castro, and Kennedy, 1958–64* (New York: Norton 1997), which itself relied on Volkogonov. One should mention that the hedgehog anecdote also appears, although in a different context, and on a different date, in V.I. Esin (ed.), *Strategicheskaya operatsiya 'Anadyr': kak eto bylo* (Moscow: MOOVVIK 1999) p. 82.

8 Bernd Greiner, 'The Cuban Missile Crisis Reconsidered: The Soviet View: An Interview with Sergo Mikoyan', *Diplomatic History*, 14/2 (Spring 1990) [my italics].

9 Richard Ned Lebow and Janice Gross Stein, *We All Lost the Cold War* (Princeton, NJ: Princeton University Press 1994) p. 30. Lebow and Stein, however, do not wholeheartedly endorse this view, leaving ample room for strategic concerns.

10 Thomas G. Paterson, 'Commentary: the Defense-of-Cuba Theme and the Missile Crisis', *Diplomatic History*, 14/2 (Spring 1990) p. 256.

11 Sergo Mikoyan, *The Soviet Cuban Missile Crisis*, ed. by Svetlana Savranskaya (Washington, DC: and Stanford, CA: Woodrow Wilson Center Press and Stanford University Press 2012). The book was first published in 2006 in Russia as Sergo Mikoyan, *Anatomiya Karibskogo Krizisa* (Moscow: Akademiya 2006), a thousand-plus-page volume. The English-language version, edited by Svetlana Savrasnkaya, is somewhat shorter, omitting much of the material that would seem repetitive to Western audiences.

12 Mikoyan, *The Soviet Cuban Missile Crisis*, p. 91.

13 Anastas Mikoyan statement to Soviet officers on 21 November as cited in Mikoyan, *The Soviet Cuban Missile Crisis*, p. 469. Differently from the Russian version of this book, Mikoyan omits this evidence in the translated volume (i.e. compare: Mikoyan, *Anatomiya Karibskogo Krizisa*, p. 140). But it does appear in the translation's documentary appendix.

14 Cited in Mikoyan, *The Soviet Cuban Missile Crisis*, p. 376. This citation comes from the documentary appendix at the end of the book, which is a more accurate reflection of the Russian text than the relevant citation on p. 96.

15 Ibid., p. 405. Compare with citation on p. 96.

16 For example, see Memorandum of Conversation between Castro and Mikoyan, 4 November, 1962 in ibid., p. 305.

17 Kremlin Decision-Making Project, Miller Center, University of Virginia, http://millercenter.org/about/kremlin (last accessed 22 September 2014).

18 Aleksandr Fursenko (ed.), *Prezidium TsK KPSS*, Vol. I (Moscow: Rosspen 2003) p. 556. See also Sergo Mikoyan, *The Soviet Cuban Missile Crisis*, p. 97. Note the difference in translation.

19 Fursenko, *Prezidium TsK KPSS*, p. 617. Mikoyan does not actually draw on this piece for evidence in defence of his view.

20 Esin, *Strategicheskaya operatsiya Anadyr*, p. 82. Also cited in Mikoyan, *Anatomiya Karibskogo Krizisa*, p. 193. The word 'hedgehog' is replaced in the translation with the words 'unpleasant surprise'. See Mikoyan, *The Soviet Cuban Missile Crisis*, p. 122.

21 It should be noted that this repetition of the hedgehog anecdote in a different context adds veracity to Volkogonov's aforementioned unreferenced anecdote. At the same time, Garbuz's hedgehog and Volkogonov's hedgehog do not refer to exactly the same line of argument, which only serves to underscore the uncertain meaning of this metaphor.

22 Mikoyan, *Anatomiya Karibskogo Krizisa*, p. 149. This sentence is missing from Mikoyan, *The Soviet Cuban Missile Crisis*, p. 99, making the author sound some-what more unequivocal than he was probably prepared to be. However, Savran-skaya is essentially correct in her interpretation of what Sergo Mikoyan perceived as the key motives for the placement of missiles. See ibid., pp. 262, 264.

23 James Hershberg, 'The Cuban Missile Crisis', in Melvyn Leffler and Odd Arne Westad (eds), *Cambridge History of the Cold War, Vol. II* (Cambridge: Cambridge University Press 2010) p. 68.

24 Vladislav Zubok and Constantine Pleshakov, *Inside the Kremlin's Cold War* (Cambridge MA: Harvard University Press 1997) p. 260.

25 Oleg Troyanovskii, *Cherez Gody i Rasstoyaniya* (Moscow: Vagrius 1997) p. 240.

26 Vladislav Zubok, *A Failed Empire: The Soviet Union and the Cold War* (Chapel Hill, NC: University of North Carolina Press 2007) p. 144. Zubok cites Troyanovskii's article, 'The Making of Soviet Foreign Policy', in William Taubman, Sergei Khrushchev and Abbott Gleason (eds), *Nikita Khrushchev* (New Haven, CT: Yale University Press 2000) pp. 218–41.

27 Mikoyan, *Anatomiya Karibskogo Krizisa*, p. 135. This criticism is toned down in the translation. See Mikoyan, *The Soviet Cuban Missile Crisis*, p. 94. For Gaddis' discussion of Khrushchev's desperation, see John Lewis Gaddis, *We Now Know: Rethinking Cold War History* (New York: Oxford University Press 1997) p. 262.

28 Gaddis, *The Cold War*, p. 78.

29 Ibid., p. 76.

30 For this observation, I relied on the Russian version of *'One Hell of a Gamble'*, which, Fursenko claimed in his introduction, cited the original Russian docu-ments rather than re-translations from English. Aleksandr Fursenko and Timothy Naftali, *Adskaya Igra: Sekretnaya Istoriya Karibskogo Krizisa, 1958–1964* (Moscow: Geiya 1999).

31 Sergey Radchenko, *Two Suns in the Heavens: The Sino-Soviet Struggle for Supremacy* (Washington, DC/Stanford, CA: Woodrow Wilson Center Press/Stanford University Press 2009) p. 37.

32 David Priestland, *The Red Flag: A History of Communism* (New York: Grove Press 2009) p. 384.

33 Odd Arne Westad, *The Global Cold War: Third World Interventions and the Making of Our Times* (Cambridge: Cambridge University Press 2006) p. 174. Westad, however, errs on the side of caution, suggesting that saving Cuba was only one of Khrushchev's 'key purposes' – a much more careful argument than, for instance, the claims in Gaddis' latest book, or in Zubok and Pleshakov.

34 Piero Gleijeses, *Conflicting Missions: Havana, Washington, and Africa, 1959–1976* (Chapel Hill, NC: University of North Carolina Press 2002) p. 18.

35 Hal Brands, *Latin America's Cold War* (Cambridge, MA: Harvard University Press 2010) p. 31.

36 Lebow and Stein, *We All Lost the Cold War*, p. 28.

37 Mervyn Bain, *Soviet-Cuban Relations, 1985–1991: Changing Perceptions in Moscow and Havana* (Plymouth: Lexington Books 2007) p. 20.

38 Odd Arne Westad, 'Introduction: Reviewing the Cold War', in Odd Arne Westad (ed.), *Reviewing the Cold War: approaches, interpretations, theory* (London: Frank Cass 2000) p. 1. It has been more than a decade since the publication of this important volume. In recent years – in the opinion of this author – there

has been some movement in the historiography in the opposite direction – away from 'beliefs and ideas' towards 'interests and power.'

39 See Aleksandr Fursenko and Timothy Naftali, *Khrushchev's Cold War* (London: W.W. Norton 2006) chapter 19.

40 Mikoyan, *The Soviet Cuban Missile Crisis*, pp. 156–9. Fursenko and Naftali, *Khrushchev's Cold War*, pp. 478–80.

41 Fursenko, *Prezidium TsK KPSS*, Vol. I, p. 620.

42 Aleksandr Fursenko and Timothy Naftali, 'Using the KGB Documents: The Scali-Feklisov Channel in the Cuban Missile Crisis', *Cold War International History Project Bulletin*, Issue 5 (Spring 1995) 58.

43 Fursenko and Naftali, *Khrushchev's Cold War*, pp. 487–8.

44 Fursenko, *Prezidium TsK KPSS*, Vol. I, p. 623.

45 Hershberg, 'The Cuban Missile Crisis', p. 83.

46 Fidel Castro's 26 October 1962 letter to Khrushchev is in James G. Blight, Bruce J. Allyn, and David A. Welch, *Cuba on the Brink: Castro, the Missile Crisis, and the Soviet Collapse* (New York: Pantheon 1993) pp. 509–10. Khrushchev cited in Hershberg, 'The Cuban Missile Crisis', p. 82.

47 'Mikoyan's Mission to Havana: Cuban-Soviet Negotiations, November 1962', *Cold War International History Project Bulletin*, Issue 5 (Spring 1995), pp. 93–109, 159. Mikoyan, *The Soviet Cuban Missile Crisis*, pp. 293–504.

48 See James Hershberg and Sergey Radchenko, with Zhang Qian, 'Sino-Cuban Relations and the Cuban Missile Crisis, 1960–62: New Chinese Evidence', *Cold War International History Project Bulletin*, Issues 17–18 (October 2012) 21–116.

49 Flora Lewis, 'Worse Than We Knew', *New York Times*, 1 February 1989, A25.

50 Ibid., A25

51 Raymond Garthoff, 'The Havana Conference on the Cuban Missile Crisis', *Cold War International History Project Bulletin*, Issue 1 (Spring 1992) pp. 2–3.

52 Mark Kramer, 'Tactical Nuclear Weapons, Soviet Command Authority, and the Cuban Missile Crisis', *Cold War International History Project*, Issue 3 (Fall 1993) p. 40; James G. Blight, Bruce J. Allyn, and David A. Welch, 'Kramer vs. Kramer: or, How Can You Have Revisionism in the Absence of Orthodoxy?', *Cold War International History Project*, Issue 3 (Fall 1993), 40.

53 Kramer, 'Tactical Nuclear Weapons', 45.

54 Fursenko and Naftali, *'One Hell of a Gamble'*.

55 Anatoly I. Gribkov and William Y. Smith, *Operation Anadyr: US and Soviet Generals Recount the Cuban Missile Crisis* (Chicago: Edition Q 1994). See also Scott D. Sagan, *The Limits of Safety: Organisations, Accidents, and Nuclear Weapons* (Princeton, NJ: Princeton University Press 1993).

56 V.I. Esin (ed.), *Operatsiya Anadyr: Fakty, Vospominaniya, Dokumenty* (Moscow: TSIPK 1997).

57 Mikoyan, *The Soviet Cuban Missile Crisis*, p. 187.

58 The document is reprinted in full in *Cold War International History Project Bulletin*, Issue 14/15 (Winter 2003 – Spring 2004) p. 387.

59 Fursenko, *Prezidium TsK KPSS*, Vol. I, p. 618.

60 *Cold War International History Project Bulletin*, Issue 14/15 (Winter 2003 – Spring 2004) p. 388.

61 Michael Dobbs, *One Minute to Midnight: Khrushchev, and Castro on the Brink of Nuclear War* (London: Knopf 2008) p. 346.

62 John C. Wohlstetter, 'Cuba 1962: Lessons for Today', *The American Spectator*, 22 October 2009.

63 Mikoyan, *The Soviet Cuban Missile Crisis*, p. 266.

64 Ibid., pp. 223–5.

65 See Thomas S. Blanton, 'The Cuban Missile Crisis Just Isn't What It Used to Be', *Cold War International History Project Bulletin*, Issues 17–18 (October 2012), p. 15.

66 Svetlana Savranskaya, 'Cuba Almost Became a Nuclear Power in 1962: The Scariest Moment in History Was Even Scarier Than We Thought,' *Foreign Policy*, 10 (October 2012).

67 The author is grateful to Svetlana Savranskaya for pointing his attention to the available evidence. See also Svetlana Savranskaya, 'Last Nuclear Weapons Left Cuba in December 1962,' 11 December 2013, www2.gwu.edu/~nsarchiv/ NSAEBB/NSAEBB449/. (last accessed 28 September 2014).

68 Mikoyan, *The Soviet Cuban Missile Crisis*, pp. 355–6.

69 Ibid., p. 398.

70 Mikoyan, *The Soviet Cuban Missile Crisis*, p. 480.

71 Dobbs, *One Minute to Midnight*, p. 260.

72 Khrushchev mentioned the U-2 incursion in his 28 October public letter to Kennedy. But there is no information on the internal Soviet deliberations on the matter.

73 John Ibbitson, 'He Almost Blew up the World, but Kennedy Learned – So Would Obama', *Globe and Mail*, 30 July 2008, A13.

74 Dobbs, *One Minute to Midnight*, p. 179. Raymond Garthoff's comments on the cruise missile document and other Guantánamo-base related evidence in Raymond L. Garthoff, 'New Evidence on the Cuban Missile Crisis: Khrushchev, Nuclear Weapons, and the Cuban Missile Crisis', *Cold War International History Project Bulletin*, Issue 11 (Winter 1998) pp. 251–62.

75 Aleksandr Mozgovoi, *Kubinskaya Samba Kvarteta Fokstrotov* (Moscow: Voennyi Parad 2002).

76 Mozgovoi, *Kubinskaya Samba Kvarteta Fokstrotov*.

77 Svetlana Savranskaya, 'New Sources on the Role of Soviet Submarines in the Cuban Missile Crisis', *Journal of Strategic Studies*, 28/2 (April 2005) 233–59. See also William Burr and Thomas S. Blanton (eds), 'The Submarines of October: U.S. and Soviet Naval Encounters during the Cuban Missile Crisis', *The National Security Archive Electronic Briefing Book No. 75*, 31 October 2002, www2.gwu. edu/~nsarchiv/NSAEBB/NSAEBB75/, last accessed 15 December 2014.

78 Tim Reid, 'Soviet Submariner "Saved the World" in Cuban Crisis', *The Times*, 14 October 2002, 16.

79 For example, see James Hershberg (ed.), *Cold War International History Project Bulletin*, Issues 17–18 (October 2012).

9   Beyond the smoke and mirrors

The real JFK White House Cuban missile crisis

Sheldon M. Stern

The great enemy of the truth is very often not the lie – deliberate, contrived and dishonest – but the myth – persistent, persuasive, and unrealistic.

(John F. Kennedy, Yale University Commencement Address, 11 June 1962)

JFK: a politician's quarrel with history

President Kennedy, much like his predecessors going back at least to Lincoln, recognized the political benefits of managing news and, in the long run, trying to shape the historical record. An avid reader of history since his early teens, JFK understood precisely what Winston Churchill meant when he declared that he would leave his Second World War record to the verdict of history – but he himself would be one of the historians. Kennedy, on multiple occasions, is known to have alerted aide Ted Sorensen when he thought that some statement or document should be set aside for the book they would later write about his presidency.

JFK the politician was instinctively wary of historians. He was comfortable having Pulitzer Prize winner and Democratic party activist Arthur Schlesinger Jr. as a White House special assistant; but he nonetheless groused to David Herbert Donald in 1962 about historians' facile hubris – as revealed in surveys that rated presidents as 'below average' or even as 'failures'. 'Thinking, no doubt, about how his administration would look in the backward glance of history', Donald recalls,

> he resented the whole process. With real feeling he said, 'No one has the right to grade a President – not even poor James Buchanan – who has not sat in his chair, examined the mail and information that came across his desk, and learned why he made his decisions.'

In a less guarded moment, Kennedy grumbled about historians to his friend Ben Bradlee: 'Those bastards, they are always there with their pencils out.'[1]

Historians, therefore, should hardly have been surprised to learn from the now declassified White House ExComm tape recordings that Kennedy had been apprehensive about the political – and ultimately the historical – judgements of the Cuban missile crisis. On 22 October, for example, just hours before his televised speech to the nation, JFK met with the National Security Council and the Joint Chiefs and stressed that everyone would be expected to fully back the quarantine (naval blockade) in order to maximize domestic political support. Every administration voice, Kennedy demanded, was to 'sing one song in order to make clear that there was now no difference among his advisers as to the proper course to follow.' He described the quarantine as 'a reasonable consensus' and grimly noted that if the wrong choice had been made, we may not even have had 'the satisfaction of knowing what would have happened if we had acted differently. ... I think we've done the best thing', he added fatalistically, 'at least as far as you can tell in advance.' He also reminded his advisors, in the event that anyone should later have second thoughts (probably recalling the aftermath of the Bay of Pigs fiasco), 'I don't think there was anybody ever who didn't think we shouldn't respond'. His meaning was plain in spite of his grammar.[2]

Attorney General Robert Kennedy, with a habitual eye on the imminent mid-term congressional elections and his brother's 1964 re-election prospects, warned about potentially damaging press reaction after the President's speech – possibly accusing the administration of incompetence or duplicity for not acting much sooner. JFK replied that without hard evidence, which had not become available until 16 October,[3] it would have been very difficult to get OAS support and NATO would have regarded risking Soviet retaliation in Berlin as proof of 'almost a fixation on the subject of Cuba'. And, he added, 'no one at that time was certain that Khrushchev would make such a far-reaching step, which is wholly a departure from Soviet foreign policy, really, since I would say the Berlin Blockade'. JFK pointedly reminded his colleagues that none of the Eastern European satellites had nuclear weapons on their territory and 'this would be the first time the Soviet Union had moved these weapons outside their own borders'. And, RFK grumbled, Ambassador Anatoly Dobrynin, and Foreign Minister Andrei Gromyko had privately insisted 'that this was not being done'.[4]

The President seemed confident that the administration could make a convincing case in the court of world public opinion and in the judgement of history that the blockade of Cuba was not comparable to the Soviet Berlin blockade in 1948: 'we're permitting goods to move into Cuba at this point, food and all the rest. This is not a blockade in that sense. It's merely an attempt to prevent the shipment of weapons there.'[5]

Kennedy was also determined to publicly defend the naval blockade decision as a reasonable and restrained response to an unwarranted and gratuitous Soviet provocation. The American public, of course, knew nothing about the sabotage and terrorism of Operation Mongoose or about the efforts of the CIA to assassinate Fidel Castro; the President also did not want to hand Moscow a propaganda bonanza by revealing that surprise air attacks against Cuba had even been seriously considered by the administration; he was entirely willing to mislead the press and tersely ordered his advisers to 'scratch that from all our statements and conversations, and not ever indicate that that was a course of action open to us. *I can't say that strongly enough,*' he instructed. 'Now it's gonna be very difficult to keep it quiet, but I think we ought to because … it may inhibit us in the future.'[6]

Six days later, on Sunday 28 October, hours after Nikita Khrushchev had agreed publicly to remove 'those weapons you describe as offensive' (verified by on-site United Nations inspectors), in return for a United States pledge not to reinvade Cuba and a secret American commitment to remove the Jupiter missiles from Turkey, President Kennedy began purposefully to manipulate the historical record. He phoned former Presidents Eisenhower, Truman and Hoover – and shrewdly lied to his predecessors. He accurately reported that Khrushchev had privately suggested (on Friday 26 October) withdrawing the Cuban missiles in exchange for an American promise not to invade Cuba, but had then made a public announcement early the next day offering to remove the missiles if the US pulled its Jupiter missiles out of Turkey. Kennedy informed Eisenhower, 'we couldn't get into that [Turkey] deal', told Hoover that Khrushchev had gone back 'to their more reasonable [Friday] position' and assured Truman, 'we rejected … [the trade and] they came back with and accepted the earlier proposal'. Eisenhower, who had personally dealt with Khrushchev, seemed doubtful and asked if the Soviets had tried to attach any other conditions. 'No', Kennedy replied disingenuously, 'except that we're not gonna invade Cuba.' Ike expressed concern that Khrushchev might try to extract an American commitment that 'one day could be very embarrassing'. Nonetheless, the former President, knowing only half the truth, concluded, 'this is a very, I think, conciliatory move he's made'.[7]

Such deceptions shaped the administration's cover story – which required concealing the fact that the President had, in fact, cut a deal with the Soviets. In a very real sense, JFK's phone calls on that thirteenth day represent the first step in creating the myths that were later elaborated and embellished by Robert Kennedy in *Thirteen Days*.

RFK: inventing the secret Cuban missile crisis

Robert F. Kennedy apparently began working on his account of the missile crisis sometime late in 1962. The draft manuscript of *Thirteen Days* was almost certainly intended for release in time for President Kennedy's 1964 re-election effort – a familiar campaign tactic for the Kennedys. In 1946, when JFK first ran for Congress, his campaign had disseminated reprints of John Hersey's 1944 *New Yorker* article about Kennedy's PT 109 exploits. Likewise, in 1960, copies of *Profiles in Courage* were distributed and a signed, gold-edged, leatherette edition was prepared for major donors. Initially however, the drafts of RFK's missile crisis memoir were so tightly held within the White House inner circle that many senior administration officials did not even know about its existence.

Of course, 22 November 1963 changed everything. No one knows precisely when Robert Kennedy, devastated by his brother's assassination, returned to work on the book. However, in the spring of 1964, he asked JFK's former special assistant and confidante Kenneth O'Donnell to read a draft of the manuscript. O'Donnell responded several days later and was characteristically blunt and to the point: 'I thought your brother was President during the missile crisis!' Bobby replied, 'He's not running, and I am' (RFK was seeking, successfully, a US Senate seat from New York). Another version has RFK replying, 'Jack wouldn't mind.'[8]

O'Donnell had obviously perceived that the focus of the manuscript had shifted; it was now intended to boost RFK's personal political fortunes. This concern about his own political future was neither surprising nor completely unprecedented. On 29 October 1962, a day after Khrushchev had agreed to remove the missiles from Cuba, Soviet Ambassador Dobrynin delivered a letter from the Kremlin to Bobby Kennedy. The message identified the terms of the agreement reached on that fateful weekend and specifically mentioned the secret American commitment to remove the Jupiter missiles from Turkey.

After consulting with the President, RFK met with Dobrynin again the next day. The attorney general returned the letter and explained that the White House was not prepared to 'engage in any correspondence on so sensitive an issue ... even by means of strictly confidential letters'. More to the point, Dobrynin later recalled: 'Very privately, Robert Kennedy added that someday – who knows? – he might run for president, and his prospects could be damaged if this secret deal about the missiles in Turkey were to come out.'[9]

When O'Donnell first read the draft manuscript nearly two years later, Robert Kennedy was very likely already thinking about seeking the presidency – perhaps as soon as 1968. He must have recognized that his persistently hawkish stance during the missile crisis meetings would not appeal to an electorate increasingly and bitterly divided over the war in Vietnam (which he had initially supported). The tapes of the ExComm meetings were, it must be emphasized, classified and legally regarded as the President's personal property, to be preserved or disposed of according to his wishes (or that of his estate) after he left office; no one at the time could have foreseen Watergate or imagined the sequence of events that would lead to the Freedom of Information Act, the Presidential Records Act, and the eventual declassification of these one-of-a-kind primary sources.

The existence of the Kennedy tape recordings was not even publicly acknowledged until 1973 – in the wake of the revelations about the Nixon tapes during the Senate Watergate hearings.

The manuscript (still unfinished at the time of the 1968 campaign), presented Robert Kennedy with a unique and unparalleled opportunity, as it were, to invent the past and design a politically expedient historical persona for himself (on 9 August 1963, JFK's secretary sent 18 *very rough* transcripts to Attorney General Robert Kennedy's office in the Justice Department. RFK likely read these transcripts and, far less likely, listened to some of the tapes. In any case, these transcripts help to explain the origin of a number of fairly accurate quotes from the ExComm meetings scattered throughout *Thirteen Days*).[10]

Ted Sorensen completed the manuscript (published in 1969) after RFK's assassination in June, 1968. *Thirteen Days* has never been out of print and has shaped – *and warped* – our understanding of the Cuban missile crisis for nearly half a century. It is the only account of the ExComm meetings by one of the actual and principal participants. Indeed, the very term, 'Thirteen Days', has now become indelibly identified with the events of October 1962. RFK's extremely general recollections (a total of only 80 pages) quickly became the core source – if not the iconic source – for most journalistic and scholarly writing on the missile crisis.

The real Thirteen Days

RFK played a unique role in the missile crisis meetings because he was the President's brother and most trusted advisor. A different attorney general would likely not even have been invited to participate in the ExComm meetings. Indeed, the relationship between the Kennedy brothers was unique in the history of the American presidency. I can clearly recall, for example, first listening to their recorded telephone conversations and initially finding it very difficult to understand what they were saying. Typically, the brothers would immediately burst into an exchange of barely coherent verbal fragments and interjections before abruptly concluding with 'OK', 'good', or 'right' or just hanging up. Somehow, they always understood each other.

If the President was temporarily out of the room during the ExComm discussions, RFK was considered 'the President's alternate' and was viewed as the 'fearless watchdog on behalf of the President. He had enormous possessive pride in the President, and he was looking after the President's interests in a way which, he felt, the President could not do.'[11] At one meeting, RFK may even have turned on the tape recorder after the President had turned it off and left the room. The ExComm, of course, was also aware that RFK chaired the Special Group (Augmented) which oversaw covert operations against Cuba. Bobby Kennedy was a steadfast hawk on the Cuban question and an ardent supporter of plots to oust or assassinate Castro. RFK's stance during the ExComm meetings, which can only be fully understood in the context of his role in Mongoose, turns out to be very different from the idealized and sanitized view he consciously crafted for *Thirteen Days*.

In sharp contrast to his brother, RFK was one of the most consistently hawkish and confrontational members of the ExComm. The tape recordings fundamentally and irrefutably contradict many of RFK's most important recollections and conclusions. In fact, the recordings expose *Thirteen Days* as not just selective or skewed history, which is the common affliction of personal diaries and memoirs, but rather as the capstone of an effort to manipulate the history of the missile crisis to Robert Kennedy's perceived political advantage.

Thirteen Days is, in fact, unintended proof of the unique value of the secret ExComm tapes as an essential and reliable historical source. History based on personal recollections rarely transcends the author's motives in writing it. This flaw has been particularly striking among the small, closed, and inevitably shrinking group of ExComm participants, who, until the release of the tape recordings, had successfully preserved and promoted their supposedly unique authority to shape our understanding of those historic meetings.

In 1978, Arthur M. Schlesinger Jr., admittedly 'a great admirer and devoted friend' of Robert Kennedy, published a thousand-plus-page biography of his friend – whose career in public office had spanned less than a decade. Schlesinger's conclusion about RFK's role in the ExComm meetings was unequivocal:

> Robert Kennedy was the indispensable partner. Without him, John Kennedy would have found it far more difficult to overcome the demand for military action.... It was Robert Kennedy ... who stopped the air strike madness in its tracks.... Within the closed meetings of the so-called Executive Committee of the National Security Council, Robert Kennedy was a dove from the start.[12]

Schlesinger cited a quote from the first ExComm meeting on 16 October that he had discovered in RFK's papers: 'You're droppin' bombs all over Cuba.... You're covering most of Cuba. You're gonna kill an awful lot a people, and we're gonna take an awful lot a heat on it.'[13] This quote, which Schlesinger claimed demonstrated RFK's opposition to the use of military force, was, in fact, extremely misleading – if not intentionally deceptive. Bobby Kennedy was actually arguing that bombing the missile sites or blockading Cuba were weak and inadequate responses; he was instead demanding *nothing short of a full land, sea, and air invasion* of Cuba.

Before the opening of the ExComm recordings, Schlesinger presumably could not have been certain about the actual, intended meaning of RFK's words. However, two years after the 1997 declassification of the tapes and the publication of a volume of transcripts which he described as 'a historical triumph', he nonetheless continued to insist that this 'New testimony supplements and reinforces Robert Kennedy's account in *Thirteen Days*'. It appears that loyalty to his friend continued to trump his commitment to a candid assessment of the historical record.[14]

It is now clear as well that many of RFK's own still widely accepted generalizations in *Thirteen Days* fly in the face of the incontrovertible evidence on the ExComm tapes. RFK claimed, for example:

1   'That kind of pressure does strange things to a human being, even to brilliant, self-confident, mature, experienced men. For some it brings out characteristics and strengths that perhaps even they never knew they had, and for others the pressure is too overwhelming.' As a result, some ExComm members, 'because of the pressure of events, even appeared to lose their judgment and stability'.[15] There is absolutely nothing on the tapes, or in the available documentary record, to support this claim. It is, on the contrary, remarkable that the round-the-clock physical and emotional stress of those two weeks did not result in nervous or physical breakdowns – perhaps because of the relative youth of JFK and most of his inner circle who were at least a generation younger than, for example, Eisenhower and his key advisors.

2   'We spent more time on this moral question [whether the US should attack a small nation like Cuba without warning] during the first five days than on any other single matter.' The Pearl Harbor analogy was in fact only very briefly discussed – for minutes rather than hours or days.[16]

3   President Kennedy 'had asked the State Department to conduct negotiations' for removal of the Jupiter missiles from Turkey and 'had ordered their removal some time ago'. JFK did direct the State and Defense departments to study 'What action can be taken to get Jupiter missiles out of Turkey', but never issued a presidential order to actually do so. On the contrary, Kennedy gave the go-ahead to activating the missiles in Turkey and one site was scheduled to be turned over to Turkish authorities in October 1962 – key factors in Khrushchev's decision to send MRBMs and IRBMs to Cuba.[17]

4   UN Ambassador Adlai Stevenson proposed trading the missiles in Cuba for those in Turkey, but President Kennedy 'rejected Stevenson's suggestion' because 'this was not the appropriate time to suggest this action'.[18] It is ironic, of course, that the proposal Stevenson first suggested on 17 October and then personally defended against harsh ExComm criticism on 26 October, was essentially identical to the one JFK secretly adopted the very next day.

5   Soviet Ambassador Anatoly Dobrynin was explicitly told 'that there could be no [public] *quid pro quo*' for mutually withdrawing the missiles from Turkey and Cuba. Ted Sorensen, however, confirmed at the

1989 Moscow missile crisis conference that RFK's secret diary was quite explicit that a trade was part of the final settlement. And, of course, the tapes prove that JFK insisted, despite tough ExComm resistance, on an unequivocal (if secret) agreement to remove missiles from Cuba and Turkey.[19] Of course, concealing the secret deal was one of the principal purposes of *Thirteen Days* (Khrushchev had been considering a trade before Dobrynin's message about meeting with RFK – and even before he received Castro's cable on 27 October urging a nuclear first strike against the US if Cuba were attacked).

6   'To keep the discussions from becoming inhibited and because he did not want to arouse attention', the President 'decided not to attend all the [ExComm] meetings.' 'This was wise', RFK explained. 'Personalities change when the President is present, and frequently even strong men make recommendations on the basis of what they believe the President wishes to hear.'[20] Notwithstanding Bobby Kennedy's perceptive behavioural insight, his assertion about JFK's presence at the ExComm meetings is demonstrably false. JFK attended all the sessions, except when, in an effort to keep the crisis discussions secret during the first week, he left Washington to campaign in New England (Wednesday 17 October) and in the Midwest (Friday afternoon, 19 October, to Saturday afternoon, 20 October). The President did not deliberately stay away from any of the White House meetings when he was in Washington.

The real Robert Kennedy

RFK's invention of his own role as peace-maker in the missile crisis is, without question, the most enduring and ironic historical legacy of *Thirteen Days*. The attorney general had engaged in secret contacts with a Soviet embassy official in an effort to caution and deter Khrushchev over Cuba. But, Soviet deception had negated these efforts and RFK's strikingly personal sense of betrayal was often palpable at the ExComm discussions.

The attorney general first spoke up about an hour into the first meeting (discussed above). He rejected any military action short of an all-out invasion and warned that the Russians would simply send the missiles in again if they were destroyed and possibly retaliate against the US Jupiter sites in Turkey in response to either bombing or a blockade. Only an all-out invasion, he demanded, could justify so much destruction and loss of life.

It would be better, he insisted, 'If you could get it in, get it started, so that there wasn't any turning back'.[21] RFK seemed oblivious to the fact that once military action began it might be impossible to turn back. From these first remarks through the entire 13 days of discussions, he never seemed to connect the dots between a US attack on Cuba and the chance of escalation to global nuclear war (Ted Sorensen later claimed that Robert Kennedy had been 'particularly good' during the first week of ExComm meetings: 'Never stating a position of his own, he was persistent in trying ... to get people to agree.'[22] In fact, as revealed by his first remarks, RFK made his own extremely provocative positions clear from the very first meeting).

That evening, RFK warned again that a blockade would require the US Navy 'to sink Russian ships' and could become 'a very slow death' over several months. It was better to stand up to Khrushchev right now – 'we should just get into it, and get it over with and take our losses if he wants to get into a war over this. Hell, if it's war that's gonna come on this thing, you know, he sticks those kinds of missiles in after the warning, then hey, he's gonna get into a war six months from now or a year from now.' He even suggested using the American naval base at Guantánamo Bay to stage an incident that would justify a military attack: 'You know, sink the *Maine* again or something!'[23]

Bobby Kennedy briefly modified his belligerent posture later that evening and agreed that Cuba and the Soviet Union should be informed before bombing in order to affirm 'what kind of a country we are'. For fifteen years, RFK avowed, the US had worked to prevent a Russian first strike against us. 'Now, in the interest of time, we do that to a small country. I think it's a hell of a burden to carry.' He also recommended sending a personal emissary to inform Khrushchev before the air attacks began.[24]

But, when the recorded meetings resumed on 18 October, after the President's return from New England, RFK once again pressed for an invasion and in response to speculation about whether the blockade 'has a chance of bringing down Castro', responded contemptuously, 'Has a blockade ever brought anybody down?' The blockade amounts to telling the Soviets, he commented acerbically, that 'they can build as many missiles as they want.'[25]

'It would be better for our children and grandchildren', he asserted on 20 October, 'if we decided to face the Soviet threat, stand up to it, and eliminate it, now. The circumstances for doing so at some future time were bound to be more unfavorable, the risks would be greater, the chances of success less good.'[26] The President finally decided, by the end of the first week, to start with a blockade. He did however agree to RFK's insistence that preparations for an invasion of Cuba should also continue.

During the second week of discussions, after the President's speech revealed the crisis to the world, Robert Kennedy's hawkish advice continued unabated. On 23 October, he insisted that it would be 'a hell of an advantage' and 'damn helpful' to take advantage of the blockade to seize a Soviet vessel carrying missiles in order to photograph and examine their weapons – even if the ship had reversed course to return to the USSR. Secretary of State Dean Rusk lectured him that the Soviets were already 'as sensitive as a boil' about the blockade and that its announced, limited purpose was to keep nuclear weapons out of Cuba, not to seize them on the high seas.[27] The President delayed a decision, in essence siding with Rusk.

On 25 October, with the blockade in effect, RFK revived the bombing option shelved during the first week, insisting that 'rather than have the confrontation with the Russians at sea ... it might be better to knock out their missile base as the first step'. He circumvented the issue of an American Pearl Harbor by proposing to warn Soviet personnel 'to get out of that vicinity in ten minutes [!] and then we go through and knock [out] the base'. He insisted that air strikes would demonstrate 'that we're not backing off and that we're still being tough with Cuba. That's really the point we have to make.' He also expressed concern about delaying the seizure of a ship: 'The only weakness in my judgment, is the idea to the Russians that you know ... backing off and that we're weak.... And we've got to show them that we mean it' [*sic*].[28]

And then, there is Black Saturday – 27 October 1962 – doubtless the most dangerous day in human history. 'I suggested', RFK wrote, in what turned out to be the most important and influential line in *Thirteen Days*, 'and was supported by Ted Sorensen and others, that we ignore the latest [27 October] Khrushchev letter [demanding a mutual withdrawal of missiles from Cuba and Turkey] and respond to his earlier [Friday evening, 26 October] letter's proposal' to remove the missiles from Cuba in return for an American promise not to invade the island.[29] This allegedly stunning diplomatic strategy came to be called the 'Trollope ploy' – a reference to a plot device by novelist Anthony Trollope, in which a woman interprets a pro-forma romantic gesture as a proposal of marriage.

The myth of this inspired proposal began with Stewart Alsop and Charles Bartlett, writing in the *Saturday Evening Post* barely two weeks after the crisis. Their article launched the argument that Robert Kennedy had conceived of the 'Trollope ploy' as a way out of the deadlock. Arthur Schlesinger Jr. soon claimed as well that RFK 'came up with a thought of breathtaking simplicity and ingenuity'.[30] Ted Sorensen, who completed RFK's manuscript, did not challenge Bobby Kennedy's claim to have suggested this breakthrough strategy. Dean Rusk, Robert McNamara, and McGeorge Bundy, with slight variations, endorsed it as well and Sorensen did not budge from his original position in his 2008 personal memoir.

Despite the fact that the ExComm tapes have been declassified for more than 15 years, the Trollope ploy myth continues to thrive – much like the fable that Lincoln dashed off the Gettysburg Address on the train ride to the Pennsylvania battlefield. However, the crisis was not resolved so cleverly or melodramatically and Robert Kennedy's role in the final settlement is fundamentally at odds with his account in *Thirteen Days*.

At the morning ExComm meeting on that fateful Saturday, some twelve hours after receiving Khrushchev's Friday evening letter – the first of the two messages – JFK read aloud: 'Premier Khrushchev told President Kennedy in a message [broadcast over Moscow Radio] today he would withdraw offensive weapons from Cuba if the United States withdrew its rockets from Turkey.'[31] The President and the ExComm were startled and confused but soon received confirmation that a new Khrushchev message had indeed been announced on Moscow Radio.

The trade proposal was new from the Soviets, but Ambassador Stevenson had first proposed it on 17 October and the President had raised that possibility twice on 18 October and had been exploring the Jupiter option for more than a week. It became immediately apparent that his advisors were firm and united in their opposition to a missile 'trade'. Paul Nitze, McGeorge Bundy, George Ball, Llewellyn Thompson, and Dean Rusk urged Kennedy to promptly reject any Cuba–Turkey link, but JFK responded impatiently:

> We're gonna be in an insupportable position on this matter if this becomes his proposal. In the first place, we last year tried to get the missiles out of there because they're not militarily useful, number one. Number two, to any man at the United Nations or any other rational man, it will look like a very fair trade.[32]

RFK disagreed emphatically, 'I don't see how we can ask the Turks to give up their defense'. The first priority had to be the removal of the threat to the US and Latin America – which required making

> doubly clear that Turkish NATO missiles were one problem and that Cuba was an entirely separate problem.... We can have an exchange with him [Khrushchev] and say, 'You've double-crossed us and we don't know which deal to accept'.... In the meantime, he's got all the play throughout the world.

The attorney general also warned about the possible erosion of the US position if talks with the Soviets dragged on for weeks or longer and the Cubans refused to allow UN inspectors to verify that the missiles were inoperable – but, he added with unmistakable enthusiasm, 'we could then decide to attack the bases by air'.[33]

The attorney general opposed taking Khrushchev's public offer seriously because it 'blows the possibility of this other one, of course, doesn't it?' 'Of what?' JFK replied impatiently. 'Of getting an acceptance', RFK explained, 'of the [Friday] proposal', and he urged keeping the pressure on so that 'We don't look like we're weakening on the whole Turkey complex'. The President responded: 'You see, they [NATO] haven't had the alternatives presented to them. They'll say, "Well, God! We don't want to trade 'em off!" They don't realize that in 2 or 3 days we may have a military strike [on Cuba]' which could lead to the seizure of Berlin or a strike on Turkey. 'And then they'll say, "By God! We should have taken it!"'[34]

Bobby Kennedy urged his brother not to 'abandon' Cuba to the Communists: 'Send this letter', he pleaded, 'and say you're accepting his

[Friday] offer. He's made an offer and you're in fact accepting it. ... God, don't bring in Turkey now. We want to settle [Cuba first].' Khrushchev 'must be a little shaken up or he wouldn't have sent the [Friday] message to you in the first place.' 'That's last night', JFK retorted yet again. 'But it's certainly conceivable', Bobby replied, 'that you could get him back to that. I don't think that we should abandon it.'[35]

JFK finally agreed, despite a transparently audible lack of enthusiasm, that there was no harm in trying. 'All right', he conceded, 'Let's send this letter dealing with Cuba first.' But, he persisted yet again that the key question remained how to overcome likely NATO and Turkish opposition to a trade. 'I think we oughta', JFK repeated, 'be able to say that the matter of Turkey and so on, in fact all these matters can be discussed if he'll cease work. Otherwise he's going to announce that we've rejected his proposal.' He paused dramatically for some six seconds before reiterating darkly,

> And then where are we?... That's our only, it seems to me, defense against the appeal of his trade. I think our message oughta be that we're glad to discuss this [Turkey] and other matters but we've gotta get a cessation of work....

'Let's start with our letter', JFK continued. 'It's got to be finessed ... we have to finesse him.' But he had no illusions about Khrushchev's response to US pressure to go back to Friday's proposal, 'which he isn't gonna give us. He's now moved on to the Turkish thing. So we're just gonna get a letter back saying, "Well, he'd be glad to settle Cuba when we settle Turkey."' The real question remained, 'what are we gonna do about the Turks?'[36]

'Actually, I think Bobby's formula is a good one', Sorensen observed; 'we say, "we are accepting your offer of your letter last night and therefore there's no need to talk about these other things.".' The President seemed willing to go along with this scheme on the slim chance that Khrushchev might agree to a cessation of work, but he clearly remained sceptical and unenthusiastic: 'As I say, he's not gonna [accept] now [after his public offer on Turkey]. But anyway, we can try this thing, but he's gonna come back on Turkey.'[37]

The 27 October tapes prove that ExComm participants and scholars have read far too much into the so-called Trollope ploy. President Kennedy stubbornly contended that Khrushchev's Saturday offer could not be ignored precisely because it had been made publicly. In fact, JFK's eventual message to Khrushchev did *not* ignore the Saturday proposal on Turkey, but left the door open to settling broader international issues once the immediate danger in Cuba had been neutralized. The President ultimately offered the Kremlin a calculated blend of Khrushchev's 26 and 27 October proposals: the removal of the Soviet missiles from Cuba, an American non-invasion pledge (coupled with UN inspection of the missile sites – which Castro refused), a readiness to talk later about NATO-related issues, and a secret commitment to withdraw the Jupiters from Turkey.

It is also essential to understand the importance of the ExComm discussions in helping the President to make up his mind, especially in those final crucial hours of the crisis. Painstaking attention to the recordings proves beyond question that the often rough give-and-take with the ExComm (as well as the Joint Chiefs and the leaders of Congress) played a decisive role in shaping JFK's views. The President, for example, clearly understood the alarming implications of Bundy's claim that everyone in the administration involved in alliance issues would oppose a Cuba–Turkey missile trade; and Nitze's stubborn inflexibility over amending JCS procedures to prevent the immediate firing of the Turkish Jupiter missiles at the USSR in the event of a Soviet strike in Turkey; as well as RFK's insistence that rejecting the Cuba–Turkey link was the only way to demonstrate American toughness.[38]

In several of these cases, JFK barely managed to conceal his disdain in the face of dogmatic and doctrinaire thinking and lack of imagination. Even in the final days and hours of the crisis, the ExComm had an enormous emotional and psychological impact on President Kennedy's determination to avert nuclear war. Every major option was discussed, frequently in exhaustive and exhausting detail – providing both the context and sounding board for the President in making his final decisions.

The President repeatedly rejected provocative and dangerous ExComm advice, refusing for example: to mine international waters around Cuba; to declare war on Cuba when announcing the quarantine; to seize Soviet weapons from a ship that had reversed course before reaching the quarantine line; to provoke an armed clash in Berlin by denying Soviet demands to inspect US trucks entering East Germany; to extend the quarantine to Soviet aircraft flying to Cuba 'because the only way you can stop a plane is to shoot it down';[39] to arm US photo reconnaissance planes flying over Cuba; to return ground fire from Soviet/Cuban forces; to initiate night surveillance using flares; and to immediately destroy the Surface-to-Air Missile site(s) if a U-2 were shot down. Ironically, the one time that Kennedy did agree to potentially catastrophic counsel – by approving the use of supposedly harmless 'practice' depth charges against Soviet submarines near Cuba – led directly to one of the most dangerous flashpoints of the crisis. A Soviet submarine *was* damaged by the 'practice' depth charges (the air circulation system was disabled, the temperature rose to over 122 degrees, and some crewmen lost consciousness). The grenade-like explosions felt to the crew like hammer blows inside a metal barrel; the frantic captain, unable to communicate with Moscow and assuming that nuclear war had already begun, nearly fired a nuclear-tipped torpedo at a US Navy vessel.[40]

President Kennedy's inclination to pursue the Turkish trade option actually seems to have hardened in response to the dogged intractability of his advisors at the 27 October meetings. The ExComm toughened JFK's determination simply by consistently and almost unanimously attacking his preferred course of action – a deal on the Turkish missiles. It is a serious mistake for historians to underestimate the importance of these discussions in prodding the President to implement this possible settlement – while there was still time to avoid a nuclear conflagration (we now know, of course, that Khrushchev's fear of an imminent US attack on Cuba, especially in the context of Castro's 'nuclear first strike' cable, had a greater impact on the Kremlin than the secret American concession on the Turkish missiles). The key participants in the White House meetings, notwithstanding, worked for decades to minimize, if not conceal, their own fierce resistance to the missile trade agreement imposed on the ExComm by the President. The Trollope ploy – and RFK's role in coming up with it to save the peace – was, like *Thirteen Days* itself, essentially a myth and cover story from the start.

The evidence from the White House missile crisis tapes is both ironic and contradictory. JFK and his administration, without doubt, bear a significant share of responsibility for bringing about the crisis; the secret war against Cuba was effectively kept from the American people, but it was well known in Moscow and Havana. During those perilous two weeks, however, President Kennedy often stood essentially alone against bellicose counsel from the ExComm, the leaders of Congress, and the Joint Chiefs. Nonetheless, after the crisis, Kennedy continued to support covert plans to destabilize the Cuban revolution and eliminate Fidel Castro.

The real Dean Rusk

In December 1960, President-elect Kennedy announced the appointment of career diplomat Dean Rusk as Secretary of State. JFK had considered more well-known individuals but settled on Rusk because he intended, in practice, to personally oversee foreign affairs. The relationship between the President and his top diplomat was cordial and proper, but never approached the comfort level enjoyed by Sorensen, Bundy, or McNamara.

Stories soon circulated in Washington that the President was disenchanted with Rusk – particularly after the Secretary's allegedly conflicting advice about the Bay of Pigs invasion. But it was Rusk's reported conduct in October 1962 that established his reputation as a bureaucrat who 'would sit quietly by, with his Buddha-like face and half-smile, often leaving it to Bundy or to the President himself to assert the diplomatic interest'.[41] In retrospect, it now seems clear that Rusk, like Adlai Stevenson, was a poor fit for the hard-hitting, alpha-male, best and brightest image that typified media and public perceptions of the youthful new administration.

Robert Kennedy's hostility to Rusk was well known in Washington – particularly as a source of rumours that Rusk would be discarded after JFK's re-election. Only a month before the missile crisis, at a meeting 'generated by Secretary Rusk's concern over Cuban overflights and his desire to avoid any incidents', RFK had sneered, 'What's the matter, Dean, no guts?'[42] But it was in *Thirteen Days* that RFK had the unique opportunity – which could not be effectively verified at the time – to shape the historical reputation of the Secretary of State. He claimed that Rusk had first been in favour of air strikes, but subsequently he was either silent or missing:

> During all these deliberations, we all spoke as equals. There was no rank, and, in fact, we did not even have a chairman. Dean Rusk – who as Secretary of State, might have assumed that position – had other duties during this period of time and could not attend our meetings. As a result, with the encouragement of McNamara, Bundy, and Ball, [Rusk's subordinate] the conversations were completely uninhibited and unrestricted. Everyone had an equal opportunity to express himself and to be heard directly. It was a tremendously advantageous procedure that does not frequently occur within the executive branch of the government, where rank is often so important.[43]

These allegations have become part of the accepted lore of the missile crisis. In 1969, for example, former Secretary of State Dean Acheson declared, in a review of *Thirteen Days*, 'One wonders what those "other duties and responsibilities" were, to have been half so important as those they displaced'.[44] What indeed could have been more important for a Secretary of State than confronting the genuine possibility of a nuclear world war?

There is, however, one insurmountable problem with this claim about Rusk's frequent absence from the ExComm meetings: *it is not true!* There were twenty meetings convened by the President between 16 October and 29 October. Dean Rusk attended nineteen; the only one he missed was on 18 October when he was obligated to host a dinner at the State Department for visiting Soviet Foreign Minister Andrei Gromyko. Most of the nineteen ExComm meetings Rusk participated in were recorded and his presence and contributions are indisputable. The notes from the unrecorded meetings are equally authoritative about Rusk's substantive role.

The ExComm participants, RFK also declared, were

> men of the highest intelligence, industrious, courageous, and dedicated to their country's well-being. It is no reflection on them that none was consistent in his opinion from the very beginning to the very end. That kind of open, unfettered mind was essential.

But, as discussed above, he also alleged that some members were unable to cope with the unrelenting pressure. RFK clearly had Rusk in mind; in a 1965 oral history interview, he had specifically accused Rusk of having 'had a complete breakdown mentally and physically' during the Cuban missile crisis.[45]

Rusk's children recall that their father was tense and preoccupied during the crisis but promptly returned to his normal routine at the State Department after 28 October.[46] If such a collapse had in fact happened, would JFK and LBJ have retained Rusk as Secretary of State for six more years? There is no evidence from the tapes or any other source to substantiate this claim.

Finally, Bobby Kennedy rebuked Rusk for being indecisive and for not articulating the diplomatic perspective at the meetings. He even claimed to have asked Rusk about this alleged failure and the Secretary of State purportedly replied that he had wanted to prevent the group from 'moving too far or too fast' and that 'he had been playing the role of the "dumb dodo" for this reason. I thought it was a strange way of putting it.'[47] The alleged 'dumb dodo' remark is invariably cited (particularly online) as if it were Rusk's personal assessment of his own role in the ExComm meetings – rather than RFK's totally unsubstantiated allegation.

It is implausible, to say the least, that Rusk would have made such a belittling statement about himself to someone he neither trusted nor liked – particularly since the charge is entirely fictitious. Rusk constantly injected the diplomatic perspective into the meetings, stressing that unilateral action was untenable for a nation that had treaty commitments to 40-plus allies. If anything, his colleagues felt that he spoke too often and too long about diplomatic options.

In short, Dean Rusk did not miss most of the ExComm meetings; was not silent, passive, indecisive, or reluctant to recommend tough decisions; did not play the role of 'dumb dodo' by failing to introduce the diplomatic perspective; did not fortuitously allow the discussions to become 'completely uninhibited and unrestricted' by virtue of his absence; and did not have a physical or mental breakdown during the crisis.

Dean Rusk was the only ExComm participant who regularly challenged RFK's persistently hawkish advice. The Secretary's professorial tone also came across as condescending to the instinctively short-tempered attorney general. Rusk was, undeniably, one of the most cautious and restrained participants in the discussions and before joining the essentially unanimous opposition to the Turkish trade on 27 October, came closest to personifying the role of 'dovish' adviser which RFK shrewdly appropriated for himself in his memoir. Rusk decided in 1969 that it would be unseemly to respond to the publication of *Thirteen Days* in the wake of RFK's 1968 assassination. He preferred instead 'to leave it to professional historians, working from a perspective of several decades, to reach their judgments about his time in office. He was particularly sceptical of ' "instant histories" by "insiders", real or self-proclaimed'.[48] The missile crisis tape recordings have, finally, vindicated this historical forbearance.

Hollywood's Cuban missile crisis

The Hollywood film, *Thirteen Days*, was released in 2000, but I became
aware of it about a year earlier after receiving a call at the JFK Library from
director Roger Donaldson. He explained that he was directing a film
about the crisis and expressed interest in the fact that I had been the first
non-ExComm participant and the first historian to hear all the missile
crisis tapes. We agreed to meet in my office about a week later. I learned
during our discussion that the script had already been written, but asked
who was playing the lead role. He told me it was Kevin Costner. I volun-
teered that it was hard to imagine Costner playing either JFK or RFK; Donaldson explained that Costner had been cast as Kenneth O'Donnell. I
thought to myself, 'Kenny O'Donnell? What on earth did he have to do
with the missile crisis?' The rest is not history.

Prominent figures from the Kennedy administration were predictably
dismayed by the film's depiction of O'Donnell's central role in the crisis.
McNamara, Sorensen, and Schlesinger pointed out that O'Donnell, the
President's political appointments secretary, was on the periphery of
events in October 1962 and did not attend the ExComm meetings
(O'Donnell's son, Kevin, founder of Earthlink.net, purchased the film
production company Beacon Entertainment in 1999 after work on *Thirteen
Days* had begun; he has revealed, however, that he was in touch with the
scriptwriter even before buying the company, but nonetheless insists that
the film does not falsify his father's role in the crisis).[49] Critics have also
pointed to other inaccuracies – such as the claim that JFK approved the
use of conventional depth charges against Soviet submarines near the
naval blockade line. In fact, Kennedy agreed to use 'practice' depth
charges (discussed above) only after he was assured by JCS chairman
Maxwell Taylor and Defense Secretary McNamara that they would not
damage the submarines. General Taylor, a D-Day veteran, is also depicted
in the film as an unreserved hawk; in fact, he initially disagreed with RFK
about an invasion and warned the President against getting bogged down
'in that deep mud of Cuba'.[50]

These legitimate concerns, however, only scratch the surface of the substantive historical problems with the film – which purports to be based on
Ernest May and Philip Zelikow, *The Kennedy Tapes: Inside the White House
during the Cuban Missile Crisis* – the first transcripts of the ExComm tape
recordings (published by Harvard University Press in 1997). Nonetheless,
the film takes its title directly from RFK's book. And there, indeed, is the
historical rub.

The 1997 transcripts (notwithstanding serious transcription inaccuracies)[51] and the editors' accompanying analysis began the public exposure
of what the tapes actually reveal, puncturing the reliability of *Thirteen Days*
by confirming, for example, the open discussion of the administration's
secret war against Cuba, the extent of Robert Kennedy's self-serving

invention of his role as peace-maker, Dean Rusk's previously unacknow-ledged and central role in the meetings, JFK's rebuff of the virtually unanimous ExComm demands to reject the Cuba–Turkey missile trade, and the misleading claims about the brilliance and importance of the Trollope ploy in resolving the crisis.

Thirteen Days, a film supposedly based on a book about the declassified White House tapes, instead validates the deceptions and half-truths in *Thirteen Days*. RFK is shown (accurately) arguing against bombing Cuba without warning because of the comparison to the attack on Pearl Harbor. But, there is not a hint about his insistence that the blockade was weak and inadequate; his persistent demands for an invasion; his readiness to concoct a phoney *casus belli* to justify using force; his revival of the bombing option late in the second week; and his fierce opposition to the Cuba–Turkey trade – described in the film as 'Jack *and Bobby's idea*' (italics added).

In one particularly counterfactual scene, RFK begs McNamara (who also opposed the trade) to find any solution that would not 'force us into war'. In fact, in their final exchange on the tapes, McNamara told Bobby Kennedy that, 'before we attack them [the missile sites] you've gotta be damned sure they [the Cubans and Soviets] understand it's coming. In other words, you need to really escalate this.' RFK murmured 'Yeah', and the defence chief continued,

> And then we need to have two things ready, a government for Cuba, because we're gonna need one after we go in with 500 aircraft. And secondly, some plans for how to respond to the Soviet Union in Europe, cause sure as hell they're gonna do something there.

Robert Kennedy responded wistfully, 'I'd like to take Cuba back. That would be nice.'[52]

Thirteen Days the book and *Thirteen Days* the film are in essential agreement. The film swallows the Trollope ploy myth whole and depicts Bobby Kennedy, as Schlesinger had insisted in 1978 before the ExComm tapes were released, as 'a dove from the start'. The scriptwriter had access to the May-Zelikow transcripts but relied entirely on the book *Thirteen Days*, ignoring all the ground-breaking historical insights revealed on the tapes. The producers purchased the film rights to the 1997 transcript volume but used them, paradoxically, to breathe new life into the most enduring myths, distortions, and deceptions in Robert Kennedy's memoir. And finally, the film *Thirteen Days* fails to reveal the most important fact about the ExComm discussions: that they were being secretly recorded.

Of course, many of the evasions in RFK's book were historically explic-able – key documents were still classified in 1969 and the fact that tape recordings existed was still top secret. The filmmakers did not have that excuse three decades later; by failing to mention, for example, the Kennedy administration's covert war against Castro's regime, the film leaves viewers with the false and misleading impression that Khrushchev's decision to send missiles to Cuba was entirely unprovoked.

Thirteen Days, like the proverbial bad penny, somehow always turns up.[53]

Notes

1 David Herbert Donald, *Lincoln* (New York: Simon and Schuster 1995) p. 13; Ben Bradlee, *Conversations with Kennedy* (New York: W.W. Norton 1975) pp. 127–8.
2 Quotes from the ExComm tapes are from the author's *Averting 'The Final Failure': John F. Kennedy and the Secret Cuban Missile Crisis Meetings* (Stanford, CA: Stanford University Press 2003); this essay is adapted from ibid., and from the author's *The Cuban Missile Crisis in American Memory: Myths Versus Reality* (Stanford, CA: Stanford University Press 2012), as well as from articles in *Reviews in American History*, on www.hnn.us, and www.washington.decoded.com; Stern, *Averting*, pp. 150–1.
3 For the most up-to-date scholarship on this question, see David M. Barrett and Max Holland, *Blind Over Cuba: The Photo Gap and the Missile Crisis* (College Station, TX: Texas A&M University Press 2012).
4 In fact, the USSR had deployed nuclear weapons outside its own territory. In 1959 MRBMs were briefly based in East Germany; see Matthias Uhl and Vladimir I. Ivkin, ' "Operation Atom": The Soviet Union's Stationing of Nuclear Missiles in the German Democratic Republic, 1959', *Cold War International History Project Bulletin* (Fall/Winter 2001) 299–306. In 1961 the CIA also learned about the deployment of shorter-range ballistic missiles and their nuclear warheads in East Germany from Oleg Penkovsky, see Jerrold L. Schecter and Peter S. Deriabin, *The Spy Who Saved the World: How a Soviet Colonel Changed the Course of the Cold War* (New York: Charles Scribner's Sons 1992) pp. 68, 79, 105, 113, 116, 149. 185. JFK appears to have been unaware of these deployments at the time of the missile crisis and was not corrected by CIA Director John McCone during the ExComm meetings. Stern, *Averting*, pp. 150–3.
5 Stern, *Averting*, p. 156.
6 Ibid.
7 Ibid., p. 388.
8 Personal communication from Dan H. Fenn Jr., a member of the Kennedy White House staff and founding director of the JFK Library, 18 June 2011.
9 Anatoly Dobrynin, *In Confidence: Moscow's Ambassador to America's Six Cold War Presidents* (New York: Random House 1995) p. 90.
10 Timothy Naftali, *The Origins of 'Thirteen Days'*, Miller Center Report 15 (Virginia, VA: Miller Center, Summer 1999) pp. 23–4.
11 Roswell Gilpatric Oral History interview, John F. Kennedy Library (JFKL), Oral History Collection (OHC), 1970, p. 50; U. Alexis Johnson Oral History interview, JFKL, OHC, pp. 36–7.
12 Arthur M. Schlesinger Jr., *Robert Kennedy and His Times* (New York: Houghton Mifflin 1978), pp. xii–xiii, 507, 531; Schlesinger was granted special access to RFK's private papers by Ethel Kennedy.
13 Ibid.
14 Arthur M. Schlesinger Jr., 'Foreword', Robert F. Kennedy, *Thirteen Days: A Memoir of the Cuban Missile Crisis* (New York: W.W. Norton 1999) p. 10.
15 Kennedy, *Thirteen Days*, p. 25.

16 Ibid., pp. 30–1; CIA Deputy Director Marshall Carter and Under Secretary of State George Ball first made the pejorative comparison to Pearl Harbor.

17 Ibid., p. 83; 'Presidential Directive on actions and studies in response to new Soviet Bloc activity in Cuba', National Security Action Memorandum #181, 23 August 1962, National Security Files, JFK Library. At a 1988 Kennedy Library conference, McGeorge Bundy exclaimed: 'Jack, you never ordered the removal of the Turkish missiles. You merely expressed an opinion about their lack of strategic value. A presidential opinion is not a presidential order'.

18 Ibid., p. 39; the infamous leak to Charles Bartlett and Stewart Alsop, who charged that Stevenson had advocated a 'Munich' at the 26 October meeting, almost certainly came from one or both Kennedys.

19 Kennedy, *Thirteen Days*, p. 83; Arthur Schlesinger Jr.'s account of the settlement of the crisis (*A Thousand Days: John F. Kennedy in the White House* (New York: Houghton Mifflin 1965) pp. 828–30) comes very close to affirming that there was a secret missile trade. Schlesinger was not an ExComm member but he was likely entrusted with the secret by RFK or McNamara – his closest associates. Lyndon Johnson was never told, not even after he became President.

20 Ibid., pp. 26–7.

21 Stern, *Averting*, p. 74.

22 Ted Sorensen, Oral History Interview, JFKL, OHC, p. 68.

23 Stern, *Averting*, pp. 85, 87, 102.

24 Ibid., p. 108.

25 Ibid., pp. 114–15.

26 Ibid., p. 132.

27 Ibid., p. 193.

28 Ibid., pp. 254, 256.

29 Kennedy, *Thirteen Days*, p. 77.

30 Schlesinger, *A Thousand Days*, p. 828.

31 Stern, *Averting*, p. 291.

32 Ibid., p. 294; for the most complete study of the Jupiter missiles, see Philip Nash, *The Other Missiles of October: Eisenhower, Kennedy and the Jupiters, 1957–1963* (Chapel Hill, NC: University of North Carolina Press 1997).

33 Stern, *Averting*, pp. 299, 301, 307.

34 Ibid., p. 326.

35 Ibid., pp. 333–4.

36 Ibid., pp. 312, 331–3.

37 Ibid., p. 337.

38 Ibid., pp. 212, 316, 144–6, 255.

39 Ibid., p. 225. The US did get Guinea and Senegal to prevent refuelling stops by Soviet transport planes.

40 William Burr and Thomas S. Blanton (eds), *The Submarines of October: National Security Archive Electronic Briefing Book No. 75*, 31 October 2002. www2.gwu.edu/~nsarchiv/NSAEBB/NSAEBB75/ (last accessed 11 September 2014).

41 Schlesinger, *A Thousand Days, p.* 435.

42 'Memorandum Prepared in the Central Intelligence Agency for the Executive Director', 10 September 1962, Department of State, *Foreign Relations of the United States [FRUS], 1961–1963, Vol. X, Cuba 1961–1962* (Washington, DC: United States Government Printing Office 1997) p. 1054.

43 Kennedy, *Thirteen Days*, p. 36.

44 Dean Acheson, 'Dean Acheson's Version of Robert Kennedy's Version of the Cuban Missile Affair', *Esquire Magazine*, February 1969.

45 Kennedy, *Thirteen Days*, p. 25; Robert F. Kennedy Oral History Interview, JFKL, OHC, 1965, p. 6.

46 Personal communication from David Rusk to Sheldon M. Stern, 20 May 2011.

47 Schlesinger, *RFK*, p. 507 (citation is to a 30 November 1962 memo in the RFK papers); Rusk's children do not recall ever hearing their father use the term 'dodo' or 'dumb dodo'.

48 Rusk to Stern, 20 May 2011.

49 Ken Ringle, '"Thirteen Days" Embellishes Crisis Roles', *Washington Post*, 4 February 2001.

50 Stern, *Averting*, p. 68.

51 For critiques of the errors in the 1997 May-Zelikow transcripts, see Sheldon M. Stern, 'What JFK Really Said', *Atlantic Monthly*, 222/5 (May 2000) 122–8 and ibid., 'Source Material: The 1997 Published Transcripts of the JFK Cuban Missile Crisis Tapes: Too Good to be True?', *Presidential Studies Quarterly*, 30/3 (September 2000) 586–93.

52 Evan Thomas, *Robert Kennedy: His Life* (New York: Simon & Schuster 2007) p. 229.

53 As recently as 2012, The Belfer Center for Science and International Affairs at Harvard's JFK School of Government rated *Thirteen Days* as #4 on its top ten list of books on the missile crisis recommended for teachers.

10 'The only thing to look forward to's the past'

Reflection, revision and reinterpreting reinterpretation[1]

Len Scott

In 1986, Eliot Cohen published an article entitled, 'Why We Should Stop Studying the Cuban Missile Crisis'.[2] Supposing he had succeeded and persuaded everyone to abandon research and foreswear debate on the subject? Certainly, our understanding of events would be very different. Indeed, knowledge of important aspects and incidents would not exist. In the 1980s there were many unknown unknowns and much of our current understanding was hidden by largely unacknowledged secrets (and mysteries). Such a counterfactual is, of course, an unconvincing contrivance. Moreover, Cohen's purpose was not to halt research but to critique those who drew from the events of October 1962 theoretical approaches to managing international relations and international crises. Few of the contributors to this volume would dissent from the view that, in 1962, crisis management was a chimera if not a dangerous oxymoron.

Had the study of the crisis been abandoned in the 1980s we would not have known that, contrary to Washington's assurances, President Kennedy secretly offered to give up missiles in Turkey, and contrived, along with his senior officials, to mislead Congress, the American people and America's NATO allies. We would have learned little about Soviet or Cuban perspectives, and probably assumed that Khrushchev's motive for deploying the missiles was simply to address the imbalance in strategic nuclear forces. Our understanding of the risk of inadvertent nuclear war would have lacked evidence of Soviet tactical nuclear weapons in Cuba, the scrambling of Alaskan-based nuclear-armed US fighters or of nuclear-armed Soviet submarines being bombarded by the US Navy. Had everyone stopped researching, reflecting and debating the crisis in the 1980s our awareness of the risks of nuclear war would be greatly diminished.

If we had chosen to draw lessons on the basis of our knowledge, we would almost certainly have drawn the wrong lessons. Indeed, insofar as the architects of the American war in Vietnam in the 1960s applied lessons about the calibration of coercion and the threat of force, the ensuing American tragedy (and Vietnamese sacrifice) might have been avoided

– or at least reduced in scale. As Barton Bernstein notes, Vice-President Johnson was never apprised of JFK's offer and probably drew the wrong conclusions about his predecessor's handling of the crisis.[3]

Framing the focus

A central question in studying the Cuban missile crisis is 'What are the central questions in studying the Cuban missile crisis?' How questions are posed and answered are central themes in this collection. How the texts under scrutiny have helped frame our understanding has been the starting point for the contributors. Common concerns are apparent, though differing answers reflect how different writers start from differing theoretical assumptions and interpret evidence in differing ways. And while there is historical consensus on many facts and interpretations, the study of the missile crisis demonstrates that consensus may shift or dissipate as new sources (or interpretations) appear. An important theme in Barton Bernstein's contribution is the need to continue to ask what questions we should explore (and in what way).[4]

Several questions nevertheless loom large: 'Why did the Soviets deploy the missiles?'; 'Why did they withdraw them?'; 'What was the risk of nuclear war in 1962?' These issues have attracted the attention of scholars and former officials for the 50 years the crisis has been studied, just as they attracted the attention of political leaders and senior officials in October 1962. Many analysts and historians attached primary importance to the strategic nuclear balance in the Cuban deployment. Writing in 1987, Raymond Garthoff observed that, 'there is a general consensus that the principal motivation was to redress the publicly revealed serious imbalance in the strategic nuclear balance. No other action satisfactorily accounts for the action'.[5] New evidence nevertheless generated new discussion of various hypotheses. Interpretations based on testimony from Soviet officials soon challenged Garthoff's consensus, and also pointed away from a single explanatory factor. By 1998, Garthoff asserted that the Soviet decision 'had two principal motivations and purposes': first to redress global strategic inferiority, and second, 'to deter an anticipated US attack on Cuba'.[6]

Khrushchev's motives are explored by various contributors to this volume from different perspectives and within differing methodological frameworks. Don Munton, for example, examines Graham Allison's seminal work of American political science, *Essence of Decision* (and the revised edition of the book by Allison and Philip Zelikow).[7] Sergey Radchenko surveys Russian historiography over the last two decades or more, and demonstrates the fragility of much of the evidence on which broader interpretations and knowledge-claims are based. He reaches the striking conclusion that, 'alas, the bottom line is: we do not know why Khrushchev sent missiles to Cuba. Fifty years on, we are still struggling with this essential and perhaps impossible question.'[8] This latter point is echoed by Robert Jervis:

> [Khrushchev's] associates, even those who admired him, were keenly aware that he often failed to think things through. Politicians are less disturbed by inconsistencies than are academics, and this was particularly true for Khrushchev. We may be looking for coherence where it is absent, and what is maddeningly inconsistent to us may just be Khrushchev's normal way of proceeding.[9]

A more optimistic assessment of how new sources help re-evaluate the past is provided by Sheldon Stern.[10] In 1986, Eliot Cohen remarked on the 'the unusual quality and quantity of material available to students of this event'.[11] The material in question was primarily American, though its unusual quality became all the more unusual when it was disclosed that President Kennedy had secretly recorded key meetings with his advisors. Historians began to listen to these recordings, transcripts of which were published. As Sheldon Stern has demonstrated, the result has not only yielded unprecedented insight into Kennedy's inner counsels but provided a benchmark against which memoirs and memories could be judged. Other contributors, notably Barton Bernstein and Sergey Radchenko, also demonstrate the crucial importance of critically evaluating the provenance and integrity of historical evidence.

Harold Macmillan's approach to writing history is explained by Peter Catterall.[12] 'I much prefer the sources of history to the facile comments of clever young men', Macmillan wrote. 'From letters, memoranda and other documents you can form your own judgement.'[13] Few of the contributors to this volume could be accused of being 'young'. Yet as Sheldon Stern, Peter Catterall and R. Gerald Hughes demonstrate, memories, records and memoirs of participants reflect personal and political agendas. Clever young and (not so young) men (and women) can be much better placed to understand and represent the past than decision-makers whose world is beset by the paucity and ambiguity of information, and by conflicting diagnoses and prognoses (though such problems also afflict those who merely study the past). Moreover, as Peter Catterall demonstrates, Harold Macmillan carefully manipulated his sources to promote both his own role in the crisis and that of the British government. And as Sheldon Stern demonstrates in his evisceration of Robert Kennedy as a witness to history we need constant vigilance in reliance on our witnesses to history.

Shortly after Cohen's article appeared, Western academics began to gain access to Soviet sources, first through engagement with former officials, and then through (often controlled) access to archives. The encounters generated insight and argument. On specific issues, such as who ordered the shooting down of the American U-2 on 27 October, there was clarification: it was subordinate Soviet officers. On larger questions, such as why the Soviets sent the missiles, there was greater clarity on how decisions were made by Khrushchev, but debates about his objectives remain. In each of their essays, Robert Jervis, Don Munton, Peter Catterall and Sergei Radchenko revisit and review this crucial question, and present differing interpretations. How, when and in what context the crisis began has long been the focus of critical scrutiny and has raised important questions about how the events of October 1962 are framed and labelled. In the west there was a Cuban missile crisis, while in Moscow there was a Caribbean crisis and in Havana an October crisis. Each of these terms reflects differing assumptions about, and explanations of, the causes and courses of events.

If the essence of the crisis concerned the deployment of Medium and Intermediate Range Ballistic Missiles (MRBMs and IRBMs) within range of the principal nuclear weapon-states, then alternative starting points might be Eisenhower's deployment of Thor IRBMs in Britain from 1958 or, more plausibly, Eisenhower and Kennedy's deployment of Jupiter IRBMs in Italy and Turkey in 1961. One hundred and five IRBMs were placed within range of Moscow adding to the panoply of American nuclear weapons deployed in and around Europe, many within range of the USSR. Whatever their military and political significance, the suggestion that the starting point for discussion of events in October 1962 should be a Soviet decision (or the American discovery of that decision) prejudges more complex issues. As Robert Jervis notes, a case could be made that the crisis started when the Americans began their naval blockade.[14] The focus on 'thirteen days' may be essential but also risks ethnocentric and ideological biases. The most notable attempt to locate the crisis within broader temporal and political frameworks is Fursenko and Naftali's *'One Hell of a Gamble'* which covers 1958 to 1964.[15] Their account of Soviet and Cuban perspectives is a necessary corrective to the characterisation of the events of October 1962 in terms of Soviet action and American reaction.

Close of play

A valuable illustration of how the crisis has been debated and reinterpreted concerns its denouement. Virtually all of the contributors engage with how the crisis ended and provide differing analyses and interpretations. All nevertheless focus on how interpretations have changed significantly as new sources emerged. *How* the crisis ended is inextricably linked to *why* it ended. And why it ended is linked to what conclusions we may reach (and if we believe that lessons can be drawn what lessons we may draw). The issue of *when* the crisis ended is also now a focus of enquiry. Khrushchev's announcement on 28 October 1962 of the withdrawal of the missiles did not produce an immediate settlement. As Barton Bernstein acknowledges in his otherwise critical examination of David Coleman's *The Fourteenth Day*, that examination of the period after the announcement has only now begun to receive systematic scrutiny.[16] Details of potentially dramatic events in Soviet–Cuban relations in November 1962 also emerged in 2012.[17]

The American historiography of the 1980s was written by, or reflected testimony from, Kennedy administration officials. It presented a picture of JFK's steadfastness and statecraft. In the eloquent words of Arthur Schlesinger, special assistant to the President in 1962, 'It was this combination of toughness and restraint, of will, nerve and wisdom, so brilliantly controlled, so matchlessly calibrated, that dazzled the world'.[18] Subsequently, as various contributors have demonstrated, the resolution of the crisis appears very different and much more of a puzzle than hitherto assumed.

Why Khrushchev withdrew the missiles from Cuba has unsurprisingly attracted the attention of many scholars. The first significant reappraisal of events, which challenged the accounts of Schlesinger *et al.*, appeared in 1980.[19] In 1988 McGeorge Bundy published an account of how, on the evening of 27 October, the President tasked his brother with delivering a message to the Soviet Ambassador, Anatoli Dobrynin.[20] This included willingness to withdraw the Jupiter IRBMs in Turkey which Khrushchev had publically demanded earlier that day. The semantics of what RFK said to Dobrynin about the Turkish missiles vary: 'deal', 'offer', 'assurance', 'arrangement', 'bargain', 'secret concession', 'hedged promise'. May and Zelikow describe it as 'a unilateral statement of general intent'.[21] Don Munton considers it a 'mutual missile withdrawal pact' which resulted in the first-ever agreement on nuclear arms reduction.[22] What is clear is that, as Bundy admitted: 'we misled our colleagues, our countrymen, our successors, and our allies.'[23]

In 1989, Ted Sorensen stated that he had deliberately falsified Robert Kennedy's memoir when it was published posthumously.[24] Members of ExComm acted to preserve the myth that JFK stood firm and refused to withdraw the Jupiters from Turkey. Kennedy's willingness to remove them was made clear by his brother to Dobrynin on 27 October. Declassification of Soviet records, notably Dobrynin's report of this meeting back to Moscow, corroborates the ExComm revelations.[25] As this author's discussion of Dino Brugioni's *Eyeball to Eyeball: The Inside Story of the Cuban Missile Crisis* argues, while Khrushchev may have blinked, so too did Kennedy.[26]

In 1997 Aleksandr Fursenko and Timothy Naftali gained unprecedented access to Soviet records. This yielded significant new information on Soviet (and Cuban) perceptions and actions. *'One Hell of a Gamble'* presented the kind of archival-based study familiar in Western Cold War scholarship and illuminated how Khrushchev reached and implemented his decisions. Fursenko and Naftali's account of the meeting of the Presidium on 28 October makes clear that Khrushchev had already told his comrades it was necessary to retreat *before* he learned of Robert Kennedy's meeting with Dobrynin.[27] JFK's 'offer' on the Turkish Jupiters still compels revision of how Kennedy sought to square the circle of NATO cohesion and accommodation with Moscow. Various contributors to this volume have noted that as Khrushchev had already decided to retreat, the secret offer was not necessary to resolve the crisis. Nevertheless, Don Munton argues, 'Kennedy's offer on the Jupiters and their actual withdrawal, became integral to the deal – for both sides'.[28] Certainly Robert Kennedy made clear to Dobrynin that withdrawal of the IRBMs was dependant on Moscow not disclosing to NATO what was happening.

In 2003, fragmentary records of key meetings of the Presidium became available.[29] These were written by Vladimir Malin, chief of the General Department of the Central Committee. In 2006 Fursenko and Naftali published a new study, *Khrushchev's Cold War*, which expanded and revised their earlier work.[30] The records of the meeting of the Presidium on Thursday 25 October indicate that Khrushchev had already decided that retreat was necessary (in return for guarantees of Cuba's security) before the crisis reached its climax at the weekend.[31]

Documents do not speak for themselves. All documents are written for a purpose. Contemporaneous documents are often written to communicate, as accurately as possible, what was said or done.[32] Others record what their authors do not want known. Some of what is known to some is never written down. Documents can contain sins of omission or commission. A deeper insight is also proffered by Robert Jervis:

> What they [historians and political scientists] are less aware of is that even when people are honestly trying to describe their own motives and reasons for reaching their conclusions, they are often unable to do so. A great deal of our mental processing is unavailable to us because it occurs below the level of consciousness, and we often go about understanding why we are behaving as we do or holding our preferences in exactly the same manner that we use when analysing others – and these accounts are likely to be no more accurate. Shortly before he was assassinated, Kennedy noted that 'the essence of ultimate decision remained impenetrable to the observer – often, indeed, to the decider himself'. We try to make sense of what we have done, but this is a reconstruction. One does not have to be Freudian to recognize that, in a deep sense, we are 'strangers to ourselves'. Statements by Kennedy, Khrushchev, and their colleagues about why they held their views and why they thought others would act in specified ways may be simultaneously completely honest and untrue. Self-knowledge is inevitably limited.[33]

History, theory and policy

Relationships between history and theory are themes explored in various contributions. Many texts have multiple dimensions, and some that explore theoretical aspects also provide new empirical material. Scott

Sagan's application of organisational theory to the command and control of nuclear weapons yielded considerable evidence about the risks of inadvertent nuclear war. Richard Ned Lebow and Janice Gross Stein's use of psychological approaches drew upon significant empirical work in Moscow.

The work of all historians inevitably involves theoretical assumptions, even though these may be implicit. This volume ranges across concepts including uncertainty, trust, surprise, luck, risk, and counterfactual history. It furnishes insights into all manner of epistemological challenges and opportunities. The crisis provides fertile ground for exploring rational choice, bureaucratic politics and cognitive analysis as well as how ideas and values shape, and are shaped by, experience. Various contributors engage with these and other approaches. Most of their analyses have significant implications for policy-makers, though Campbell Craig provides a form of policy prescription in arguing that if we really want to ensure that a future Cuban missile crisis does not blow up the world, 'the solution ... is to construct a global entity powerful enough to prevent that from happening, which is to say, a world government'.[34]

One of the most notable texts to explore contending paradigms of decision-making in the crisis remains *Essence of Decision*. Other political scientists had engaged with foreign-policy making before Allison. *Essence of Decision* nevertheless stimulated a wealth of criticism and debate, and proffered alternative approaches to rational-actor assumptions that in particular pervaded thinking about nuclear deterrence. The revised edition in 1999, co-authored with Philip Zelikow, engaged with criticisms, revisited models and revised analysis in the light of new evidence and interpretation.[35] Don Munton's assessment is that historical research 'has generally not supported the claims about intra-governmental factors, and perhaps even undermined them'.[36] And as Sheldon Stern and Robert Jervis demonstrate, as the crisis reached its climax, JFK pushed accommodation on the Turkish missiles against the opposition (much of it strong opposition) of his advisors.

A central tenet in much bureaucratic politics is the axiom that where you stand depends on where you sit. Whether this has sufficient explanatory power in general to explain beliefs and actions of senior officials remains debatable. Here, new evidence and interpretation provides fertile grounds for analysis. On the Soviet side, Anastas Mikoyan emerges as the principal voice of caution (and reason) arguing against the missile deployment and the running of the blockade by Soviet submarines, and as the person who prevented the transfer of nuclear weapons to the Cubans in November 1962. How the arguments of the Soviet Deputy Premier can be attributed to his post is difficult to fathom.

A second aspect here concerns the American military. A central question in civil–military relations is whether military leaders can be expected to favour the use and escalation of force or not. The American Joint Chiefs consistently advocated an invasion of Cuba.[37] Yet there is no evidence that the American military seriously advocated the use of nuclear weapons either against Cuba or against the Soviet Union. There is one reference in *Thirteen Days* to 'one member of the Joint Chiefs' arguing that nuclear weapons could be used 'as our adversaries would use theirs against us in an attack'.[38] In 1961, the commander-in-chief of the Strategic Air Command (CINCSAC), General Thomas Power, had told Kennedy and the Joint Chiefs that 'If a general atomic war is inevitable, the U.S. should strike first'.[39] The Joint Chiefs, however, made clear to the President that there was no guarantee an American first strike would prevent some Soviet retaliation against the United States.[40] Whatever the rationality, morality and feasibility of initiating the use of nuclear weapons, no evidence has emerged to indicate the military advocated nuclear attacks. Whether they contemplated it among themselves (and whether absence of evidence is evidence of absence) awaits investigation. Where the hawks stood or sat on nuclear use, remains a matter for speculation. Moreover, how we identify 'hawks' and 'doves' reflects our knowledge of discussions that took place as well as specific ornithological assumptions. Many of the doves supported the blockade even though they anticipated Soviet retaliation against Berlin, which would in turn risk a very serious escalation in the crisis.[41] Many of the doves had talons.

Other approaches to decision-making have gathered momentum since the 1980s, drawing notably upon cognitive psychology. Benoît Pelopidas evaluates the work of Richard Ned Lebow and Janice Gross Stein, as well as that of Robert Jervis, in developing major and influential critiques of the rational decision-making that underpinned much Western thinking about nuclear deterrence.[42] Ideas about deterrence frequently reflected conceptions of states as unitary and rational actors. One legacy of the crisis was to reinforce ways of thinking in Western strategic studies in the 1960s and beyond. Evidence of the risk of inadvertent nuclear war, however, later became grist to the mill of those who focussed on the inadequacies of nuclear command, control, communications and intelligence (C3I). Yet our knowledge of C3I in 1962, in particular involving different kinds of Soviet nuclear weapons, is frequently opaque. And whatever procedural (or electronic) safeguards existed, any adjudication of the risk of unauthorised use of nuclear weapons requires exploration of military discipline, organisational culture, and the inevitably speculative question of how military decision-makers (at various levels) might have acted in war (or imminent war). These raise essential if largely unexplored (and quite possibly unanswerable) questions in assessing the risk that the nuclear threshold could have been crossed and in assessing how escalation might then have happened.

Secrets, mysteries, known unknowns and unknown unknowns

For most historians, history is evidence-based and speculation-driven. That speculation is not simply about the 'what ifs?' and 'might have beens', though as Barton Bernstein and others have shown, counterfactuals are of great value in exploring the meaning of events and decisions. Speculation is also necessary in exploring what actually happened where our knowledge may be fragmentary and/or ambiguous. Even where we believe we know, our understanding may be overtaken by new sources. Students of the crisis are very familiar with how narratives and analyses have changed as new evidence has emerged.

There are moments in the crisis where there is insufficient evidence to move beyond informed speculation about how and why decisions were made. We do have sufficient evidence to know at least some of what we do not know (and which we estimate to be significant). We do not know how Soviet military threat assessments developed during the crisis, and at specific moments such as when the Alaskan-based U-2 flew into Soviet air space on 27 October. This reflects a more general – and surely crucial issue – of our ignorance of Soviet threat assessments during the Cold War.

There are some aspects of the crisis that seem hidden in plain sight. American (and Russian) writers on the crisis seem disinterested in (or oblivious to) the activities of the third nuclear weapons state in October 1962 (whose nuclear bombers and missiles were at advanced states of readiness).[43] Disinterest in the American and nascent Russian historiography of the crisis presumably reflects the disinterest of American and (presumably) Soviet decision-makers. Apart from Macmillan's offer to involve the UK-based Thor IRBMs in a possible solution, discussed by Peter Catterall, British nuclear weapons seem invisible in October 1962. President Kennedy was greatly exercised about the command and control of the Jupiter missiles in Turkey[44] while the readiness state of the Thor missiles in Britain (less than 15 minutes) provoked no interest in ExComm.

Adjudication of the significance of British alert and readiness states awaits understanding of Soviet threat perceptions. Illustrative of American historians' lack of interest in the UK dimension is how the publication of 800 pages of documents in the Woodrow Wilson Center's *Cold War International History Project Bulletin* simply neglects British sources.[45] This is all the more curious given that British officials had access to senior Americans including Kennedy himself. These discussions generated records that provide insights into Washington decision-making and, most importantly, the disposition and perceptions of the President. When Ormsby-Gore lunched privately with JFK on 21 October, for example, something the President said in the Berlin context was so important to Ormsby-Gore that he could not commit it to a Top Secret telegram to the Prime Minister and instead offered to fly home to tell Macmillan in person.[46] Neglect of

British sources is compounded by neglect of the British Commonwealth whose study would add a further international dimension to that which the Cold War International History Project has otherwise so valuably advanced.

One foot in the grave?

The Cuban missile crisis remains one of the most intensively studied events of the twentieth century, and for the vast majority of students, the moment when humankind came closest to Armageddon. How close?[47] Historical revelations have provided much new evidence with which to address this question. Both Kennedy and Khrushchev followed a trajectory that began with belligerence and ended with accommodation. As Peter Catterall shows, the same was true of Macmillan. The closer political leaders moved to the brink, the more determined they were to draw back. Does this vindicate the hawks? Does it justify deterrence? Paul Nitze argued that American regional superiority in the Caribbean mixed with strategic nuclear superiority meant the risk of nuclear war over Cuba was nugatory.[48] At root, this is an argument that American deterrence was robust and successful.

Yet information in the last few decades has reinforced the view that we were far nearer the brink than was realised. While decision-makers were increasingly keen to avoid conflict, the risk of inadvertent nuclear war is much more apparent. Campbell Craig's analysis of Scott Sagan's *Limits of Safety* emphasises specific incidents in US nuclear command and control that require re-evaluation of the risk of inadvertent and accidental nuclear war. Craig further explores the implications of Sagan's' work for a broader assessment of nuclear risk in the Cold War and beyond.[49] Both Craig and Radchenko focus on the U-2 that strayed off course into Soviet air space on 27 October, first disclosed by Roger Hilsman in *To Move a Nation* in 1967.[50] There was fear in Washington that the Soviets might mistake the plane for pre-strike reconnaissance and launch their ICBMs pre-emptively. What is unclear is, if the Pentagon took this risk seriously, whether consideration was given in Washington to pre-empting pre-emption. *Limits of Safety* identifies more tangible risks, including how, as Soviet MiG-19s scrambled to shoot down the U-2, American F-102 fighters took off to provide support. Unbeknownst to political leaders in Washington the prevailing DEFCON alert state meant the US fighters were armed with air-to-air missiles with low-yield nuclear warheads. Sagan sketches five scenarios in which nuclear weapons could have been fired.[51]

Whilst Sagan's work focuses primarily on American nuclear command and control much new information has emerged about Soviet forces. The suggestion that the Soviets deployed a hundred or so tactical nuclear weapons in Cuba has become an accepted part of the story, though it generated fierce debates in the 1990s, including, as Sergey Radchenko describes, over whether Soviet commanders had pre-delegated authority to fire battlefield nuclear missiles. More recently, Michael Dobbs has shown that Soviet FKR cruise missiles moved to firing positions within range of the US naval base at Guantánamo Bay.[52]

How significant are these facts? Assessing the risk that tactical nuclear weapons might be fired in an American invasion raises questions both about the authority to use them and whether they could have been used without authority, as well as whether they would have survived the US aerial assault. The Americans were aware that cruise missiles were in position to threaten Guantánamo and destroying them would have been a priority for the defence of the base.[53] The larger counterfactual concerns the risk of an American invasion. Would Kennedy have invaded Cuba if the crisis had not reached its climax over the weekend of 26–28 October? If Soviet nuclear weapons had been used against the invading Americans, what then?

Kennedy's willingness to act behind the backs of his NATO allies risked the cohesion of the alliance but indicated his determination to avoid war. How far would that determination have gone? This author's commentary on Brugioni's *Eyeball to Eyeball* makes clear the strong opposition of the US military to a peaceful resolution of the crisis, but on the other hand alludes to the retrospective views of Robert McNamara and McGeorge Bundy that Kennedy would have gone the extra mile for peace. *'One Hell of a Gamble'* and *We All Lost the Cold War* have demonstrated how, as the crisis continued, both leaders manoeuvred to draw back, if necessary at personal and political cost. What if Khrushchev had not blinked? This may seem a weak counterfactual as the evidence overwhelming shows he was determined to avoid escalation. Yet it raises intriguing questions. What, for example, if Khrushchev had made clear to Kennedy (privately or publically) that action against Cuba would meet with retaliation against West Berlin? If there were circumstances in which Kennedy would have acquiesced to missiles in Cuba (as Moscow had acquiesced to missiles in Britain, Italy and Turkey) then Khrushchev's adventure looks less hazardous and, arguably, less of a gamble. On the other hand, preparations for an invasion were at an advanced state, and Robert Kennedy had, on his brother's instructions, told the Soviet ambassador an attack on the missiles could be imminent. Kennedy's close friend (and British ambassador), David Ormsby-Gore, told the Foreign Office that an attack would have come within a matter of days.[54]

'We will sink them all': losing a temper or risking a war?

Sergey Radchenko notes the complaint of Mark Kramer about predispositions to show the crisis was more dangerous than it was. Assessing the risk of nuclear war raises complex issues, not least because Soviet nuclear command and control arrangements are not yet clear. Possibly the most dramatic events involved deployment of Soviet diesel-electric submarines, each armed with a nuclear torpedo. Two of the submarines were bombarded by the US Navy using practice depth-charges and hand grenades. On at least one boat the captain is reported to been close to firing his nuclear weapon. The story of the submarines is worthy of some scrutiny as it illuminates major themes and issues in the study of the crisis.

Procedures for surfacing Soviet submarines were discussed with JFK in ExComm on 24 October (though this was *after* they were communicated to the Soviet government).[55] Neither Kennedy nor McNamara appeared aware that the submarines could be nuclear armed (even though US intelligence apparently considered that this category of submarine could be so equipped).[56] Both erroneously assumed that McNamara's ad hoc procedures would be immediately conveyed to the submarine captains, when some at least of them believed they were under real attack. The President and the Defense Secretary were greatly exercised about the need for political control over military forces, and McNamara insisted that the blockade was a means of communicating with the Soviets. Much has been made of the warning from history provided by Barbara Tuchman. Yet the Kennedy administration set in motion a train of events that could have led to nuclear war. The incident that may have generated the greatest risk of nuclear use in October 1962 may also provide the best example of the huge gap between political leaders and those who operated nuclear weapons. Yet how do we assess that risk?

Much of our understanding of the events rests on memories of Soviet submariners.[57] Whether there was pre-delegated authority for nuclear use has not yet been clarified, though accounts from two of the captains suggest that the Chief of Staff of the Northern Fleet, Vice-Admiral A.I. Rassokha, verbally specified circumstances in which the nuclear torpedo could be fired and ordered that these rules of engagement be entered into the captain's log books.[58] This delegation of authority was seemingly at variance with written instructions that made clear nuclear weapons could only be used on orders from Moscow.

Unauthorised use nevertheless remained possible. Firing the nuclear weapon apparently required three different keys. Weir and Boyle state that these were held by the captain, the political officer and the executive officer.[59] The special weapons security officer (presumably from the KGB) had one set of (presumably additional) keys with which to load the weapon, which he was responsible for arming.[60] Soviet command and control thus appears to have involved four people from three different organisations (the Soviet navy, the Communist party and – presumably – the KGB). Prima facie, this seems a more robust procedure than with many US nuclear weapons at the time, which operated on a two-man principle.

Yet procedures can be only a part of the story. Incidents on the B-59 and the B-130 have focussed attention on the plight of the submarine crews (and the extraordinary ineptitude of the senior Soviet officials who planned the operation).[61] The most dramatic account emanated from a former GRU communications officer, Vadim Orlov, who was on board the B-59 captained by Valentin Savitsky.[62] The submarine was being pursued by a carrier task group led by the USS *Randolph*. On 27 October, according to Orlov, Captain Savitsky, under intense pressure and in appalling conditions on the boat, announced his intention of firing his nuclear torpedo.[63] The brigade chief of staff, Captain Vasili Arkhipov, persuaded him to rein in his anger, Orlov recounts. The incident has received wide circulation through the writing of Svetlana Savranskaya and Michael Dobbs as well as through the efforts of the National Security Archive, and various television documentaries.

As Sergei Radchenko notes, Arkhipov has entered the history of the crisis as 'the guy who saved the world'. Weir and Boyle's account presents a less dramatic picture, even though their account was also informed by testimony from Orlov. Savranskaya also notes that at the fortieth anniversary of the crisis in Havana in 2002 Orlov

> emphasised that the utmost danger came not from an intentional launch of a nuclear torpedo, which even in the tense atmosphere of the last days before the surfacing remained very unlikely, but from malfunctioning equipment or an accident, which could have happened even under less trying conditions.[64]

Accounts record temperatures reaching 60 degrees Celsius in the engine room. Normally the temperature at which nuclear weapons are maintained is carefully controlled. What was the temperature in the forward torpedo room? Was there risk of an explosion? What assessments did the Soviet navy make of risking nuclear warheads in these environments, if any?

More (knowledge) is less (worrying)

In other episodes, evidence about activities of subordinates has lessened the sense of danger. In 1987, Raymond Garthoff, an authority on the crisis who had worked in the CIA and State Department during the Kennedy administration, published a dramatic account of an incident when the CIA received a coded message from a spy in Soviet Military Intelligence, Oleg Penkovsky.[65] While entering 'a caveat about the provenance of his information', Garthoff suggested that warning of imminent Soviet military action may have been intended by Penkovsky (who was then in KGB custody) to trigger an American attack. Garthoff suggested that the CIA withheld this information from the President (and ExComm). However, in 1992 Jerrold Schecter and Peter Deriabin provided a detailed account, based on access to CIA files, which made clear that the President was briefed on Penkovsky's arrest.[66] A second example concerns communications and intelligence. It was suggested that the CINCSAC, General Power, communicated to his airborne-alerted B-52 bombers *en clair* to intimidate the Soviets.[67] It later became clear, however, that Power's message was designed to reassure his bomber crews and make clear that if in doubt they should contact headquarters. How far this intent to reassure was comprehended by the Soviets is unknown.[68]

Learning from history

When, in the 1980s, Soviet officials began to share their recollections and reflections with their Western counterparts and Western academics, some questioned their motives. Former Deputy Director at the CIA, Ray Cline, inveighed against 'Mikhail Gorbachev's team of official intellectuals ... engaged in a program of historical revisionism serving Moscow's interest'.[69] The interest in question was promotion of Gorbachev's pursuit of global nuclear disarmament. What, then, can the missile crisis tell us about nuclear deterrence? Eliot Cohen argues:

> We should ask whether the crisis itself can and should serve as an appropriate model either for those studying policy or for those conducting it. We must, in short, ask ourselves whether the uniqueness of the crisis does not destroy its value as an archetype, or worse, make it a profoundly misleading subject for reflection.[70]

Sir Michael Howard has also warned,

> It is safer to start with the assumption that history, whatever its value in educating the judgement, teaches no 'lessons'.... The past is infinitely various, an inexhaustible storehouse of events from which we can prove anything or its contrary.[71]

Thankfully, we have had an insufficient number of nuclear crises to satisfy the yearning of social scientists for generalisability. The Cuban missile crisis is widely seen as the nearest the world came to nuclear war and is certainly the crisis about which we know most. That includes evidence of how decision-makers themselves sought to use historical analogies and draw lessons from the past, from August 1914 to Munich to Pearl Harbor.[72] As R. Gerald Hughes explains it is worth noting that before the crisis Kennedy (and other senior Washington officials) read Barbara Tuchman's *Guns of August*, which argued that war came inadvertently in 1914. Robert Kennedy suggested this history book influenced his brother's handling of the crisis.[73] Harold Macmillan also read Tuchman's account of the outbreak of a war in which he was wounded, and where so many of his generation perished. Comparisons between Kennedy's and Macmillan's attitude to alert and mobilisation are thus revealing.

While Macmillan supported American mobilisation in the Caribbean he was strongly opposed to mobilisation in Europe. On 22 October he told the Supreme Allied Commander Europe, General Lauris Norstad, 'mobilisation had sometimes caused war' echoing *The Guns of August*. The Prime Minister said that mobilisation in Europe 'was absurd since additional forces made available by "Alert" had no military significance'.[74] Even as the crisis reached its climax on 27 October, the Prime Minister made clear to the Chief of the Air Staff, Sir Thomas Pike, that he 'did not consider the time was appropriate for any overt preparatory steps to be taken such as mobilisation', and he 'did not wish Bomber Command to be alerted'.[75] Whether he fully understood the alert and readiness posture of the V-bombers and Thor missiles (a proportion of which were kept at fifteen minutes readiness under normal conditions) is unclear. Whether he knew that, on the afternoon of 27 October, Bomber Command went to Cockpit Alert (05 Readiness) is unknown.

In contrast, while in ExComm on 16 October McNamara briefly alluded to risks in changing SAC's alert condition, there was barely a pause before it was decided to raise the US DEFCON alert state. Neither the President nor his colleagues appear to have shown concern that the Soviets might mistake resolve for imminent aggression. Whether they were prudent to do so requires a fuller understanding of Soviet threat perceptions (and of American perceptions of Soviet threat perceptions).

Theories of nuclear deterrence inextricably involve consideration of how political (or military) leaders could take decisions resulting in the deaths of millions, or in Robert McNamara's phrase, the 'destruction of nations' (if not indeed the destruction of humankind).[76] However deterrence is defined, it is assumed that decision-makers will seek to avoid the annihilation of their country. In 1992, however, Fidel Castro explained his attitude to Soviet tactical nuclear weapons in Cuba 40 years earlier:

> I wish we had had the tactical nuclear weapons. It would have been wonderful. We wouldn't have rushed to use them, you can be sure of that.... Of course, after we had used ours, they would have replied with, say, 400 tactical weapons – we don't know how many would have been fired at us. In any case we were resigned to our fate.[77]

It is easy to see such ideas as irrational and dangerous. Yet the threat of a nuclear response to conventional attack remained at the heart of NATO strategy during the Cold War. Similarly Castro's exhortations to Khrushchev on 27 October to initiate strategic nuclear attacks on the USA should Kennedy invade Cuba paralleled the logic of NATO's strategy of massive retaliation that envisaged US nuclear bombardment of the USSR in response to a conventional assault on the Federal Republic of Germany. Castro's apparent willingness to provoke nuclear annihilation nevertheless appears to challenge the idea that nuclear weapons will always deter political leaders.

How far the words of political leaders denote their intentions or how they would act in particular (and especially unimaginable conditions of nuclear war) remain imponderable. Yet it is worth noting that Kennedy's televised speech on 22 October threatened 'a full retaliatory response' for the use of any Soviet missiles in Cuba against any targets in the Western hemisphere. While Kennedy obviously wished to signal his determination, is this really what he would have done, not least when he and McNamara were trying to move American and NATO strategy away from massive retaliation, and when during the crisis he was so determined to avoid escalation?

Under what circumstances Kennedy would have attacked Cuba remains central to various judgements about the risk of nuclear war. How close we came to nuclear war is inextricably linked to counterfactual questions about what might have happened. There are many 'known unknowns' about the missile crisis including what consideration was given by the respective military leaderships to nuclear war. These may well prove to be secrets rather than mysteries inasmuch as they may be amenable to archival research. The mysteries concern the minds (and souls) of those who could have faced decisions to use weapons of mass destruction. Historical evidence and cognitive insights into their moment of thermo-nuclear truth (as McGeorge Bundy termed it) are inevitably constrained.

Moreover, any evidence concerns how they *anticipated* what they would do. What they would have done could have been entirely different. Furthermore, whether it was Khrushchev or Kennedy (or Macmillan) who would have stepped across the nuclear threshold or ordered all-out attack should not be taken for granted. The issue of whether the respective militaries had authority to use strategic nuclear weapons remain crucial in adjudicating the stability of crisis management and the risk of nuclear war in 1962 (and indeed more broadly in the Cold War). Certainly, RAF Bomber Command received clear authorisation in September 1962 to initiate nuclear attacks on the Soviet Union in specified circumstances.[78] If Washington or Moscow (or London) had been destroyed who would have taken decisions on nuclear use? Would they have worn suits or uniforms? Whether those in uniforms had the power to use strategic nuclear weapons (irrespective of whether they had authority) is equally, if not more important. The Jupiters and Thors were among many nuclear weapons in NATO Europe that were not equipped with electronic locks (or Permissive Action Links as they were known) and which relied on procedural safeguards as well as the military discipline and judgement of the troops concerned.

Sergey Radchenko's discussion of Nikita Khrushchev's personality also raises important questions and counterfactuals. Would, for example, Richard Nixon or Lyndon Johnson have held back from military action against Cuba at various moments in the crisis? Or if either had been President would Khrushchev have taken his gamble in the first place? The potential importance of personality, psychology and morality are also relevant to military officials involved in decisions about using nuclear weapons, from CINSAC to the captain of the B-59. Such observations may suggest avenues of future enquiry, though ones that are self-evidently beset with difficulties not least the diminishing longevity of surviving officials.

Much of the literature on the crisis takes the use of nuclear weapons as synonymous with cataclysmic nuclear war and assumes escalation was automatic.[79] This assumption is most probably correct. Yet one of the more significant moments in the crisis was when President Kennedy chose not to retaliate against Soviet SAM sites after Major Anderson's U-2 was shot down on 27 October. Whether there would have been similar reluctance to foreswear or limit retaliation in response to the use of nuclear weapons is certainly possible, especially where that use was judged to be tactical, limited or accidental. Although the Soviets possessed a smaller strategic force whose vulnerability might have quickly raised in Moscow minds the need to 'use them or lose them', a limited or selective American attack might have prompted a limited Soviet response (or indeed no response at all). Assessments of the risk of nuclear war (and of cataclysmic nuclear war) require a dark empathy on the part of the historian. They also require attention to the organisational processes, military imperatives and the radioactive fog of war that could have hastened escalation despite the best endeavours of political leaders.

Most students of the missile crisis would agree with Eliot Cohen's antipathy to nuclear crisis management. That would certainly include Robert McNamara, who devoted much energy to re-examining the crisis, and who concluded that the decisive factor in avoiding war in 1962 was luck.[80] Captain Ketov, the skipper of the B-4 submarine, believed that it was 'mere chance' that his colleague, Captain Savitsky, did not fire his nuclear torpedo.[81] Campbell Craig endorses Scott Sagan's pessimism about the prospect of nuclear war – in Craig's words, 'if anarchical great-power politics perpetuate over the long term, a nuclear war will happen sooner or later'.[82] Robert McNamara's conclusion was that: 'it can be predicted with confidence that the indefinite combination of human fallibility and nuclear weapons carries a very high risk of a potential nuclear catastrophe'.[83] McNamara came to believe that global abolition of nuclear weapons is the solution to the problem. Otherwise, one day our luck will run out. How we conceptualise luck, and how we conceptualise the relationship between luck, judgement and risk are very important questions illuminated by Benoît Pelopidas.

The emphasis on contingency and unacknowledged risk has accelerated with more evidence. Better understanding of the role of misperception, miscalculation and mistakes, including the actions of subordinates, suggests the risk of nuclear war was greater than thought by decision-makers at the time, and by commentators subsequently. The study of the Cold War has rightly extended beyond Soviet–American relations. Previously neglected aspects have been the subject of valuable illumination, including the role and attitudes of Cuba, Latin America (notably Brazil),[84] the United Nations,[85] Europe and China.[86] The recent efforts by the Cold War International History Project and by others[87] have documented new perspectives echoing the entry in Harold Macmillan's diary for the 22 October recording the 'first day of the World Crisis'.[88]

Yet a central reason why the missile crisis remains such a focus of interest is because the events of October 1962 could have resulted in nuclear war. The risk of nuclear war and the impact of nuclear weapons on politics, culture and ideology are defining aspects of the Cold War. Yet they are seemingly neglected or marginalised in what Sergey Radchenko describes as the 'new Cold War scholarship'. Whatever the role of ideology in the Cold War it is essential to understand that the rationality and morality of nuclear deterrence (however conceived) are central to understanding the meaning of the Cold War. Yet, at the same time, ideas about nuclear weapons were often of limited and sometimes tangential relevance to the actual policies, strategies and deployments. The results, as demonstrated in the missile crisis, posed unprecedented challenges and threats to humankind. So long as we confront the problem of nuclear weapons, we should strengthen our commitment to studying the Cuban missile crisis and the nuclear history of the Cold War. How we go about that study is explored by several contributors, including Barton Bernstein and Robert Jervis. For Don Munton 'the missile crisis may be a rewarding and rich case for a fruitful marriage of rational-actor, cognitive and constructivist approaches'.[89] Underpinning Benoît Pelopidas' analysis is a combination of 'cognitive psychology, sociological investigation and historical critique'.[90]

The contributions to *The Cuban Missile Crisis: A Critical Reappraisal* await critical appraisal. The texts under scrutiny include 'essential readings' for students of the crisis. Some books fare better in critical hindsight than others, though different scholars have often differing readings of the value and limits of earlier works. Their interrogations of the texts nevertheless yield a range of insights and reinterpretations. What is beyond doubt is that *The Cuban Missile Crisis: A Critical Reappraisal* demonstrates the missile crisis will remain a focus of interest for scholars of many disciplines from many countries for many years. If anyone had been persuaded to stop studying the crisis in 1986 this would be as good a moment as any for them to change their mind.

Notes

1 I am grateful to Sheldon Stern and Bart Bernstein for their comments on earlier drafts of this chapter. This chapter contains some 15 per cent or so of material in Len Scott, 'Should We Stop Studying the Cuban Missile Crisis?', *International Relations*, 26/3 (2012) 255–66. Reproduced by permission of Sage Publications.

2 Eliot Cohen, 'Why We Should Stop Studying the Cuban Missile Crisis', *National Interest* (Winter 1985/86) 3–13.

3 Barton J. Bernstein, 'Examining *The Fourteenth Day*: Studying the Neglected Aftermath Period of the October Cuban Missile Crisis, and Underscoring Missed Analytical Opportunities', this volume.

4 Ibid.

5 Raymond L. Garthoff, *Reflections on the Cuban Missile Crisis* (Washington, DC: The Brookings Institution 1987) p. 9.

6 Raymond L. Garthoff, 'US Intelligence in the Cuban Missile Crisis', in James G. Blight and David A. Welch (eds), *Intelligence and Cuban Missile Crisis* (London: Frank Cass 1998) p. 50.

7 Don Munton, 'The Three Puzzles: *Essence of Decision* and the Missile Crisis', this volume.

8 Sergey Radchenko, 'On Hedgehogs and Passions: History, Hearsay, and Hotchpotch in the Writing of the Cuban Missile Crisis', this volume.

9 Robert Jervis, 'The Cuban Missile Crisis: What Can We Know, Why Did It Start, and How Did It End?' this volume.

10 Sheldon M. Stern, 'Beyond the Smoke and Mirrors: The Real JFK White House Cuban Missile Crisis', this volume.

11 Cohen, 'Why We Should Stop', 4.

12 Peter Catterall, 'Prime Minister and President: Harold Macmillan's Accounts of the Cuban Missile Crisis', this volume.

13 Peter Catterall (ed.), *The Macmillan Diaries: Prime Minister and After 1957–66* (London: Macmillan 2011) p. 494.

14 Jervis, 'Cuban Missile Crisis'.

15 Aleksandr Fursenko and Timothy Naftali, *'One Hell of a Gamble': Khrushchev, Castro, and Kennedy 1958–1964* (London: John Murray 1997).

16 Bernstein, 'Examining *The Fourteenth Day*'.

17 Sergo Mikoyan (edited by Svetlana Savranskaya), *The Soviet Cuban Missile Crisis: Castro, Mikoyan. Kennedy, Khrushchev, and the Missiles of November* (Washington, DC: Woodrow Wilson Press/Stanford: CA: Stanford University Press 2012).

18 Arthur M. Schlesinger Jr., *A Thousand Days: John F. Kennedy in the White House* (London: Andre Deutsch 1965) p. 716.

19 Barton J. Bernstein, 'The Cuban Missile Crisis: Trading the Jupiters in Turkey?' *Political Science Quarterly*, 95/1 (Spring 1980) 97–125.

20 McGeorge Bundy, *Danger and Survival: Choices about the Bomb in the First Fifty Years* (New York: Random House 1988) pp. 432–9. For discussion of the RFK–Dobrynin meeting see James Hershberg, 'Anatomy of a Controversy: Anatoly Dobrynin's Meeting with Robert Kennedy, Saturday 27 October 1962', *Cold War International History Project Bulletin* Issue 5 (Spring 1995) 75, 77–80.

21 Philip D. Zelikow and Ernest R. May (eds), *The Presidential Recordings: John F. Kennedy: The Great Crises, Vol. III* [hereafter *PRJFK III*], *October 22–28, 1962* (New York: W.W. Norton 2001) p. 485n.

22 Munton, 'Three Puzzles.'

23 Bundy, *Danger and Survival*, p. 434.

24 Bruce J. Allyn, James G. Blight and David A. Welch, *Back to the Brink: Proceedings of the Moscow Conference on the Cuban Missile Crisis, January 27–28, 1989* (Lanham, MD: University of America Press 1992) pp. 92–3.

25 Richard Ned Lebow and Janice Gross Stein, *We All Lost the Cold War* (Princeton, NJ: Princeton University Press 1994) pp. 523–6, discussed in Benoît Pelopidas, 'We All Lost the "Cuban Missile Crisis": Revisiting Richard Ned Lebow and Janice Stein's Landmark Analysis in *We All Lost the Cold War*', this volume.

26 Dino A. Brugioni (ed. Robert F. McCort), *Eyeball to Eyeball: The Inside Story of the Cuban Missile Crisis* (New York: Random House 1991), discussed in Len Scott, 'Eyeball to Eyeball: Blinking and Winking, Spyplanes and Secrets', *International Relations*, 26/3 (September 2012) 344–66.

27 Fursenko and Naftali, *'One Hell of a Gamble'*, pp. 283–7.

28 Munton, 'Three Puzzles'.

29 Radchenko, 'Hedgehogs and Passions'. These notes first became available in Russia in 2003 and were later translated and made accessible at the Miller Center of Public Affairs' Kremlin Decision-making Project. http://millercenter. org/about/kremlin (last accessed 7 August 2014). See Timothy Naftali, 'The Malin Notes: Glimpses Inside the Kremlin during the Cuban Missile Crisis', *Cold War International History Project Bulletin*, 17/18 (Fall 2012) 299–301.

30 Aleksandr Fursenko and Timothy Naftali, *Khrushchev's Cold War: The Inside Story of an American Adversary* (London: W.W. Norton 2006).

31 Ibid., pp. 483–6.

32 For a pessimistic comment on the reliability of ambassadors' reporting, see Jervis, 'Cuban Missile Crisis'.

33 Ibid.

34 Campbell Craig, 'Testing Organisation Man: The Cuban Missile Crisis and the Limits of Safety', *International Relations*, 26/3 (2012) 301.

35 For critical assessments of the second edition, see Barton J. Bernstein, 'Understanding Decisonmaking, US Foreign Policy and the Cuban Missile Crisis: A Review Essay', *International Security*, 25/1 (Summer 2000) 134–64 and David Patrick Houghton 'Essence of Excision: A Critique of the New Version of Essence of Decision', *Security Studies*, 10/1 (2000) 151–78.

36 Munton, 'Three Puzzles'.

37 It did, however, take the discovery of Soviet IRBM bases to persuade Maxwell Taylor of this course. Initially, on 16 October, Taylor expressed his concerns about that 'deep mud in Cuba'. More notably, the Chairman of the Joints Chiefs demurred from the Joint Chiefs' recommendation of 28 October to attack Cuba even after Khrushchev's announcement that the missiles would be withdrawn unless there was 'irrefutable evidence' that dismantling had begun.

38 Kennedy, *Thirteen Days*, p. 51. At this meeting of the National Security Council on 21 October the only member of the Joint Chiefs present was Maxwell Taylor. He was minuted as stating that, 'he did not share Secretary McNamara's fear that if we used nuclear weapons in Cuba, nuclear weapons would be used against us', Minutes of the 505th Meeting of the National Security Council, *Foreign Relations of the United States [FRUS] 1961–1963, Vol. XI, Cuban Missile Crisis and Aftermath* (Washington, DC: United States Government Printing Office 1996) p. 129. The same record makes no mention of remarks by McNamara which might have prompted Taylor's comment or of any discussion on this subject.

39 'Memorandum of Conference with President Kennedy', *FRUS, 1961–1963, Vol. VIII, National Security Policy* (Washington, DC: United States Government Printing Office 1996) p. 130.

40 Scott D. Sagan, 'SIOP-62: The Nuclear War Plan Briefing to President Kennedy', *International Security*, 12/1 (Summer 1987) 29–36.

41 For analysis of the blockade see Munton, 'Three Puzzles'.

42 Pelopidas 'We All Lost'.

43 For a significant contribution to understanding the activities of RAF Bomber

Command see Robin Woolven, 'What Really Happened in RAF Bomber Command during the Cuban Missile Crisis?' in David Gioe, Len Scott and Christopher Andrew, *An International History of the Cuban Missile Crisis: A 50-year Retrospective* (Abingdon: Routledge 2014). The main exception to American disinterest in British nuclear preparations is Scott D. Sagan, *The Limits of Safety: Organisations, Accidents, and Nuclear Weapons* (Princeton, NJ: Princeton University Press 1993) pp. 111–13.

44 Zelikow and May (eds), *PRJFK III*, pp. 33–5; Stern, *Averting 'The Final Failure'*, pp. 144–6.

45 James Hershberg and Christian Ostermann, 'The Global Missile Crisis at 50: New Evidence from Behind the Iron, Bamboo, and Sugarcane Curtains, and Beyond', *Cold War International History Project Bulletin* Issue 17/18 (Fall 2012) www.wilsoncenter.org/publication/bulletin-no-17–18 (last accessed 29 September 2014). Documents are provided from Bulgarian, Brazilian, Chilean, Cuban, Czechoslovakian, Danish, Dutch, East German, French, Hungarian, Japanese, Israeli, Italian, Mexican, Mongolian, North Korean, North Vietnamese, Polish, Romanian, Soviet, Swiss, Yugoslavian and West German sources.

46 The National Archives (TNA): Ormsby-Gore to Macmillan Tel. 2650. PM's Pers. Tel. T.505/62, 23 October 1962, PREM 11/3689.

47 On this, see Len Scott, *The Cuban Missile Crisis and the Threat of Nuclear War: Lessons from History* (London: Continuum Books, 2007), ibid., 'Intelligence and the Risk of Nuclear War', in David Gioe, Len Scott, and Christopher Andrew (eds), *An International History of the Cuban Missile Crisis: A 50-year Retrospective* (Abingdon: Routledge 2014) pp. 25–42.

48 Paul H. Nitze, *From Hiroshima to Glasnost: At the Center of Decision* (New York: Grove Weidenfeld 1989) p. 205.

49 Craig, 'Reform or Revolution?'

50 Roger Hilsman, *To Move a Nation: The Politics of Foreign Policy in the Administration of John F. Kennedy* (Garden City, NY: Doubleday 1967) p. 221.

51 Sagan, *Limits of Safety*, pp. 138–40.

52 Michael Dobbs, *One Minute to Midnight: Kennedy, Khrushchev and Castro on the Brink of Nuclear War* (London: Hutchinson 2008) pp. 124–7, 178–81, 205–6.

53 Timothy Naftali and Philip D. Zelikow (eds), *The Presidential Recordings: John F. Kennedy: The Great Crises, Vol. II, September–October 21, 1962* (New York: W.W. Norton 2001) pp. 588, 591.

54 TNA: Ormsby-Gore to Harold Caccia, AK 1261/586, 7 November 1962, FO 371/162404.

55 Zelikow and May (eds), *PRJFK III*, pp. 192–4; Stern, *Averting 'The Final Failure'*, pp. 212–14.

56 Brugioni, *Eyeball to Eyeball*, p. 386. In ExComm, McNamara said that he neglected to mention one thing about the submarine; 19 seconds of dialogue are then excised as classified information, so it is possible that ExComm may have been told of the capability, though no discussion appears to have ensued. May and Zelikow, *Kennedy Tapes*, p. 355.

57 See Svetlana V. Savranskaya, 'Soviet Submarines in the Cuban Missile Crisis', *Journal of Strategic Studies*, 28/2 (April 2005) 233–59; Dobbs, *One Minute to Midnight*, pp. 43ff.; Peter Huchthausen, *October Fury* (New York: John Wiley 2002); Gary E. Weir and Walter J. Boyne, *Rising Tide: The Untold Story of the Russian Submarines That Fought the Cold War* (New York: Basic Books 2003) pp. 75–106; Thomas S. Blanton, William Burr and Svetlana Savranskaya, 'The Underwater Cuban Missile Crisis: Soviet Submarines and the Risk of Nuclear War' *National Security Archive Electronic Briefing Book No. 399*, www.gwu.edu/~nsarchiv/NSAEBB/NSAEBB399/. (last accessed 18 August 2014).

58 Savranskaya, 'Soviet Submarines', 240; Huchthausen, *October Fury*, pp. 53, 204.

59 Weir and Boyne, *Rising Tide*, pp. 103–4.

60 Savranskaya, 'Soviet Submarines', 239.

61 This may well be an example of operational process triumphing over rational actor as a model of explanation.

62 Savranskaya, 'Soviet Submarines', 246. Savitsky's loss of temper is taken from a 2002 book, published in Moscow by the deputy editor of Russia's military trade magazine, Alexander Mozgovoi, *Kubinskaya Samba Kvarteta Fokstrotov [Cuban Samba of the Foxtrot Quartet]* (Moscow: Voennyi Parad 2002). The account was translated by Svetlana Savranskaya and is reproduced on the NSA website. It is not clear whether the provenance of the words that have now entered the vocabulary of the crisis ('We're going to blast them all! We will die, but we will sink them all. We will not disgrace our navy') is Orlov's memory or Mozgovoi's reconstructed dialogue.

63 Savranskaya, 'Soviet Submarines', 246.

64 Ibid., 247.

65 Raymond L. Garthoff, *Reflections on the Cuban Missile Crisis* (Washington, DC: The Brookings Institution 1987) pp. 39–41; second edn (1989), pp. 63–5.

66 Jerrold L. Schecter and Peter S. Deriabin, *The Spy Who Saved the World: How a Soviet Colonel Changed the Course of the Cold War* (New York: Charles Scribner's Sons 1992) pp. 246–7.

67 Garthoff, *Reflections* (1989) p. 62; Scott Sagan, 'Nuclear Alerts and Crisis Management', *International Security*, 9/4 (Spring 1985) 108.

68 Sagan, *Limits of Safety*, p. 69.

69 Ray S. Cline, 'Commentary: The Cuban Missile Crisis', *Foreign Affairs*, 68/4 (Fall 1989) 190. As Sheldon Stern demonstrates, the reliability and integrity of American officials can be every bit as problematic.

70 Cohen, 'Why We Should Stop', 5.

71 Michael Howard, *The Lessons of History* (Oxford: Oxford University Press 1993) 11.

72 For discussion of analogies see Dominic Tierney, ' "Pearl Harbor in Reverse": Moral Analogies in the Cuban Missile Crisis', *Journal of Cold War Studies*, 9/3 (Summer 2007) 49–77 and R. Gerald Hughes, *The Postwar Legacy of Appeasement: British Foreign Policy Since 1945* (London: Bloomsbury 2014) pp. 67, 76.

73 Kennedy, *Thirteen Days*, pp. 65–6. For discussion, see R. Gerald Hughes, ' "The Best and the Brightest": the Cuban Missile Crisis, the Kennedy Administration and the Lessons of History', this volume.

74 Catterall, *Macmillan Diaries*, p. 510.

75 TNA: 'Record of a Conversation between the Chief of Air Staff, First Sea Lord and the Chief of the Imperial General Staff held at the Ministry of Defence at 1430, Saturday 27 October 1962', Annex to COS 1546/29/10/62, DEFE 32/7.

76 James G. Blight and David A. Welch, 'Risking "The Destruction of Nations": Lessons of the Cuban Missile Crisis for New and Aspiring Nuclear States,' *Security Studies* 4/4 (Summer 1995) 811.

77 James G. Blight, Bruce J. Allyn and David A. Welch, *Cuba on the Brink: Castro, the Missile Crisis and the Soviet Collapse* (New York: Pantheon Books 1993) pp. 251–2. In 2005 Castro presented a rather different attitude to using 'suicidal' nuclear weapons, Fidel Castro (with Ignacio Ramonet), *My Life* (London: Allen Lane [2006] 2007) pp. 567–8.

78 Stephen Twigge and Len Scott, *Planning Armageddon: Britain, the United States and the Command of Nuclear Forces, 1945–1964* (Amsterdam: Harwood Academic Press/Routledge 2000) pp. 85–9, 321–2.

79 This, indeed, is an important element in Campbell Craig's diagnosis and prognosis. See Campbell Craig, 'Reform or Revolution? Scott Sagan's *Limits of Safety* and Its Contemporary Implications', this volume.

80 James G. Blight and Janet M. Lang, *The Fog of War: Lessons from the Life of Robert S. McNamara* (Oxford: Rowman and Littlefield 2005) p. 59.

81 Ryurik A. Ketov, 'The Cuban Missile Crisis as Seen through a Telescope', *Journal of Strategic Studies*, 28/5 (April 2005) 227.

82 Craig, 'Reform or Revolution?'

83 Robert McNamara, 'War in the Twentieth Century', in John Baylis and Robert O'Neill, *Alternative Nuclear Futures: The Role of Nuclear Weapons in the Post-Cold War World* (Oxford: Oxford University Press 2000) p. 178.

84 James Hershberg, 'The United States, Brazil, and the Cuban Missile Crisis, 1962' (Part 1) and ibid. (Part 2), *Journal of Cold War Studies*, 6/2 (Spring 2004) 3–20 and 6/3 (Summer 2004) 5–67.

85 Daniele Ganser, *Reckless Gamble: The Sabotage of the United Nations in the Cuban Conflict and the Cuban Missile Crisis of 1962* (New Orleans, LA: University Press of the South 2000); A. Walter Dorn and Robert Pauk, 'Unsung Mediator: U Thant and the Cuban Missile Crisis', *Diplomatic History*, 33/2 (April 2009) 261–92.

86 James Hershberg and Sergey Radchenko, with Zhang Qian, 'Sino-Cuban Relations and the Cuban Missile Crisis, 1960–62: New Chinese Evidence', *Cold War International History Project Bulletin*, Issues 17–18 (October 2012) 21–116, www.wilsoncenter.org/publication/bulletin-no-17–18 (last accessed 18 December 2014).

87 See Gioe, Scott and Andrew, *International History*.

88 Catterall, *Macmillan Diaries*, p. 508.

89 Munton, 'Three Puzzles'.

90 Pelopidas, 'We All Lost'.

Bibliography

Books

Abel, Elie, *The Missiles of October, The Story of the Cuban Missile Crisis* (Philadelphia, PA: J.B. Lippincott 1966).

Aldous, Richard, *Macmillan, Eisenhower and the Cold War* (Dublin: Four Courts Press 2005).

Alford, Mimi, *Once Upon a Secret: My Affair with President John F. Kennedy and Its Aftermath* (New York: Random House 2012).

Allison, Graham T., *Essence of Decision: Explaining the Cuban Missile Crisis* (Boston, MA: Little, Brown and Company 1971).

Allison, Graham and Philip Zelikow, *Essence of Decision: Explaining the Cuban Missile Crisis* (New York: Longman 1999).

Allyn, Bruce J., James G. Blight and David A. Welch (eds), *Back to the Brink: Proceedings of the Moscow Conference on the Cuban Missile Crisis, January 27–28, 1989* (Lanham, MD: University Press of America 1992).

Alterman, Eric, *When Presidents Lie: A History of Official Deception and Its Consequences* (New York: Viking 2004).

Andrew, Christopher and Vasili Mitrokhin, *The World Was Going Our Way: The KGB and the Battle for the Third World* (New York: Basic 2005).

Ashton, Nigel, *Kennedy, Macmillan and the Cold War: The Irony of Interdependence* (Basingstoke: Palgrave 2002).

Badie, Bertrand, *Diplomacy of Connivance*, trans. by Cynthia Schoch and William Snow (New York: Palgrave Macmillan 2012).

Bain, Mervyn, *Soviet-Cuban Relations, 1985–1991: Changing Perceptions in Moscow and Havana* (Plymouth: Lexington Books 2007).

Ball, George, *The Past Has Another Pattern: Memoirs* (New York: W.W. Norton 1982).

Barrett, David M. and Max Holland, *Blind over Cuba: The Photo Gap and the Missile Crisis* (College Station, TX: Texas A&M University Press 2012).

Baylis, John and Robert O'Neill, *Alternative Nuclear Futures: The Role of Nuclear Weapons in the Post-Cold War World* (Oxford: Oxford University Press 2000).

Beschloss, Michael R., *The Crisis Years: Kennedy and Khrushchev, 1960–1963* (New York: HarperCollins 1991).

Beschloss, Michael R., *Taking Charge: The Johnson White House Tapes, 1963–1964* (New York: Touchstone 1997).

Bird, Kai, *The Color of Truth, McGeorge and William Bundy: Brothers in Arms* (New York: Touchstone 2000).

Bissell, Richard M. Jr., *Reflections of a Cold Warrior: From Yalta to the Bay of Pigs* (New Haven, CT: Yale University Press 1996).

Blair, Bruce. G., *The Logic of Accidental Nuclear War* (Washington, DC: The Brookings Institution 1993).

Blight, James G., *Shattered Crystal Ball: Fear and Learning in the Cuban Missile Crisis* (Savage, MD: Rowman & Littlefield 1992).

Blight, James G. and David A. Welch, *On the Brink: Americans and Soviets Reexamine the Cuban Missile Crisis* (New York: Noonday Press 1990).

Blight, James G., Bruce J. Allyn and David A. Welch, *Cuba on the Brink: Castro, the Missile Crisis and the Soviet Collapse* (New York: Pantheon Books 1993).

Blight, James G. and Philip Brenner, *Sad and Luminous Days: Cuba's Struggle with the Superpowers after the Missile Crisis* (Oxford: Rowman and Littlefield 2002).

Blight, James. G. and Janet M. Lang, *The Fog of War: Lessons from the Life of Robert S. McNamara* (Oxford: Rowman and Littlefield 2005).

Bohlen, Charles. E., *Witness to History, 1929–1960* (New York: W.W. Norton 1973).

Bohning, Don, *The Castro Obesssion: U.S. Covert Operations Against Cuba, 1959–1965* (Washington, DC: Potomac Books 2005).

Bouchard, Joseph, *Command in Crisis: Four Case Studies* (New York: Colombia University Press 1991).

Bourdieu, Pierre with Loïc Wacquant, *Réponses: pour une anthropologie réflexive* (Paris: Seuil 1992).

Bradlee, Benjamin C., *Conversations with Kennedy* (New York: W.W. Norton 1975).

Brands, Hal, *Latin America's Cold War* (Cambridge, MA: Harvard University Press 2010).

Brugioni, Dino A., *Eyeball to Eyeball: The Inside Story of the Cuban Missile Crisis*, ed. by Robert F. McCort (New York: Random House 1991).

Bundy, McGeorge, *Danger and Survival: Choices about the Bomb in the First Fifty Years* (New York: Random House 1988).

Caesar, Gaius Julius, *The Gallic War: Seven Commentaries on The Gallic War with an Eighth Commentary by Aulus Hirtius*, trans. by Carolyn Hammond (Oxford: Oxford University Press 2008).

Castro, Fidel, with Ignacio Ramonet, *My Life*, trans. by Andrew Hurley (London: Allen Lane 2007).

Catterall, Peter (ed.), *The Macmillan Diaries: The Cabinet Years 1950–1957* (London: Macmillan 2003).

Catterall, Peter (ed.), *The Macmillan Diaries: Prime Minister and After 1957–1966* (London: Macmillan 2011).

Chang, Laurence and Peter Kornbluh (eds) *The Cuban Missile Crisis, 1962: A National Security Archive Documents Reader* (New York: The New Press 1992).

Churchill, Winston S., *The Gathering Storm: The Second World War: Vol. I* (London: Cassell 1948).

Clausewitz, Carl von, *On War*, ed. and trans. by Michael Howard and Peter Paret (Princeton, NJ: Princeton University Press 1984 [1832]).

Coleman, David G, *The Fourteenth Day: JFK and the Aftermath of the Cuban Missile Crisis* (New York: W.W. Norton 2012).

Craig, Campbell and Sergey Radchenko, *The Atomic Bomb and the Origins of the Cold War* (New Haven, CT: Yale University Press 2008).

Craig, Gordon A., and Alexander L. George, *Force and Statecraft: Diplomatic Problems of Our Time*, third edn. (New York/Oxford: Oxford University Press 1995).

Dallek, Robert, *John F. Kennedy: An Unfinished Life 1917–1963* (Boston, MA: Little, Brown and Company 2003).

Dallek, Robert, *Camelot's Court: Inside the Kennedy White House* (New York: Harper 2013).

Department of State, *Foreign Relations of the United States, 1961–1963, Vol. V, Soviet Union* (Washington, DC: Government Printing Office 1998).

Department of State, *Foreign Relations of the United States, 1961–1963, Vol. VI, Kennedy–Khrushchev Exchanges* (Washington, DC: Government Printing Office 1996).

Department of State, *Foreign Relations of the United States, 1961–1963, Vol. X, Cuba 1961–1962* (Washington, DC: United States Government Printing Office 1997).

Department of State, *Foreign Relations of the United States, 1961–1963, Vol. XI, Cuban Missile Crisis and Aftermath* (Washington, DC: United States Government Printing Office 1996).

Department of State, *Foreign Relations of the United States, 1961–1963, Vol. XV, Berlin Crisis, 1962–1963* (Washington: Government Printing Office 1994).

Devine, Robert A. (ed.), *The Cuban Missile Crisis* (Chicago, IL: Quadrangle 1971/ New York: Marcus Wiener 1988, second ed.).

Dobbs, Michael, *One Minute to Midnight: Kennedy, Khrushchev, and Castro on the Brink of Nuclear War* (New York: Knopf 2008).

Dobrynin, Anatoli, *In Confidence: Moscow's Ambassador to America's Six Cold War Presidents* (New York: Random House 1995).

Donald, David Herbert, *Lincoln* (New York: Simon and Schuster 1995).

Donovan, Hedley, *Roosevelt to Reagan: A Reporter's Encounters with Nine Presidents* (New York: Harper & Row 1985).

Dorrien, Gary, *Kantian Reason and Hegelian Spirit: The Idealistic Logic of Modern Theology* (Chichester: Wiley-Blackwell 2012).

Dulles, Allen, *The Craft of Intelligence* (London: Weidenfeld and Nicolson 1963).

Duncan, Jason K., *John F. Kennedy: The Spirit of Cold War Liberalism* (New York: Routledge 2014).

Esin, V.I. (ed.), *Strategicheskaya operatsiya 'Anadyr': kak eto bylo* (Moscow: MOOVVIK 1999).

Evans, Harold, *Downing Street Diary: The Macmillan Years 1957/63* (London: Hodder and Stoughton 1981).

Fischer, Fritz, *Griff nach der Weltmacht: Die Kriegzielpolitik des kaiserlichen Deutschland 1914–1918* (Düsseldorf: Droste 1961).

Fontova, Humberto, *Fidel: Hollywood's Favorite Tyrant* (New York: Regnery Publishing 2005).

Freedman, Lawrence, *Kennedy's Wars: Berlin, Cuba, Laos and Vietnam* (Oxford: Oxford University Press 2000).

Fursenko, Aleksandr and Timothy Naftali, *'One Hell of a Gamble': Khrushchev, Castro Kennedy, and the Cuban Missile Crisis, 1958–1964* (New York: W.W. Norton 1997).

Fursenko, Aleksandr and Timothy Naftali, *Khrushchev's Cold War: The Inside Story of an American Adversary* (New York: W.W. Norton 2006).

Fursenko, Aleksandr (ed.), *Prezidium TsK KPSS, Vol. 1* (Moscow: Rosspen 2003).

Gaddis, John Lewis, *We Now Know: Rethinking the Cold War* (Oxford: Oxford University Press 1997).

Gaddis, John Lewis, *The Cold War* (New York: Allen Lane 2006).

Ganser, Danielle, *Reckless Gamble: The Sabotage of the United Nations in the Cuban*

Conflict and the Cuban Missile Crisis of 1962 (New Orleans, LA: University Press of the South 2000).

Garthoff, Raymond L., *Détente and Confrontation: American-Soviet Relations from Nixon to Reagan* (Washington, DC: The Brookings Institution 1985).

Garthoff, Raymond L, *Reflections on the Cuban Missile Crisis* (Washington, DC: The Brookings Institution 1989).

Gavin, Francis J., *Nuclear Statecraft: History and Strategy in America's Atomic Age* (Ithaca, NY/London: Cornell University Press 2012).

George, Alice L., *Awaiting Armageddon: How Americans Faced the Cuban Missile Crisis* (Chapel Hill, NC: The University of North Carolina Press 2003).

Gibson, David R., *Talk at the Brink: Deliberation and Decision during the Cuban Missile Crisis* (Princeton, NJ: Princeton University Press 2012).

Giglio, James N., *The Presidency of John F Kennedy* (Lawrence, KS: University Press of Kansas 1991).

Gioe, David, Len Scott and Christopher Andrew (eds), *An International History of the Cuban Missile Crisis: A 50-year Retrospective* (Abingdon: Routledge 2014).

Gitlin, Todd, *The Sixties: Years of Hope, Days of Rage* (New York: Bantam Books 1987).

Glaser, Charles L., *Rational Theory of International Politics* (Princeton NJ: Princeton University Press 2010).

Gleijeses, Piero, *Conflicting Missions: Havana, Washington, and Africa, 1959–1976* (Chapel Hill, NC: University of North Carolina Press 2002).

Goldstein, Gordon, *Lessons in Disaster: McGeorge Bundy and the Path to War in Vietnam* (New York: Times/Henry Holt 2008).

Gribkov, Anatoli, I. and William Y. Smith, *Operation Anadyr: US and Soviet Generals Recount the Cuban Missile Crisis* (Chicago, IL: Edition Q 1994).

Grow, Michael, *US Presidents and Latin American Interventions: Pursuing Regime Change in the Cold War* (Lawrence, KS: University of Kansas Press 2008).

Haig, Jr., Alexander M. with Charles McCarry, *Inner Circles: How America Changed the World* (New York: Warner 1992).

Halberstam, David, *The Best and the Brightest* (New York: Harper & Row 1972).

Hanhimäki, Jussi M., *The Rise and Fall of Détente: American Foreign Policy and the Transformation of the Cold War* (Washington, DC: Potomac 2013).

Hansen, Olaf, *Aesthetic Individualism and Practical Intellect: American Allegory in Emerson, Thoreau, Adams, and James* (Princeton, NJ: Princeton University Press 1990).

Haslam, Jonathan, *Russia's Cold War* (New Haven, CT: Yale University Press 2010).

Hegel, Georg W.F., *The Philosophy of History* (New York: Dover 1956 [1837]).

Hernández, José M., *Cuba and the United States: Intervention and Militarism, 1868–1933* (Austin, TX: University of Texas Press 1993).

Herring, Eric, *Danger and Opportunity* (Manchester: Manchester University Press 1995).

Hersh, Seymour M., *The Dark Side of Camelot* (London: HarperCollins 1998).

Hilsman, Roger, *To Move A Nation: The Politics of Foreign Policy in the Administration of John F. Kennedy* (New York: Dell Publishing 1967).

Hilsman, Roger, *The Cuban Missile Crisis: The Struggle over Policy* (Westport, CT: Praeger 1996).

Horne, Alastair, *Macmillan 1957–1986, Vol. II of The Official Biography* (London: Macmillan 1989).

Howard, Michael, *The Lessons of History* (Oxford: Oxford University Press 1993).

Huchthausen, Peter A., *October Fury* (Hoboken, NJ: John Wiley & Sons 2006).

Hughes, R. Gerald, *The Postwar Legacy of Appeasement: British Foreign Policy since 1945* (London: Bloomsbury 2014).

Ikenberry, John G., *Liberal Leviathan* (Princeton NJ: Princeton University Press 2011).

Ikenberry, John G., William Wohlforth and Michael Mastanduno, *International Relations Theory and the Consequences of Unipolarity* (Cambridge: Cambridge University Press 2011).

Jeffreys-Jones, Rhodri, *The CIA and American Democracy* (New Haven, CT: Yale University Press 1989/1998/2003).

Jervis, Robert, *The Logic of Images in International Relations* (Princeton NJ: Princeton University Press 1970); second edn. (New York: Columbia University Press 1989).

Jervis, Robert, *Perception and Misperception in International Politics* (Princeton, NJ: Princeton University Press 1976).

Jervis, Robert, *The Illogic of American Nuclear Strategy* (Ithaca, NY: Cornell University Press 1984).

Jervis, Robert, *The Meaning of the Nuclear Revolution: Statecraft and the Prospect of Armageddon* (Ithaca, NY: Cornell University Press 1989).

Jervis, Robert, Richard Ned Lebow and Janice Gross Stein, *Psychology and Deterrence* (Baltimore, MD: Johns Hopkins University Press 1985).

Johns, Andrew L., *Vietnam's Second Front: Domestic Politics, the Republican Party, and the War* (Lexington, KY: University Press of Kentucky 2012).

Johnson, Walter (ed.), *The Papers of Adlai E. Stevenson, Vol. 8* (Boston, MA: Little, Brown and Company 1979).

Jones, Howard, *The Bay of Pigs* (Oxford/New York: Oxford University Press 2008).

Kagan, Donald, *On the Origins of War and the Preservation of Peace* (New York: Doubleday 1995).

Kaiser, David, *American Tragedy: Kennedy, Johnson, and the Origins of the Vietnam War* (Cambridge, MA: Harvard University Press 2000).

Kaussler, Bernd, *Iran's Nuclear Diplomacy: Power Politics and Conflict Resolution* (Abingdon: Routledge 2014).

Kennan, George, *The Nuclear Delusion* (New York: Pantheon 1983).

Kennedy, John F., *Why England Slept* (London: Hutchinson 1940/Westpost, CT: Greenwood Press Reprint 1981).

Kennedy, John F., *Profiles in Courage*, 'Foreword' by Robert F. Kennedy (London: Hamish Hamilton 1965/Perennial Classics 2000).

Kennedy, Robert, *Thirteen Days: A Memoir of the Cuban Missile Crisis* (New York: W.W. Norton 1969).

Khrushchev, Nikita, *Khrushchev Remembers*, ed. and trans. by Strobe Talbott (Boston, MA: Little, Brown, and Company 1970).

Khrushchev, Nikita, *Khrushchev Remembers: The Last Testament*, ed. and trans. by Strobe Talbott (Boston, MA: Little, Brown and Company 1974).

Khrushchev, Nikita, *Khrushchev Remembers: The Glasnost Tapes*, ed. and trans. by Jerrold L. Schecter and Vyacheslav Luchkov (Boston, MA: Little, Brown and Company 1990).

Khrushchev, Sergei, *Nikita Khrushchev and the Creation of a Superpower*, trans. by Shirley Benson (University Park, PA: Pennsylvania State University Press 2000).

Kissinger, Henry, *Nuclear Weapons and Foreign Policy* (New York: Council on Foreign Relations 1957).

Kissinger, Henry, *White House Years* (Boston, MA: Little, Brown and Company 1979).

Kurzban, Robert, *Why Everyone (Else) Is a Hypocrite* (Princeton, NJ: Princeton University Press 2010).

Lebow, Richard Ned, *Nuclear Crisis Management: A Dangerous Illusion* (Ithaca, NY: Cornell University Press 1987).

Lebow, Richard Ned, *A Cultural Theory of International Politics* (New York: Cambridge University Press 2008).

Lebow, Richard Ned and Janice Gross Stein, *We All Lost the Cold War* (Princeton, NJ: Princeton University Press 1994).

Lechuga, Carlos, *In the Eye of the Storm: Castro, Khrushchev, Kennedy and the Missile Crisis* (Melbourne: Ocean Press 1995).

LeoGrande, William M. and Peter Kornbluh, *Back Channel to Cuba: The Hidden History of Negotiations between Washington and Havana* (Chapel Hill, NC: University of North Carolina Press 2014).

Ling, Peter J., *John F. Kennedy* (London: Routledge 2013).

McAuliffe, Mary S. (ed.), *CIA Documents on the Cuban Missile Crisis 1962* (Washington, DC: Central Intelligence Agency 1992).

McDermott, Rose, *Presidential Leadership, Illness, and Decision Making* (New York: Cambridge University Press 2008).

McDonald, David MacLaren, *United Government and Foreign Policy in Russia, 1900–1914* (Cambridge, MA: Harvard University Press 1992).

Machiavelli, Niccolò, *The Prince*, trans. by Peter Bondanella. (Oxford: Oxford University Press 2005 [1532]).

Maclean, Alan, *No, I Tell a Lie, It Was the Tuesday . . .* (London: Kyle Cathie 1997).

McMahon, Patricia, *Essence of Indecision* (Kingston and Montreal: McGill-Queens 2009).

McMeekin, Sean, *The Russian Origins of the First World War* (Boston, MA: Harvard University Press 2011).

Macmillan, Harold, *At the End of the Day, 1961–1963* (London: Macmillan 1973).

McNamara, Robert S. with Brian VanDeMark, *In Retrospect: The Tragedy and Lessons of Vietnam* (New York: Vintage 1996).

McNamara, Robert S., James Blight and Robert K. Brigham with Thomas J. Biersteker and Col. Herbert Schandler, *Argument Without End: In Search of Answers to the Vietnam Tragedy* (New York: PublicAffairs 1999).

Mahan, A.T., *The Influence of Sea Power upon History: 1660–1783* (Boston, MA: Little, Brown and Company 1890).

Mann, Robert, *A Grand Delusion: America's Descent into Vietnam* (New York: Basic 2001).

May, Ernest R. *The Making of the Monroe Doctrine* (Cambridge, MA: Harvard University Press 1975).

May, Ernest R and Philip D. Zelikow (eds), *The Kennedy Tapes: Inside the White House during the Cuban Missile Crisis* (Cambridge, MA: Harvard University Press 1997/ New York: W.W. Norton 2002).

Mearsheimer, John, *The Tragedy of Great Power Politics* (New York: W.W. Norton 2001).

Mikoyan, Sergo, The Soviet Cuban Missile Crisis: Castro, Mikoyan, Kennedy, Khrushchev, and the Missiles of November, ed. by Svetlana Savranskaya (Stanford, CA: Stanford University Press 2012).

Mikoyan, Sergo, *Anatomiya Karibskogo Krizisa* (Moscow: Academia 2006).

Monteiro, Nuno, *Theory of Unipolar Politics* (Cambridge: Cambridge University Press 2014).

Morgenthau, Hans J., *Truth and Power: Essays of a Decade* (New York: Praeger 1970).

Mozgovoi, Aleksandr, *Kubinskaya Samba Kvarteta Fokstrotov* (Moscow: Voennyi Parad 2002).

Mueller, John, *Atomic Obsession: Nuclear Alarmism from Hiroshima to al Qaeda* (Oxford: Oxford University Press 2009).

Münger, Christof, *Die Berliner Mauer, Kennedy und die Kubakrise: Die westliche Allianz in der Zerreißprobe 1961–1963* (Paderborn: Schöningh 2003).

Munton, Don and David A. Welch, *The Cuban Missile Crisis: A Concise History* (Oxford: Oxford University Press 2007/2012).

Musicant, Ivan, *Empire by Default: The Spanish-American War and the Dawn of the American Century* (New York: Henry Holt 1998).

Naftali, Timothy, *The Origins of 'Thirteen Days'*, Miller Center Report, 15/2 (Richmond, VA: Miller Center 1999).

Naftali, Timothy (ed.) *The Presidential Recordings, John F. Kennedy, The Great Crises, Vol. I, July 30–August 1962* (New York: W.W. Norton 2001).

Naftali, Timothy and Philip Zelikow (eds), *The Presidential Recordings, John F. Kennedy, The Great Crises, Vol. II, September–October 21, 1962* (New York: W.W. Norton 2001).

Nasaw, David, *The Patriarch: The Remarkable Life and Turbulent Times of Joseph P. Kennedy* (New York: Penguin Press 2012).

Nash, Philip, *The Other Missiles of October: Eisenhower, Kennedy, and the Jupiters 1957–1963* (Chapel Hill, NC: University of North Carolina Press 1997).

Nathan, James A. (ed.), *The Cuban Missile Crisis Revisited* (New York: St Martin's Press 1992).

Neustadt, Richard E., and Ernest R. May, *Thinking in Time: The Uses of History for Decision Makers* (New York: Free Press 1986).

Nitze, Paul, *From Hiroshima to Glasnost: At the Center of Decision* (New York: Grove Weidenfeld 1989).

Nunnerley, David, *President Kennedy and Britain* (London: The Bodley Head 1972).

O'Donnell, Kenneth and David Powers, with Joe McCarthy, *'Johnny, We Hardly Know Ye': Memories of John Fitzgerald Kennedy* (Boston, MA: Little, Brown and Company 1972).

Olson, Lynne, *Troublesome Young Men: The Rebels Who Brought Churchill to Power in 1940 and Helped to Save Britain* (London: Bloomsbury 2007).

Parmet, Herbert, *Jack: The Struggles of John F. Kennedy* (New York: Dial Press 1980).

Paterson, Thomas G. (ed.), *Kennedy's Quest for Victory: American Foreign Policy, 1961–1963* (Oxford: Oxford University Press 1989).

Pedlow, George W. and Donald E. Weizenbach, *The CIA and the U-2 Program, 1954–1974* (Washington DC: Central Intelligence Agency 1988).

Pérez Jr., Louis A., *Cuba in the American Imagination: Metaphor and the Imperial Ethos* (Chapel Hill, NC: University of North Carolina Press 2008).

Polmar, Norman and John D. Gresham, *DEFCON-2: Standing on the Brink of Nuclear War during the Cuban Missile Crisis* (Hoboken, NJ: John Wiley & Sons 2006).

Poole, Walter S., *The Joint Chiefs of Staff and National Policy, 1961–1964* (Washington, DC: Government Printing Office 2011).

Preble, Christopher, *Kennedy and the Missile Gap* (DeKalb, IL: Northern Illinois Press 2004).

Priestland, David, *The Red Flag: a History of Communism* (New York: Grove Press 2009).

Priestland, Jane, *British Archives on the Cuban Missile Crisis 1962* (London: Archival Publications International 2001).

Prior, Robin, *Churchill's World Crisis as History* (Beckenham: Croom Helm 1983).

Radvanyi, Janos, *Hungary and the Superpowers: The 1956 Revolution and Realpolitik* (Stanford, CA: Hoover Institution Press 1972).

Ramsden, John, *Man of the Century: Winston Churchill and His Legend since 1945* (London: HarperCollins 2002).

Reed, Craig W., *Red November: Inside the Secret U.S. Soviet Submarine Base* (New York: HarperCollins 2010).

Reagan, Ronald, *An American Life* (New York: Simon and Schuster 1990).

Reynolds, David, *In Command of History: Churchill Fighting and Writing the Second World War* (London: Allen Lane 2004).

Roy, Raj, and John W. Young (eds), *Ambassador to Sixties London: The Diaries of David Bruce 1961–1969* (Dordrecht: Republic of Letters Publishing 2009).

Ruffner K.C. (ed.), *Corona: America's First Satellite* (Washington, DC: CIA Center for the Study of Intelligence 1995).

Rusk, Dean, as told to Richard Rusk, *As I Saw It* (New York: W.W. Norton 1990/ London: Penguin 1991).

Sabato, Larry J., *The Kennedy Half-Century: The Presidency, Assassination, and Lasting Legacy of John F. Kennedy* (New York: Bloomsbury 2013).

Sagan, Scott D., *The Limits of Safety: Organisations, Accidents, and Nuclear Weapons* (Princeton, NJ: Princeton University Press 1993).

Sagan, Scott D. and Kenneth N. Waltz, *The Spread of Nuclear Weapons: A Debate* (London: W.W. Norton 1995).

Sand, G.W. (ed.), *Defending the West: The Truman-Churchill Correspondence, 1945–1960* (Westport, CT: Praeger 2004).

Sandler, Martin W. (ed.), *The Letters of John F. Kennedy* (London: Bloomsbury 2013).

Schecter, Jerrold L. and Peter S. Deriabin, *The Spy Who Saved the World: How a Soviet Colonel Changed the Course of the Cold War* (New York: Charles Scribner's Sons 1992).

Schelling, Thomas, *The Strategy of Conflict* (Cambridge, MA: Harvard University Press 1960).

Schlesinger, Arthur M. Jr., *A Thousand Days: John F. Kennedy in the White House* (Boston, MA: Houghton Mifflin 1965/New York: First Mariner 2002).

Schlesinger, Arthur M. Jr., *Robert Kennedy and His Times* (Boston, MA: Houghton Mifflin 1978).

Schlesinger, Arthur M. Jr., *Journals, 1952–2000*, ed. by Andrew and Stephen Schlesinger (New York: Penguin Press 2007).

Schlesinger, Arthur M. Jr., *The Letters of Arthur Schlesinger, Jr.*, ed. by Andrew and Stephen Schlesinger (New York: Random House 2013).

Schlosser, Eric, *Command and Control: Nuclear Weapons, the Damascus Accident, and the Illusion of Safety* (New York: Penguin 2013).

Scott, L.V. *Macmillan, Kennedy and the Cuban Missile Crisis: Political, Military and Intelligence Aspects* (Basingstoke: Macmillan 1999).

Scott, Len, *The Cuban Missile Crisis and the Threat of Nuclear War: Lessons from History* (London: Continuum Books 2007).

Shapley, Deborah, *Promise and Power: The Life and Times of Robert McNamara* (Boston: MA: Little, Brown and Company 1993).

Slantchev, Branislav L., *Military Threats: The Costs of Coercion and the Price of Peace* (Cambridge: Cambridge University Press 2011).

Sorensen, Theodore C., *Decision-making in the White House* (New York: Columbia University Press 1963).

Sorensen, Theodore C., *Kennedy* (New York: Hodder and Stoughton 1965).

Sorensen, Theodore C., *Counselor: A Life at the Edge of History* (New York: Harper-Collins 2008/Harper Perennial 2009).

Snyder, Glenn and Paul Diesing, *Conflict Among Nations* (Princeton, NJ: Princeton University Press 1977).

Steel, Ronald, *Walter Lippmann and the American Century* (Boston, MA: Atlantic Monthly Press/Little, Brown and Company 1980).

Stern, Fritz (ed.), *The Varieties of History: From Voltaire to the Present*, second edn. (London: Macmillan 1970).

Stern, Sheldon M., *Averting 'The Final Failure': John F. Kennedy and the Secret Cuban Missile Crisis Meetings* (Stanford, CA: Stanford University Press 2003).

Stern, Sheldon M., *The Week the World Stood Still: Inside the Secret Cuban Missile Crisis* (Stanford, CA: Stanford University Press 2005).

Stern, Sheldon M., *The Cuban Missile Crisis in American Memory: Myths versus Reality* (Stanford, CA: Stanford University Press 2012).

Steury, Donald (ed.), *Sherman Kent and the Board of National Estimates: Collected Essays* (Washington, DC: Center for the Study of Intelligence, Central Intelligence Agency 1994).

Taubman, W., S. Khrushchev and A. Gleason (eds), *Nikita Khrushchev* (New Haven, CT: Yale University Press 2000).

Taubman, William, *Khrushchev: The Man, His Era* (New York: W.W. Norton 2003).

Taylor, Gen. Maxwell D., *Swords and Plowshares: A Memoir* (New York: Da Capo 1972).

Thomas, Evan, *Robert Kennedy: His Life* (New York: Simon & Schuster 2007).

Thompson, Nicholas, *The Hawk and the Dove: Paul Nitze, George Kennan, and the History of the Cold War* (New York: Henry Holt 2009).

Trachtenberg, Marc, *History and Strategy* (Princeton, NJ: Princeton University Press 1991).

Troyanovskii, Oleg, *Cherez Gody i Rasstoyaniya* (Moscow: Vagrius 1997).

Tuchman, Barbara, *The Guns of August* (New York: Macmillan 1962/London: Robinson 2000).

Twigge, Stephen and Len Scott, *Planning Armageddon: Britain, United States and the Command of Nuclear Forces, 1946–1964* (Amsterdam: Routledge 2000).

Ulam, Adam, *Expansion and Coexistence: The History of Soviet Foreign Policy, 1917–67* (New York: Praeger 1968).

Ulam, Adam, *The Rivals: America and Russia Since World War II* (New York: Viking 1971).

Uslu, Nasuh, *The Turkish-American Relationship between 1947 and 2003* (New York: Nova 2003).

Volkogonov, Dmitrii and Harold Shukman, *Autopsy for an Empire: The Seven Leaders Who Built the Soviet Regime* (New York: Free Press 1998).

Waltz, Kenneth, *Theory of International Politics* (Reading, MA: Addison-Wesley 1979).

Waltz, Kenneth, *The Spread of Nuclear Weapons: More May be Better*, Adelphi Papers No. 171 (London: International Institute for Strategic Studies 1981).

Weiner, Tim, *Legacy of Ashes: The History of the CIA* (New York: Doubleday 2008).

Weir, Gary E. and Walter J. Boyne, *Rising Sun: The Untold Story of the Russian Submarines That Fought the Cold War* (New York: Basic Books 2003).

Weldes, Jutta, *Constructing National Interests: The United States and the Cuban Missile Crisis* (Minneapolis, MN: University of Minnesota Press 1999).

Westad, Odd Arne, *The Global Cold War: Third World Interventions and the Making of Our Times* (Cambridge: Cambridge University Press 2006).

Westad, Odd Arne (ed.), *Reviewing the Cold War: approaches, interpretations, theory* (London: Frank Cass 2000).

White, Theodore H., *In Search of History: A Personal Adventure* (New York: Harper & Row 1978).

Wiener, Jon, *How We Forgot The Cold War. A Historical Journey Across America* (Oakland, CA: University of California Press 2012).

Wilson, Timothy, *Strangers to Ourselves: Discovering the Adaptive Unconscious* (Cambridge, MA: Belknap Press of Harvard University Press 2002).

Woodward, Bob, *Obama's Wars: The Inside Story* (London: Simon & Schuster 2010).

Zaloga, Steven J., *The Kremlin's Nuclear Sword: The Rise and Fall of Russia's Strategic Nuclear Forces 1945-2000* (Washington, DC: Smithsonian Institution Press 2002).

Zelikow, Philip and Ernest May (eds), *The Presidential Recordings, John F. Kennedy, The Great Crises, Volume Three, October 22–28, 1962* (New York: W.W. Norton 2001).

Zubok, Vladislav, *A Failed Empire: The Soviet Union and the Cold War* (Chapel Hill, NC: University of North Carolina Press 2007).

Zubok, Vladislav and Constantine Pleshakov, *Inside the Kremlin's Cold War* (Boston, MA: Harvard University Press 1996).

Journal articles/book chapters

Abedul, Hugo and R. Gerald Hughes, 'The Commandante in His Labyrinth: Fidel Castro and His Legacy', *Intelligence and National Security*, 26/ 4 (2011) 531–65.

Aldrich, Richard J., 'CIA History as a Cold War Battleground: The Forgotten First Wave of Agency Narratives' in Christopher Moran and Christopher Murphy (eds), *Framing Intelligence History: The Historiography of British and American Secret Services since 1945* (Edinburgh: Edinburgh University Press 2012), pp. 19–46.

Allyn, Bruce. J., James G. Blight and David A. Welch, 'Essence of Revision: Moscow, Havana and the Cuban Missile Crisis', *International Security*, 14/3 (1989/90) 136–72.

Bendor, Jonathan and Thomas H. Hammond, 'Rethinking Allison's Models', *American Political Science Review*, 86/2 (1992) 301–22.

Bernstein, Barton, J., 'Bombers, Inspection, and the No Invasion Pledge', *Foreign Service Journal*, 56/7 (1979) 8–12.

Bernstein, Barton, J., 'The Cuban Missile Crisis: Trading the Jupiters in Turkey?' *Political Science Quarterly*, 95/1 (1980) 97–125.

Bernstein, Barton, J., 'Reconsidering the Missile Crisis: Dealing with the Problems of the American Jupiters in Turkey' in James Nathan (ed.), *The Cuban Missile Crisis Revisited* (New York: St Martin's Press 1992) pp. 94–104.

Bernstein, Barton, J., 'Understanding Decisonmaking, US Foreign Policy and the Cuban Missile Crisis: A Review Essay', *International Security*, 25/1 (2000) 134–64.

Blanton, Thomas S., 'The Cuban Missile Crisis Just Isn't What It Used to Be', *Cold War International History Project Bulletin*, Issues 17–18 (2012), www.wilsoncenter. org/publication/bulletin-no-17-18 (last accessed 18 December 2014).

Blight, James G. and David A. Welch, 'Risking "The Destruction of Nations": Lessons of the Cuban Missile Crisis for New and Aspiring Nuclear States', *Security Studies*, 4/4 (1995) 811–50.

Blight, James G. and David A. Welch, 'What can Intelligence Tells Us about the Cuban Missile Crisis, and What can the Cuban Missile Crisis Tell us about Intelligence?', *Intelligence and National Security*, 13/ 3 (1998) 1–17.

Blight, James. G., Bruce J. Allyn and David A. Welch, 'Kramer vs. Kramer, Or How Can You Have Revisionism in the Absence of Orthodoxy?', *Cold War International History Project Bulletin* Issue 3 (1993), www.wilsoncenter.org/publication/bulletin-no-3-fall-1993 (last accessed 12 January 2013).

Bostdorff, Denise M. and Steven R. Goldzwig, 'Idealism and Pragmatism in American Foreign Policy Rhetoric: The Case of John F. Kennedy and Vietnam', *Presidential Studies Quarterly*, 'Conduct of Foreign Policy', 24/3 (1994) 515–30.

Brenner, Philip, 'Thirteen Months: Cuba's Perspective on the Missile Crisis' in James Nathan (ed.), *The Cuban Missile Crisis Revisited* (New York: St Martin's Press 1992) pp. 187–218.

Buhite, Russell D., 'From Kennedy to Nixon: The End of Consensus' in Gordon Martel (ed.), *American Foreign Relations Reconsidered: 1890–1993* (London: Routledge 2002), pp. 125–44.

Burlatskiy, Fedor, 'The Lessons of Personal Diplomacy', *Problems of Communism*, 41 (1992) 8–13.

Burr, William and Thomas S. Blanton (eds), 'The Submarines of October', *National Security Archive Electronic Briefing Book No. 75*, 31 October 2002, www2. gwu.edu/~nsarchiv/NSAEBB/NSAEBB75/ (last accessed 18 December 2014).

Campus, Leonardo, 'Italian Political Reactions to the Cuban Missile Crisis' in David Gioe, Len Scott and Christopher Andrew (eds), *An International History of the Cuban Missile Crisis: A 50-year Retrospective* (Abingdon: Routledge 2014) pp. 236–57.

Catterall, Peter, 'At the End of the Day: Macmillan's Account of the Cuban Missile Crisis', *International Relations*, 26/3 (2012) 267–89.

Catterall, Peter, 'Identity and Integration: Macmillan, "Britishness" and the Turn towards Europe' in Gilbert Millat (ed.), *Angleterre ou Albion entre fascination et répulsion* (Lille: Presses de l'Université Charles de Gaulle – Lille 3 2006) pp. 161–178.

Catterall, Peter, 'Modifying "a Very Dangerous Message": Britain, the Non-aligned and the UN during the Cuban Missile Crisis' in David Gioe, Len Scott and Christopher Andrew (eds), *An International History of the Cuban Missile Crisis: A 50-year Retrospective* (London: Routledge 2014) pp. 72–98.

Cline, Ray, 'Commentary: The Cuban Missile Crisis', *Foreign Affairs*, 68/4 (1989) 190–6.

Cohen, Eliot, 'Why We Should Stop Studying the Cuban Missile Crisis', *National Interest*, 2 (1985/6) 3–13.

Coleman, David G., 'After the Cuban Missile Crisis: Why Short-Range Nuclear Weapons Delivery Systems Remained in Cuba', *Miller Center Report*, 18/4 (2002) 36–39.

Coleman, D., 'Camelot's Nuclear Conscience', *Bulletin of the Atomic Scientists*, 62/3 (2006) 40–5.

Coleman, David G., 'The Missiles of November, December, January, February…: The Problem of Acceptable Risk in the Cuban Missile Crisis Settlement', *Journal of Cold War Studies*, 9/3 (2007) 5–48.

Conze, Eckart, 'Konfrontation und Détente: Überlegungen zur historischen Analyse des Ost-West-Konflikts', *Vierteljahrshefte für Zeitgeschichte*, 46/2 (1998) 269–82.

Craig, Campbell, 'Testing Organisation Man: The Cuban Missile Crisis and the Limits of Safety', *International Relations*, 26/3 (2012) 291–303.

Craig, Campbell, 'The Nuclear Revolution: A Product of the Cold War, or Something More?' in Richard Immerman and Petra Goedde (eds), *Oxford Handbook of the Cold War* (Oxford: Oxford University Press 2013), pp. 360–76.

Craig, Campbell and Jan Ruzicka, 'The Nonproliferation Complex', *Ethics and International Affairs*, 27/3 (2013) 329–48.

Criss, Nur Bilge, 'Strategic Nuclear Missiles in Turkey: The Jupiter Affair, 1959–1963', *Journal of Strategic Studies*, 20/3 (1997) 97–122.

Drent, Jan, 'Confrontation in the Sargasso Sea: Soviet Submarines during the Cuban Missile Crisis', *Northern Mariner/Le Marin du nord*, 13/3 (2003) 1–19.

Fearon, James, 'Rationalist Explanations for War', *International Organization*, 49/3 (1995) 379–414.

Fursenko, Aleksandr and Timothy Naftali, 'Using KGB Documents: The Scali-Feklisov Channel in the Cuban Missile Crisis', *Cold War International History Project Bulletin*, Issue 5 (1995) 58–62.

Garthoff, Raymond L., 'Handling the Cienfuegos Crisis', *International Security*, 8/1 (1983) 46–66.

Garthoff, Raymond L., 'Berlin 1961: The Record Corrected', *Foreign Policy*, 84 (1991) 142–56.

Garthoff, Raymond L., 'U.S. Intelligence in the Cuban Missile Crisis', *Intelligence and National Security*, 13/3 (1998) 18–63.

Garthoff, Raymond L., 'New Evidence on the Cuban Missile Crisis: Khrushchev, Nuclear Weapons, and the Cuban Missile Crisis', *Cold War International History Project Bulletin*, Issue 11 (1998) 251–62.

Garthoff, Raymond L., 'The US–Soviet Tank Confrontation at Checkpoint Charlie' in Stephen Cimbala (ed.), *Mysteries of the Cold War* (London: Ashgate 1999) pp. 73–87.

Gavin, Francis *et al.*, 'What We Talk About When We Talk About Nuclear Weapons', H-Diplo/ISSF forum, http://issforum.org/ISSF/PDF/ISSF-Forum-2.pdf (last accessed 18 December 2014).

Ghent, Jocelyn Maynard, 'Canada, the United States, and the Cuban Missile Crisis', *Pacific Historical Review*, 48/2 (1979) 159–84.

Glaser, Charles, 'Will China's Rise Lead to War?' *Foreign Affairs*, 90/2 (2001) 80–91.

Glazer, Nathan, 'Cuba and the Peace Movement', *Commentary*, 34/12 (1962) 514–19.

Gromyko, Andrei, 'The Caribbean Crisis' in V.V. Zhurkin and Ye.M. Primakov (eds), *Mezhdunarodnye konflikty* (Moscow: Mezhdunarod- nye Otnosheniya 1972).

Hafner, Donald L., 'Bureaucratic Politics and "Those Frigging Missiles": JFK, Cuba, and U.S. Missiles in Turkey', *Orbis*, 21/2 (1977) 307–33.

Harken, Gregg, review of Thomas C. Reed, *At the Abyss: An Insider's History of the*

Cold War (New York: Ballantine 2004) in *Journal of Cold War Studies*, 9/2 (2007) 148–50.

Hershberg, James G., 'Before "The Missiles of October": Did Kennedy Plan a Military Strike Against Cuba?', *Diplomatic History* 14/4 (1990) 163–98.

Hershberg, James G., 'Anatomy of a Controversy: Anatoly Dobrynin's Meeting with Robert Kennedy, Saturday 27 October 1962', *Cold War International History Project Bulletin*, Issue 5 (1995) 75–80.

Hershberg, James G., 'The United States, Brazil, and the Cuban Missile Crisis, 1962 (Part 1)', *Journal of Cold War Studies*, 6/2 (2004) 3–20.

Hershberg, James G., 'The United States, Brazil, and the Cuban Missile Crisis, 1962 (Part 2)', *Journal of Cold War Studies*, 6/3 (2004) 5–67.

Hershberg, James G. (ed.), 'Mikoyan's Mission to Havana: Cuban–Soviet Negotiations, November 1962', *Cold War International History Project Bulletin*, Issue 5 (1995) 93–109.

Hershberg, James G. and Sergey Radchenko, with Zhang Qian, 'Sino-Cuban Relations and the Cuban Missile Crisis, 1960–62: New Chinese Evidence', *Cold War International History Project Bulletin*, Issues 17–18 (2012) 21–116.

Holland, Max, 'A Luce Connection: Senator Keating, William Pawley, and the Cuban Missile Crisis', *Journal of Cold War Studies*, 1/3 (1999) 139–67.

Holland, Max, 'The "Photo Gap" that Delayed Discovery of Missiles in Cuba', *Studies in Intelligence*, 49/4 (2005) 15–29.

Horelick, Arnold .L. 'The Cuban Missile Crisis: An Analysis of Soviet Calculations and Behavior', *World Politics*, 16/3 (1964) 363–89.

Houghton, David Patrick, 'Essence of Excision: A Critique of the New Version of *Essence of Decision*', *Security Studies*, 10/1 (2000) 151–78.

Howard, Michael, 'The Lessons of History', *The History Teacher*, 15/4 (1982) 489–501.

Howard, Michael, review of Lawrence Freedman, *The Official History of the Falklands Campaign* (London: Routledge 2005), *English Historical Review*, 121/490 (2006) 260–1.

Hughes, R. Gerald, ' "In the Final Analysis, It Is Their War": Britain, the United States and South Vietnam in 1963', and Hughes, R. Gerald and Len Scott, ' "Knowledge Is Never Too Dear": Exploring Intelligence Archives', in R. Gerald Hughes, Peter Jackson and Len Scott (eds), *Exploring Intelligence Archives: Enquiries into the Secret State* (London: Routledge 2008) pp. 183–212, 13–39.

Hughes, R. Gerald, 'The Ghosts of Appeasement: Britain and the legacy of the Munich Agreement', *Journal of Contemporary History*, 48/4 (2013) 688–716.

Iriye, Akira, 'Culture and International History' in Michael J. Hogan and Thomas G. Paterson (eds), *Explaining the History of American Foreign Relations*, second edn. (Cambridge: Cambridge University Press 2004) pp. 241–56.

Jackson, Peter, 'Pierre Bourdieu, the "Cultural Turn" and the Practice of International History', *Review of International Studies*, 34/1 (2008) 155–81.

Jervis, Robert, 'Deterrence Theory Revisited', *World Politics*, 31/2 (1979) 289–324.

Jervis, Robert, 'Explaining the War in Iraq' in Trevor Thrall and Jane Cramer (eds), *Why Did the United States Invade Iraq?* (New York: Routledge 2012) pp. 25–48.

Kaplan, Fred, 'JFK's First Strike Plan', *The Atlantic Monthly*, 288/3 (2001) 81–6.

Kent, Sherman, 'A Crucial Estimate Relived', originally published in CIA's classified *Studies in Intelligence* in 1964 and reprinted in Donald Steury (ed.), *Sherman*

Kent and the Board of National Estimates: Collected Essays (Washington, DC: Center for the Study of Intelligence, Central Intelligence Agency 1994).

Ketov, Ryukik A., 'The Cuban Missile Crisis as Seen through a Periscope', trans. Yuri Zhukov, *Journal of Strategic Studies,* 28/2 (2005) 217–31.

Kornbluh, Peter (ed.), 'Kennedy Sought Dialogue with Castro Aborted by Assassination, Declassified Documents Show', *National Security Archive Electronic Briefing Book 103,* 26 September 2014, www2.gwu.edu/~nsarchiv/news/20140926/ (last accessed 18 December 2014).

Kramer, Mark, 'Tactical Nuclear Weapons, Soviet Command Authority, and the Cuban Missile Crisis', *Cold War International History Project Bulletin,* Issue 3 (Fall 1993), www.wilsoncenter.org/publication/bulletin-no-3-fall-1993 (last accessed 18 December 2014).

Kramer, Mark., Bruce J. Allyn, James G. Blight and David A. Welch, 'Correspondence: Remembering the Cuban Missile Crisis: Should We Swallow Oral History?', *International Security,* 15/1 (1990) 212–18.

Kristensen, Hans M and Robert S. Norris, 'The Cuban Missile Crisis: A Nuclear Order of Battle, October and November 1962', *Bulletin of the Atomic Scientists,* 68/6 (2012) 85–91.

Kroenig, Matthew, 'Nuclear Superiority and the Balance of Revolve: Explaining Nuclear Crisis Outcomes', *International Organization,* 67/1 (2013) 141–7.

Kunz, Diane, 'Camelot Continued: What If John F. Kennedy Had Lived?' in Niall Ferguson (ed.), *Virtual History: Alternatives and Counterfactuals* (London: Picador 1997) pp. 368–91.

Kurth, James, 'U.S. Policies, Latin American Politics, and Praetorian Rule' in Phillippe Schmitter (ed.), *Military Rule in Latin America* (Beverly Hills, CA: Sage 1973) pp. 244–58.

Lippmann, Walter, 'Cuba and the Nuclear Risk', *The Atlantic,* 211/2 (1963) 55–8.

Lebow, Richard Ned, 'The Traditional and Revisionist Interpretations Reevaluated: Why Was Cuba a Crisis?' in James Nathan (ed.), *The Cuban Missile Crisis Revisited* (New York: St Martins Press 1992) pp. 161–86.

LeoGrande, William, 'Cranky Neighbors: 150 Years of U.S.–Cuban Relations', *Latin American Research Review,* 49/2 (2010) 217–27.

Mercer, J., 'Rational Signaling Revisited' in James Davis (ed.), *Psychology, Strategy and Conflict* (New York: Routledge 2013) pp. 64–81.

Munton, Don, 'The Fourth Question: Why Did John F. Kennedy Offer Up the Jupiters in Turkey', in David Gioe, Len Scott and Christopher Andrew (eds), *An International History of the Cuban Missile Crisis: A 50-year Retrospective* (Abingdon: Routledge 2014) pp. 258–78.

Munton, Don and Elizabeth Rennie, 'The Cuban Missile Crisis' in Rüdiger Wolfrum (ed.), *Max Planck Encyclopedia of Public International Law* (Oxford: Oxford University Press 2011).

Naftali, Timothy, 'The Malin Notes: Glimpses inside the Kremlin during the Cuban Missile Crisis', *Cold War International History Project Bulletin,* 17/18 (Fall 2012) 299–301.

Nuti, Leopoldi, 'Dall'operazione "Deep Rock" all'operazione "Pot Pie": una storia documentata dei missili SM Jupiter in Italia', *Storia delle Relazioni Internazionali,* 11/12 (1996–7) 95–149.

Nuti, Leopoldi, 'Italy and the Cuban Missile Crisis', *Cold War International History*

Project Bulletin, 17/18 (2012), www.wilsoncenter.org/publication/bulletin-no-17-18 (last accessed 18 December 2014).

Osgood, Josiah, 'The Pen and the Sword: Writing and Conquest in Caesar's Gaul', *Classical Antiquity*, 28/2 (2009) 328–58.

Paterson, Thomas, 'Commentary: The Defense of Cuba Theme and the Missile Crisis', *Diplomatic History*, 14/2 (1990) 249–57.

Paterson, Thomas G. and William J. Brophy, 'October Missiles and November Elections: The Cuban Missile Crisis and American Politics, 1962', *The Journal of American History*, 73/1 (1986) 87–119.

Payne, Keith, 'The Future of Deterrence: The Art of Defining How Much Is Enough', *Comparative Strategy*, 29/1 (2010) 217–22.

Payne, Keith and Colin Gray, 'Victory is Possible', *Foreign Policy*, 39 (1980) 14–27.

Pendas, Devin O., 'Testimony' in Miriam Dobson and Benjamin Ziemann (eds), *Reading Primary Sources: The Interpretation of Texts from Nineteenth- and Twentieth-century History* (London: Routledge 2009), pp. 226–42.

Pomper, Philip, 'Historians and Individual Agency', *History and Theory*, 35/3 (1996) 281–308.

Powers, Thomas, 'And After We've Struck Cuba?' (1997) in *Intelligence Wars: American Secret History from Hitler to Al-Qaeda* (New York: New York Review Books 2004), pp. 171–84.

Pressman, Jeremy, 'September Statements, October Missiles, November Elections: Domestic Politics, Foreign Policy, and the Cuban Missile Crisis', *Security Studies*, 10/3 (2001) 80–114.

Rabe, Stephen G., 'After the Missiles of Cuba: John F. Kennedy and Cuba, November 1962 to November 1963', *Presidential Studies Quarterly*, 30/4 (2000) 714–26.

Radchenko, Sergey, 'The Cuban Missile Crisis: Assessment of New, and Old, Russian Sources', *International Relations*, 26/1 (2012) 327–43.

Reynolds, David, 'Churchill's Writing of History: Appeasement, Autobiography and *The Gathering Storm*', *Transactions of the Royal Historical Society*, Sixth Series, 11 (2001) pp. 221–48.

Sagan, Scott D., 'Nuclear Alerts and Crisis Management', *International Security* 9/4 (1985) 90–139.

Sagan, Scott D., 'SIOP-62: The Nuclear War Plan Briefing to President Kennedy', *International Security*, 12/1 (1987) 22–51.

Sagan, Scott D., 'The Case for No First Use', *Survival*, 51/3 (2009) 163–82.

Sagan, Scott D., 'Shared Responsibilities for Nuclear Disarmament', *Daedalus*, 138/4 (2009) 157–68.

Savranskaya, Svetlana V., 'Tactical Nuclear Weapons in Cuba: New Evidence', *Cold War International History Project Bulletin*, 14/15 (Winter 2003/Spring 2004), www.wilsoncenter.org/sites/default/files/CWIHP_Bulletin_14-15.pdf (last accessed 18 December 2014).

Savranskaya, Svetlana V., 'Soviet Submarines in the Cuban Missile Crisis', *Journal of Strategic Studies*, 28/2 (2005) 233–59.

Savranskaya, Svetlana V., 'Cuba Almost Became a Nuclear Power in 1962: The Scariest Moment in History Was Even Scarier Than We Thought', *Foreign Policy*, 10 October 2012, www.foreignpolicy.com/articles/2012/10/10/cuba_almost_became_a_nuclear_power_in_1962 (last accessed 18 December 2014).

Schlesinger Jr., Arthur M., 'On the Inscrutability of History', *Encounter*, 27/5 (1966) 10–7.

Scott, Len, 'Espionage and the Cold War: Oleg Penkovsky and the Cuban Missile Crisis', *Intelligence and National Security*, 14/3 (1999) 23–47.

Scott, Len, 'Intelligence and the Risk of Nuclear War', in David Gioe, Len Scott and Christopher Andrew (eds), *An International History of the Cuban Missile Crisis: A 50-year Retrospective* (Abingdon: Routledge 2014), pp. 25–42.

Scott, Len and Steve Smith, 'Lessons of October: Historians, Political Scientists, Policy-makers and the Cuban Missile Crisis', *International Affairs*, 70/4 (1994) 659–84.

Seydi, Süleyman, 'Turkish–American Relations and the Cuban Missile Crisis, 1957–63', *Middle Eastern Studies*, 46/3 (2010) 433–55.

Stern, Sheldon M., 'What JFK Really Said', *Atlantic Monthly*, 225/5 (2000) 122–8.

Stern, Sheldon M., 'Source Material: The 1997 Published Transcripts of the JFK Cuban Missile Crisis Tapes: Too Good to be True?', *Presidential Studies Quarterly*, 30/3 (2000) 586–93.

Twigge, Stephen and Len Scott, 'The Other Other Missiles of October: The Thor IRBMs and the Cuban Missile Crisis', *Electronic Journal of International History*, 3 (2000) 1–11, http://sas-space.sas.ac.uk/3387/ (last accessed 18 December 2014).

Uhl, Matthias and Vladimir I. Ivkin, ' "Operation Atom": The Soviet Union's Stationing of Nuclear Missiles in the German Democratic Republic, 1959', *Cold War International History Project Bulletin*, 12/13 (2001) 299–306.

Walt, Stephen, 'Rigor or Rigor Mortis? Rational Choice and Security Studies' *International Security*, 23/4 (Spring 1999) 5–48.

Welch, David A., 'The Organizational Process and Bureaucratic Politics Paradigms: Retrospect and Prospect', *International Security*, 17/2 (1992) 112–46.

Welch, David A., 'The Cuban Missile Crisis', in Andrew E. Cooper, Jorge Heine and Ramesh Thakur (eds), *The Oxford Handbook of Modern Diplomacy* (Oxford: Oxford University Press 2013), pp. 826–39.

Welch, David A. and James Blight, 'The Eleventh Hour of the Cuban Missile Crisis: An Introduction to the ExComm Transcripts', *International Security*, 12/3 (1987–8) 5–29.

Wenger, Andreas, 'Der lange Weg zur Stabilität: Kennedy, Chruschtschow und das gemeinsame Interesse der Supermächte am Status quo in Europa', *Vierteljahrshefte für Zeitgeschichte*, 46/1 (1998) 69–99.

Wohlforth, William and Stephen Brooks, 'Assessing the Balance', *Cambridge Review of International Affairs*, 24/2 (2011) 201–19.

Wohlstetter, Albert, 'The Delicate Balance of Terror', *Foreign Affairs*, 37/1 (1959) 211–34.

Woolven, Robin, 'What Really Happened in RAF Bomber Command during the Cuban Missile Crisis?' in David Gioe, Len Scott and Christopher Andrew (eds), *An International History of the Cuban Missile Crisis: A 50-year Retrospective* (London: Routledge 2014) pp. 176–95.

Index